T0292870

SCHOOL FARMS

This book highlights the potential of school farms to fight hunger and malnutrition by providing access to locally produced, fresh, and healthy food as well as providing young students with educational opportunities to learn, interact with nature, and develop their skills.

Hunger is one of the most pressing concerns we face today and there is a clear need to provide alternative sources of food to feed a fast-growing population. School farms offer a sustainable opportunity to produce food locally in order to feed students who rely on school meals as an integral part of their daily diet. Approaching the concept of school farms through four themes, Problem, People, Process, and Place, the book shows how they can play an essential role in providing sustainable and healthy food for students, the critical role educational institutions can play in promoting this process, and the positive impact hands-on farming can have on students' mental and physical wellbeing. Utilizing the authors' personal hands-on experiences, and drawing on global case studies, the book provides a theoretical framework and practical guidance to help with the establishment of school farms and community-based gardening projects and an education system which promotes a sustainable and healthy approach to food, agriculture, and the environment.

This book will be essential reading for students and scholars of food security, agriculture, healthy and sustainable diets, education for sustainable development, and urban studies. It will also be of great interest to practitioners and policymakers involved in food policy, developing school and community projects, global health and international development, as well as education professionals.

Alshimaa Aboelmakarem Farag is a researcher, educator, and urban designer, who has a special passion for creating public spaces that are smart, inclusive, livable, healthy, and people oriented. She is Assistant Professor at Zagazig University, Egypt.

Her most recent book is *Humanizing Cities Through Car-Free City Development and Transformation* (2020).

Samaa Badawi is Associate Professor of Architecture and Urban Design at Mansoura University, Egypt. She has worked in both the academic and research fields for 18 years where her interest lies in livable cities, human-friendly urban environments, and urban conservation.

Gurpinder Lalli is Senior Lecturer in Education and Inclusion Studies at the University of Wolverhampton, UK. He is the author of *Schools, Food and Social Learning* (Routledge, 2019).

Maya Kamareddine is Lecturer of Architecture at Effat University, College of Architecture and Design, Saudi Arabia.

Routledge Studies in Food, Society and the Environment

For more information about this series, please visit: www.routledge.com/books/series/RSFSE

SCHOOL FARMS

Feeding and Educating Children

Edited by Alshimaa Aboelmakarem Farag,
Samaa Badawi, Gurpinder Lalli,
and Maya Kamareddine

LONDON AND NEW YORK

First published 2022
by Routledge
2 Park Square, Milton Park, Abingdon, Oxon OX14 4RN

and by Routledge
605 Third Avenue, New York, NY 10158

Routledge is an imprint of the Taylor & Francis Group, an informa business

British Library Cataloguing-in-Publication Data
A catalogue record for this book is available from the British Library

Library of Congress Cataloging-in-Publication Data
Names: Farag, Alshimaa Aboelmakarem, 1979- editor.
Title: School farms: feeding and educating children/
edited by Alshimaa Aboelmakarem Farag, Samaa Badawi,
Gurpinder Lalli, and Maya Kamareddine.
Description: Milton Park, Abingdon, Oxon;
New York, NY: Routledge, 2022.|
Series: Routledge studies in food, society and the environment |
Includes bibliographical references and index.
Subjects: LCSH: School farms.
Classification: LCC S531 .S355 2022 (print) |
LCC S531 (ebook) | DDC 630.71–dc23
LC record available at https://lccn.loc.gov/2021028166
LC ebook record available at https://lccn.loc.gov/2021028167

ISBN: 978-1-032-00961-2 (hbk)
ISBN: 978-1-032-00960-5 (pbk)
ISBN: 978-1-003-17655-8 (ebk)

DOI: 10.4324/9781003176558

Typeset in Bembo
by Deanta Global Publishing Services, Chennai, India

This book is dedicated to our mothers
Fatmah, Zeinab, and Pal
and
to mothers worldwide,
who are the first to feed and educate their children,
with love, devotion, and care.

CONTENTS

PICTURES

FIGURES

TABLES

LIST OF EDITORS AND CONTRIBUTORS

Editors

Alshimaa Aboelmakarem Farag is Assistant Professor at Zagazig University, Egypt. She has a special passion for innovating and adapting smart, sustainable, and inclusive built environments. Her research interest lies in Urban Sustainability and Ecological Psychology that concern human responsive reactions and sustainable behavior within the built environments. Through several research contributions, she has built a deeper understanding of sustainable urbanization knowledge and practices through people-oriented approaches, which results in several publications in indexed journals, books, and conferences. Her most recent book is *Humanizing Cities Through Car-Free City Development and Transformation* (2020). She endeavors to continue investigations into the development of new urban measures to promote sustainable urban alternatives to contribute to cleaning the environment and eliminating the impact of the climate change crisis, jointly with creating healthy and human-oriented spaces and cities where people live and work, enjoying a healthy life. https://orcid.org/0000-0003-1539-6928

Samaa R. Badawi is Associate Professor of Architecture and Urban Design at Mansoura University, Egypt. She has worked in both the academic and research fields for 18 years. Her PhD concerned 'The Role of The Urban Form-Based Code in Achieving Sustainable Urban Communities in Egypt'. She has many published papers and book chapters. Her research interest focuses on livable cities, human-friendly urban environments, and urban conservation. In addition, she works as a reviewer for international journals and conferences. She won the Queen Effat Award for Excellence in Teaching for the Academic Year 2015–2016, and The University PhD Award in 2014. https://orcid.org/0000-0001-9318-7326

Gurpinder Singh Lalli is Course Director and Senior Lecturer in Education and Inclusion Studies, based in the School of Education at the University of Wolverhampton, UK. Gurpinder has a vested interest in school food policy and is interested in curriculum. He is the author of *Schools, Food and Social Learning*, published in 2019. He undertook undergraduate studies in Sociology and Social Policy, Master's degrees in Social and Cultural Theory; Corpus Linguistics, and a PhD in Education at University of Leicester, UK. Gurpinder taught in further education colleges prior to joining academia and therefore holds qualified teachers status. He is Senior Fellow of the Higher Education Academy and has led funded research projects. Published work includes peer-reviewed articles in world-leading journals, including the Cambridge Journal of Education, British Journal of Sociology of Education, and International Journal of Qualitative Studies in Education. Gurpinder is a trustee of food education charity, Taste Education, and continues to advocate for curriculum development for food in schools. https://orcid.org/0000-0002-7493-4813

Maya Kamareddine is Senior Lecturer of Architecture at Effat University, College of Architecture and Design, Saudi Arabia. Mrs. Kamareddine received her Master's degree in Architecture from Lebanese University, Lebanon, in 2004. Her thesis discussing the 'development of the rural areas through expansion of agricultural research − Bsharee' was her first interest in sustainability and environmental solutions. As a registered architect in Lebanon, she developed her expertise in design and project management working for international consultants and developers inside and outside her country. As an academic and researcher, she brings a multicultural background eager to build a new generation of leading women in the Arab world.

Authors

Abel Ebiega Enokela is a doctoral student at the Guidance and Counselling Department, Faculty of Education, Ambrose University, Edo State, Nigeria. He has a Bachelor's degree in English and Linguistics, a Post Graduate Diploma in Education, a Master's degree in English Language, and a Master's degree in Guidance and Counselling. He is a professional member of the Nigerian Institute of Management, NIM (chartered); Counselling Association of Nigeria (CASSON); Association of Professional Counsellors in Nigeria (APROCON); and the International Society for Policy Research and Evaluation in School-Based Counseling (ISPRESC). The author hopes to round off his doctoral program soon with post-data defenses. https://orcid.org/0000-0003-4488-8614

Ali Fouad Bakr is Professor of Urban and Regional Planning, Faculty of Engineering, Alexandria University, Egypt. Ali has supervised over 100 PhD and Master Theses. He is also a consultant at the Bibliotheca Alexandrina, Un-Habitat, and General Organization of Physical Planning, Egypt, reviewer for several architectural and planning journals, and a strong believer in the concept of creativity and free thinking in his studios and postgraduate courses. https://orcid.org /0000-0002-9728-602X

Amani Jamal Momani has been the leading college counselor and outreach specialist to the Harmony Independent School District, Texas, United States, for the last six years. She also works as a career coach in advising students on how to best aid themselves and their communities. Amani specializes in the support of low-income families by their surrounding communities. Her time spent in the Middle East as a child and adult has led to her focus on research regarding the efforts of disenfranchised communities to uniquely adapt to their regional qualities to benefit local children and essential businesses. She has a Master's in Public Administration with a focus on public health and has been recognized by multiple school districts for her work on public health in relation to children's nutrition and physical well-being. Amani lives in Dallas with her family. https://orcid.org/0000-0002-6430 -4447

Chris Blythe is Director of Social Farms & Gardens, Bristol, UK and has been involved in the community growing and green space movement in various roles over the last ten years. A geographer by background, Chris is particularly interested in the social impacts of urban farming and growing, and how it is used to improve people's lives. Chris is also a board member/trustee of the European Federation of City Farms and The Birmingham Open Spaces Forum, working with wider green spaces to improve people's lives. https://orcid.org/0000-0001-8517-2458

Divya Chandrasenan is Assistant Professor of Education at the Department of Education, University of Kerala, Kerala, India, with 17 years of professional and teaching experience and with expertise in the development and implementation of educational technology tools and constructive curricular applications in the classroom. She is a motivated researcher looking to further advance understanding of energy and sustainable education by conducting independent research on energy curricula at different educational levels. She is a winner of the Best Teacher Educator Award, Govt. of India, Fulbright-Nehru Post-doctoral Fellowship, Raman Post-doctoral fellowship for Indian scholars in the United States, Precourt fellowship, BECC fellowship, and Outreach Lecturing Fund Travel award IIE, United States. https://orcid.org/0000-0002-7972-0734

Donna Ashlee is Assistant Principal at Brockhill Park Performing Arts College, Kent, UK. Brockhill is a mixed comprehensive secondary school, where Donna is responsible for the attainment and pastoral care of the students in Stour Academy. She is a Geography teacher and leads the schools working farm. As a farmer's wife and daughter, Donna is passionate about the benefits outdoor learning brings, food security issues and where food comes from, sustainability, and the link to children's health. She is part of the team that has fully embedded the Rural Dimension across the whole school curriculum at Brockhill. She is also the current Chair of the School Farms Network and is a FarmerTime ambassador.

Elisabetta Antonucci has a degree in Cultural Anthropology from Ca' Foscari University, Venice, Italy, a PhD in Social Sciences from the FISPA Department of Padua, Italy, a specialization in Urban Regeneration from the University of Milano, Italy, and is a member of the Advisors on Public Space network of City Space Architecture, Italy. During the PhD, her research interests concerned the processes of urban regeneration on a social and cultural basis. This field of interest includes the observation of some experiences of educational experimentation between school and territory that have been launched in the Venice area for some years and which look to the school as a potential resource for initiating a process of change.

Erling Krogh is the leader and coordinator of further education related to school gardens and farms as a pedagogical resource at the Norwegian University of Life Sciences, Norway. Together with Linda Jolly, he has arranged more than 40 further education courses, given all over Norway. Since 2001, he has been responsible for the development and implementation of practical pedagogical education in agriculture, forestry, fishery, and management of natural resources at the university. In the last decade, he has initiated coordination and implementation of school/farm cooperation and other community development projects in the Uluguru Mountains, Tanzania. https://orcid.org/0000-0001-8963-4242

Frans Ari Prasetyo is Research Associate at the York Centre for Asian Research, York University, and Visiting Fellow at the University of Toronto, Canada. He works on urban-ecology politics with various grassroots communities, underground collectives, and the urban-rural marginalized population. He has written several articles, journals, and visual publications. https://orcid.org/0000-0003-0556-8546

Ian Egginton-Metters has been involved with the community and school farming and growing sector for over 40 years and received an OBE in 2014 for his services to City Farms. Initially working with farms supporting young people/adults with learning difficulties, and later running a residential Crisis Centre for young people. Ian joined The Federation of City Farms & Community Gardens in 1984 and led the organization for 14 years before retiring in 2017. During this time, Ian established the Access to Farms partnership, Growing Schools program, School Farms Network (SFN), and helped set up Care Farming UK, which later merged with FCFCG to form SF&G. https://orcid.org/0000-0002-6586-3662

Iman S. Hamza El Gemae is a PhD and independent researcher, Egypt. She received her PhD in Theories of Architecture from Ain Shams University, Egypt. Her research interest falls under the Environmental Psychology of the built environment and users' behaviors within diverse built environments, especially special needs users. She has several published papers in the field of Experiential Architecture, working with requirements and guidelines of different spaces for users with different disabilities, and with emphasis on wayfinding approaches in Architecture Design. https://orcid.org/0000-0002-3655-8765

Imana Pal is Research Scholar in the University of Calcutta, Department of Home Science (Food and Nutrition), Kolkata, India. She has about ten years' teaching and research experience in the field of Food and Nutrition. Her research papers have been published in several national and international journals. She has presented papers at various national and international conferences. https://orcid.org/0000-0001-5636-889X

Jayapraveen J is currently an ICSSR Doctoral Fellow of University of Kerala, India, researching 'Research culture' and 'Quality of work life'. He has more than six years' teaching experience at professional colleges, including Engineering and Teacher Education. He bagged the silver medal for his Master's in Education. He has to his credit a good number of journal publications and paper presentations. He is an excellent team leader and was short-listed for the Best Programme Officer for President's Award. http://orcid.org/0000-0002-6547-5619

Kathryn R. Terzano is Assistant Professor of Community and Regional Planning in the College of Design at Iowa State University, Iowa, United States. Her research interests center on how people perceive and respond to their built, natural, and social environments, with the larger aim of understanding and improving our changing neighborhoods, towns, cities, and regions. https://orcid.org/0000-0001-6942-7991

Kholoud Jamal Moumani has been Senior Architect at the Ministry of Public Works and Housing for nearly 12 years, 2008–2020 at Jordan. She was Assistant Professor at the College of Architecture & Design-Architecture Department. She has been Chair for the Architecture Department and Director of the Master Program for the last two years at Effat University, Saudi Arabia. She joined Effat University, Saudi Arabia, in Fall 2008. She received her PhD in 2015, and has more than 15 years of academic and practice experience. Through her private firm, Kholoud participated in the design and construction of several projects, and she was the sole Architect and the main Architectural/Senior Consultant for different residential, office, medical and educational buildings. https://orcid.org/0000-0001-7821-6416

Linda Jolly is a Lecturer based at Norwegian University of Life Sciences, Norway, and has worked as a teacher in Biology, Gardening, and Agriculture with children and youth of all ages. She now works in Teacher Education for Natural Science and Agriculture. Together with Erling Krogh, she has held courses to initiate partnerships between farms and schools, such that practical work on farms and in gardens can be incorporated with learning in school subjects. The learning theory, presented in this book, has arisen from experience with youth in agricultural activities, both in Norway and in Tanzania. https://orcid.org/0000-0003-2816-6152

Mike Hardman is Senior Lecturer in Urban Geography at the University of Salford, UK, and Lead for the Salford Care and Urban Farm Hub. Mike's research explores informal and formal approaches to Urban Agriculture at a global level. His research is impact-driven and has led to enabling urban farming on the ground. He is an interdisciplinary researcher who has explored business models for urban farming to conducting Social Return on Investment studies and ethnographic studies of food-producing guerrilla gardeners. Mike holds a PhD in Planning from Birmingham City University, UK, and currently leads the Geography, Environment, Archaeology, and Sustainability courses at the University of Salford, UK. https://orcid.org/0000-0002-4282-0766

Nehad A. Gawad is a passionate PhD candidate at Alexandria University, Egypt. Her passion extends from Urban Development and City Planning to Fine Art. She discussed the concept of Urban Revitalization comprehensively through her Master's thesis. Her publications focus on Neglected Urban Spaces. Nehad aspires to re-imagine city planning to empower community resilience. https://orcid.org/0000-0001-9051-6083

Ramshad Khan Rawther is currently Chairman of the Department of the Students Union, University of Kerala, India. He is pursuing an M.Phil degree in Islamic History. He completed his Master's in Islamic History with a gold medal from University of Kerala. He has a proven track record of leadership as former General Secretary and Chairman of student unions at various colleges. http://orcid.org/0000-0003-1804-0070

Robyn Fuller is Middle Leader at Brockhill Park Performing Arts College, Kent, UK. Robyn is a Science teacher and has responsibility for the school's Rural Studies department with oversight of the development and delivery of a range of subjects that make use of the school's farm as the center point for learning. Robyn's interest mainly focuses on enriching learning by being outdoors with a particular focus on attendance, engagement, self-fulfillment, and mental health. Robyn is also part of the team which has developed the whole school's Rural Dimension and created outreach programs to feeder primary schools with the aim to widen the understanding of current issues such as food security.

Victoria Schoen is Agricultural Economist currently working on the productivity of urban gardens at the University of Kent, UK. She is also Project Officer for the European Federation of City Farms. Victoria is interested in the social benefits that community and school gardens can offer and has worked on placing a monetary value on such outputs. She previously worked at the Centre for Food Policy, City, University of London, UK, and is also an online tutor for SOAS. Victoria holds a PhD from Wye College, University of London, UK, examining the economics of Bedouin sheep farming in Jordan. https://orcid.org/0000-0001-6695-1747

FOREWORD

School farms: anachronism or innovation

Michael Corbett, Acadia University, Canada

When I arrived at the University of Tasmania in the new role of professor of Rural and Regional Education in 2015, I began looking at the rural education landscape. Rural education there bore many of the features I had become familiar with in Canada. Rural schools were smaller, less well-resourced, and contained fewer specialist teachers than their urban counterparts. Many were a long way from larger population centers and struggled to find teachers. While often considered the heart of the communities in which they operated, rural schools were also ambivalent spaces. They provided what were often seen as exit opportunities for many community youths. But I also found something that I had not seen in Canada, a network of small school farms.

In Canada, agricultural education in schools has a long history that in some ways continues to this day. School gardens are not uncommon. Nevertheless, it is generally conceded that school-based agricultural education never really took off as a core component of the school curriculum. The Agricultural Education Act of 1913 was a rare piece of federal education legislation in Canada's decentralized education system in which 13 provinces and territories fund and control schools and curriculum. The 1913 Act was designed to transmit the principles of scientific agriculture and to keep rural populations stable in the face of advancing industrialization. Somewhat ironically, a Canadian tobacco magnate William MacDonald also sponsored both university- and college-based agricultural education, but also a number of consolidated schools that brought rural youth out of dispersed villages to attend a model school focused on modern agriculture. Each of these initiatives was a practical project meant to create sustainable and efficient farming and rural communities.

The Act failed in its objectives, and the MacDonald school in Nova Scotia only operated as a school farm for a short number of years before it became simply a large consolidated academically focused primary school in a rural area. Consolidation was a successful part of the initiative, which brought rural children out of their small, dispersed villages, and ironically led to the disconnection between school life and life in a rural village. I am in my seventh decade and have never seen a school farm in Canada. But in Tasmania, I found a network of close to 40 more or less functional school farms which operated in primary and secondary schools around the state, mostly in small rural communities.

The farms were controversial when I arrived, and elements in the state education bureaucracy were keen to see them closed because many were considered to be liability concerns and because there seemed to be a sense that these facilities represented the very anti-modern, place-based backwardness that was holding back rural and state development. When the government threatened (or rather let slip) that the school farms might be closed, a political firestorm erupted, which was serious enough to cause rural politicians to stand up and defend the school farms. They may have been falling down and poorly resourced, but they meant something important to the people in rural communities. They were often run with adult volunteer labor using donated materials, but this illustrated how they served as an important bridge between community and school. Following these threats, school farm activists who were committed community members, farm organizations, rural politicians, and educators organized to pressure the government to take seriously and support not just the existing school farms but to consider what agricultural education should look like going forward in the 21st century. This work continues, and the government now supports human resources, curriculum work, and the support necessary for a coordinated pipeline to link school-based educational experiences to both community values represented by the presence of the school farm, but also to the needs of contemporary agricultural careers. The school farm has moved from the periphery to, if not the core, at least into the official curriculum.

This collection provides a challenge to educators to consider what the school farm means today in different contexts. The chapters in this book cut a broad swath through a complex set of problems, processes, and issues that relate to the connection between schooling and agriculture around the world. Some of these accounts relate to the problems of developing community and workforce capacity. Others relate to questions of food security, children's psychological wellbeing, experiential learning, inclusion, ecological stewardship, urban farming, and land use. The chapters take up specific located initiatives, but each in its own way points to how farming is fundamentally about stewardship, sustainability, and the relationship between the human and the more-than-human world. This work is not anachronistic; it is cutting-edge, materially engaged education for sustainability.

When I encountered the school farms in Tasmania, I must admit I saw them as a curiosity at best and an anachronism at worst. But I came to see how entangled our ideas about schooling are with the narrative of modernity, urbanization, and industrialization and with preparing young people to leave rural spaces. This approach creates foundational ambivalences and segregates the life practices of many people from what is taught in school. While urbanization seems relentless, let us remember that it is not the only game in town, and nearly half of us who share this planet still live in rural areas where most of us are engaged in agriculture.

PREFACE

Alshimaa A. Farag, Gurpinder Singh
Lalli, and Samaa R. Badawi

The school farm is one of the educational models that has developed over many years, providing young students with educational opportunities to learn, interact with nature, and develop their farming skills, as well as providing them with locally sourced, fresh, and healthy school meals. Yet, its crucial role has emerged recently in many countries of the world as one of the thriving urban features, contributing to face critical challenges such as child malnutrition and hunger.

Child malnutrition and hunger consequently emerged as a result of climate change, depletion of natural resources, and sacrificing of agricultural lands for the development and extension of the built environment. They are pressing problems that continually spread and threaten world peace and the security of peoples. They lead to severe harm to children's health, and are expected to be a significant threat for human beings in the future with the accelerating increase of the urban population. Recently and while proceeding with this book, the world has been facing a global pandemic (COVID-19) outbreak that aggravated an already acute and chronic food problem. In some countries, all school feeding programs were canceled. With the lack of access to food as people's incomes fall, production ceases, and in some contexts, food prices rise, and the need for alternative food production solutions becomes more pressing than ever.

Given the criticality and complexity of such a problem, a comprehensive and interdisciplinary effort is essential to redefine a sustainable relationship between children and their food resources. Although the United Nations set the second goal of its 2030 Sustainable Development Goals to fight hunger worldwide, there is a need for concerted efforts from all stakeholders to overcome the urgent global problems through scientific response and reasonable solutions.

This book mixes methodological and empirical approaches to discuss educational institutions' integral role in restoring the balance between humans and the local environment. The book investigates the school farm as one of the developed urban and educational trends that aim to fight hunger and malnutrition and provide children with locally produced, fresh, and healthy food as well as maintain development of their sustainable knowledge, behavior, and attitude.

Within this multidisciplinary book, scholars and practitioners from across the globe introduce various theoretical and empirical studies that represent the implication of school farms in different communities to provide the readers with distinctive perceptions, insights, and experiences worldwide. All participants in this book contribute either with their theoretical knowledge, academic and research experience, or practical field experience. They all have extensive experience that significantly guarantees academic quality with an argumentative discussion or practical experience. The authors approach the concept of school farm in four themes (Problem, People, Process, and Place), in which four important complementary aspects shape the sustainable recommendation through: 1) understanding the problem of food insecurity, 2) promoting a healthy learning community, 3) developing agricultural curriculum and educational practices, and operational systems, and 4) the efficient use and adaptation of open spaces for school farms. However, the reader can choose to read the chapters individually according to their interest or cumulatively to see how the 14 chapters are set to complement the knowledge with practice to feed into the four book themes.

The authors present multiple scenarios for school farms as an educational model introducing young generations to better nutrition, enhanced education and livelihood, and eventually resilient and sustainable communities. This book offers an in-depth explanation for a sustainable opportunity to produce food locally to feed students who rely on school meals as an integral part of their daily diet. Simultaneously, it provides the reader with how school farms can provide students with educational opportunities to gain practical farming skills, which in turn sensitizes them to their environment, promotes subsistence farming and kitchen gardens in households, and ignites a passion for growing food in young minds.

This book tackles an interdisciplinary topic which links different specialties to provide the readers with a guideline for establishing the school farm as a community-based gardening project. It provides compelling content that would be informative and relevant to an extensive range of readers, from educators to policymakers, researchers, designers, urban developers, and undergraduate and postgraduate students. Therefore, although much has been written, this exciting, edited book offers a comprehensive perspective on the role of the school farm in feeding and educating children.

ACKNOWLEDGMENTS

We would like to take this opportunity to thank the participants in the respective studies for bringing such a rich collection of work together, as without their involvement, much of this work would not have been possible. They contributed their knowledge and experience with sincerity and dedication to enrich this scholarly publication. Equally, we would like to show our deep appreciation to the reviewers for offering their valuable comments, which contributed to improving the criticality of the book content. We would like also to expand our deepest gratitude to Professor Michael Corbett, who, in his foreword, put our publication into the wider context of current academic discourses, sharing his own interesting experience that we enjoyed reading and benefited from. Special thanks to Hannah Ferguson and John Baddeley, Routledge editors Nancy Antony and team, for their positive support and efforts during the book editing process. At last, we thank our families, who work on providing a supportive environment to work in. We wish to express our gratitude to all who contributed to the development and delivery of this book.

INTRODUCTION

Samaa Badawi, Alshimaa A. Farag,
and Gurpinder Singh Lalli

Proper nutrition is an essential need for children's balanced biological, psychological, mental, and social development. The shortage of proper nutrition, either in quantity or quality, will impact the child's health, causing many diseases and even death (WHO, 2021). Malnutrition has different forms, including undernutrition and hunger, and overweight and obesity due to a deficiency of micronutrients, which play an essential role in growth, bone health, fluid balance, and several other processes. Children's hunger is a pressing challenge facing the global community as around 10,000 children worldwide die from hunger each day (Chinyoka, 2014). Accordingly, there is severe pressure on governments and international organizations to fight malnutrition and hunger and provide multiple alternatives to healthy food sources.

Providing appropriate nutrition for children requires providing them with healthy food, educating them about healthy nutrition and food sources, and involving them in developing appropriate local solutions. This book tackles malnutrition and hunger as contemporary pressing challenges facing the global community and sheds light on the role of educational institutions in providing children with the essential food sources and food education and spreading the culture of farming among young generations.

The school farm is an effective solution that imposes its presence on the scene since it has been an important intervention program for several decades (Hardman & Larkham, 2014). School farms have deep historical roots as school gardens have been widely used in Europe in education since 1811, while the United States developed one of the earliest educational school garden programs in 1891. Then, the school garden movement received a massive boost during World War I and World War II, followed by the environmental movement of the 1970s that brought renewed interest to the idea, and another period of intense growth began in the early 1990s (Hayden–Smith, 2015). Recently, school farms

DOI: 10.4324/9781003176558-101

are a strategy that enhances the availability, utilization, and sustainable access of healthy and local food to school meals to address the nutritional needs of students (Gottlieb & Hasse, 2004; Adebayo & Mudaly, 2019; Korani, 2012; Vallianatos et al., 2004), and consequently fighting hunger and malnutrition (Foodtank, 2021).

On this approach, the Food and Agriculture Organization (FAO) promotes the idea of school farms and encourages schools to create moderate-sized learning gardens/farms, producing various fruit and vegetables, using simple techniques, so that teachers and parents can easily manage the garden/farm and students can apply learned gardening/farming techniques easily (Georges, 2019).

This book uses the comprehensive definition of school farms to refer to an educational model, which includes two main sectors (Roche et al., 2012; Foeken et al., 2010):

- School gardens.
- Farm-to-school programs.

School gardens refer to a wide range of farm activities that depend on the scale and category of the schools. School gardens as a concept are built upon enhancing hands-on or 'learning by doing' by providing educational lessons to investigate where food comes from, how it is grown, and the value and joy of eating fresh foods (Savoie-Roskos et al., 2017; Berezowitz et al., 2015). Therefore, students acquire authentic and positive experiences within the agricultural field (Vallianatos et al., 2004). Moreover, school gardens provide an active learning context and serve as living classrooms or outdoor laboratories where students can apply academic subjects such as science, mathematics, languages, and even fine arts (Hayden-Smith, 2015). However, the perception of school gardens now focus more on food production, better nutrition, and environmental protection (FAO, 2010); one needs to keep in mind that school gardens are first and foremost an educational tool and are not often regarded as an exit strategy to school feeding (FAO, 2006).

Similarly, there are many successful initiatives of school gardens worldwide, such as in the United States, Canada, Indonesia, Japan, Finland, Ireland, Kenya, and Zambia. One of the most prominent examples of school gardens is the Australian school garden, where the community engagement involving families, teachers, and students is at the core of establishing the school garden; for example, the Stephanie Alexander Kitchen Garden, where Australian students of all ages learn to grow, harvest, and prepare healthy food with their peers. This helps them build robust social relationships with peers, encourages critical thinking and teamwork skills, and increases observation levels among students. The Stephanie Alexander Kitchen Garden is established with a productive garden space, a kitchen and dining space, regular garden classes, and regular kitchen classes (Alexander, 2021).

Farm-to-school program is the second sector of school farms and the viral initiative that led to the concept of school farms. It was founded in 1990 in the United States and spread worldwide. The farm-to-school program aims to increase the integration of fresh food from local and regional farms into school meals (New York Department of Agriculture and Markets, 2015), enriching the communities' connection with fresh, healthy, and local food (National Farm to School Network, 2021).

Although the primary purpose of farm-to-school programs is food production, their priorities vary depending on the local circumstances and the target group. In the global south, food production, fighting hunger, and malnutrition are the main aim of farm-to-school programs, while the educational use of school farms is mainly for vocational agricultural training (Schreinemachers et al., 2020). In comparison, in the global north, farm-to-school programs function in the educational field, providing students with food education and developing hands-on farming skills (Gonsalves, Hunter, and Lauridsen, 2020). Besides, 'garden-based learning' has predominated, using gardens as laboratories for learning science, environmental studies, and other subjects such as art and language, in addition to providing children with fresh organic vegetables and fruit (FAO, 2010).

Across the globe, farm-to-school has 19 inspiring and innovative programs, making a demonstrated difference in child health, school attendance rates, food security, and farmer livelihoods in many communities (Social Farms & Gardens, 2018). Many countries worldwide have adopted farm-to-school programs, such as the 'School Feeding Program' in Ghana and 'Purchase from Africans for Africa Program' in Ethiopia, Malawi, Mozambique, Niger, and Senegal. Moreover, there is the 'School Meals Program' in Italy, 'Farm to Cafeteria' program in Canada, 'National School Feeding Programme' in Brazil, and 'Garden to Table' program in New Zealand. In Oceania, 'Australian Organic Schools' is the largest organic industry body in Australia. All of those initiatives aim to grow farming and cooking skills and build awareness of individual and collective responsibility for the environment, healthy eating, and community connectedness (Foodtank, 2021). According to the World Food Programme (WFP), nearly every country globally has a national school feeding program, serving an estimated 368 million children worldwide (Tembon et al., 2015). Studies reveal the lasting impact of school feeding programs on shaping children's future, as creating school farms and boosting agriculture education can raise students' awareness on how to grow nutritious food crops, to cook, share, and enjoy at mealtimes (Bundy et al., 2009).

This book shows several case studies from different countries and cultures that have adopted school farm initiatives with different and innovative approaches, presented in 14 chapters. Cases from the UK, Norway, England, Italy, Germany, the United States, Canada, the Middle East, Nigeria, India, Nepal, Bhutan, Indonesia, Tanzania, Vietnam, and China are presented and the concepts and applications of the school farm from different perspectives are discussed. In order to avoid dispersion and disorganization between the different ideas represented in the 14 chapters, all chapters are mapped together around four main themes/

sections, which are Problem, People, Process, and Place. The four themes are considered the four pillars to create a school farm that prompt the phycological, social, and physical health for young students and the community at large.

Book themes and chapters

Problem

This section comprises three chapters, emphasizing the critical need to adopt the school farm for two crossed purposes; first, revolving around mitigating food scarcity worldwide; second, to redefine the relationship between children and their food resources through education and direct interaction with nature. In this section, the school farm is introduced as a restorative practice to guarantee sustainable education and food security.

In the first chapter *Food education and food for life*, *Lalli* highlights critical issues in school gardening and engaging food education in the curriculum. He conducted critical discussions regarding the role of school gardens/farms in promoting students' engagement with school gardening programs and food education from an English perspective. From another perspective, in Chapter 2 *The impact of hunger on children and Adolescents: School farming as a panacea*, *Enokela* discusses the adverse impact of hunger on children and adolescents. The author investigates the potentials of school farms as a sustainable tool to face the urgent challenge of hunger of children and adolescents in the global south countries, and in Nigeria in particular. Similarly, in Chapter 3 *Fighting malnutrition and reaching Sustainable Development Goals through school farming (during the COVID-19 pandemic): Scenario in some South Asian countries – India, Nepal, and Bhutan*, *Pal's* discussion confirms and complements the previous review of Enokela's study, but with emphasis on South Asian countries, where 70% of the world's malnourished children reside. The author focuses on the food crisis during the COVID-19 pandemic.

People

This section handles different people's issues on different scales regarding school farming; some concern the School Farm Network and participatory initiatives on a broad scale, and others concern the benefits students will gain by being involved in farming-based education. Four chapters provide innovative examples from four countries, the UK, Indonesia, the United States, and India. All present models that involve students and sometimes the broader community in school gardening and farming experiences to change their perception toward the environment and promote their sense of belonging toward their communities.

This section starts with the fourth chapter of this book *The School Farms Network in the UK: History, context, and adding value*. *Blythe, Egginton, Hardman, and Schoen* present case studies from the UK to illustrate the breadth of the school farms concept and the role of networks. This chapter, combined with

Chapter 9, confirms the significant role of networking in promoting the initiatives of school farms and overcoming many considerable challenges beyond school grounds. From a socio-political perspective, in Chapter 5 *Foodways, farms, and ecology: School farms and cultivation of precision agriculture in Bandung upland*, *Prasetyo* displays two community participatory scenarios and cooperation between social entrepreneur farming/ecology NGOs and a local farmer society at school farms in the rural peri-urban area of Bandung upland in Indonesia. In Chapter 6 *Psychological benefits of school farms to students*, *Terzano* displays the psychological benefits of school farms to students by exploring research background and providing a case study of a successful model of a school farm in the United States. In Chapter 7 *Harithalayam campus farming mission: A case study in Kerala, India*, *Chandrasenan, Khan*, and *Jayachandran* present a quantitative study conducted at the University of Kerala, India to assess how the dimensions of students' sustainability literacy are enhanced through the campus farming initiative.

Process

This section comprises three chapters, introducing innovative ideas to enhance the school education and management systems. It focuses on the efficiency of the study curriculum and school learning activities in accommodating horticultural activities and investigates the methods to enhance the hands-on learning experiences to show how students could grow, increase preference for, and consume fresh fruit and vegetables.

This section starts with Chapter 8, *How do children and youth learn through farming and gardening activities?*, in which *Jolly* and *Krogh* discuss a learning theory based on practical experiences from the cooperation between farms and schools in Norway and Tanzania. They present a new learning model that could stimulate the students' interest to learn through farming and gardening activities. In Chapter 9 *Using the outdoors to enhance learning experiences at secondary school*, *Ashlee* and *Fuller* continue to interpret how to promote student learning through hands-on experience. The authors have been extensively involved in developing the school farm in Brockhill Park Performing Arts College in Kent. They explain in detail innovative strategies developed in a case study from the UK to engage students and teaching staff, make the farm an integral part of the curriculum, appeal to teenagers, extend the provision of their unique resource, and use the farm to encourage attendance and promote health and wellbeing. In Chapter 10 *Working towards the garden: A case study of Middle East agricultural preservation, school farming, and alternative horticultural programs*, *K. Moumani* and *A. Moumani* evaluate the farm-to-school and horticulture farming programs across the Middle East in terms of the impact of alternative horticultural farming systems and farm-to-school programs on school culture, food service, farmers and producers, community partnership, as well as gains in awareness towards health and proper diet. The chapter provides guidelines to minimize the cost of the farm-to-school programs, which is considered the most significant obstacle that faces less fortunate schools from adopting the program on campus.

Place

This section includes four chapters, providing a guideline for designing and developing the built environment of school farms. It shows how productive planting can be woven into urban spaces and how sustainability, food security, and environmental quality can be linked through innovative, sustainable, and inclusive urban design to produce food in an urban educational setting without diminishing its functionality.

Antonucci, in Chapter 11 *The school as a potential resource for the transformation of the territory*, opens this section with a discussion on case studies which present the role of school farms and green areas in transforming the territory and the spaces of learning, realized through a partnership between schools and local institutions in Venice. Following this is Chapter 12 *School roof farms: Challenges and success pillars*. By narrowing down the scope to a micro-architectural scale, *Badawi* presents six case studies of constructing school roof farms in different contexts. The chapter explores the challenges and the pillars of implementing roof farms within school buildings and the benefits for the school and the broader community. In Chapter 13, *Building community resilience: The synergy between school farms and neglected urban open spaces*, *Bakr* and *Gawad* introduce the concept of Neglected Urban Open Spaces as a potential resource for adapting school farms meanwhile achieving community resilience. In the last chapter of this book *Inclusive learning school farm environment*, *Farag* and *Hamza* present a thought-provoking discussion of inclusive education and detailed consideration of guidelines and requirements essential to design an inclusive learning environment in a school farm, where all students together, regardless of their abilities, could access nature, learn, improve their skills, and participate physically, sensory, and mentally in an inclusive learning experience and environment.

The final chapter of this book concludes with inclusive remarks for the general design and management guidelines that would help the reader implement the idea of the school farm. This book's conclusion elucidates the 4Ps framework that connects the four pillars of the successful school farm: Problem, People, Process, and Place. The final sections of the chapter outline any closing thoughts and future directions.

References

Adebayo, O. & Mudaly, R., 2019. Creating a Decolonised Curriculum to Address Food Insecurity among University Students. *Problems of Education in the 21st Century*, 77(2):179–194.

Alexander, S., 2021. Program Fundamentals. Retrieved March 2021, from Stephen Alexander Kitchen Garden Foundation: https://www.kitchengardenfoundation.org.au/content/program-fundamentals

Berezowitz, C.K., Yoder, A.B.B. & Schoeller, D.A., 2015. School Gardens Enhance Academic Performance and Dietary Outcomes in Children. *The Journal of School Health*, 85 (8):508–518.

Bundy, Donald, Carmen Burbano, Margaret E. Grosh, Aulo Gelli, Matthew Juke & Drake Lesley, 2009. *Rethinking School Feeding: Social Safety Nets, Child Development, and the Education Sector.* The World Bank.

Chinyoka, K., 2014. Impact of poor nutrition on the academic performance of grade seven learners: a case of Zimbabwe. *International Journal of Learning & Development*, 4(3).P.73-84

FAO, September 2006. School Gardens. Retrieved April 19 from: http://www.fao.org/ schoolgarden/concept_en.htm

FAO, 2010. Promoting Lifelong. Retrieved April 19 from: http://www.fao.org/home/ en/

Foeken, D., Owuor, S.O. & Mwangi, A.M., 2010. School Farming for School Feeding: Experiences from Nakuru, Kenya. *The Journal of Field Actions*, 20(1).P.1-6

Foodtank, 2021. National Farm-to-School Month: Highlighting Cutting-Edge Programs. Retrieved March 2021, from Foodtank: https://foodtank.com/news/2017 /10/national-farm-school-initiatives/

Georges, W., 2019. Introducing the School Farm Program. Retrieved March 2021, from Ybard: https://docs.google.com/document/d/14nMh_rQva7FmXko5z0RvT0jC gpMvXj_XJ0eZ7n_xjRg/edit

Gonsalves, J., Hunter, D. & Lauridsen, N., 2020. School Gardens: Multiple Functions and Multiple Outcomes. In Hunter, D., Monville-Oro, E., Burgos, B., Roel, C.N., Calub, B.M., Gonsalves, J. & Lauridsen, N. (eds.) *Agrobiodiversity, School Gardens and Healthy Diets: Promoting Biodiversity, Food and Sustainable Nutrition.* Routledge, pp. 1–32.

Gottlieb, R. & Hasse, M., 2004. Farm-to-School. *Journal of Planning Education and Research*, 23(4):414–423.

Hardman, M. & Larkham, P.J., 2014. *Informal Urban Agriculture.* Springer.

Hayden-Smith, Rose, 2015. A History Of School Gardens…and How the Model is Getting a Boost Today from Foodcrops. *Uc Food Observer.* Retrieved March, 2021 from: http://ucfoodobserver.com/2015/05/06/a-history-of-school-gardens-and-how-the-model-is-getting-a-boost-today-from-food-corps/

Korani, Z., 2012. Application of Teaching Methods, Promoting Integrated Pest Management on the Farm School in Order to Achieve Sustainable Agriculture. *Procedia: Social and Behavioral Sciences*, 47: 2187–2191.

National Farm to School Network, n.d. About Farm to School What is Farm to School, and How Does it Contribute to Vibrant Communities? Retrieved December 2021 from: http://www.farmtoschool.org/about/what-is-farm-to-school.

New York Department of Agriculture and Markets, 2015. Getting Local Food into New York State Schools: A local procurement toolkit to bring together producers and schools in New York State. Retrieved December 2021 from: https://www.agricult ure.ny.gov/f2s/index.html.

Roche, E. et al., 2012. Social Cognitive Theory as a Framework for Considering Farm to School Programming. *Childhood Obesity*, 8 (4): 357–363.

Savoie-Roskos, M.R., Wengreen, H. & Durward, C., 2017. Increasing Fruit and Vegetable Intake among Children and Youth through Gardening-Based Interventions: A Systematic Review. *Journal of the Academy of Nutrition and Dietetics*, 117 (2): 240–250.

Schreinemachers, P., Yang, R.Y., Bhattarai, D.R., Rai, B.B. & Ouedraogo, M.S., 2020. The Impact of School Gardens on Nutrition Outcomes of Low-Income Countries.

In Hunter, D., Monville-Oro, E., Burgos, B., Roel, C.N., Calub, B.M., Gonsalves, J. & Lauridsen, N. (eds.) *Agrobiodiversity, School Gardens and Healthy Diets: Promoting Biodiversity, Food and Sustainable Nutrition.* Routledge, pp. 115–125.

Social Farms & Gardens, 2018. School Farms Network. Retrieved January 2021from: https://www.farmgarden.org.uk/resources#filter

Tembon, A.C., Schultz, L.B. & Fernands, E., 2015. *School Feeding: A Tool for Social Inclusion.* Education for Global Development.

Vallianatos, M., Gottlieb, R. & Haase, M.A., 2004. Farm-to-School: Strategies for Urban Health, Combating Sprawl, and Establishing a Community Food Systems Approach. *Journal of Planning Education and Research,* 23(4):414–423.

WHO, 2021. Adolescent Health in the South-East Asia Region. Retrieved April, 2021 from: https://www.who.int/southeastasia/health-topics/adolescent-health

PART 1

Problem-focused perspective

1

FOOD EDUCATION AND FOOD FOR LIFE

Gurpinder Singh Lalli

Introduction

This chapter aims to draw together the most recent developments within the school food curriculum and draws on school food policy, food growing, school gardens, and sustainability. Educating children about food growing supports the development of food literacy through which culinary capital is being fostered. The first school lunches were documented as being served in Germany as early as 1790 by an American-born individual known as Count Rumford. Mass feedings were introduced for children living in deprivation, who worked part-time in exchange for schooling and food. In the UK, the introduction of a National Food Strategy (Defra, 2020) after 75 years has seen a renewed focus on food which is identified as vital to life, and for one in eight of us, it is the source of our livelihoods. Food is said to shape our sense of self, and cooking and eating together have been identified as arguably the most defining communal act. The strategy aims to banish pollution and poverty for sustainability, and the current global pandemic has brought into painful focus the flaws in the UK's food system, most notably its effect on the nation's physical and mental health (The Guardian, 2020). The School Standards and Framework Act (1998) saw the introduction of nutritional standards for school meals in the UK.

We know that food is a public right, not a privilege, and we need a systems approach in ensuring children and young people have access to nutritious foods which provide fuel for their engagement and learning. The role of school in society includes a duty of care and to work towards reducing inequalities to strive for social justice and developing good citizens. Cognitive development is influenced by many factors, including nutrition. There is an increasing body of literature that suggests a connection between improved nutrition and optimal brain function (Nyaradi et al., 2013). So why has the concern for children's

DOI: 10.4324/9781003176558-1

health increased, and what do we already know? How does the introduction of school food gardens affect children and young people's attitudes to food? What are the implications for designing a food-based ethos in a school, and how could this fit into the curriculum? There is much to be said about advocacy and the focus on children's rights more recently, which has led to the focus on developing a more sustainable future for all. In light of such questions and issues, this chapter brings the field of school food up to date and is organized into two sections: 1) food education, 2) school food growing, gardens, and eating spaces. These allow for presenting discussions on the formal curriculum structures within which food is 'placed' and informal spaces through which engagement with food begins to grow.

School food in England

Compliance with school food standards is mandatory for all maintained schools, and the revised standards came into force on January 1, 2015 (DfE, 2019). The regulations are typically cited as 'Requirements for School Food Regulations 2014', and it is also important to note these apply to England (DfE, 2014). I present two key schedules extracted from the requirements below (Schedule 1 and 2). From September 2014, every child in reception, year 1, and year 2 in state-funded schools is entitled to a free school lunch.

Food education

Food education in school varies across school types, curriculum focus, and even differs in terms of the importance of food to a school. A framework developed by Public Health England (2015) details the knowledge and skills expected of primary school teachers who would typically engage with children and teach about food. The guidelines introduce the idea of adopting a whole school approach which involves planning and working collaboratively with colleagues in order to enhance learning opportunities. The aim is to use food lessons to motivate change in behavior, i.e., to influence the uptake of healthier school lunches. The aim also consists of developing schemes of work that take into consideration the thinking and advice from professional associations, which include the Design and Technology Association, School Food Plan, and Public Health England. Having introduced school food in a UK context, I draw attention to the broader picture and the variables that play a role in school feeding. Inevitably, this led me to review feeding programs in the globalized south. Some of the work that explores school food has been written about extensively using ethnographic design and draws on implications and the messy nature of research on the school food space (Lalli, 2020), school food policy (Earl and Lalli, 2020), and through reviewing school mealtime (Lalli, 2021). This part of the chapter outlines the impact of food on learning.

The impact of school food on learning

The interest of the public has consisted of trying to establish links between food and learning, and for some time, I have tried to develop proposals that offer a suitable methodology in trying to capture or observe such links. Given that a number of variables need to be considered, I outline these here. Firstly then, is it about establishing links to attainment so that we can compare to PISA league tables? Or is it about trying to capture the unseen benefits of how food has a wider impact on learning? While I have written about the social aspect of food, what about cognition and educational attainment? What about breakfast? In order to delve deeper into such debates, I review a number of papers, all of which are highly cited and stem from a wide range of disciplines such as public health, psychology, medicine, nutrition, and sociology, to name a few. I highlight a key resource at this stage which is a bank of research papers published in a public health journal that draws together leading research on the impact of school food consumption on children's cognition, educational attainment, and social development (Drake et al., 2017). An important point raised in the editorial is that 'healthy children learn better' and in order for them to learn, they need to be in school, and to yield the most benefit from their attendance, they need to be healthy.

We know that hunger affects children's concentration and ability to learn. In 2019, 17.3 million schoolchildren received nutritious meals and snacks from the World Food Program (WFP) in 59 countries. In light of this, school feeding programs have gained traction in terms of being recognized for their dual roles as a long-term social protection investment and productive safety net for children and their families in the short term (Drake et al., 2017: 1). It is estimated that nearly half of the world's schoolchildren, approximately 310 million, in low- and middle-income countries eat a daily meal at school (WFP, 2019). For instance, India now feeds over 100 million children; Brazil 48 million; China 44 million; South Africa and Nigeria each more than 9 million. The role of school feeding then clearly needs investment as this is about developing human capital and local economies which offer social stability alongside national development.

School feeding programs have had a positive impact on school enrolment, and interventions are implemented in nearly every country as they offer the potential to support the education, health, and nutrition of children in school (Gelli, 2015). In the globalized north, perhaps something we take for granted is highlighted by Gelli (2015), who observes the improvements to primary education across multiple low- and middle-income countries. More specifically, a number of key observations are noted as follows: 1) 58 million children are still not in school, 2) poor nutrition and health among schoolchildren are said to contribute to the inefficiency of the education system, 3) children with diminished cognitive abilities perform less well, and are more likely to be subject to grade repetition and drop out of school, 4) short-term hunger in children is said to result in a loss in concentration and the ability to take part in complex tasks, 5) the increase

in school feeding programs has been a key education sector response to the economic crises, 6) school feeding programs are said to be able to ensure children
reach school and stay there (ibid., 4). The main issue with these observations is
that the government response is usually one which adopts an approach of using
feeding as a 'response to a problem' rather than considering feeding as a fundamental part of the economic system and wellbeing. In the study by Gelli (2015),
an observational study involving a meta-analysis of published data was developed
to investigate the impact of the school feeding programs. The method involved
dividing school types and the length of the program. In terms of intervention, it
consisted of two types of school feeding: onsite meals alone or onsite meals plus
take-home rations. Overall, school feeding programs were identified to have statistically significant increases in enrolment with an effect size of approximately
10%. Therefore, school feeding programs had a positive impact on school enrolment. This work identifies the impact of food on enrolment and engagement,
which is relevant to all contexts.

The work of Nelson et al. (2015) highlighted the impact of school lunch
uptake in relation to attainment across primary and secondary schools in England.
The introduction of school food standards resulted in an overall improvement in
relation to the nutritional quality of the food served in schools, namely between
2005 and 2011 (Haroun et al., 2010; Nicholas et al., 2013). Based on an international review, it was suggested that across a wide range of nutrition, better
nutrition is associated with better learning outcomes (Ells et al., 2008). This
highlights the impact of food on learning. Furthermore, research undertaken
in UK schools highlighted that healthier eating during lunchtime was linked
with better learning behaviors within the classroom directly after lunch (Golley
et al., 2010; Storey et al., 2011). In their study, the relationship between levels
of attainment and school lunch uptake was explored, namely during the following years: 2008–2009, 2009–2010, and 2010–2011. The data was extracted from
local authority level or school level, whichever was available with the following
hypothesis being tested: 'average levels of attainment at ages 11–12 (KS2) and
15–16 (KS4 GCSE) in 2010 and 2011 in schools and local authorities in England
are positively associated with changes in average school lunch uptake between
2008–2009 and 2010–2011' (ibid., 2). Overall, the analyses identified some positive links between KS2 and KS4 results in 2010 and 2011 alongside changes
in school lunch uptake during previous years, although overall, the results are
variable. As a result, this study highlighted the significant links between food
and attainment as while findings are variable, the data is able to contribute to a
growing corpus of evidence that identifies how in the correct circumstances, an
increase in levels of consumption of healthier food choices in schools can support
an increase in levels of attainment at both primary and secondary school level in
the UK.

To continue along the path of identifying key studies on school food to date,
the work of Hilari and Franco (2015) in El Salvador was critical in relation to
perspectives on food sales in schools. Save the Children International (SCI) is

an organization that has implemented a school health and nutrition program in 45 schools across El Salvador with the aim to increase consumption of protein and micronutrients while making an attempt to reduce sugar and fat intake in schoolchildren. The reason for considering this project was due to the consumerism of school food, and it is important to learn lessons from other countries. The governmental recommendation involved regulating the sale of soft drinks in schools and proposed as law. Similar to the UK, which is now imposing laws on banning junk food advertisements within a close reach of schools. Schools' stores have a written contract that regulates the vendor's services and forms the basis of a model from the Ministry of Education in El Salvador. A number of interesting findings emerged from the study, which ultimately aimed to develop interventions to improve the quality of food that children buy in school (ibid., 2). It was interesting to learn about children's involvement in the intervention, which involved training children through which a 'student brigade' was introduced. While we can make an attempt to control food consumption and choices in school, students who leave the school often gain access to unhealthy foods. A number of vendors highlighted how children would be less likely to bring junk food to school if taught and motivated by the student volunteer brigade.

In order to look more closely at the food served in schools, it is useful to review the work of Aliyar et al. (2015), who conducted a review of nutritional guidelines and menu compositions for school feeding programs across 12 countries. A reported 805 million people across the globe do not have enough food to eat, and approximately 98% of these individuals live in low- and middle-income countries (United Nations, 2014). Furthermore, Aliyar et al. (2015) identify the shared public health concern of overweight and obesity across the global north and south, which of course include high-, middle- and low-income countries which have become a social problem and key challenge, i.e., overweight- and obesity-related issues in schoolchildren. More specifically, it was identified that children at school consumed unhealthy foods and were lacking adequate knowledge in healthy eating habits alongside lifestyle choices (ibid., 2). We must acknowledge that issues surrounding school feeding in low- and middle-income countries are considerably different compared to high-income countries. For instance, school food provision in high-income countries is determined by evidence that suggests foods consumed by children are deficient in terms of the calorific content, which usually involves a focus on high sugars and fats. Conversely, school feeding programs in low- and middle-income countries aim to reduce hunger in children and increase enrolment into schools, and arguably the longer-term focus is also different with aims of improving attendance, retention, and cognitive development. Although, it could be argued that the policy which drives the policy agenda of high-income countries is much too focused on the policing of obesity which is a multifaceted issue. The foods children consume are not the single contributing factor that determines overweightness and obesity in children.

School breakfast and learning

A widely cited paper explored the relationship between breakfast consumption and academic performance in UK schools (Adolphus et al., 2015). We know that breakfast is recommended as part of a healthy diet due to the association with healthier macro and micronutrient intakes, Body Mass Index (BMI), and lifestyle (Hoyland et al., 2009). Hoyland et al. (2009) conducted a systematic review of the effect of breakfast on the cognitive performance in children as breakfast, in particular, had been widely cited as promoting improvement in cognitive function and academic performance. Therefore, it is useful to explore some of these studies as too often we focus on the lunch hour in schools and on-task behaviors in children immediately after this period. What about on-task behavior after breakfast? How much do we know about children's breakfast consumption and whether school breakfast clubs are as important as school lunches? Following a systematic review of 45 studies published in 42 articles between 1950 and 2008, it was found that many lacked scientific rigors. Overall, the evidence suggests that breakfast consumption has positive effects on cognitive performance when compared to not having breakfast. More importantly, it is difficult to identify and recommend an optimal breakfast that links to cognitive function based on existing research. To return to the more recent work by Adolphus et al. (2015), in their study, they examined the association between habitual breakfast consumption frequency and cognitive ability test performance. It was found that finding more comprehensible ways to measure habitual breakfast consumption with academic performance would involve measuring achievement tests within the taught curriculum. Therefore, contrary to the positive association identified in the systematic review (Hoyland et al., 2009), Adolphus et al. (2015) found no evidence to suggest that habitual breakfast consumption was associated with academic performance.

So, what about breakfast then? While I have reviewed some key studies on quantitative measures between food and performance, what else has been written about its effectiveness? Harvey-Golding et al. (2015) highlight how only a few qualitative studies attempt to examine the relationship of school food experiences which highlight the gap in the sociocultural impacts of school breakfast. We know that the provision of school breakfast has increased in the UK and for this reason, very little research exists on this topic, but I review some of the work that has been done so far. Therefore, the study focused on the views and attitudes in relation to breakfast consumption which included children, school staff, and parents, with a key focus on children's self-reported breakfast behaviors. The study was conducted in the North West of England within an area of high socioeconomic deprivation and was conducted on the basis of the council-wide universal free school breakfast initiative (Harvey-Golding et al., 2015). In terms of reporting, a number of breakfast consumption behaviors were identified, which included the timing of breakfast consumption, skipping breakfast, consuming breakfast multiple times, and breakfast consumption on the journey to school.

Furthermore, to note some further observations which influenced breakfast consumption, these included socioeconomic factors such as poverty, food insecurity, work, educational commitments, and school holidays. On the whole, the free school breakfast scheme reduced the number of barriers to breakfast consumption, most notably relating to socioeconomic factors. Due to the lack of research on this particular topic, more work is needed that covers broader geographical regions and in relation to school and family.

What impact have breakfast clubs had on children's behavior? 'School breakfast clubs are a type of before school provision that typically take place on the school premises prior to the beginning of the formal school day' (Graham et al., 2015a: 1). The aim of such breakfast clubs is to provide children with the opportunity to start the school day on a full stomach and food that is nutritious in which adult supervision occurs. While we know that breakfast clubs are said to have a positive benefit in schools, only very few studies have investigated such an impact. Graham et al. (2015a) carried out observations using both real-time and filmed breakfast club footage in the North East of England, UK, to investigate the occurrence of positive and negative behaviors. In total, a sample of 30 children aged between three and 11 years was recruited from three breakfast clubs using an opportunity sample. It was interesting to note that children's behaviors were classified into three positive and three negative behavioral categories. Firstly, it is important to highlight the underpinning links between on-task behavior and its association to learning. It is argued that the time a schoolchild spends on concentrating is possibly the most important feature of learning (Grantham-McGregor, 2005). It is also important to note how the research places emphasis on the start of the school day being particularly important as core subjects, including literacy and numeracy, are taught during this period. Overall, the results demonstrated that children displayed more positive than negative behaviors when engaged with both quiet and active tasks. It was interesting to read about the level of supervision during breakfast clubs, as this was identified as a critical factor in determining children's behavior. Previous research suggests that a lack of and inadequate supervision during breakfast clubs links to poor behavior in children (Shemilt et al., 2004).

Breakfast clubs are known to offer a unique opportunity for children to access and consume breakfast in school with some of their peers, and recognizing these opportunities for children is important (Defeyter et al., 2015). To return to the original focus for this section of the chapter, links to the benefits of school food provision on children's health, cognitive performance, and academic attainment have been discussed in the context of research (Adolphus et al., 2013; Rampersaud, 2009; Hoyland et al., 2009) and policy (Dimbleby and Vincent, 2013). Another avenue that is identified as providing children with space for developing social relationships is after-school clubs. The aim of the study was to investigate whether breakfast clubs and after-school clubs have an impact on children's social experiences. While the benefits of school food provision are closely linked to children's health and cognition, research that places a focus on eating spaces that offer children opportunities to socialize with peers is under-researched (Graham et al., 2014). More importantly, research indicates that consuming a meal alongside others can promote interaction among individuals through which children are able to potentially develop social skills (Lalli, 2019a, b; Fulkerson et al., 2006; Eisenberg et al., 2004). This particular piece of research offers a somewhat important overview of the nature of friendships in school and the multifaceted nature through which development is shaped. Overall, attendance at breakfast clubs was identified as having a positive impact on children's friendships. Most importantly, this research highlighted how engagement with breakfast clubs and after-school clubs reported to reduce levels of peer victimization significantly. This work highlights the importance of social relationships for children, and the spaces in which such activity takes place involve food consumption and therefore need to be taken more seriously, as opposed to merely a space for eating.

To provide the final review paper, which explores school breakfast clubs, it is important to highlight the view of parents, children, and school staff, which have largely been neglected in this area (Graham et al., 2015b). The study aimed to investigate the views of these key stakeholders on breakfast clubs in the North East of England using semi-structured interviews. Findings revealed breakfast clubs provided children with a structure and positive start to the school day alongside the varied food choices and opportunities for social interaction. Children were asked to highlight the advantages and disadvantages of breakfast clubs, and children reported the likeness for meal choices and social opportunities that emerged as they were able to spend informal time with peers before going to class. Some children reported tiredness in the morning, but no one reported a dislike for the breakfast clubs. The views of staff and parents were similar, and themes cut across, which include food options and opportunities for social interactions. However, the exclusion of breakfast clubs which incurred charges meant some children who wanted to access them were unable to do so. Most important of all here is that the benefits of breakfast clubs are apparent and echo the views of policymakers and charities who state that access to breakfast clubs could lead to a reduction in child hunger and poverty.

What has not been discussed so far is the impact of school feeding programs in relation to the inclusivity of children with disabilities. This is another aspect of mealtime which has been under-researched. I draw some attention to this here and want to highlight how much more work needs to be done to observe such settings and listen to perspectives from these groups. Based on statistics from the World Health Organization and World Bank, approximately 93 million children across the globe, which equates to one in 20 children, have identified having a moderate or severe disability (Meresman and Drake, 2016). It was found that several barriers prevent children with disabilities from receiving adequate nutrition, and some of these were identified as structural in terms of challenges to access health and social services. The lack of data available on this group is problematic, and a number of related systemic barriers which relate specifically to the functional characteristics of programs include: 1) dining halls and other important spaces in a school such as washrooms and toilets are not accessible to those with disabilities, 2) a lack of experience from teachers in working with those individuals with disabilities, 3) special dietary restrictions, 4) lack of access to resources for individuals with disabilities, 5) discrimination due to stigma (ibid., 2). Teacher training in this regard is crucial, but the functional requirements of school buildings need to be adapted too. The work on mitigating such exclusion rests on having an understanding of the term 'inclusion'. The term 'inclusive education' has typically been used to refer to children with disabilities, but inclusive education is equally important for those who may not speak the typical classroom language of instruction or those who may be too hungry to participate. Therefore, to understand inclusion better is to recognize the importance of proactive policies and plans that ensure learning for all children regardless of their circumstances (FRESH, 2006). Overall, two main ways were established for feeding children with disabilities, and these involve: 1) regularly feeding children through mainstream education, 2) providing a provision for feeding throughout special education institutions.

The research on school holiday provision has recently gained traction as access to an adequate supply of food that is nutritious is a basic human right (Graham et al., 2016), not a privilege. As many families across the UK face food insecurity, research suggests such insecurities are worsened during school holiday periods. Consequently, a select few schools and clubs introduced holiday clubs. We know that the numbers of families accessing food banks in the UK are growing, and according to the Trussell Trust, an estimated 1,085,640 people were provided with a three-day emergency food parcel from 2014–2015. Between April 2019 and March 2020, a record 1.9 million food bank parcels had been provided as both individuals and families struggle to access food (Trussell Trust, 2020). The study by Graham et al. (2016) involved conducting semi-structured interviews in order to capture the perspectives of participants on food insecurity. The overall aim of the study was to investigate the need for holiday club provision and its benefits. Findings revealed that staff believed there is a need for holiday club provision in order to relieve the financial strain on families and to encourage them to stay actively engaged within their communities through the school holidays. Another benefit of such provision was the opportunity to learn about nutrition and sports coaching. A recommendation of the study was for more research to be conducted on this topic in order to support UK policymakers and practitioners in more discussions and investment on such provision.

School gardens

What are the health and wellbeing impacts of school gardening? This final part of the chapter aims to draw on the evidence discussed in the form of a review. School gardening programs have become increasingly popular based on the notion that healthier eating and an increase in physical activity can lead to improved overall health outcomes. A number of schools have very little space for gardening and food growing, as school grounds become paved with concrete. Very little has been covered on the subject of school food gardens from a sociological perspective, as much of the work is concentrated on the impact of school gardening on children's eating habits (Leuven et al., 2018). Work on healthy and alternative approaches to food has also been explored by Hayes-Conroy (2014), which involved studying two North American School Garden and Cooking Program (SGCP) case studies which included a public school in Berkeley, California, and a public school in a rural community in Nova Scotia. Both projects took inspiration from the work of the Edible Schoolyard (ESY) project (Waters and Duane, 2008), which embraced growing, cooking, and sharing healthy food and have grown into the idea of 'Edible Education' from which five key principles were developed. These were: 1) food is an academic subject, 2) schools provide lunch for every child, 3) schools support farms, 4) children learn by doing, 5) beauty is a language. This chapter provides a review of such discussions, which highlight the function and impact of school garden programs.

A brief social history of school garden programs

So, what is the history behind school gardens, and how were they defined? Why were school gardens introduced, and in relation to what problem? Over the past 100 years, in Europe and the United States, school gardens have been situated to support initiatives surrounding hunger. School gardens played a crucial role in reducing hunger in children, and this dates back to as early as 1811 in Europe and the purpose of school gardens was to provide a place where children and young people could learn about natural sciences alongside developing vocational skills. Friedrich Fröbel was the founder of kindergarten and taught between 1805 and 1835, and his thinking rested on a fundamental set of features. These included: 1) people need to be educated to think for themselves, 2) there should be tolerance such that we can place our ideas into the public without fear, 3) to identify with the past as a resource to inform and transform the present and future (Bruce, 2012: 6). Late 19th century pioneering educators such as Maria Montessori and John Dewey built upon educational theories, and they highlighted a focus on gardening and agriculture for children and young people. Furthermore, they identified the vocational aspect of skills acquisition as only a part of the gardening experiences. Today, the focus on the 'whole child' has become a term almost overused but also so important. Of course, this represents different things to different people, but ultimately it was about putting the child into context, and this needs to be reflected for the world in which we live today. A considerable amount of literature on school gardens covers the United States, which appears to be more accessible. With immigration and child labor laws, the number of schoolchildren increased, and gardens were identified as a way of keeping such demands on the state under control (Mader, 2010). By 1905, school gardens had become popularized, and WW1 led to the addition of funding through the

Victory Garden grants. As part of the WW1 effort, schoolchildren were involved in producing food, but school gardens diminished as the years went by. In the latter part of 1906, the US Department of Agriculture (USDA) reported that there were 75,000 school gardens which had been referred to as relief gardening (Hunter et al., 2020). The Cleveland Public Schools ran a garden program that aimed to build character, teach the ways of nature, furnish fun for leisure hours, and yield products of use and beauty (Mader, 2010: 16).

During the mid-60s and 70s, particularly in the developing world, school gardens were introduced as food security interventions through which children are encouraged to gain a sense of appreciation for how food is harvested and produced. School gardens have been associated with having multiple benefits and continue to do so, particularly in relation to teaching agricultural and horticultural skills alongside capacity building. Therefore, the power of engaging with such spaces historically has been known to yield multiple benefits, and such activities cover the full spectrum of the growing cycle from the design of the garden, selection of planting material and agricultural biodiversity, growing and management through harvesting, and preparation for consumption as well as processing for longer-term storage (Hunter et al., 2020: 17). The societal benefit includes the knowledge-building activity, which can support the sustainable management of natural resources.

School garden programs

School garden programs have clearly become a popular development intervention, although it has been observed that the objectives for school gardens have differed significantly. In the globalized south, such activities have included teaching improved farming skills, support with community-based food production, fundraising, and identifying agricultural practices. In the industrialized world, school gardens appear to serve a much broader educational function which includes supporting children to understand science, nature, and the environment, although such activities are also gaining much-needed traction in the developing world (Hunter et al., 2020). More importantly, we have also seen a recognition of the role of school gardens in environmental education, food biodiversity and conservation, diets, nutrition, health, and agricultural education (ibid., 1). In their work, Hunter et al. (2020) acknowledge how the nutrition agenda directing the current interest in supporting school garden initiatives, and this is a major focus of their work; the importance of school gardens as a tool for developing food and nutrition education.

What evidence has been published on the links between school gardens and learning? Passy (2014) conducted projects and reports on the impact of school gardens on primary children's learning with a focus on exploring the pedagogies used in teaching children. I am interested in learning more about such links as the research on learning outside of the classroom develops. The idea is based on being able to engage with problem-solving and team working. The two projects explored by Passy (2014) focused on the impact of school gardens on children's learning, and the other one was to investigate the pedagogies which link to school gardens. While a number of projects which explore Forest Schools have been conducted, very little explores research on the school grounds, which include gardens. School gardens in England have grown in popularity and have encouraged both teaching practitioners alongside local communities to take an interest in growing their own fruit and vegetables. Overall, it was observed that gardens can be demanding places in terms of the time and effort required but also a place that fosters social cohesion and where success can be shared through growing.

The school gardens attracted local communities such as pensioners to join as volunteers in their maintenance. One of the key themes that emerged from the research was the contribution gardens offered in terms of price, pleasure, and enjoyment for those involved. When eating together, we take pride in the relationships we are able to build and growing shares a very similar intimate experience (Passy, 2014). In terms of learning then, teachers reported how school gardens are able to engage children in a number of ways, but further research is required to ascertain such links. The key focus for me within these projects is on the school culture and how they are said to determine attitudes towards such initiatives. School culture has been defined as 'the integration of environmental, organizational and experimental features of school existence to offer a context for teaching and learning and its subsequent improvement' (Glover and Coleman, 2005: 266). The ethos of the school is crucial, and the head teacher's vision plays a crucial role in creating a culture that is inviting of ideas involving school gardening. Finally, school gardens are noted as having more advantages compared with other forms of outdoor learning. For instance, firstly, gardens are onsite or in the case of school allotments, they are within walking distance so, therefore, are more accessible. School gardens are also fairly inexpensive and relatively small in size, with very little equipment and transportation required. The interest for me is in the pedagogy of school gardens, and we are beginning to see more research being published on this area (Earl and Thompson, 2020). This more recent work maps out the complex history of the gardening movement in schools and examines why gardens should be built in schools offering practical guidance for teachers.

Following a systematic review of the health and wellbeing impacts of school gardening, it is important to reflect on the breadth of studies which include 40 journal articles, 21 of which are quantitative, 16 qualitative, and three mixed methods studies (Ohly et al., 2016). Since the 1990s, we have observed an increase in the number of research studies that have made an attempt to evaluate the effectiveness of school gardening programs. Several reviews of the literature on school gardening have been published (Nelson et al., 2011; Langellotto and Gupta, 2012; Oxenham and King, 2010; Robinson-O'Brien et al., 2009; Blair, 2009; Ozer, 2007), and five of these were based on a US context and while some empirical evidence was found supporting the health and wellbeing of school gardening on children, most of the conclusions were based on theoretical models.

A comprehensive review on food-growing activities in schools was conducted by Nelson et al. (2011) and submitted to the Department for Environment, Food and Rural Affairs (DEFRA) on behalf of the National Foundation for Educational Research (NFER). The aim of the review was to investigate the impact of food growing in schools for pupils, schools, and communities and the cost benefits of growing. Another aim of the review was to conduct a survey to examine the extent to which schools and early years settings were involved in food-growing activities. Overall, it was found that the strongest evidence of impact relates closely to health and educational outcomes, which include healthy eating and nutrition and particularly on science and horticultural knowledge. This extensive review highlighted limitations in terms of methodological robustness, which has an impact on the evidence base, but on the whole, a number of positive messages emerged for children, schools, and communities. The review also highlighted modest evidence for social wellbeing benefits, and these observations were particularly evident in children identified as having lower abilities who had become disengaged from learning. Despite the popularity of school gardens, evidence to support health benefits and engagement is limited, and the evidence is largely self-reported. In terms of the qualitative evidence, a wide range of data suggests an engagement with school gardens has a range of health and wellbeing benefits. Although school gardens have been identified as complex interventions, there is limited research suggesting a need for a more complex design approach as consistency is required in terms of the way in which food intake is being measured (Ohly et al., 2016).

Gardening for learning

What about the interactions with the garden beyond the school gates? How does this connect with learning, and how does it offer to the school premises? What about allotments off the school premises and garden spaces that extend beyond the school gates? My experience of growing up included watching my parents cultivate food and then also preserving space for us to play in the garden, all of which was handled with pride. We know that school gardening programs have been identified as the most promising interventions to improve children's vegetable intake, yet this remains a problem and is a public health challenge (Nury et al., 2017). What we also need to consider are the connections between gardening at home or with grandparents and relatives. In terms of socioeconomic status, this has an impact on children who may not have grown up with access to a garden. We have also started to observe community-funded gardening programs and projects through which those children who may not have access to a garden at home can interact with the sensory aspect and void they may have experienced. Moreover, some children who live in urban settings may not have access to gardens regardless of socioeconomic status. What is particularly interesting is the perspective of McLennan, who accounts for the experiences of a class that participated in a community-funded gardening project titled 'Ready, Set, Grow!' in Montverde, Costa Rica, and presents the view of a school principal who supports the point about needing vision. For example, the principal at Cloud Forest School (2009) made the following statement,

> Must we always teach our children with books? Let them look at the stars and the mountains above. Let them look at the waters and trees and flowers on earth. Then they will begin to think, and to think is the beginning of a real education.

While thinking of gardening, we also know that whether at home or in school, it is arguably one of the most educational experiences we can share with children, and Cooper and Holmes (2006) highlight how children interact differently with gardens at different ages. For example, pre-school children may wish to plant a seed, dig for worms, or even pluck strawberries, although this does not necessarily make the connection between growing and preparing food (ibid., 108). As children enter formal education, they may be able to use the garden as a tool for play which includes storytelling and a place for exploring the imagination. Therefore, at a young age, gardening can be about reading, writing, drawing, math, science, and learning about food. So, links between gardening and children's intake of vegetables tend to dominate the published literature, and of course, fruit and vegetable consumption plays an important role in maintaining a healthy diet (Benkowitz et al., 2019). Gardening experiences are known to help children to acquire a liking for certain vegetables, and such exposure is also said to have a positive impact on children's food consumption in their adult lives. In order to improve the school gardening outcomes, researchers need to focus on developing a robustly designed longitudinal study that combines both qualitative and quantitative (descriptive and statistical) elements using an appropriate sample design (Blair, 2009). The research design also needs to focus on the effects of class, gender, and race as contributing factors in the participation and engagement with school garden spaces.

Lessons to be learned

So, what is the role of school food education, and what potential does it have to support children's capabilities to adopt positive and healthy behaviors? In response to high levels of childhood obesity, a focus on protecting children's health has gained the attention of policymakers and practitioners (Dimbleby and Vincent, 2013; Rose et al., 2019). In terms of those suffering most, the social gradient in health outcomes as a whole is known to affect those from lower socioeconomic groups (Marmot et al., 2010, 2020). Conversely, it is argued that adopting a moral stance on what is said to constitute a healthy diet is another mechanism for surveillance (Hart and Page, 2020). As this piece of research was conducted in England, this relates to my work at Peartree Academy and Maple Field Academy in terms of context, and more leadership and governance is required in pushing the vision forward, particularly the school food standards in secondary schools. On the whole, healthy eating, as mentioned in the healthy rating scheme for schools, is not yet a priority across schools in England, and there is also no cultural priority (Hart and Page, 2020).

It is particularly promising to see a number of publications surfacing on food education both in the curriculum (Rutland and Turner, 2020) and on school gardens (Earl and Thompson, 2020). The work of Rutland and Turner (2020) provides a refreshing collection of works that explore the place of food in education and stems from a number of contexts which include primary, secondary, and vocational school education. Furthermore, the book also draws on teacher education programs and the focus on food technology within the design and technology curriculum. The multitude of issues explored includes health, obesity, design, sustainability, and global warming, which all contribute to critical global issues. Therefore, the link between food and learning extends beyond the classroom and is able to shape children into critical thinkers and potential adversaries and advocates to growing debates on the environment. Much can be learned from understanding the issues involved in learning how to teach about food in schools successfully and developing sound knowledge skills in food teaching on a more practical basis. In a book written by Earl and Thompson (2020), the connection between educational theory and gardening is examined closely and is based on case studies of the school that develops a new garden while another tries to maintain one. In terms of lessons to be learned, four key issues are highlighted which need consideration prior to setting up a garden. These include: 1) the wider social context, 2) public policy, 3) the whole school, and 4) the formal and informal curriculum.

The links between nutrition and cognitive function are widely known to be strong. We know pupil scores vary considerably in terms of school performance and are influenced by a number of factors, including health and wellbeing. School food policy also varies and, in an attempt to update standards, the School Food Plan was introduced in 2015. All schools are encouraged to provide healthy, tasty, and nutritious food and drink, and compliance with the school food standards is mandatory. However, the implementation of food policy is sporadic, and the picture is unclear. While there are a number of insights from cognitive science about how nutrition affects learning, no one is yet to link this to school food standards which I wish to take seriously. We also know that school gardens promote engagement with agricultural and horticultural education, which means the capacity for knowledge building is extremely rich for future generations. What has become problematic is the multifaceted nature of engaging with research in such spaces, and it would be fascinating to conduct research to find ways of developing suitable methodological tools which capture children's experiences. For success in school gardening, in particular, the need to support teachers is vital, and the vision of the school's principal needs to focus on school gardening as a fundamental element of curriculum design. Ultimately, researchers and educators need to pay close attention to the design of gardens and the learning experience but in a way that lightens the teacher's burden (Blair, 2009) as opposed to creating additional work at a time where workload issues have become commonplace. The major teacher issues are lack of interest and limited capabilities, knowledge, and time, so these barriers need to be addressed (Blair, 2009). Clearly, the power of such spaces in forging positive sensory relationships with nature and people is a key talking point.

Conclusion

Clearly, much more work is needed, and the way in which schools are designed needs to take account of spaces for gardening activities. These offer rich experiences for children, schools, and local communities, which enrich children's lives, and evidence demonstrates a positive impact on their wellbeing. This is a particularly important aspect of schooling, and we need to think more creatively about the way in which school spaces are being utilized. While the pressure for securing space remains problematic in schools, the amount of space and resources required is minimal compared to the potential benefits that are offered. It is clear that more attention needs to be paid to food and sustainability education in schools and a whole school approach through which the leadership team is able to portray a vision for schools. While the literature on school garden programs is based in the United States, we need to closely examine how such programs have been developed for use elsewhere, and we should not think of gardening as an isolated activity but a way of life as children are able to forge positive and lasting social relationships and if this has an impact on their eating choices, then this has a positive impact on future generations. How do we push for policymakers to prioritize food education? How can we develop a robust methodology to develop a bank of evidence, both statistical and descriptive, to document the importance of such sensory and personal interactions? What is the meaning of food for life, and how does such a philosophy impact our values and beliefs? Questions I continue to ponder as I continue to write about the school food space.

References

Adolphus, K., Lawton, C.L., Dye, L. 2013. The effects of breakfast on behaviour and academic performance in children and adolescents, *Frontiers in Human Neuroscience*, 7, p. 425, DOI: 10.3389/fnhum.2013.00425.

Adolphus, K., Lawton, C.L., Dye, L. 2015. The relationship between habitual breakfast consumption frequency and academic performance in British adolescents, *Frontiers in Public Health: Children and Health*, 3 (68), DOI: 10.3389/fpubh.2015.00068.

Aliyar, R., Gelli, A., Hadjivayanis Hamdani, S. 2015. A review of nutritional guidelines and menu compositions for school feeding programs in 12 countries, *Frontiers in Public Health: Children and Health*, 3, p. 148, DOI: 10.3389/fpubh.2015.00148.

Benkowitz, D., Schulz, S., Lindemann-Matthies, P. 2019. The impact of gardening experiences on children's intake of vegetables, *Journal of Health, Environment and Education*, 11, pp. 1–5.

Blair, D. 2009. The child in the garden: An evaluative review of the benefits of school gardening, *Journal of Environmental Education*, 40 (2), pp. 15–38.

Bruce, T. 2012. *Early Childhood Practice: Froebel Today.* London: Sage.

Cloud Forest School. 2009. Environmental education at the CEC [Online]. Available at: http://cloudforestschool.org/ Accessed 10 December 2020.

Cooper, A. and Holmes, L. M. 2006. Lunch Lessons: Changing the way we feed our children. London: Harper Collins.

Defeyter, M.A., Graham, P.L., Russo, R. 2015. More than just a meal: Breakfast club attendance and children's social relationships, *Frontiers in Public Health: Children and Health*, 3, p. 183, DOI: 10.3389/fpubh.2015.00183.

Defra. 2020. National Food Strategy. https://www.gov.uk/government/publications/developing-a-national-food-strategy-independent-review-2019/developing-a-national-food-strategy-independent-review-2019-terms-of-reference. Accessed 6 August 2021.

Department for Education. 2014. Requirements for school food regulations [Online]. Available at: https://www.legislation.gov.uk/uksi/2014/1603/pdfs/uksi_20141603_en.pdf. Accessed 6 November 2020.

Department for Education. 2019. School food in England: Advice on governing boards [Online]. Available at: https://www.gov.uk/government/publications/standards-for-school-food-in-england Accessed 6 November 2020.

Dimbleby, H. and Vincent, J. 2013. The school food plan [Online]. Available at: http://www.schoolfoodplan.com/wp-content/uploads/2013/07/School_Food_Plan_2013.pdf Accessed 2 December 2020.

Drake, L., Russo, R., Defeyter, M.A. 2017. Editorial: The impact of school food consumption on children's cognition, educational attainment and social development, *Frontiers in Public Health: Children and Health*, 5, 204, DOI: 10.3389/fpubh.2017.00204.

Earl, L. and Lalli, G. 2020. Healthy meals, better learners: Debating the focus of school food policy in England, *British Journal of Sociology of Education*, 41(4), pp. 476 – 489.

Earl, L. and Thompson, P. 2020. *Why Garden in Schools?* London: Routledge.

Eisenberg, M.E., Olson, R.E., Neumark-Sztainer, D., Story, M., Bearinger, L.H. 2004. Correlations between family meals and psychosocial wellbeing among adolescents, *Archives of Pediatric and Adolescent Medicine*, 158 (8), pp. 792–796.

Ells, L.J., Hillier, F.C., Shucksmith, J., Crawley, H., Harbige, L., Shield, J., Wiggins, A., Summerbell, C.D. 2008. A systematic review of dietary exposure that could be achieved through normal dietary intake on learning and performance of school-aged children of relevance to UK schools, *British Journal of Nutrition*, 100 (5), pp. 927–936.

Focusing Resources on Effective School Health. 2006. A FRESH approach for achieving education for all [Online]. Available at: http://www.unicef.org/lifeskills/files/FreshDocument.pdf Accessed 4 December 2020.

Fulkerson, J.A., Story, M., Mellin, A., Leffert, N., Neumark-Sztainer, D., French, S.A. 2006. Family dinner meal frequency and adolescent development: Relationships with developmental assets and high-risk behaviours, *Journal of Adolescent Health*, 39, pp. 337–345.

Gelli, A. 2015. School feeding and girls' enrolment: The effects of alternative implementation modalities in low-income settings in Sub-Saharan Africa, *Frontiers in Public Health: Children and Health*, 3, p. 76, DOI: 10.3389/fpubh.2015.00076.

Glover, D. and Coleman, M. 2005. School culture, climate and ethos: Interchangeable or distinctive concepts? *Journal of In-service Education*, 31 (2), pp. 251–271.

Golley, R., Baines, E., Bassett, P., Wood, L., Pearce, J., Nelson, M. 2010. School lunch and learning behaviour in primary schools: An intervention study, *European Journal of Clinical Nutrition*, 64 (11), pp. 1280–1288.

Graham, P.L., Crilley, E., Stretesky, P.B. Long, M., Palmer, K.J., Steinbock, E., Defeyter, M.A. 2016. School Holiday Food Provision in the UK: A qualitative investigation of needs, benefits, and potential for development, *Frontiers in Public Health: Children and Health*, 4, p. 172, DOI: 10.3389/fpubh.2016.00172.

Graham, P.L., Russo, R., Blackledge, J., Defeyter, M.A. 2014. Breakfast and beyond: The dietary, social and practical impacts of a universal free school breakfast scheme in the North West of England, UK, *International Journal of Sociology of Agriculture and Food*, 21, pp. 261–274.

Graham, P.L., Russo, R., Defeyter, M.A. 2015a. Breakfast clubs: Starting the day in a positive way, *Frontiers in Public Health Children and Health*, 3, p. 172, DOI: 10.3389/fpubh.2015.00172.

Graham, P.L., Russo, R., Defeyter, M.A. 2015b. The advantages and disadvantages of breakfast clubs according to parents, children and school staff in the North East of England, UK, *Frontiers in Public Health: Children and Health*, 3, p. 156, DOI: 10.3389/fpubh.2015.00156.

Grantham-McGregor, S. 2005. Can the provision of breakfast benefit school performance? *Food Nutrition Bulletin*, 26 (Supplement 2), pp. 144–158.

Haroun, D., Harper, C., Wood, L., Nelson, M. 2010. The impact of the food-based and nutrient-based standards on lunchtime food and drink provision and consumption in primary schools in England, *Public Health Nutrition*, 14 (2), pp. 209–218.

Hart, C.S. and Page, A. 2020. The capability approach and school food education and culture in England: 'gingerbread men ain't gonna get me very far', *Cambridge Journal of Education*, DOI:10.1080/0305764X.2020.1764498.

Harvey-Golding, L., Donkin, L.M., Blackledge, J., Defeyter, M.A. 2015. Universal free school breakfast: A qualitative model for breakfast behaviours, *Frontiers in Public Health: Children and Health*, 3, p. 154, DOI: 10.3389/fpubh.2015.00154.

Hayes-Conroy, J. 2014. *Savoring Alternative Food: School Gardens, Healthy Eating and Visceral Difference.* London: Routledge.

Hilari, C. and Franco, M. 2015. What is needed to improve food sales in schools? Food vendors' opinion from El Salvador, *Frontiers in Public Health, Children and Health*, 3, p. 168, DOI: 10.3389/fpubh.2015.00168.

Hoyland, A., Dye, L., Lawton, C.L. 2009. A systematic review of the effect of breakfast on the cognitive performance of children and adolescents, *Nutrition Research Reviews*, 22, pp. 220–243, DOI: 10.1017/S0954422409990175.

Hunter, D., Monville-Oro, E., Burgos, B., Rogel, C.N., Calub, B., Gonsalves, J., Lauridsen, N. 2020. *Agrobiodiversity, School Gardens and Health Diets.* London: Routledge.

Lalli, G. 2021. A review of the English School Meal: 'Progress or a recipe for disaster?', *Cambridge Journal of Education*, DOI: 10.1080/0305764X.2021.1893658.

Lalli, G. 2019a. School mealtime and social learning in England, *Cambridge Journal of Education*, 50 (1), pp. 55–75.

Lalli, G. 2019b. *Schools, Food and Social Learning*, Abingdon: Routledge.

Lalli, G. 2020. The school restaurant: Ethnographic reflections in researching children's food space, *International Journal of Qualitative Studies in Education*, DOI: 10.1080/09518398.2020.1797210.

Langellotto, G.A., Gupta, A. 2012. Gardening increases vegetable consumption in school-aged children: A meta-analytical synthesis, *Horttechnology*, 22 (4), pp. 430–445.

Leuven, J.R.F.W., Rutenfrans, A.H.M., Dolfing, A.G., Leuven, R.S.E.W. 2018. School gardening increases knowledge of primary school children on edible plants and preference for vegetables, *Food Science and Nutrition*, 6 (7), pp. 1960–1967.

Mader, J. 2010. *Cleveland School Gardens*. South Carolina: Arcadia Publishing.

Marmot, M., Allen, J., Boyce, T., Goldblatt, P., Morrison, J. 2020. *Health Equity in England: The Marmot Review 10 Years On*. London: Institute of Health Equity.

Marmot, M., Allen, J., Goldblatt, P., Boyce, T., McNeish, D., Grady, M., Geddes, I. 2010. *Fair Society, Healthy Lives*. London: The Marmot Review.

Meresman, S. and Drake, L. 2016. Are school feeding programs prepared to be inclusive of children with disabilities, *Frontiers in Public Health: Children and Health*, 4, p. 45, DOI: 10.3389/fpubh.2016.00045.

Nelson, J., Martin, K., Nicholas, J., Easton, C., Featherstone, G. 2011. *Food Growing Activities in Schools: Report Submitted to DEFRA*. National Foundation for Educational Research.

Nelson, M., Gibson, K., Nicholas, J. 2015. School lunch take up and attainment in primary and secondary schools in England, *Frontiers in Public Health: Children and Health*, 3, p. 230, DOI: 10.3389/fpubh.2015.00230.

Nicholas, J., Wood, L., Harper, C., Nelson, M. 2013. The impact of the food-based and nutrient-based standards on lunchtime food and drink provision and consumption in secondary schools in England, *Public Health Nutrition*, 16 (6), pp. 1052–1065.

Nury, E., Sarti, A., Dijkstra, C., Seidell, J.C. 2017. Sowing seeds for healthier diets: Children's perspectives on school gardening, *International Journal of Environmental Research in Public Health*, 14 (7), DOI: 10.3390/ijerph14070688.

Nyaradi, A., Li, J., Hickling, S., Foster, J., Oddy, W.H. 2013. The role of nutrition in children's neurocognitive development, from pregnancy through childhood, *Frontiers in Human Neuroscience*, 7(97), pp. 1–16.

Ohly, H., Gentry, S., Wigglesworth, R., Bethel, A., Lovell, R., Garside, R. 2016. A systematic review of the health and wellbeing impacts of school gardening: Synthesis of quantitative and qualitative evidence, *BMC Public Health*, 16, p. 286, DOI: 10.1186/s12889-016-2941-0.

Oxenham, E. and King, A.D. 2010. School gardens as a strategy for increasing fruit and vegetable consumption, *Journal of Child Nutrition and Management*, 34 (1), pp. 5.

Ozer, E.J. 2007. The effects of school gardens on students and schools: Conceptualisation and considerations for maximising healthy development, *Health Education and Behaviour*, 34 (6), pp. 846–863.

Passy, R. 2014. School gardens: Teaching and learning outside the front door, *Education 3–13: International Journal of Primary, Elementary and Early Years Education*, 42 (1), pp. 23–38.

Public Health England. 2015. Food teaching in primary schools: A framework of knowledge and skills [Online]. Available at: https://www.gov.uk/government/publications/food-teaching-in-primary-schools-knowledge-and-skills-framework Accessed 11 November 2020.

Rampersaud, G.C. 2009. Benefits of breakfast for children and adolescents: Update and recommendations for practitioners, *American Justice of Lifestyle Medicine*, 3 (2), pp. 86–103.

Robinson-O'Brien, R., Story, M., Heim, S. 2009. Impact of garden-based youth nutrition intervention programs: A review, *Journal of American Dietetic Association*, 109 (2), pp. 273–280.

Rose, K., Lake, A.A., Ellis, L.J., Brown, L. 2019. School food provision in England: A historical journey, *Nutrition Bulletin*, 44 (3), pp. 283–291.

Rutland, M. and Turner, A. 2020. *Food Education and Food Technology in School Curricula: International Perspectives*. New York: Springer.

Shemilt, I., Harvey, I., Shepstone, L., Swift, L., Reading, R., Mugford, M. 2004. A national evaluation of school breakfast clubs: Evidence from a cluster randomised controlled trial and an observational analysis, *Child: Care, Health and Development*, 30, pp. 413–427.

Storey, C., Pearce, J., Ashfield-Watt, P.., Wood, L., Nelson, M. 2011. A randomised controlled trial of the effect of school food and dining room modifications on classroom behaviour in secondary school children, *European Journal of Clinical Nutrition*, 65, pp. 32–38.

The Guardian. 2020. National food strategy set out: Banishing pollution and poverty for sustainability, by Patrick Butler [Online]. Available at: https://www.theguardian.com/uk-news/2020/jul/29/national-food-strategy-set-out-banishing-pollution-and-poverty-for-sustainability Accessed 30 November 2020.

Trussell Trust. 2020. Latest statistics [Online]. Available at: https://www.trusselltrust.org/news-and-blog/latest-stats/ Accessed 4 December 2020.

United Nations. 2014. Food and Agriculture Organization of the United Nations, The State of Food Insecurity in the World (SOFI) [Online]. Available at: http://www.fao.org/publications/sofi/2014/en/ Accessed 26 November 2020.

Waters, A. and Duane, D. 2008. *Edible Schoolyard*. San Francisco: Chronicle Books.

World Food Programme. 2019. The impact of school feeding programmes [Online]. Available at: https://www.wfp.org/publications/impact-school-feeding-programmes Accessed 25 November 2020.

2

THE IMPACT OF HUNGER ON CHILDREN AND ADOLESCENTS

School farming as a panacea

Abel Ebiega Enokela

Introduction

Agriculture as a human endeavor dates to antiquity as a means of food security, sustainability, and continued existence. Nature endows man with all the necessary resources with which to sustain food security and a healthy environment. Back then, healthy and natural food was available, and man's longevity was guaranteed because his food and environment were healthy and safe. Unfortunately, we have a different story to tell today. The natural food and the healthy environment that used to be the pride of humankind at some point in history are facing serious threats due to food insecurity, environmental pollution, erosion, loss of virgin land for farming, and other human-made adverse conditions. The days of forests providing humankind with a healthy and beautiful environment to behold, surplus land for farming, and a conducive environment to rear animals have become elusive. In addition to the fact that human beings have tampered with the natural setting of land and other natural resources that can guarantee food security, other problems like pandemics, terrorism, banditry, wars, earthquakes, and similar natural disasters are also threatening agricultural ventures. Dunn (2018), in a study entitled 'The impact of the Boko Haram insurgency in Northeast Nigeria on childhood wasting: a double-difference study', noted poor children's health situation that was attributable to destabilized social services and rising food insecurity occasioned by the activities of the insurgents in the region. With all these challenges, it is evident that there is an impending famine or starvation in the days ahead. Fawole, Ilbasmis and Ozkan (2015) hinted that undernourishment, food inadequacy and the number of undernourished individuals in Nigeria was high and required urgent attention. The challenge of impending hunger even goes beyond Nigeria, as Gamer (2020) reported that Catholic Relief Services (CRS) in the United States, in an evaluation of Guatemala, discovered

DOI: 10.4324/9781003176558-2

that 85% of households in one area were affected by hunger compared to 22% in April 2020. The report noted that CRS also cited the situation report of the Famine Early Warning Systems Network of June 29, 2020, which confirmed that Yemen, Niger, South Sudan, Honduras, El Salvador, Uganda, Somalia, and Kenya were at risk of famine. In response to this challenge, CRS and other humanitarian bodies, according to the source, requested Congress to provide at least $12 billion in COVID-19 supplemental legislation for humanitarian support overseas (Gamer, 2020). This report shows that the world is heading towards a time of terrible famine, and it requires timely intervention to save lives, especially those of children and adolescents.

Children and adolescents are likely to be in danger as food shortages and environmental degradation continue to hold sway. Food is essential for the developmental processes of children and adolescents. Shortage of food will lead to starvation of many children across Africa and other parts of the world if no proactive measures are taken early. Children and adolescents are still in their formative stages and require the right quality and quantity of food to biologically, psychologically, and socially develop in a balanced way. Lack of food can lead to malnourishment, sickness, and even death, particularly among young children (WHO, 2016, 2021; UNICEF, 2018a; Glicken, 2010). Psychologically, a hungry child could have difficulty coping with his or her study and could manifest disruptive behavior (Foodbank, 2015), such as bullying, poor peer interaction, aggressiveness, and criminal tendencies. A hungry child can exhibit an inferiority complex, low self-esteem, depressive mood, and very poor attention span. To avoid this looming danger of global famine, all countries need to go back to the land and produce sufficient food to save children and adolescents from starvation, and to prevent distorting their developmental processes and even sending some to early graves.

The school farm, as a long-established practice, has been filling the gaps in food sustenance. Olaitan and Mama (2001) posited that a school farm is an area of land specially dedicated to a school's agricultural activities; it may be within the school premises or walking distance. Students engage in farm activities like crop farming and animal husbandry. Through this process, communities could be fed; students could eat fresh and nutritious food and enjoy a green environment that can enhance effective learning. Students also learn valuable vocational skills from the exercise of school farming (Emeya and Ojimba, 2012). Students' engagement in school farming can be a form of extracurricular activity which is an opportunity for them to put into practice what they learn in the classroom, thereby harmonizing formal classroom learning outcomes with practical experiences (Lunenburg, 2010; Massoni, 2011). However, the school farming system, which was very much active in Nigeria and many other parts of the world, is gradually facing threats of extinction due to neglect of the system by stakeholders (Falaju, 2018, Famiwole, 2013). According to the National Aeronautics and Space Administration (NASA) (1998), cited in Azare et al. (2019), Nigeria has the world's highest annual deforestation rate of primary forest at 55.7%, and is one of the two largest losers of annual natural forests in Africa. This means that fertile land for school farming could be a serious challenge in the country. Furthermore, Nigeria's dependence on oil resources for funds has shifted emphasis from the agricultural sector, which was generating 70% GDP before the oil boom in 1970 (Pettinger, 2015). Reliance on oil has regrettably led the country to vigorous extensive and intensive oil exploration and drilling in the oil-rich regions of the country where farmlands and ecosystems have been destroyed as a result of oil spillage (Saleh et al., 2017); and thereby adding to the problem of not having sufficient farmlands in some areas.

Addressing the ailing state of school farming and the danger of impending hunger in the world requires the concerted efforts of researchers and necessitates a multidisciplinary and interdisciplinary approach to foster a broad understanding of the phenomenon, its likely impacts, and solutions. The challenge of food insecurity is enormous and should be a shared burden since everybody needs food and a green environment to survive. On this note, this study looked at foreseeable challenges of global famine and its possible adverse effects on children and adolescents and how to revive the workability of school farms through the lens of counseling. School-based counselors have many roles to play to strengthen the school farm system. Counseling is a professional interaction that empowers diverse individuals, families, and groups to accomplish mental health, wellness, education, and career goals (Kaplan, Tarvydas, and Gladding, 2014). Considering this definition of counseling, one can say that the counselors' concern towards children's and adolescents' feeding is inevitable because hunger affects students' wellbeing and academic performance.

Similarly, counselors' advocacy for the resuscitation of school farms is germane because school farms promote mental health, wellness, and career goals. Counseling can be divided into three areas: vocational counseling, educational counseling, and personal/social counseling. From all three domains, counseling has a crucial role in addressing the impacts of hunger on children with a view to raising hope of surmounting the looming danger of food insecurity through school farming instrumentality. Looking at it from the side of vocational counseling, a school farm is a vocational training tool and should attract counselors' attention with respect to vocational counseling. Considering it from the educational counseling point of view, a school farm is a part of the subject of agricultural science and should attract counselors' concern in terms of educational counseling.

Furthermore, viewing it from the personal/social counseling angle, which is concerned with the psychological health of individuals, the school farm still maintains relevance to counseling as the counselor is interested in the psychological health of the clients. Hence, the school farm, being a catalyst for a green environment with accompanying aesthetic and serenity, promotes psychological health. In a nutshell, counselors have influential roles to play in championing and promoting the course of school farms to eradicate hunger, poverty, and a myriad of other challenges associated with food insecurity, hunger, malnutrition, and interference with the ecosystem.

It is worth mentioning that this study, though it addressed a universal challenge of hunger among children and adolescents and the need to prioritize school farming as a panacea to lingering and impending global food insecurity, the situation of Nigeria in connection to the subject matter was the focal point throughout this chapter. This study is significant since it contributes to understanding the impact of hunger on children and adolescents, and how it can be minimized through the instrumentality of school farming. Though Nigeria is used as a microcosm, the study has international relevance and significance because hunger has devastating psychosocial and biological effects on children and adolescents worldwide. Children's and adolescents' developmental processes have both immediate and future impacts on them and society and should therefore attract the attention of scholars in interdisciplinary and multidisciplinary research. This study particularly portrays its uniqueness by looking at school farming's importance as an antidote to children's and adolescents' hunger. Children and adolescents are the leaders of tomorrow and require much attention for balanced development. Hence, this study is expected to help agriculturists, school administrators, governments, counselors, parents, researchers, and the public as it intends to be an eye-opener for everyone to prioritize feeding children and adolescents.

Method and procedure

This study explores the potentialities of school farming in fostering food security to curb hunger among children and adolescents. It also explores some of the benefits of school farming in terms of vocational and pedagogical benefits. The target population for this study is Nigerian children and adolescents. Research data were drawn from findings of both local and international researchers, but with greater emphasis on those from Nigeria to portray local content. The researcher adopted a mixed approach to obtain data for the purpose of this study. On the one hand, the study adopted a theoretical approach and relied on secondary data based on existing literature findings. On the other hand, the researcher visited Hope Eden Community School, located at Kuje, a suburb in the Federal Capital Territory, Abuja, Nigeria, on October 14, 2020, to obtain primary data on its school farm through observation and interview methods. The school representatives provided information related to the purpose of the school farm, students' and parents' participation in the school farm, types of crops produced by the school farm, how the food was used to feed the schoolchildren who were from less privileged homes, among others. The researcher also took pictures of various growing crops on the farm. Thus, the secondary data gleaned from reliable sources and the first-hand information obtained based on the researcher's visit to Hope Eden Community School, located at Kuje, a suburb in the Federal Capital Territory, Abuja, Nigeria, provided the source of data for this study. It is worth mentioning that the researcher was guided by the following research questions while carrying out this research: 1. Can school farming enhance food sustainability to curb hunger among children and adolescents? 2. Can school farms also foster vocational and pedagogical benefits? Thus, these questions formed the thrust of this chapter, though with greater emphasis on question 1.

Feeding children and adolescents for proper psychological development

The concepts of children and adolescents are fundamental and central to this study. There is the need to address the stages of children's and adolescents' development with the utmost care. Understanding these stages and the psychological dynamics that go with them will help one to appreciate the need to feed children and adolescents with food that contains all the necessary nutrients that can enhance proper developmental processes. Childhood is the period between infancy and puberty (0–9 years), and according to the WHO (2021), adolescence is the period of transition between childhood and adulthood (10–19 years). Growing up for children and adolescents involves several things. At the center of their developmental processes is the need for a good diet. Hunger or malnutrition affects children and adolescents psychologically, biologically, and socially. The WHO (2014) posited that patterns of present and future health conditions which can also impact behavioral patterns are established during childhood and adolescence. According to Omotayo and Aliyu (2020), children's and adolescents' mental, physical, and social wellness are the most significant tools that can guarantee good economic growth and development in society. Hence, promoting healthy eating habits and breastfeeding is needed to enhance the nutritional level of children and adolescents, as breastfeeding alone has been estimated to prevent 12% of fatalities in children below five years of age in Europe (WHO, 2014). The risk of children dying early or developing illnesses that can be triggered by hunger or undernutrition is equally high (WHO, 2016; UNICEF, 2018a; Glicken, 2010).

Psychologically, the growing child undergoes multidimensional developmental processes. The child undergoes personality, cognitive, psychosocial, and moral development. The 'psychoanalytical theory' of Sigmund Freud, 'psychosocial theory' of Erik Erikson, 'cognitive theory' of Jean Piaget, 'morality theory' of Lawrence Kohlberg, 'ecological system theory' of Urie Bronfenbrenner, 'choice theory' of William Glasser, and 'need theory' of Abraham Maslow are relevant to children's and adolescent's development and of interest to this study. Freud's psychoanalytical theory talks about five stages a child goes through in terms of personality development. These stages are: oral stage (0–18 months); anal stage (1.5–3 years); phallic stage (3–7 years); latency stage (6–11 years); and genital stage (11–14+ years) (Freud, 1949; McLeod, 2018a). The oral stage is particularly essential to this study, considering that it is the first stage of developing a child in the world. Freud postulated that the child's most attention-seeking part of the body is the mouth at this stage. The child longs for food to satisfy his or her psychosexual urge. It is believed that a child that is starved at this stage of personality development is prone to oral personality disorders like excessive eating and drinking, dependency, and aggressiveness in adulthood. This suggests that children should be properly fed for them to develop an adaptive oral personality. The psychosocial theory of Erikson looks at eight stages for an individual's psychosocial developments: trust vs. mistrust (0–12 months); autonomy vs. shame (1–3 years); initiative vs. guilt (3–6 years); industry vs. inferiority (6–12 years); identity vs. role confusion (12–18 years); intimacy vs. isolation (young adulthood); generativity vs. stagnation (middle adulthood); and integrity vs. despair (late adulthood) (Erikson, 1963, Erikson, 1964; McLeod, 2018b). Erikson thought that an individual who went through these stages successfully would have a sense of fulfillment as an adult. The first stage, which is trust vs. mistrust (0–12 months), sets the stage for all the other stages. This is the stage of bonding among the child, mother, and caregivers. The mother and other caregivers' attitudes will determine the child's worldview in terms of trust or mistrust at this stage. Proper feeding of the child forms part of the bonding processes that can enhance trust on the part of the growing child. Dollard and Miller (1950), in their behaviorist attachment theory, posited that attachment is a set of learned behavior; and that through the provision of food by a mother, a child will associate food with satisfaction (classical conditioning), and by extension, discover that the relationship with the mother brings satisfaction or reward. Thus, food is a catalyst for bonding and attachment. A starved child may not be attached to the mother and is likely to have a maladjusted worldview of trust and tend to see the world as hostile and unapproachable. The early maladjusted worldview of a child can affect their behavior in the future. The stage of trust vs. mistrust of Erikson's theory coincides with Freud's oral stage, which emphasizes proper feeding of children to avert maladjusted behavior in adulthood. Piaget (1936, 1957) emphasized four stages of cognitive development of children and adolescents: sensorimotor stage (0–2 years); preoperational stage (2–7 years); concrete operational stage (7–11 years), and formal operational stage (11 years and above). According to Piaget, these stages are steps of cognitive development of children and adolescents. The point to note is that hungry children may find it difficult to develop properly in terms of cognition (World Food Programme, 2012; Foodbank, 2015; Winicki and Jemison, 2003). A hungry person may not think properly and likely have an attention deficit. The morality theory of Kohlberg posits that the morality development of a growing child is on three levels. The levels are pre-conventional morality, conventional morality, and post-conventional morality (Kohlberg, 1984; McLeod, 2013). These moral development levels of a child can be truncated if the child's basic need of feeding is neglected. The ecological system theory of Bronfenbrenner explains that the child interacts with his or her environment as part of his or her psychosocial development. These psychosocial environments are the microsystem, mesosystem, exosystem, macrosystem, and chronosystem (Bronfenbrenner, 1979, 2005; Ettekal and Mahoney, 2017). The children are expected to interact with these environments to develop adaptive emotionality. They are to interact with their family members, peers, teachers, and significant others in line with their eco-logical system. However, hungry children do not usually get along well with others because they are usually depressed, angry, and moody. The need theory of Maslow categorized man's needs in a hierarchy: physiological needs, safety needs, love, affection, and belongingness needs, esteem needs, and self-actualiza-tion needs (Maslow, 1943, 1954; Tay and Diener, 2011). Similarly, Glasser (1998, 2001, 2003) emphasized that man has five needs: survival, sense of belonging, power, freedom, and fun. Food is one of the basic needs that must be met before an individual can proceed to other needs. Food is a physiological and basic need since, without it, survival needs will be threatened. Psychological theories help us to understand children's and adolescents' developmental processes. Proper feeding plays a major role in their overall psychosocial developmental processes.

Hunger or malnutrition affects children's and adolescents' health and poses challenges to their survival. Oruamabo (2015) reported that approximately half of deaths among children under five years of age worldwide could be traced to undernutrition, making children susceptible to infectious diseases. David, Megan, and Brigitte (2013) also postulated that adolescence is a stage when many mental disorders, such as binge drinking and illegal drug use, emerge. Antisocial behavior could be attributable to faulty psychological development during child-hood or adolescence. Therefore, one of the predictors of faulty developmental processes in children and adolescents is hunger.

Global cases of the impact of hunger on children and adolescents

Hunger is an uncomfortable or painful sensation caused by lack of food intake below the average level (Cook and Jeng, 2009; USDA, 2017); or a condition of weakness because of lack of food or the appetite to eat (Yafi, 2018). A look at the surging cases of the impact of hunger on children and adolescents globally paints a picture of doom as they are becoming an at-risk population with a high pos-sibility of health challenges and fatalities. This is even more worrisome, as it has been estimated that 815 million people worldwide are hungry or cannot afford a proper meal each day (Yafi, 2018).

Food with appropriate nutritional content is vital for all human beings, espe-cially for children and adolescents, to guarantee healthy growth, organ forma-tion, and function. Children that are hungry or not fed well can be stunted (UNICEF, 2018a; Vishwambhar, 2015); underweighted (World Bank, 2017; Krasevec et al., 2014); and nutrient deficient (UNICEF, 2018b; Gernand et al., 2016). Research shows that kindergartners from food-insecure homes had lower Mathematics scores and manifest poor learning abilities than children from food-secure homes over a period of an academic year (Winicki and Jemison, 2003). Cook and Jeng (2009) also posited that food insecurity, resulting in hun-ger, could affect the commencement and continuation of a child's educational endeavors at the kindergarten level.

Foodbank (2015), in its findings, observed that children in Australia were affected by hunger. The research confirmed that 67% of teachers who participated in the study confirmed that children came to school hungry or without breakfast. The report also stated that, on average, students lost more than two hours a day of learning time because of hunger. 82% of the research participants also confirmed that children found it difficult to pay attention because of hunger, thereby increasing staff's workload. The survey also hinted that hungry schoolchildren were lethargic and exhibited behavioral challenges. The report of Foodbank (2015) confirms the impacts of hunger on schoolchildren. It corroborates that of the World Food Programme (2012), which reported that 66 million primary school-age children attended classes hungry and experienced difficulties with learning across developing countries, with 23 million of these children living in Africa.

Furthermore, there are reports from the United States which confirm hunger among its children. In particular this affects low-income families who could not eat healthy food like fresh fruit and vegetables because they were scarce, dear, and of low quality (Haynes-Maslow et al., 2013); 15.3 million children faced challenges of food insecurity (Weinfeld et al., 2014); and families living below the poverty line faced food inadequacy and food insecurity (Coleman-Jenson et al., 2015). The reports provide evidence of food insecurity and show that hunger seems to have come a long way – not even sparing the world's wealthiest nations.

Children's and adolescents' hunger cases in Nigeria

Nwagbara (2020) credited a report to the Food and Agricultural Organization (FAO) in which it forecasted that about 7 million Nigerians would face the challenge of food insecurity from June to August 2020. Also, it stressed that states like Borno, Adamawa, Yobe, Benue, Gombe, Taraba, Katsina, Jigawa, Kano, Bauchi, Plateau, Kaduna, Kebbi, Sokoto, Zamfara, and Niger would be confronted with the challenge of food insecurity. The World Poverty Clock (2018) cited in Kalu (2020) reported that over 40% of Nigerian citizens were living below the poverty line. These reports portend danger for children and adolescents as Nigeria, a highly populated country, is likely to be hunger-stricken. Similarly, Nextier SPD (2020) reported that Boko Haram insurgency activities in the states of Borno, Adamawa, and Yobe had increased hunger, shelter inadequacy, and a high risk of exposure to diseased conditions.

Furthermore, Adedokun (2018), in a study entitled 'Fighting Hunger and Poverty for Child's Sustainability: A Case Study of Ibadan, Metropolis, Oyo State, Nigeria', with a sample of 153 participants drawn from civil servants, market people, artisans, and children between the ages of 10 and 15, confirmed that children in Ibadan, in Oyo State, were denied rights to education, good health care, adequate nutrition, and safe water, among others, due to poverty. This research report points out that Ibadan, the capital city of Oyo State, was under the asphyxiating impact of hunger. With the ongoing pandemic, which has resulted in economic hardship in the country, the situation is likely to worsen.

As a result of the COVID-19 pandemic, food security predictions for Nigeria seem unfavorable. VOA (2020) credited a report to the World Food Programme where it postulated that the pandemic would provoke widespread hunger in the country; and posited that about 90 million citizens lived on less than $2 per day. The report further stated that Kano, Abuja, and Lagos were explicitly affected by the socio-economic challenges occasioned by the COVID-19 pandemic; and noted that adults and children in Borno, Adamawa, and Yobe States who had been affected by a decade-long insurgency would need food support. This report clarifies that the ongoing COVID-19 pandemic would pose challenges of hunger in many parts of Nigeria. This situation is worrisome because some parts of the country have even been experiencing insurgency and other forms of violence, making farming difficult even before the emergence of the COVID-19 pandemic. With these challenges, it may be safe to hypothesize that Nigerian children and adolescents are likely to be hard hit by hunger and famine in the days ahead.

The reports so far in this section show that food insecurity and hunger prevail in many parts of the world. More precisely, Nigeria seems to be gliding towards one of its worst periods of hunger with devastating consequences on children and adolescents if necessary precautionary measures are not put in place in time.

School farming as a tool for food sustainability

School farming could play a vital role in school feeding efforts and reducing the cost of providing meals for learners in schools as some parents cannot afford to provide lunch for their kids (Dick, Owuor, and Mwangi, 2010). Olaitan et al. (2001) observed that, apart from the provision of food for students, school farms could also serve many other purposes such as helping the school to generate money, develop skills in students, and create aesthetics, among others. Hence school farms can be a source of food and vocational sustainability for students. They provide students the opportunity to have access to fresh food instead of processed or canned foods that are generally perceived as unhealthy. Chukwudum and Ogbuehi (2013) postulated that a school farm, which includes both crop and livestock farms, is an effective teaching and learning avenue for practical knowledge of agriculture to students. This shows the importance of the school farm as a tool in the teaching and learning processes of agriculture, aside from its enormous advantages in terms of food security and enhancement of the green environment.

The benefits of the school farm as a tool of food security and means of a vocational channel for students are evident in several research studies from Nigeria. Emeya and Ojimba (2012), in a study in Rivers State, noted that 23.21% of schools had barns and livestock pens, and 22.79% had well-established and managed fishponds. The study provides evidence of the potentialities of school farms as a tool for food sustainability. Similarly, Mbanaso et al. (2013), in a study appraising young farmers' club programs in Abia State, reported that about 27% of secondary schools in the state had functional young farmers' clubs which engage in farming activities that could boost food availability. The report confirms the viability of the school farm in providing food for students and the community.

Furthermore, Onwumere, Modebelu, and Chukwuka (2016) confirmed in a study that school farms had a positive influence on the learning of agricultural science in senior secondary schools in the Ikwuano Local Government Area of Abia State. The knowledge of agricultural science could translate to the high output of crop farming and animal husbandry, which in the long run enhance food sustainability. The study also shows that the school farm has pedagogical benefits, aside from making food available for students. A study involving 300 farm children was conducted by Adewale, Oladejo, and Ogunniyi (2005) in Ekiti State, and also observed that children contributed immensely towards agricultural production in the area of study. Although the research did not emphasize whether the children were students, it shows that children and adolescents can contribute significantly to food security if school farms are in place.

So far, studies have shown evidence of the existence of school farms in Nigeria with proof of their importance for food security and pedagogy. Specifically, a case study of Hope Eden Community School is presented in this study. Hope Eden Community School is situated in a serene environment with many trees in Kuje, a suburb of the Federal Capital Territory, Abuja. The school farm could contribute food to assist the school in feeding the less privileged children and parents who could not afford school fees. The community school is an initiative of a German-Nigerian couple and a team of assistants who are devoted to helping children and adolescents to have a chance at a bright future. The school farm, owned by this school for the less privileged, produces basic food crops like maize, guinea corn, sweet potatoes, and yams. The school also has a young farmers' club, and its members meet twice a week where the children learn practical things about farming. The children under the farm club cultivate vegetables like tomatoes, peppers, and pumpkins. The farming activities for children at this school present hope for the continuity school farm system; and put a means of food sustainability into the hands of the children.

Parents are also involved in the school farm program, in addition to the generous donation of food items to the school from their own personal farms. Participation of parents in the school farm enhances the children's interest in farming. Foods from the school farm are used to feed the children in addition to the food items given to the school by donors. Hope Eden Community School's school farm initiative is testament to the fact that school farms can be a source of food sustainability to curb children's and adolescents' hunger in Nigeria and other parts of the world.

Conclusion

This study looked at the impacts of hunger on children and adolescents and the role of school farming as a panacea. The study rode on two research questions: 1. Can school farming enhance food sustainability to curb hunger among children and adolescents? 2. Can school farms also foster vocational and pedagogical benefits? However, greater emphasis was placed on providing answers to research question 1, since food sustainability is the thrust of this chapter. Nevertheless, research question 2 also received adequate answers in the study to justify its inclusion. These questions were adequately addressed based on available literature and the data collected by the researcher from Hope Eden Community School.

Hunger can affect children and adolescents in all areas of development. This study highlighted the psychological, biological, and social impacts of hunger on children. Hunger impacts negatively on their health, emotion, education, peer interaction, and attentional capacity. School farms from available literature in this study showed potentialities of being an antidote to the problem of hunger in the world, and in particular Nigeria. The study drew a lot of research evidence showcasing the importance of the school farm with its positive effects on students and even the community. In Rivers, a state in southern Nigeria, 23.21% of schools had barns and livestock pens, and 22.79% had well-established and managed fishponds (Emeya et al., 2012). Barns of food and livestock are indicative of the availability of food. If the trend is maintained, children's and adolescents' hunger would be reduced drastically. About 27% of secondary schools had functional young farmers' clubs in Abia, a state in the country's south-east (Mbanaso et al., 2013). Having young farmers' clubs in schools is a good omen as the clubs are expected to produce food for Nigerian children and adolescents. This chapter has revealed that children contributed to agricultural production in Ekiti, a state in the country's south-west (Adewale et al., 2005). The northern part of the country also showcased the benefits of school farms in terms of food sustainability through the Hope Eden Community School's school farm in Kuje, a suburb of Abuja, the capital city of Nigeria. All the cases cited in this chapter are indicators of school farms' availability and effectiveness in Nigeria. There is proof of the benefits of school farms both to the school and community at large.

Without adequate food and required nutrients both in quality and quantity, there cannot be any sustainable development in any country because children and adolescents who are supposed to be future drivers of the nation may not be able to do much as a result of an impoverished childhood and adolescent developmental processes. Hunger has far-reaching implications on children and adolescents and should be tackled by all means necessary.

Implications of study and recommendations

A study of this nature requires recommendations that can help policymakers and key people who are responsible for driving the educational system in various capacities. The study has implications for curriculum planners. Hence, it is recommended that curriculum planners and implementers should prioritize agriculture with emphasis on the establishment and utilization of school farms to foster students' practical knowledge of agriculture, and enhance students' involvement in farming, so that they are able to provide fresh and adequate food for themselves and the community (Chukwudum et al., 2013). Similarly, schools should ensure that functional school farms are in place to serve their purposes (Chukwudum et al., 2013; Onwumere et al., 2016).

Furthermore, agriculture should be encouraged as a vocational subject in all schools, emphasizing the school farm. Research findings revealed that very few students offer agricultural science as a vocational subject (Azubuike, 2011; Otekunrin, Otekunrin, and Oni, 2019; Obayelu and Fadele, 2019). Even though research evidence shows that practical agriculture was attractive to students (Diise et al., 2018), the quest for white-collar jobs still remains a major hindrance to farming in Nigeria. Hence, children and adolescents should be encouraged to participate in farming exercises both in school and at home. School management, teachers, and parents should encourage farming (Adewale et al., 2005).

Governments, organizations, and spirited individuals should provide funds for the procurement of farm instruments and farmlands for schools (Adewale et al., 2005; Emeya et al., 2012; Mbanaso et al., 2013). In addition, community leaders should help to provide land for school farms. Similarly, communities should collaborate with schools within their environments to make school farms effective. For instance, community leaders can organize their subjects to provide materials like tractors, harvesters, fertilizers, hoes, cutlasses, among others, to support school farms. Communities should promote community farms to serve as models for schoolchildren to emulate and make farming attractive. Members of the general public should be encouraged to promote a green environment.

The government at all levels needs to prioritize agriculture and school farms. This can be achieved through policies that can help to promote agriculture. For instance, deforestation and destruction of farmlands should be discouraged through appropriate laws and implementations to ensure land preservation for agricultural purposes. Government and agricultural research experts and institutes should work hand in hand with student farmers to enhance the use of technology to boost agricultural practices (Abdulahi and Sheriff, 2017). In a nutshell, the government must be at the forefront to lead the war against hunger in Nigeria, Africa, and beyond through the instrumentality of school farms, especially in an era like the COVID-19 pandemic, where global farming is under the spotlight.

This study also has implications for school-based counselors. Career or vocational development involves a range of vocational activities and programs in schools to help school-aged individuals identify essential tasks that can help them in life (Dik et al., 2011). The school-based counselor, being a special expert in the school system, is saddled with organizing and implementing students' orientation services which could help them to adjust appropriately to a school system.

Thus, the school counselor has the responsibility to enlighten students about school farms and arouse their interest in school farming since it is a potential tool for food security, a green environment, and vocation. Furthermore, in countries like Nigeria, where farming is still stigmatized and labeled a profession for the illiterates, the school-based counselor needs to change students' mindset by engaging them with appropriate counseling approaches that can lead to cognitive restructuring. Cognitive Behavioral Therapy, for instance, has been found to be effective in restructuring individuals' cognition in terms of maladaptive beliefs or misconceptions upheld by them (Teater, 2010; Frojan-Parga, Calero-Elvira, and Montano-Fidalgo, 2009).

Moreover, the Parents Teachers' Association (PTA), or School's Open Days where parents come to school to get updates about their wards academic progress, should be utilized to talk to parents on the need to embrace farming for food security and a green environment. Again, the school counselor is a partner to teachers of all subjects, including the teacher of agriculture. Students or pupils who do not show interest in school farms should be identified by the school counselor for counseling interventions so as to help them emotionally adjust to the school farm system.

Researchers should carry out empirical research on the effects of hunger on children and adolescents to provide data to enhance the level of understanding. Again, empirical research assessing perceived levels of school farms' effectiveness should be carried out by researchers as research evidence will go a long way to aid policymakers and planners.

References

Abdullahi, H.S. and Sheriff, R.E., 2017. Case study to investigate the adoption of precision agriculture in Nigeria using simple analysis to determine variability on a maize plantation, *Journal of Agricultural Economics and Rural Development*, 3(3), pp.279–292.

Adedokun, M.O., 2018. Fighting hunger and poverty for child's sustainability: a case study of Ibadan, metropolis, Oyo State, Nigeria, *IOSR Journal of Research & Method in Education*, 8(4), pp.15–21.

Adewale, J.G., Oladejo, J.A. and Ogunniyi, L.T., 2005. Economic contribution of farm children to agricultural production in Nigeria: a case study of Ekiti State of Nigeria, *Journal of Social Science*, 10(2), pp.149–152.

Azare, I.M., Abdullahi, M.S., Adebayo, A.A., Dantata, I.J. and Duala, T., 2019. Deforestation, desert encroachment, climate change and agricultural production in the Sudano-Sahelian region of Nigeria, *Journal of Applied Sciences and Environmental Management*, 24(1), pp.127–132.

Azubuike, O.C., 2011. Influential factors affecting the attitude of students towards vocational/technical subjects in secondary schools in south-eastern Nigeria, *Journal of Educational and Social Research*, 1(2), pp.49–56.

Bronfenbrenner, U., 1979. *The Ecology of Human Development: Experiments by Nature and Design*. Cambridge, MA: Harvard University Press.

Bronfenbrenner, U., 2005. *Making Human Beings Human: Bioecological Perspectives on Human Development*. Thousand Oaks, CA: Sage.

Chukwudum, E.O. and Ogbuehi, U.G., 2013. Effective utilization of the school farm as instructional initiative for developing agricultural interest among primary school children in Nigeria, *Academic Journal of Interdisciplinary Studies*, 2(6), p.113.

Coleman-Jenson, A., Rabbit, M.P., Gregory, C. and Singh, A., 2015. *Household Food Security in the United States in 2014* (Report No. ERR-194). Washington, DC: United States Department of Agriculture Economic Research Service.

Cook, J. and Jeng, K., 2009. Child food insecurity: the economic impact on our nation: a report on research on the impact of food insecurity and hunger on child health, growth and development [online]. Available at: www.feedingamerica.org (Accessed 10 October 2020).

David M., Megan Barry and Brigitte Vaughn, 2013. Adolescent health highlight: mental disorders [Online]. Available at: https//www.childtrends.org (Accessed 10th October, 2020).

Dick, D. Owuor, O.S. and Mwangi, A.M., 2010. School farming for school feeding: experiences from Nakuru, Kenya. *Field Actions Science Reports*, 1, pp.1–6.

Diise, A.I., Zakaria, H. and Mohammed, A.A., 2018. Challenges of teaching and learning of agricultural practical skills: the case of deploying project method of teaching among students of Awe Senior High School in the Upper East Region, Ghana, *International Journal of Agricultural Education and Extension*, 4(2), pp.167–179.

Dik, B.J., Steger, M.F., Gibson, A. and Peisner, W., 2011. Make your work matter: development and pilot evaluation of a purpose-centered career education intervention, *New Directions for Youth Development*, 132, pp.59–73.

Dollard, J. and Miller, N.E., 1950. Personality and psychotherapy. New York: McGraw-Hill.

Dunn, G., 2018. The impact of the Boko Haram insurgency in Northeast Nigeria on childhood wasting: a double-difference study, *Conflict and Health*, 12(6), pp. 2–12.

Emeya, S. and Ojimba, T.P., 2012. Benefits of secondary school farms in Rivers State, Nigeria, *International Journal of Arts and Humanities Social*, 1(4), pp.274–290.

Erikson, E.H., 1963. *Youth: Change and Challenge*. New York: Basic Books.

Erikson, E.H., 1964. *Insight and Responsibility*. New York: Norton.

Ettekal, A.V. and Mahoney, J.L., 2017. Ecological systems, in Kylie, P. (ed.) *Theory in the Sage Encyclopedia of Out-of-School Learning*. Thousand Oaks: Sage.

Falaju, J., 2018. Mbaram: there must be conscious effort to make youth fall in love with agriculture, *The Guardian* (Saturday-magazine), 6th May [Online]. Available at: https //guardian.ng/saturday-magazine/cover/mbaram-there-must-be-conscious-effort -to-make-youth-fall-in-love-with-agriculture/ (Accessed 20 March 2021).

Famiwole, R.O., 2013. Measures to improve the declining usage and operation of school farm in secondary schools in Ekiti State, Nigeria, *International Journal of Computational Engineering Research*, 3(7), pp.20–27.

Fawole, W.O., Ilbasmis, E. and Ozkan, B., 2015. Food insecurity in Africa in terms of causes, effects and solutions: a case study of Nigeria. A paper presentation at the 2nd International Conference on Sustainable Agriculture and Environment held at the Selcuk University and Bahri Dagdas International Agricultural Research Institute Campus in the City of Konya, Turkey between September 30 and October 3, 2015 [online]. Available at: https://www.researchgate.net/publication/293814921 (Accessed 11 November 2020).

Foodbank, 2015. Hunger in the classroom [Online]. Available at: https://foodbank.org .au (Accessed 10th October, 2020).

Frojan-Parga, M.X., Calero-Elvira, A. and Montano-Fidalgo, M., 2009. Analysis of the therapist's verbal behavior during cognitive restructuring debates: a case study, *Psychotherapy Research*, 19, pp.30–41.

Freud, S., 1949. An outline of psychoanalysis. New York: Norton.

Gamer, N., 2020. Global hunger worsening due to COVID-19: humanitarian groups look to congress [Online]. Available at: https://reliefweb.int/report/world/global-hunger-worsening-due-covid-19 humanitarian-groups-look-congress (Accessed 15 September 2020).

Gernand, A.D., Schulze, K.J., Stewart, C.P., West Jr, K.P. and Christian, P., 2016. Micronutrient deficiencies in pregnancy worldwide: health effects and prevention, *Nature Reviews Endocrinology*, 12(5), p.274.

Glasser, W., 1998. *Choice Theory: A New Psychology of Personal Freedom.* New York: Harper Collins.

Glasser, W., 2001. *Counseling with Choice Theory: The New Reality Therapy.* New York: Harper Collins.

Glasser, W., 2003. *Warning: Psychiatry Can Be Hazardous to Your Mental Health.* New York: Harper Collins.

Glicken, M.D., 2010. *Social Work in the 21st Century: An Introduction to Social Welfare, Social Issues, and the Profession.* Thousand Oaks, CA: Sage.

Haynes-Maslow, L., Parsons, S.E., Wheeler, S.B. and Leone, L.A., 2013. Peer-reviewed: a qualitative study of perceived barriers to fruit and vegetable consumption among low-income populations, North Carolina, 2011. *Preventing Chronic Disease*, 10, 1-10

Kalu, B., 2020. COVID-19 in Nigeria: a disease of hunger [Online]. Available at: www.thelancet.com/respiratory (Accessed 15 September 2020).

Kaplan, D.M., Tarvydas, V.M. and Gladding, S.T., 2014. A vision for the future of counseling: the new consensus definition of counseling, *Journal of Counselling and Development* [Online]. Available at https://onlinelibrary.wiley.com/doi/full/10.1002/j.1556-6676.2014.00164.x (Accessed 15 September 2020).

Kohlberg, L., 1984. *Essays on Moral Development*, Vol. 2: The psychology of moral development. San Francisco, CA: Harper & Row.

Krasevec, J., Thompson, A., Blössner, M., Borghi, E., Feng, J. and Serajuddin, U., 2014. Levels and trends in child malnutrition: UNICEF-WHO-The World Bank joint child malnutrition estimates [Online] Available at: http://www.who.int/nutgrowthdb/summary_jme (Accessed 15 September 2020).

Lunenburg, F.C., 2010. Extracurricular activities, *Schooling*, 1(1), pp.1–4.

Maslow, A.H., 1943. A theory of human motivation, *Psychological Review*, 50(4), pp.370–396.

Maslow, A.H., 1954. *Motivation and Personality.* New York: Harper and Row.

Massoni, E., 2011. The positive effects of extracurricular activities on students, *Essai*, 9(27), pp.84–87.

Mbanaso, E.O., Ajayi, A.R., Ironkwe, A.G. and Onunka N.A., 2013. Appraisal of young farmers' club programme in Abia state, Nigeria, *Journal of Agriculture and Social Research*, 13(1), pp.31–38.

McLeod, S.A., 2013. Kohlberg [Online]. Available at: www.simplypsychology.org/kohlberg.html (Accessed 25 October 2020).

McLeod, S.A., 2018a. Erik Erikson's stages of psychosocial development [Online]. Available at: https://www.simplypsychology.org/Erik-Erikson.html (Accessed 10 October 2020).

McLeod, S.A., 2018b. Sigmund Freud [Online]. Available at: www.simplypsychology.org/SigmundFreud.html (Accessed 25 October 2020).

Nextier SPD, 2020. Looking beyond the bombs [Online]. Available at https://nextierspd.com/looking-beyond-bombs (Accessed 15 September 2020).

Nwagbara, C., 2020. 7 million Nigerians, 13 states to experience food shortage: FAO. [Online] Available at https://nairametrics.com/2020/03/20/7-million-nigerians-to -experience-food-shortage/ (Accessed 15 September 2020

Obayelu, O.A. and Fadele, I.O., 2019. Choosing a career path in agriculture: a tough calling for youths in Ibadan metropolis, Nigeria, *Agricultura Tropica Et SubTropica*, 52(1), pp.27–37.

Olaitan, R.O. and Mama, R.O., 2001. *Principles and Practice of School Farm Management*. Nigeria, Cape Publishers International Ltd.

Omotayo G. O and Aliyu I.N., 2020. Implementation of school health policy: echoing its prospects in combating emerging health challenges in Nigeria, *World Journal of Innovative Research*, 8(4), pp.125–130.

Onwumere, M., Modebelu, M.N. and Chukwuka, I.E., 2016. Influence of school farm on teaching of agricultural science in senior secondary schools in Ikwuano local government area, Abia State, *Open Access Library Journal*, 3, p.e2742 [Online]. Available at: http://dx.doi.org/10.4236/oalib.1102742 (Accessed 20 October 2020).

Oruamabo, R.S., 2015. Child malnutrition and the millennium development goals: much haste but less speed?, *Archives of Disease in Childhood*, 100 (1) Supplement 1, pp.19–22.

Otekunrin, O.A., Otekunrin, O.A. and Oni, L.O., 2019. Attitude and academic success in practical agriculture: evidence from public single sex high schools students in Ibadan, Nigeria, *Asian Journal of Advanced Research and Reports*, 4(3), pp.1–18.

Pettinger, T., 2015. Impact of falling oil prices. Available at: http://www.economics help.org/blog/11738/oil/impactof-falling-oil-prices/ (Accessed 20 September 2020).

Piaget, J., 1936. *Origins of Intelligence in the Child*. London: Routledge & Kegan Paul.

Piaget, J., 1957. *Construction of Reality in the Child*. London: Routledge & Kegan Paul.

Saleh M.A., Ashiru M.A., Sanni J.E., Ahmed T.A. and Muhammad, S., 2017. Risk and environmental implications of oil spillage in Nigeria (Niger-Delta Region), *International Journal of Geography and Environmental Management*, 3(22), pp.44–53.

Tay, L. and Diener, E., 2011. Needs and subjective well-being around the world, *Journal of Personality and Social Psychology*, 101(2), pp.354–356.

Teater, B., 2010. *An Introduction to Applying Social Work Theories and Methods*. Basingstoke: Open University Press.

The World Bank, 2017. Prevalence of underweight, weight for age (% of children under 5) [Online]. Available at: https://data.worldbank.org/indicator/SH.STA.MALN.ZS ?view=chart (Accessed 27th September, 2020).

UNICEF, 2018a. Malnutrition rates remain alarming: stunting is declining too slowly while wasting still impacts the lives of far too many young children [Online]. Available at: https://data.unicef.org/topic/nutrition/malnutrition/ (Accessed 12 October 2020).

UNICEF, 2018b. Micronutrients [Online]. Available at: https://www.unicef.org/nutriti on/index_iodine.html (Accessed 15 September 2020).

USDA, 2017. Economic research service (ERS). Food security in the US: overview [Online]. Available at: https://www.ers.usda.gov/topics/food-nutrition-assistance/fo od-security-in-the-us.aspx (Accessed 15 September 2020).

Vishwambhar, P.S., 2015. Issues and options of food security and poverty: an empirical study of Mizoram, the eastern extension of Hilamaya, *Journal of Food Security*, 3(4), pp.107–114.

VOA, 2020. COVID-19 is threatening food security in Nigeria [Online]. Available at: https://www.voanews.com/africa/covid-19-threatening-food-security-nigeria (Accessed 27 September 2020).

Weinfeld, N.S., Mills, G., Borger, C., Gearing, M., Macaluso, T., Montaquila, J. and Zedlewski, S., 2014. *Hunger in America 2014: National report prepared for Feeding America.* Washington, DC: Westat and the Urban Institute.

WHO, 2014. Regional office for Europe [Online]. Available at: http://www.euro.who .int/data/assets (Accessed 5 September 2020).

WHO, 2016. Global health observatory [Online]. Available at: http://www.who.int/gho /child_health/mortality/mortality_under_five/en/ (Accessed 20 September 2020).

WHO, 2021. Adolescent health in the South-East Asia region [Online]. Available at https://www.who.int/southeastasia/health-topics/adolescent-health   (Accessed 26 October 2020).

Winicki, J. and K. Jemison, 2003. Food insecurity and hunger in the kindergarten classroom: its effect on learning and growth, *Contemporary Economic Policy* 21(2), pp. 145–157.

World Food Programme, 2012. Two minutes to learn about: school meals [Online]. Available   at: https://documents.wfp.org/stellent/groups/public/documents/c ommunications/wfp220221 (Accessed 7 October 2020).

Yafi, N.A., 2018. A perspective from Cameroon: hunger, poverty, and terrorism in the north [Online]. Available at: https://www.worldhunger.org/hungerpovertyandt errorisminnortherncameroon/ (Accessed 20 September 2020).

3

FIGHTING MALNUTRITION AND REACHING SUSTAINABLE DEVELOPMENT GOALS THROUGH SCHOOL FARMING (DURING THE COVID-19 PANDEMIC)

Scenario in some South Asian countries – India, Nepal, and Bhutan

Imana Pal

Introduction

The increasing population of the world is estimated to achieve 9 billion by the year 2050 and providing food to this increasing population possesses serious concerns about food quality and safety (Buttriss and Riley, 2013, pp. 402–407). A secure and adequate food supply for populations, particularly those from resource-limited economies, seems to be difficult over the next few decades. Inadequate food supply and unstable economy, both are making people susceptible to poor nutritional status leading to a compromised immune system. Inadequate nutrition also has a negative impact on the growth of children and their cognitive development. Developing communities in African and South Asian areas face highly prevalent malnutrition in villages, tribal areas, and urban slums. The impact of malnutrition is greater among developing children (Srivastava et al., 2012, p. 8).

In most cases, malnutrition manifests itself in the form of stunting, and around 90% of children suffering from stunting live in 36 countries worldwide. Asia is home to 70% of malnourished children, in particular South Asia, and ~61 million malnourished stunted children reside in India alone (Black et al., 2008, pp. 243–260). Numerous reports identified several causes of stunting, including inadequate food consumption, insufficient intake of nutrients, and recurrent infection in childhood (Psaki et al., 2012, p. 24; Khor, 2003, pp. 113–122; Akhtar, 2015 pp. 219–226).

Malnutrition directly or indirectly causes 54% of deaths among under-fives in developing countries. Poor nutrition and deficiency of micronutrients among mothers and children are a significant concern for half of the world's population

DOI: 10.4324/9781003176558-3

(Ahmed et al., 2012, pp. 8–17). The highest malnutrition rate is prevalent mainly in three South Asian countries: India, Bangladesh, and Pakistan. Micronutrient deficiencies that are predominantly widespread in South Asia include vitamins A and D and minerals like iron, zinc, and iodine. Preschool children and school-children are particularly susceptible to vitamin A deficiency, and very few initiatives have been taken to combat the problem of zinc and iron deficiency in South Asian nations. Several studies on the physiological manifestations of micronutrient deficiencies showed retarded physical and psychological development of children, iron deficiency anemia, a high rate of maternal deaths, poor cognitive accomplishment as well as reduced productivity, and loss of vision. In particular, economic insecurity, lack of nutrition, and malabsorption among vulnerable sections of the population were correlated with vitamin A deficiency as a public health problem in developing economies (Akhtar, 2016, pp. 2320–2330).

Enhancing the nutritional status of these children, as described in the Second International Conference on Nutrition (ICN2), the Sustainable Development Goals (SDGs), the Non-Hunger Challenge, and the United Nations Decade of Action on Nutrition 2016–2025 will be crucial to human development and the achievement of human rights. Many children worldwide, especially from low-income communities, start school with stunted growth, underweight, and/ or with multiple micronutrient deficiencies. In mid- and high-income countries too, nutritional and dietary issues are still prevalent. Every country suffers from at least one type of malnutrition which covers undernutrition to being overweight or obesity; all extremes are sometimes coupled with a deficiency of micronutrients.

School farms play a vital role in this context, where schools could offer a chance to avoid and handle malnutrition problems and contribute to quality education. Students who have taken part in various nutrition-related activities in schools will be able to influence and minimize the number of malnourished children and have an effect on their families and siblings (United Nations System Standing Committee on Nutrition, September 2017). School-based approaches to health and nutrition program implementation are an efficient tool because the education system's current structure frequently provides the most economical way for health and nutrition interventioncompared to what health organizations can offer (Holmer R, n.d.). This chapter investigates the school farming scenario of three of South Asia's developing nations, namely, India, Bhutan, and Nepal. The problem is crucial because these nations have a high malnutrition rate, as manifested by stunting and wasting away of children.

Methodology

This chapter aims to explore the combined impact of school farming that can not only improve the nutritional status of schoolchildren, especially in the COVID-19 pandemic, and hands-on learning experience, but also maintain food security and Sustainable Development Goals in South Asia. Therefore, the present study is entirely based on a narrative review structure and explanatory case study method. Various scientific databases, such as Scopus, Google Scholar, PubMed, and ScienceDirect, and direct articles and relevant research papers and studies are all considered for the study. The chapter focuses primarily on school farming, school gardens, sustainable development, malnutrition, COVID-19, school lunches, and food security. Reports, observations, fundamental studies, book chapters, relevant reviews, preferably with global data, were selected. The present study focuses on more recent studies, reviews, and original papers, published mainly in the last ten years. From the literature review, approximately 140 studies were generated. After excluding duplicates and those that did not fit into the inclusion criteria, 38 articles were analyzed; analysis of these studies provided few evaluations of the direct or indirect impact of school farms on nutrition. Compared to developed countries, the number of reports and articles related to school-based farms in South Asian countries was inadequate.

Impact of COVID-19 on malnutrition of school-going children in South Asia

Insufficient dietary intake is one of the main reasons for PEM (Protein Energy Malnutrition), which in turn makes children vulnerable to infectious diseases. The immune system is compromised by infections that increase the risk of malabsorption, increased catabolism, or decreased nutrient intake. All these factors are responsible for malnutrition, and this vicious cycle continues.

While COVID-19 infections themselves can amplify the danger of malnutrition, the risk of malnutrition is directly proportional to food insecurity due to the economic emergency and social segregation secondary to COVID-19 (Handu et al., 2020, pp. 979-987).

Since the second week of March 2020, most countries worldwide have been in lockdown due to the COVID-19 infection, leading to food shortages on the markets and inflation of food prices. These factors directly link with the infant mortality rate, especially in undernourished children infected with COVID-19 in developing countries (Kabir et al., 2020, pp. 2322-2323).

Almost 1.5 billion children – more than half of the school population worldwide – are kept out of school by the pandemic. In more than 180 countries, schools are closed nationwide, and in some places, schools are being closed locally, but the pandemic threatens to close them all over the country. As a result, children are deprived of routine school feeding and nutrition programs during the COVID-19 pandemic.

For schoolchildren's health and safety, proper nutrition is essential. Nutrient-deficient, vulnerable, or at-risk children could already be seen to benefit from school nutrition programs. These children are highly reliant on these programs either as only a meal or snack, as everyday meals, or they contribute significantly to their daily nutritional needs.

It is difficult to say how long school closures will last, so the well-being, food safety, and nutrition of the most vulnerable children have to be prioritized. Anticipated adverse economic effects and the possible disturbance of the local food system will further limit children's access to sufficient foods and dietary quality along with household mitigation behavior (WFP, FAO, and UNICEF, April 2020).

School farm: a sustainable source for bridging the gap of malnutrition

Proper nutrition, good nutritional status, well-being, and education are crucial factors for children to develop and have a better livelihood in the future. Sustainable Development Goals (SDGs) cover all these priorities adequately (MHRD, Govt. of India, 2014, pp. 1-64).

The health risk to humans has been greatly accelerated by poor-quality diet (Willett et al., 2019, pp. 447-492). Awareness of the population about proper eating habits is necessary to maintain a good nutritional status and health. Tastes and food preferences are considered to be important drivers alongside lifestyle, comfort, affordability, knowledge of nutrition, and policies. Preferences of taste and attitudes towards food are decided at an early age and continue throughout adulthood. This understanding has fostered an interest in actions that encourage children to follow healthy eating practices. School farms are such kinds of intervention programs (Schreinemachers et al., 2020, pp. 115-125).

For several decades, school farms have been an important intervention program. However, school farms' goals vary greatly, depending on the aims, target groups, and proponents. Improvement of farming with proper guidance, encouraging food production of the community, collecting funds, and demonstrating remarkable farming practices to the area adjoining the schools are some of the benefits of school farming in developing countries. In the developed and industrialized world, school farms served an extensive function in the educational field. They broadenchildren's knowledge of science, and helpto better understandnature and the environment. They are also essential to reconnect urban schools withthe reality of rural life, local food history, traditional food biodiversity, and agricultural tourism. The role played by school farms is now widely recognized in the fields of education related to nature and ecology, biodiversity and conservation of traditional food, environmental literacy, diet, well-being, and agricultural education (Gonsalves, Hunter, and Lauridsen, 2020, pp.1–32). School farms are also the source of fresh vegetables that can be utilized to prepare midday meals in schools. Children learn to grow fruit and vegetables using organic methods and develop an interest in consuming them instead of junk food and fast food. Concisely, a school farm is a means to promote good health and education (MHRD, Govt. of India, 2014, pp. 1-64).

However, the dietary agenda also drives existing interest with donors and the government in funding school farming programs. Nutrition-related activities in schools and promoting school farms and other related feeding programs in South Asia are sponsored by mainstream institutional and policy support. Frameworks to support universal school feeding initiatives are being established in several countries. This broader emphasis on the school's nutritional agenda has taken school farms back to the development phase by sensitizing the value of nutrition on agriculture with the participation of a diverse range of funding agencies. The increasing awareness of the wider range of benefits and functionalities of school farms, irrespective of geographical variations, is the driving force for this grow-ing interest in school farms (Gonsalves, Hunter, and Lauridsen, 2020, pp.1–32).

In low-income countries, the use of school farms for healthy eating is con-ceptually interesting as the malnutrition rate among children is very high, and it causes a dramatic increase in such services in these countries. However, the evidence to establish its effect on food behavior is inadequate, as there is limited literature available for low-income countries (Schreinemachers et al., 2020, pp. 115-125).

Promoting sustainable development through school farming to meet the basic needs of schoolchildren

A school farm is an inventive educational tool and strategy that allows educators to incorporate practical activities into a range of interdisciplinary, standards-based lessons. The farm invites students to observe, discover, investigate, foster, and learn through a dynamic setting. It is a living lab that takes lessons from real-life experiences rather than examples from a textbook, which enables students to participate actively in the learning process. Students achieve an understanding of the environment, an appreciation of food sources and nutrition, and knowledge of life cycles of plants and animals through the farm. They also learn practical, life-long horticultural skills (Introduction to School Gardens, n.d.)

The school farm has historically played and continues to play a significant role in the teaching of agricultural, horticultural, and related learning and capacity building. This frequently covers all the cycles of cultivation: planting and biodi-versity selection, production and management through harvesting, consumption planning, as well as long-term storage processing. Such preparation also involves enhancing awareness and skills for sustainable natural resource management, and environmental approaches like improving school farms' biodiversity coupled with cultural approaches. This increases students' understanding and capabil-ity, including their contribution to a more sustainable food system in renewable agriculture.

With increasing recognition of the value of local and indigenous vegetables in people's diets, an effort to revive food culture and encourage the develop-ment of recipes for such crops is a new window of opportunity for using school farms as a platform for conserving agrobiodiversity including native tree spe-cies. Local vegetable agrobiodiversity is hard to conserve on-farm but can also be effectively maintained in school farms, where they can continue changing according to environmental changes. Children in urban areas are particularly likely to be disconnected from nature and to lack understanding of where their food comes from. Specific challenges face urban schools in addressing these challenges, from limited space to food production to the logistical challenges of rural and farm visits. Trends in greening urban areas and creating liveable, sustainable urban cities provide opportunities for these challenges to be addressed. Although it is increasingly hard to preserve local agrobiodiversity in urban areas, school farms may provide sufficient space for this to be achieved, providing a significant forum for urban schoolchildren to better understand nature, biodiversity, and the variety of foods they provide, and the role they play in healthy eating (Gonsalves, Hunter, and Lauridsen, 2020, pp.4–13).

The scenario of school farming in South Asian countries

The experimental basis for the nutritional effects of children's school farming, however, remains diminutive. Earlier reports have obtained records from one or a small number of schools that are difficult to generalize from. Biases in selection may also be a concern since there is a shortage of experimental techniques being used. Most notably, almost all recent studies have been done in countries with high incomes, mostly conducted in the United States. As the form and degree of malnutrition are quite different in developed and developing countries, as are

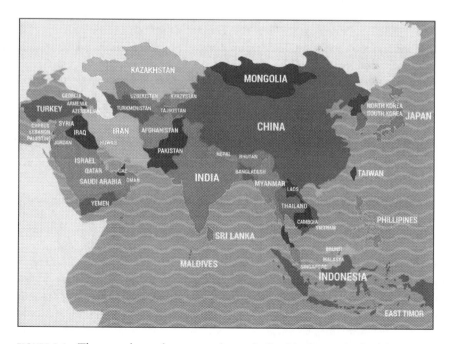

FIGURE 3.1   The map shows the areas under study for this chapter (India, Bhutan, and Nepal) and their location in Asia (New Era of Regional Cooperation, n.d.).

the social and financial backgrounds in which educational institutions work, the findings from these studies cannot be generalized to developing nations. This chapter investigates the school farming scenario in three of South Asia's developing nations, namely, India, Bhutan, and Nepal See Figure 3.1. The problem is crucial because these nations have a high malnutrition rate, as manifested by stunting and wasting away of children. The following data are available for school farming in South Asian developing nations (Schreinemachers et al., 2017, pp. 635–648).

India

India is South Asia's largest country and has a unique position there. India has become the natural leader in this region due to its size, location, and future economic prospects. India's economy is among the world's fastest growing, with GDP expected to increase by 12% in 2021. In the past two decades, the Indian economy has developed steadily but has grown unevenly in relation to the various social and economic classes, geographic areas, and rural and urban regions (Mishra, 2021). However, India failed to combat malnutrition, despite economic progress that is adversely affecting socio-economic progress in the country (World Bank, 2010). According to the UN's Global Hunger Index, India ranks 94 among the 107 nations on the list (Global Hunger Index, One Decade to Zero Hunger Linking Health and Sustainable Food Systems, 2020). In India, the number of malnourished children is almost double compared to sub-Saharan Africa and affects the country's mortality, productivity, and economic growth. Almost half of India's children suffer from malnutrition every year, and nearly a million die before the age of one month. Moreover, 43% of children under five in India are underweight, whereas 48% suffer from stunting due to severe malnutrition (Narayan, John, and Ramadas, 2019, pp. 126–141).

In this regard, the school could serve as a focal point and a place for teaching and implementing government initiatives on good health practices for achieving behavioral change in households (Holmer R, n.d.). The main aim of establishing a school farm, as stated by the Ministry of Human Resource Development (MHRD), is to reduce India's rates of malnutrition and encourage the consumption of fresh fruit and vegetables rich in micronutrients. The MHRD has directed all schools in urban and rural areas to set up Nutrition Gardens or school farms on the school campus. The farms will not only deal with the nutritional aspect but also act as experimental learning for students. Since then, school farms have acted as a resource builder for children regarding the nutritional importance of vegetables and the injurious properties of fast food and junk food. Aside from these, school farms can reduce the effects of climate change. The use of locally available foods for midday meals reduces the dependence on food transportation, which ultimately reduces carbon emissions from fossil fuels and minimizes greenhouse gas emissions. The number of Government and Government-aided schools in India is about1.17 million, and setting up one school farm in each school would have a significant impact on climate change.

According to the MHRD guidelines, schools may teach nutritional farming for one or two hours per week, with children taking up extra responsibility on a voluntary or rotational basis. Children should look after the crops they have planted and monitor them on their way to class or home and even during the holidays. The initiative will also create encouragement among students to learn and practice composting and harvesting water. Composting uses organic wastes and helps the gardening process; water harvesting will sensitize young children to water scarcity and the need for water conservation. The Government provides the schools with technical, infrastructural, and other assistance, and it is the schools' responsibility to involve parents, teachers, and non-teaching staff to promote the children's skills in growing their food (MHRD, Govt. of India, 2014, pp. 1–64).

Various states in India have successfully implemented the program but very little data are available to compare the nutritional status enhancement of schoolchildren who have school farms on their campus. One recognizable school farming program in Bihar, known as 'Ankuran' and started in 2016, was successfully implemented by the United Nations Children's Fund in public schools across Bihar. The program's main aim is to add variety to children's diet, including various foods from different food groups. This program engages students in organic farming and cultivates fruit and vegetables which are rich in vitamins, minerals, and other protective nutrients, and these vegetables are used in the preparation of midday meals (Raman, 2017).

India's child nutrition and school lunch scenario during COVID-19 pandemic

Globally, the corona virus (COVID-19) pandemic has impacted social protection programs.. Both the government and the community in India are fighting to contain this pandemic. As a strategy to prevent the spread of coronavirus, the Government of India (GOI) imposed a national lockdown.

To combat the problem of malnutrition among school children, the Union Government of India has announced additional expenditure for 16 billion US dollars to provide midday meals. The Indian Government has issued instructions for states and other union territories to keep feeding children during the school day. A recent circular issued on July 31, 2020, allowed children to receive food security benefits. The grants are permitted for both primary and upper primary students, and include food grains, pulses, and oil. Some states distribute dry foods as rations. On the other hand, some states arrange both financial assistance and rations for school-going children. However, these efforts are not enough. Owing to the closure of schools and meal programs, students have been forced to return to other practices such as rag-picking, begging, and so on to satisfy their hunger (Goutam, 2020, pp. 1–12).

Bhutan

The Kingdom of Bhutan is situated in the Himalayan Mountains, sandwiched between India and the People's Republic of China, making it one of the most isolated and least-developed nations in the world (Raghuram, 2008, pp. 1–56). Bhutan's development agenda has made significant progress over the last two decades, as has the betterment of its people's health. Its development success story is well-known, but many challenges continue to hamper the health of school-going children (Report on Bhutan Global School-Based Student Health Survey, 2016).

Malnutrition among children has been a serious problem in Bhutan. According to Bhutan's 2008 National Nutrition Survey, 34.9% of preschool children were stunted, 10.4% were underweight, and 4.7% experienced wasting (Zangmo, de Onis, and Dorji, 2012, pp. 1–7).

The Bhutan Government inaugurated the School Agricultural Programme (SAP) in 2000, including about 300 schools out of 549 schools across the country, including primary to higher secondary schools. The SAP program, jointly introduced by the Ministry of Agriculture and Forestry and the Ministry of Education, aims to supplement schoolchildren's diets. Schools that are part of the initiative can supply about 20% of the fresh vegetable requirements of their school feeding program and 35% of the needs for animal products such as pork and eggs.

The SAP program also examined the initiative on school farms financed by the Swiss Agency for Development and Cooperation (SDC) in the World Vegetable Center in the context of the project 'Vegetables Go to School'. This pilot framework builds on the SAP experience but has created a stronger connection between agriculture and learning in school. Unlike SAP, the main emphasis is on educating students about the value of the cultivation and consumption of vegetables for their nutrition and health, as well as the importance of good water, sanitation, and hygiene, which are otherwise independent events in schools. A significant aspect of the project was to enhance the partnership between agriculture, nutrition, and education to boost the nutritional status of schoolchildren. The intervention has three aspects that have been incorporated simultaneously in all participating schools. The first part was a school farm for schoolchildren, guided by teachers and supported by parents and the local community, to cultivate nutritionally rich vegetables. The second component consisted of teaching materials in gardening, nutrition, water, sanitation, and hygiene (WASH) weekly lessons. School farming was initiated in secondary schools where agriculture was an integral part of school curricula as a teaching tool for science and geography. The third component comprised promotional activities to emphasize the lessons learned and to consolidate their impact.

The study suggested that a greater supply of vegetables from school farms would contribute directly to schoolchildren's growing consumption of vegetables. However, the school farm areas are comparatively small, and the cultivated garden products were insufficient to feed many of the children. Farm products were sold to the school feeding program for a supplementary meal in the school canteen at a low price or where no canteen was present, and distributed for home consumption to the children and the teachers. Produce was sold to the community on occasion to raise money to support farm programs in schools.

The study design was based on a randomized controlled trial to measure the collective effect of the three above-mentioned intervention aspects. Here randomization decreases the chances of possible selection bias. To make it easier for the project team to access during the pilot plan, the research schools were chosen in 11 of the 20 districts in Western and Central Bhutan. Thirty-five schools were randomly chosen and distributed randomly into three categories: 15 participating schools for 2014, ten participating schools for 2015, and 10 schools used as controls.

The study report supported the idea that an extensive intervention in school farms, combining horticulture with learning and promotion, may control low-income nations' dietary preferences and behavior. There is a positive effect on the amount of vegetables consumed, but the variety in vegetable consumption was not markedly increased. The findings of this research support previous studies that indicate that school nutrition training focused on farming appears to improve understanding, knowledge, and preferences for children but does not always increase the amount of vegetable intake.

This Bhutan-based study on school farming concluded that Governments and non-governmental organizations are becoming particularly involved in supporting school farming in developed countries to counter child malnutrition. Based on the study findings in 18 schools and 468 students in Bhutan, it was evident that school farming increases children's awareness about vegetables and knowledge of sustainable farming, stimulates their food preferences, and increases the probability of school farm interventions in combination with nutrition education, WASH (water, sanitation, and hygiene) and promotional activities (by 11.7 percent). However, the amount of different vegetables consumed has not increased significantly. The implementation of school farms in countries with lower incomes needs a distinct approach from those with higher incomes, as improvements to children's diets entail additional changes in both the environment and homes (Schreinemachers et al., 2017, pp. 635–648).

Bhutan's child nutrition and school lunch scenario during COVID-19 pandemic

Schools in Bhutan were closed throughout the country on March 18, 2020, affecting approximately 180,00 students. Bhutan's school feeding program reaches 74,726 students (2019) (WFP), nearly half of the country's schoolchildren. Many kids and young people rely on healthy food in schools. Many children lack school meals due to school closures, thus compromising food security and nutrition (The impact of school closure on children, UNICEF, 2020). As a mitigation measure, WFP and UNICEF have started providing take-home rations to support 10,000 vulnerable families in collaboration with the Education Ministry. However, this emergency measure is unable to cover all the students who were previously covered by the school lunch program (WFP Bhutan Country Brief, 2020).

Nepal

Nepal, which is situated between India and China, is one of the world's most impoverished countries, with 25% of the population living below the national poverty line (US$ 0.50/day) and ranks 144th out of 188 nations on the UNDP's 2016 Human Development Index (World Bank, n.d.).

According to the Nepal Demographic and Health Survey, 2016, about 35.8% of children in Nepal were suffering from stunting, 27.1% of children under-five were underweight, and the proportion of wasted children was 9.6% (Tiwari et al., 2020, pp. 1–13).

With the Nepalese Government's help, a project called 'Vegetables Go to School', a broad school farm program was initiated, which deals with malnutrition among Nepalese children. The project's findings indicated that this program significantly increased children's awareness about consumption of fruit and vegetables, improved their familiarity with farming, nutritional practices, and WASH and fruit and vegetable preferences between 10- and 15-years-old students in Nepal's rural areas.

Another study explored the effects of vegetable gardening at schools in Nepal as a learning instrument to enhance education, understanding, and preference for vegetable consumption. To classify the nutritional outcomes of school vegetable gardens, the Randomized Control Trial (RCT) design was used, and 30 high-level schools (Dolakha and Ramechhap districts) were randomly selected (World Vegetable Center, 2017, p. 64).

Students participating in the program attended the 23-week farm-based nutritional exercises. The participating schools were analyzed using data (pre-and post-intervention data) obtained from grade 6 and 7 students (n = 1275). The results from the post-intervention analysis greatly resembled the higher degree of knowledge and preference in participating schools ($p < 0.01$) for the consumption of nutrient-dense vegetables. In comparison to students in the control group, participants that engaged in farm-based interventions raised their level of awareness (7.80%) on vegetables and nutrition (Bhattarai et al,, 2015, pp. 1–7).

One more piece of research on school farms in Nepal evaluated the cumulative effect of school farms on nutritional awareness, information, attitudes, food, complimentary lessons, and promotional activities on farming and food of 10- to 15-year-old schoolchildren in Nepal. For the 2014 and 2015 classes, the study used a cluster of randomized controlled trials design to obtain information from 30 institutions and a sample of 1275 and 785 students. The experiment revealed a substantial ($p < 0.01$) increase in the child's understanding of fruit and vegetables, their knowledge of sustainable farming, food, nutrition, and health, and their reported preferences for fruit and vegetables after one year. However, these intermediate results did not result in major fruit and vegetable consumption or dietary improvements. It might be important to work more intensively with parents and to increase the availability of fruit and vegetables at home and in communities to influence food decision-making by children (Schreinemachers et al., 2017, pp. 329–343).

Nepal's child nutrition and school lunch scenario during COVID-19 pandemic

Based on a recent national survey, 12% of children in Nepal are suffering from acute malnutrition, including 2.9% who have Severe Acute Malnutrition (SAM). During the COVID-19 pandemic, UNICEF has led efforts to communicate the risks, and the importance of water, sanitation, and hygiene (WASH), nutrition and child protection, and education (Humanitarian Action for Children Nepal HIGHLIGHTS, 2021). Nevertheless, no particular data is currently available on the school lunch program or food security of children.

Discussion

Though the chapter focuses on the impact of school farming on South Asian countries, there is no such data available in countries like Bangladesh, Sri Lanka, and Pakistan. The impact of school farming and its role in reducing malnutrition in developing countries should be more clearly investigated in future research.

The whole school and community are concerned with children's health. The curriculum of the classroom, extra-curricular programs, the establishment of schools, and the school environment should make sure that children have their fundamental rights to education and proper nutrition with the help of their families and communities (MHRD, Govt. of India, 2014, pp. 1–64).

The studies on school farming in low-income nations showed that school farming noticeably increases children's awareness, knowledge, and food preferences, but they cannot increase children's consumption of fruit and vegetables. The major reason behind this is the size of the school farms is minimal, so that they cannot adequately supply the daily need of vegetables for students. Another reason indicated that paying extra attention to school farms seriously hampers the school programs and diverts teachers' and students' minds. The objective of a school farm is, therefore, generally solely educational because of the irregular and inadequate production of vegetable crops. Therefore, school farms can only have an indirect influence on nutrition by encouraging awareness among students about fruit and vegetables and improving their knowledge of the importance of consuming a variety of fruit and vegetable products for good health. Combining these effects is intended to enable students to change their diet and consume more fruit and vegetables. Generally, the meals provided in the schools are a combination of staple cereal grain and pulses and are devoid of fresh vegetables, and many families in low-income countries are unable to provide enough vegetables to the students. As a result, the students have no alternative even though they may have decided to eat fruit and vegetables. However, this can happen by integrating school farm initiatives with school meals that serve fruit and vegetables in the household or within a neighborhood to meet these objectives and offer children a healthier food choice (Schreinemachers et al., 2020, pp. 120–125).

In India, school farming programs are running successfully. In some states in India, such as Kerala, school farming has become popular as children have gained a lot of passion and commitment about cultivating in a small area. It is profoundly inspiring in itself because farming is not seen as a chore. Children have a sense of motivation by savoring seasonal crops, investigating unknown plants, and learning new measures to combat pests (MHRD, Govt. of India, 2014, pp. 1–64).

In countries like Bhutan and Nepal, the 'Vegetables Go to School' project was very successful and motivated the governments to run several school-based projects combining different aspects such as farming, health, and diet. Bhutan has a comprehensive approach that incorporates school feeding with WASH (water, sanitation, hygiene) and school planting to counter child malnutrition. As a result, Nepal's government has also introduced a Green School Program to establish school farms in the country for public schools, while the Ministry of Education has developed a school farm curriculum that includes food, agriculture, and health. These initiations need to be closely observed to gain a deeper insight into how such interventions can have an optimal effect on children's and parents' healthy eating behavior, along with lessons to those with similar programs.

During the COVID-19 pandemic, all three countries have almost suffered from the same problem of child malnutrition and food security. The uncertainties about future strategies to combat this pandemic have forced the governments to make various health interventions a priority and prepare them for further development. The closure of schools can offer immediate benefits to contain the disease and avoid further burden on an already overwhelmed health system, but it also has the potential to leave children undernourished in the wake of the COVID-19 pandemic. An agenda that policymakers would have to prioritize amid urgent health needs is to ensure food availability to maintain children's nutritional status during this crisis.

With the closing of schools, the supply of nutritional services throughout India, Bhutan, and Nepal has been interrupted. They could have been the only primary source of nutrition for many children in their daily lives, and this may have long-lasting consequences. The economic downturn that will result from this pandemic will also aggravate food insecurity. Loss of employment can lead to extreme poverty among vulnerable sections of the population. This will limit people's ability to access nutritious food in various ways, including low income and unemployment. In India's case, the closure of businesses results in a mass exodus of workers and their families from metropolitan towns. Nevertheless, the nutritional needs of these children who are moving with their families are facing an unknown challenge.

Though several initiatives have been adopted to maintain the nutritional status of schoolchildren during this pandemic, they are not sufficient. Even during short-term food deprivation, children can become affected by various forms of nutritional disorders, including PEM (Protein Energy Malnutrition). Accordingly, a multi-faceted approach involving government and non–governmental stakeholders would be required under the present scenario to coordinate and support and expand community child nutrition services. As a short-term interim measure, the public distribution system must be strengthened until schools are reopened, food banks are established, and food parcels are delivered at home, especially for the beneficiaries of child nutrition programs (Upadhyay, Patra, and Khan, 2020, pp. 251–254). However, they still may lack the supply of fresh vegetables from school farms, as the rations provided during this time mainly consist of dry foods.

It is also a matter of great concern that these countries have no specific data available for the rate of malnutrition among schoolchildren, their drop-out rates, and how many of them benefited from the supply of food during the COVID-19 pandemic. It is expected that, when the schools reopen, the school farms may act as a source of nutrition and make up for the nutritional deprivation of the children. As millions of families worldwide struggle to sustain their lives, increased social protection measures like the school lunch program are crucial to reduce and prevent millions of children from becoming nutrient deficient in the future.

Conclusion

Research findings on school farms in low-income countries can effectively increase children's knowledge, understanding, and preferences towards nutrient-rich vegetables. They would also help them to understand the effect of fresh fruit and vegetables on human nutrition. Students can also act as a mediator to disseminate the knowledge for promoting home kitchen gardens. Nevertheless, the increase in vegetable consumption should be combined with school farming and home kitchen gardening to improve its effectiveness among children.

Very little data are available for low-income countries in South Asia, and there is no particular research data available on the improvement of nutritional status of schoolchildren receiving midday meals enriched with vegetables from school farms. Schools are closed now as a result of the COVID-19 pandemic, and there is no such project that supplies fresh fruit and vegetables during this time. There is even no specific data that discloses the exact number of students in these countries receiving a midday meal. Nevertheless, after the COVID-19 pandemic is over, these school farms can act as a source of nutrients to the children living in poverty and unable to acquire adequate food during the lockdown and keep the incidence of malnutrition under control. Therefore, governments should encourage the formation of school farms in both government and private schools to provide a better future for students.

References

Ahmed, T., Hossain, M. and Sanin, K.I., 2012. Global burden of maternal and child undernutrition and micronutrient deficiencies. *Annals of Nutrition and Metabolism*, 61(Suppl. 1), pp.8–17.

Akhtar, S., 2015. Food safety challenges: A Pakistan's perspective. *Critical Reviews in Food Science and Nutrition*, 55(2), pp.219–226.

Akhtar, S., 2016. Malnutrition in South Asia: A critical reappraisal. *Critical Reviews in Food Science and Nutrition*, 56(14), pp.2320–2330.

Asia, C.A.C.E., n.d. New era of regional cooperation. *Belt & Road News* [online]. Available at: https://www.beltandroad.news/new-era-of-regional-cooperation/ [Accessed 1 Apr. 2021].

Bhattarai, D.R., Subedi, G.D., Acharya, T.P., Schreinemachers, P., Yang, R.Y., Luther, G., Dhungana, U., Poudyal, K.P. and Kashichwa, N.K., 2015. Effect of school vegetable gardening on knowledge, willingness and consumption of vegetables in mid-hills of Nepal. *International Journal of Horticulture*, 5(20), pp. 1–7.

Black, R.E., Allen, L.H., Bhutta, Z.A., Caulfield, L.E., De Onis, M., Ezzati, M., Mathers, C., Rivera, J. and Maternal and Child Undernutrition Study Group, 2008. Maternal and child undernutrition: Global and regional exposures and health consequences. *The Lancet*, 371(9608), pp. 243–260.

Buttriss, J. and Riley, H., 2013. Sustainable diets: Harnessing the nutrition agenda. *Food Chemistry*, 140(3), pp. 402–407.

Global hunger index one decade to zero hunger linking health and sustainable food systems. 2020. [online]. Available at: https://www.globalhungerindex.org/pdf/en /2020.pdf. [Accessed 1 Apr. 2021].

Gonsalves, J., Hunter, D. and Lauridsen, N., 2020. School gardens: Multiple functions and multiple outcomes. In Hunter, D., Monville-Oro, E., Burgos, B., Roel, C.N., Calub, B.M., Gonsalves, J. and Lauridsen, N. (eds.) *Agrobiodiversity, School Gardens and Healthy Diets: Promoting Biodiversity, Food and Sustainable Nutrition*. London and New York: Routledge, pp. 1–32.

Goutam, N., 2020. COVID-19 and its impact on Mid-Day Meal program in India,*Sanrachna*, pp. 1–12.doi 10.31219/osf.io/t4ghu

Handu, D., Moloney, L., Rozga, M. and Cheng, F., 2020. Malnutrition care during the COVID-19 pandemic: Considerations for registered dietitian nutritionists evidence analysis center. *Journal of the Academy of Nutrition and Dietetics*,121(5), pp. 979–987.

Holmer, R., n.d. Home, community and school vegetable gardens: Nutrition-sensitive food system intervention for changing rural and urban livelihoods in East and Southeast Asia [online]. Available at: https://www.jircas.go.jp/sites/default/files/ publication/proceedings/2013-session-41_0.pdf [Accessed 1 Apr. 2021].

Humanitarian Action for Children Nepal HIGHLIGHTS, 2021. [online]. Available at: https ://www.unicef.org/media/87426/file/2021-HAC-Nepal.pdf [Accessed 2 Apr. 2021].

Introduction to School Gardens, n.d. [online]. Available at: http://www.csgn.org/sites/ default/files/GFL_1.pdf [Accessed 31 March, 2021].

Kabir, M., Saqib, M.A.N., Zaid, M., Ahmed, H. and Afzal, M.S., 2020. COVID-19, economic impact and child mortality: A global concern. *Clinical Nutrition*, 39(7), pp. 2322–2323.

Khor, G.L., 2003. Update on the prevalence of malnutrition among children in Asia. *Nepal Medical College Journal*, 5(2), pp.113–22.

Ministry of Human Resource Development (MHRD), 2014.*School Nutrition Gardens: Mid-day Meal Scheme*. New Delhi: Ministry of Human Resource Development (MHRD), Government of India, pp. 1–64

Mishra, A.R., 2021. Moody's upgrades India's GDP growth to 12% in 2021 [online]. Available at: https://www.livemint.com/news/india/moodys-analytics-upgrades-ind ia-s-growth-forecast-to-12-for-2021-11616082021410.html [Accessed 1 Apr. 2021].

Narayan, J., John, D. and Ramadas, N., 2019. Malnutrition in India: Status and government initiatives. *Journal of Public Health Policy*, 40(1), pp.126–141.

Psaki, S., Bhutta, Z.A., Ahmed, T., Ahmed, S., Bessong, P., Islam, M., John, S., Kosek, M., Lima, A., Nesamvuni, C. and Shrestha, P., 2012. Household food access and child malnutrition: Results from the eight-country MAL-ED study. *Population Health Metrics*, 10(1), p.24.

Raghuram, S., 2008. ISAS working paper South Asia-social development: Country perspectives and regional concerns † for the institute of South Asian studies [online]. Available at: https://www.files.ethz.ch/isn/46845/35.pdf [Accessed 1 Apr. 2021].

Raman, S., 2017. In public schools across Bihar, students are growing their own vegetables in 'nutrition gardens [online]. Available at: https://scroll.in/article/946395/in-publ ic-schools-across-bihar-students-are-growing-their-own-vegetables-in-nutrition-g ardens [Accessed 19 October, 2020].

Schreinemachers, P., Bhattarai, D.R., Subedi, G.D., Acharya, T.P., Chen, H.P., Yang, R.Y., Kashichhawa, N.K., Dhungana, U., Luther, G.C. and Mecozzi, M., 2017. Impact of school gardens in Nepal: A cluster randomised controlled trial. *Journal of Development Effectiveness*, 9(3), pp. 329–343.

Schreinemachers, P., Rai, B.B., Dorji, D., Chen, H.P., Dukpa, T., Thinley, N., Sherpa, P.L. and Yang, R.Y., 2017. School gardening in Bhutan: Evaluating outcomes and impact. *Food Security*, 9(3), pp.635–648.

Schreinemachers, P., Yang, R.Y., Bhattarai, D.R., Rai, B.B. and Ouedraogo, M.S., 2020. The impact of school gardens on nutrition outcomes of low-income countries. In Hunter, D., Monville-Oro, E., Burgos, B., Roel, C.N., Calub, B.M., Gonsalves, J. and Lauridsen, N. (eds.) *Agrobiodiversity, School Gardens and Healthy Diets: Promoting Biodiversity, Food and Sustainable Nutrition*. London and New York: Routledge, pp. 115–125.

Srivastava, A., Mahmood, S.E., Srivastava, P.M., Shrotriya, V.P. and Kumar, B., 2012. Nutritional status of school-age children: A scenario of urban slums in India. *Archives of Public Health*, 70(1), p.8.

The impact of school closure on children, 2020. [online]. Available at: https://www.uni cef.org/bhutan/impact-school-closure-children#:~:text=An%20Op%2DEd%20b y%20the%20UNICEF%20Bhutan%20Representative.&text=Teachers%2C%20S chool%20Counsellors%2C%20and%20ECCD [Accessed 1 Apr. 2021].

Tiwari, I., Acharya, K., Paudel, Y.R., Sapkota, B.P. and Kafle, R.B., 2020. Planning of births and childhood undernutrition in Nepal: Evidence from a 2016 national survey. *BMC Public Health*, 20(1), pp. 1–13.

UNICEF, 2020. Mitigating the effects of the COVID-19 pandemic on food and nutrition of school children. WFP, FAO and UNICEF, April 2020 [online]. Available at: https ://www.wfp.org/publications/mitigating-effects-covid-19-pandemic-food-and-n utrition-schoolchildren

UNSCN, 2017. Schools as a system to improve nutrition: A new statement for school-based food and nutrition interventions. United Nations System Standing Committee on Nutrition, September 2017 [online]. Available at: https://www.unscn.org/upl oads/web/news/document/School-Paper-EN-WEB.pdf

Upadhyay, M.K., Patra, S. and Khan, A.M., 2020. Ensuring availability of food for child nutrition amidst the COVID-19 pandemic: Challenges and way forward. *Indian Journal of Community Health*, 32(2) Supplement, pp. 251–254.

WFP Bhutan Country Brief, 2020. [online]. Available at: https://reliefweb.int/sites/re liefweb.int/files/resources/WFP-0000116793.pdf [Accessed 1 Apr. 2021].

Willett, W., Rockström, J., Loken, B., Springmann, M., Lang, T., Vermeulen, S., &Murray, C.J., 2019. Food in the anthropocene: The EAT–Lancet commission on healthy diets from sustainable food systems. *The Lancet*, 393(10170), pp. 447–492.

World Bank, 2010. *World Development Indicators 2010*. Washington, DC: The World Bank.

World Bank, n.d.Overview [online]. Available at: https://www.worldbank.org/en/c ountry/nepal/overview#2 [Accessed 1 Apr. 2021].

World Vegetable Center, 2017. *Vegetables Go to School NEPAL: School Vegetable Gardens: Linking Nutrition, Health and Communities*. Tainan,Taiwan: World Vegetable Center. Publication no. 17-817, pp. 64.

Zangmo, U., de Onis, M. and Dorji, T., 2012. The nutritional status of children in Bhutan: results from the 2008 National Nutrition Survey and trends over time. *BMC Pediatrics*, 12(1), pp.1–7.

PART 2

People-focused perspective

4

THE SCHOOL FARMS NETWORK IN THE UK

History, context, and adding value

Chris Blythe, Ian Egginton-Metters,
Michael Hardman, and Victoria Schoen

Introduction

Networks and connections are an important part of the School Farms Network (SFN) in the UK. In this chapter, members, and organizers of the network, as well as participant school farmers and academics, come together to present an overview of the SFN. Using case studies as examples, we show how the network has supported schools, as well as highlight some of the challenges faced by the network and by individual member school farms. Finally, we discuss the School Farms Network's role in supporting projects and make some recommendations for the future.

In the UK, the School Farms Network defines a school farm as:

> a teaching facility within school grounds or directly managed by a school that provides some of the following: Access to a range of farm livestock, the facilities and land needed for their up-keep, machinery, incubators or other farming equipment, small scale food growing, greenhouses or polytunnels.
>
> *(Saunders et al., 2014)*

There is a vast array of evidence demonstrating the significant benefits of school farms and gardens (Hardman & Larkham, 2014). Schreinemachers et al. (2020) have shown how the spaces can impact students' health and wellbeing, enabling them to eat more fruit and vegetables. Adding to this, Burt et al.'s (2019) statistical analysis of school gardens and their impacts demonstrated the important value of these assets, particularly within urban communities. Consistently, studies have shown the value of these spaces in terms of tackling obesity, improving access to nutritional products, and improving mental health (Howarth et al., 2017, 2020; Wells et al., 2018; Mead et al., 2021).

DOI: 10.4324/9781003176558-4

Background

In the UK, the United States, and other countries (see, for example, Christie & Gaganakis, 1989; Corbett et al., 2017; Wells, 2014), there is a long record of using agriculture and horticulture in the education system (Viljoen & Wiskereke, 2012). This includes more radical concepts in the United States, such as horticultural aquaponics, aiming to be embedded in the school curriculum by the Government. A similar initiative, Agriculture in the Classroom, aims to embed more conventional agricultural practice into the school setting and educate students about the importance of food production (National Agriculture in the Classroom, 2013).

North America also has innovative work around food procurement linked to school farms and gardens. Food Tank (2019) provides an overview of innovative school gardens revolutionizing lunches; from Texas to Canada, they provide evidence to show how the food menu is healthier through this approach, and other benefits can be felt from investing in the concept. Healthy Plymouth (2021), a scheme in Massachusetts, adds weight to these examples by showing how produce is used in school gardens across their area and contributes to students' health and wellbeing. Boston and New York pioneered the practice of urban agriculture and school growth in the United States, with early examples dating from around 1891. The modern community growing movement in New York also helped to push forward the practice, with policy tools and funding fueling the concept's growth (Hardman and Larkham, 2014).

To this day in the United States, *The Agricultural Education Magazine*, a long-established publication, charts the challenges and opportunities of the School Farm Sector in the United States over the years. In the UK, the growth of school farms and gardens varies and is very much dependent on the local authority (municipality). An example is in Oldham, where the mayor's school gardens program enabled the widespread development and growth of the practice in both primary and secondary schools (Get Oldham Growing, 2021). University Technical Colleges (UTC) have also often pioneered practice through embedding high-tech growing into curriculums. Examples here include the first vertical farm in Wigan's UTC (now defunct since the demise of the UTC) to underground hydroponics at Liverpool's UTC (Farm Urban, n.d.). The aim here was to embed both the science behind growing and the practicalities of so doing into the classroom environment.

History of school farm education in the UK

Historically in the UK, as far back as the 18th century, farming and gardening were included in the school curriculum, particularly in those schools established in 'schools of industry' and developed as a result of the Poor Law system (Goodson, 1993). By around 1912, it is estimated that about 2,500 schools in the UK had gardens (personal correspondence, HMI), and the use of gardening and farming as a means of bringing students closer to nature was very much part of the curriculum.

The 1920s saw the emergence of Rural Studies, with an increasing focus on outdoor education within the curriculum. By the 1940s, there was a growth in gardening in schools as a result of the 'Dig for Victory' campaign, where school gardens were the main way in which children became involved in the national campaign to grow fruit and vegetables and rear animals as part of the war effort (Smith, 2011), alongside other youth organizations such as the Scouting and Guiding movements. Similar patterns were seen in the United States (Burt, 2016). In rural areas, farms were increasingly involving school pupils and evacuated children and refugees in farming activities, providing them with an agricultural education as well as an opportunity to increase farm productivity, when many of the male laborers had been conscripted (Moore-Colyer, 2004; United States Holocaust Memorial Museum, 2020).

Following the end of World War 2, rural subjects were even incorporated into some emergency teacher training, and the 1950s saw the emergence of regional networks for teachers of Rural Studies (Goodson, 1993). In the 1960s, the credibility of Rural Studies increased, and the National Association of Rural Studies (NARS) was founded. By 1963 nearly 900 schools offered the subject (41% of Secondary Moderns and 5% of Grammars). The year 1964 saw the introduction of the Certificate of Secondary Education, and by 1966, there were over 2,000 entries for rural subjects, and 14 out of 15 examination boards offered them. By the 1970s Rural Science (rather than Rural Studies) emerged only to be challenged by the rise of the environmental movement, and the NARS changed its name to the National Association for Environmental Education. By the late 1970s, there were approximately 13,500 entries nationally.

The 1980s saw a rise in vocational education, starting with the Training and Vocational Education Initiative (TVEI) in 1984. City & Guilds, BTEC, and RSA then emerged, and a further increase to over 18,000 Rural Science entries nationally was recorded. At this time, 112 schools had Young Farmers' Clubs. However, the numbers then gradually reduced, and examination boards lost interest.

The 1990s saw the domination of the National Curriculum. Local Management of Schools (LMS) was introduced, and many schools and Local Education Authorities saw the opportunity to sell land. There was a return to the twin-track route of academic and vocational: NVQs/GNVQs/GCSEs/Diplomas.

The DfES (now Department for Education [DfE]) Growing Schools program was started in 2001 by the Federation of City Farms and Community Gardens (now Social Farms & Gardens), just before the Foot and Mouth outbreak, with the aim of reintroducing hands-on farming and horticultural education opportunities for all pupils. Its first endeavor was to check on the barriers involved and analyze the work of school farms, and from this, a network was developed. Growing Schools in the early days provided support to develop the network and subsidized some of the costs of network meetings and training. The commitment by the government in the 2003 *Every Child Matters* report, along with the Growing Schools program, led to the creation of the *Learning Outside the Classroom Manifesto* in 2006 and the creation of the Learning Outside the Classroom Council (later renamed as the Council for Learning Outside the Classroom).

It also paid for the development of the resource *Get Your Hands Dirty* which was initially aimed at supporting new school farm teachers and technicians. However, it was realized that many teachers needed some affirmation of what they were currently doing and some introduction to what might be involved in progression to more complicated and resource-intensive horticulture and rearing of livestock. The resource was then divided into seven sections rising in the complexity of knowledge and skills, buildings, and funding and includes a bibliography and other support materials. The SFN in the UK is unique in being developed by and for practitioners who are very small in number due to there being few school farms and a lack of qualifications to encourage Headteachers to develop farm resources in support; they are a 'rare breed'!

Other networks focus on broader outdoor and environmental education and play (e.g., National Association for Environmental Education) but include a wide range of settings rather than just school farms. Current estimates, based on Social Farms & Garden internal surveys, suggest that some two-thirds of UK schools now involve students in growing, and an increasing proportion of these are food plants.

Background and development of the School Farms Network

The School Farms Network (SFN) was created by Social Farms & Gardens (SF&G) with experienced practitioners to develop a framework for mutual support and raise the status and understanding of the benefits school farms bring to education.

SF&G is a leading charity supporting over 2000 member groups across the UK to farm, garden, and grow together. The organization originated in the late 1970s when city farms and community gardens wanted an organization that represented them and provided a network to support them while being accountable to members.

With Local Education Authorities selling off school land, a lack of suitable qualifications that schools were willing to invest in, and experienced school farm teachers retiring, SF&G were initially approached to help save many school farms in danger of being closed. Bringing practitioners together, producing a printed newsletter dedicated to school farms, and surveying all Local Education Authorities, generated an enthusiasm to identify peers and create a voice for a network of schools with farm units.

The network brings together experienced practitioners and those interested in the concept of providing livestock experience within schools for mutual support, to develop a framework for mutual support, and to raise the status and understanding of the benefits that school farms bring to education.

Objectives of the network

- Offers support and assistance to existing school-based farms and those wishing to start a new school farm (teachers, assistants, and parents).
- Facilitates the exchange of ideas and information, including peer teacher support.
- Produces a regular newsletter for those interested in promoting opportunities for young people to take part in farming and agricultural/land-based learning across the education sector.
- Operates a Facebook forum for the exchange of information and ideas.
- Arranges network meetings and conferences, which are an excellent opportunity for school farm staff and volunteers to swap ideas, gain inspiration from the work of their colleagues, and discuss how to stimulate understanding and support for school farms.
- Advocates for and promotes school farming.

Technical support for gardening is available through organizations such as the Royal Horticultural Society, Learning through Landscapes, and Council for Learning Outside the Classroom. The Access To Farms partnership of agricultural organizations, and Countryside Classroom (the successor to Growing Schools) help schools to identify farms they can visit, and for some, they help establish a long-term supportive relationship. Access to Farms also supports and trains farmers to understand what teachers need on a farm visit.

Several local and regional Agricultural Societies run education programs, including visits to schools. Some specialist programs such as Tractors into Schools and most livestock breed societies will provide enthusiastic breeders to visit and advise schools. In summary:

- The use of agriculture and hands-on farming, and horticultural education, is not new!
- Recognition of multiple intelligences and learning styles means there is a responsibility to ensure that every pupil can learn in environments best suited to the individual.
- Ofsted reports and other evidence demonstrate the learning and achievement benefits of hands-on farming and horticultural education.
- Schools with farm units attract pupils they otherwise would not, and those who gain the most are not just the low achievers.
- The School Farms Network and others are there to help any teacher develop their knowledge and skills.

Teachers and pupils should all get their hands dirty!

The network today

Today the SFN in the UK operates with support from Social Farms & Gardens and has over 400 members, including active and prospective school farms, other teachers, and other interested parties, including some agricultural organizations. The membership crosses a wide range of educational establishments, age ranges, and focus. SF&G continues to support the SFN and provide resources and staff time to support the network. The SFN is seen as a key part of Social Farms & Gardens' future strategy and work.

The leadership of the network is provided by a management and advisory group, chaired by an experienced school farm educator and senior educational professional, and supported in a volunteer capacity by an SF&G secretary/convenor. Membership of this group includes school farm managers, practitioners, and staff from Social Farms & Gardens.

There are currently 116 schools and Pupil Referral Units in the UK with functioning farms ranging from those keeping a few sheep and hens in a small area to a 120-acre mixed farm in Banbury. Approximately two-thirds of UK schools have some form of gardens tended by teachers and pupils, most growing some food plants. From there being no interest for many years and a gradual decline in the number of school farms (down to 66 in 2006), there is now an increasing interest in both urban settings and primary schools.

Challenges faced by the network

As with any support network, the SFN faces many challenges concerning its role. The capacity of teachers in terms of time and pressures to deliver on targets means that it is difficult to find time in the calendar to attend training, conferences, and events, although the use of online approaches developed during the pandemic will certainly mitigate this in the future. Funding for the network will always be a challenge, with many funders preferring to support 'on the ground' activity as opposed to the just as vital support role that networks such as the SFN can offer.

Case studies

The case studies below show three examples of how the SFN has supported school farms and some of the values and benefits that the schools, their staff, and pupils, as well as the local community, get from being a part of the network. Case studies were selected from members of the SFN to provide examples of different school farm approaches and were provided by senior teachers within the schools.

Case study 1: SF&G and SFN Awards for school farms

For several years Social Farms & Gardens (SF&G), supporting the School Farms Network, has worked in partnership with the Royal Agricultural University

(RAU) to deliver a conference for school farms and promote and judge a series of awards. In this case study, we examine two award winners and how their involvement in the SFN has benefited them. The material in this case study is taken from the award entries submitted.

Development of the awards

The conference and awards were developed to recognize the importance of school farms and that to do this, a flagship project was needed that could be used to interest people beyond the schools with farms, while also being exciting and useful to engage teachers and pupils within the school.

The RAU offered to host a reception and presentation of awards during the joint SFN/SF&G conference as both an incentive to enter and to give due recognition for the tremendous and important work undertaken by school farms.

Entry categories were agreed to ensure they would be of interest to most school farms, and a simple application form and guidance were developed to ensure fairness. The criteria for judging were:

- Clarity of vision and strategic direction, leadership, and management.
- Evidence of social, environmental, and/or community impact.
- Evidence of creativity and innovation.
- Positive impact on student development and learning.
- Reflections upon success, learning points, and areas for development.

RAU staff volunteered to help judge the entries, and wooden plaques were awarded inscribed with the winner and runner-up names and categories. That format has been repeated except where COVID-19 has intervened; 2021 will be a virtual online presentation of awards.

In 2018, Kian Halliwell from St Michael's Church of England High School won the award for School Farms Student Leadership Award 2018. Despite barriers to learning, Kian has not only completed his BTEC (Business and Technology Education Council) qualification, secured a place in further education in the agricultural sector, and had the stress of his other General Certificate of Secondary Education examinations, but he also consistently found time to be in school from 8am every day of the week and stayed till 4pm every evening on the farm.

He also got involved in community events and helped to forge strong links with companies in the community in order to develop the school farm; he asked local companies for materials to be donated, including the local supermarket who now donate fresh fruit and vegetables to the school farm which Kian picked up every morning before he came to school. He has also helped to landscape the area with the materials that he has collected.

Kian has attended the Royal Cheshire Show with some of the farm rare breed sheep and has taken part in young handler competitions. With Kian spending so much time on the farm, he knows the animals very well and understands their normal behavior patterns. Due to this, he can spot abnormalities in these patterns and always flags up any issues he suspects.

At the 2019 awards, Alice Codner from Elsey Primary School won the School Farm Leader Award.

Elsley is over a mile's walk away from the nearest public green space, which means that for many of their pupils, the school provides their only access to nature. 32% of children in the constituency live below the poverty line; a figure reflected in families being made homeless in emergency accommodation. In general, they are ineligible for pupil premium due to being recent arrivals from overseas or lacking the necessary paperwork. Alice started Elsley Farm to combat the low levels of physical and mental health and wellbeing witnessed as a result of this. Many of these children work on the farm regularly in one-to-one or small group sessions. This allows them to regulate their emotions and build their confidence in learning new skills. Meanwhile, having the animals right in the middle of the school grounds means that all children have access during break times.

Working with a tight school budget that would not have allowed for creating a school farm, Alice fundraised tirelessly to ensure that it was possible. Calling on the help of volunteers in the community and doing much of it herself, they were able to create a farm at the school that has grown considerably. It also created an opportunity for the 620 children living in London to have green space on the school site and have access to various animals.

Alice raised money to buy initial materials, and awareness grew, resulting in a local company coming forward to help with manual labor. Another company then paid for a year's supply of vegetable plants for the school. Alice was a full-time class teacher, but due to her work, she was given leadership of a new Outdoor Learning Team. She took them on training events and ran an INSET day for all staff. She gained confidence and knowledge by volunteering at a city farm and was later employed solely as an outdoor learning leader, a testament to the impact she had had in the school. In the first term, she supported each teacher in taking their curriculum lessons outside while also building connections with other schools with farms, taking the Outdoor Learning Team across London to get inspiration and training. Alice leads assemblies for the whole school, ensuring the children know why the animals are there and how to be safe around them. She also takes children one-to-one and runs two eco-clubs after school for children who want to spend more time outside.

Impact of the awards

All entry schools report an increased interest in the farm and its potential for learning and social development, with some engaging teachers for the first time in using the resource. Publicity within the school and beyond generates increased feelings of pride, enjoyment, and a desire to develop the resource even further.

For some, it helps with fundraising for the farm, and for all, increases status within the school community (Egginton-Metters, 2019).

Nationally, it helps to demonstrate that school farms have a clear role in developing the whole person and delivering the government aspirations, such as contained within *Every Child Matters(2003)*, They also help to raiseinterest across the agricultural sector where most companies and individuals are oblivious to the existence of school farms and how so many thousands of pupils get the opportunity to experience farm livestock, albeit on a small scale.

RAU staff involved in judging the entries have been extremely impressed and humbled by the variety of activity, ingenuity, and passion demonstrated, and recognize that the pupil experience leads to greater understanding and appreciation for agriculture and generates interest in higher education towards employment.

Case study 2: Gloverspiece

The value of horticulture and agriculture has long been recognized as a means of working with students with additional needs. Using a care farm approach, the case study described here, Gloverspiece, exemplifies this. In this case, care farming is defined as the therapeutic use of farming practices (SF&G, 2020).

Gloverspiece Minifarm was established as a care farm in 2010 on 11 acres of land close to the Worcestershire town of Droitwich. It developed an outdoor provision for pupils of local schools as well as adults with additional needs and saw a need to offer qualifications around animal care to these clients, providing them with a tangible outcome alongside the meaningful but softer achievements of social skills, workplace skills, and confidence-building. The proprietor started the care farm after seeing the positive impact on her own five children (two of whom have additional needs) of being on the farm and with the animals. All of her now-adult children have worked on the care farm or in the school and remain committed to its vision, having grown a lifelong bond with the land, nature, animals, and the hope is that every child that comes to the farm grows that too.

In 2017, Gloverspiece Independent School was established on the site, providing education for those outside of the mainstream school system. Using the principles of care farming, the school delivers tailored services to both primary and secondary aged clients that are unable to engage with their main placement school. This is often anxiety-based, especially in older clients; many have been school 'refusers' or are unable to cope with a school environment. Younger clients are all supported on a one-to-one basis and focus on connecting with the animals through real farm work: cleaning out stables, feeding, and grooming. Clients aged 14 or over can enroll in animal care courses that are practically based, from Level 1 to 3. These clients can be 'unsupported', in that they work alongside the farm technicians rather than have an assigned support worker and are treated as part of the team. Expectations are that of the workplace but with a softer, therapeutic approach to choosing and engaging with tasks. Behaviors that prevent them from engaging positively with mainstream school life or classroom learning are usually left at the gate. For some, the farm is the only provision they actively engage with. The Department for Education's cap on such provision is 18 hours per week. Gloverspiece works closely with schools to help address the needs of the client. Examples include struggling with the pressures of studying for exams and a desire to work with animals in the future, separation issues, anxiety around busy school environments, mental health, and low-level behavioral concerns that are under investigation. Often consultation is underway to obtain an Education and Health Care Plan for the child and to find them a more suitable school: in some cases, this results in them then being enrolled full time at Gloverspiece School.

The school provides education for up to 25 children with additional needs, all of whom require close staff support. Initially, the age range was 5–12, but this has been extended to 16 to accommodate the current cohort and give them the option of remaining at the school for the majority of their education. Animal care is an optional subject for secondary pupils, and it is expected that 100% of the current class will choose it. The farm is a key element in the bespoke programs to re-engage children with learning. Some have been out of formal education for over a year before they join the school. They have a range of needs from anxiety to ADHD, PDA, and autistic spectrum disorders. A large percentage of pupils are looked after or have been in care at some point previously and come with additional attachment disorders or associated traumas. The farm is essential in creating an environment where each pupil can feel like they can cope with the day, remain calm and settled enough to engage with meaningful learning, and find ways to deal with their emotions if they become dysregulated. This is achieved in a variety of ways. Often, new pupils will begin by being entirely out on the farm with no pressure to be in the classroom at all. Others need encouragement to engage with nature and the outdoors, but it builds confidence and resilience when they do. The curriculum offers academic subjects alongside a broad land-based timetable, including animal care, horticulture, forest schools, and various nature-focused programs. Land-based activities are timetabled for everyone with the addition of being able to access the farm whenever needed throughout the day. This can be as a reward, a cross-curricular learning resource, or a place to get away from everyone and have space and calm to cope (from cuddling a ferret to feeding the pigs). Hope was one such pupil. Her mother explains:

> She went to a mainstream school, which she found quite difficult. She was quite anxious there; she used to tear the walls to pieces basically. She used to get excluded quite a lot. And then we found Gloverspiece, and things have completely changed. It is a more open space; obviously, she is an animal lover anyway. She seems a lot happier, calmer, loves coming to school now. I love the fact that she comes here and she is happier. She plays with the animals and comes on to the farm sometimes too, but her academics are doing better as well. Last year we found this place, and we could not do without it, to be honest; it has been brilliant, absolutely brilliant.

There is a large crossover between the care farm, college, and school: staffing, policies, and training are all pooled and resourced together to build on the strengths throughout. This means that the farm is used as broadly and creatively as possible, with thorough safeguarding, behavior, health, and safety protocols. The *Care Farming Code of Practice* is essential in shaping how Gloverspiece stays true to its ethos. They have added in being a Nurture School, a trauma-informed school, and a Disability Confident employer. It is embedded in everything from recruitment to parental engagement. Every staff member is asked at interview whether they are willing and confident to take their pupil out on the farm. The majority of consultations for school places come from the fact that it is within a farm.

For Gloverspiece, being part of the School Farms Network has meant that the journey from caring for animals to caring for people to educating people has had support. For many of the staff, the journey happens in the other direction: a move from education to working with pupils through their connection with animals and the land. Sharing ideas and best practices, guiding each other through legislative changes, risk assessments, curriculum demands, and management changes is vital for the growth and sustainability of a school farm. Also, knowing that you are not the only one whose pig ran through a PE lesson is too reassuring for words.

Case study 3: Thomas Alleyne's school farm

Martin Wedgwood qualified as a teacher in 1978 with a B.Ed. in Rural Science which included the basic skills needed for running a school farm. Martin was appointed as a teacher in Charge of Rural Science with minimal resources and a muddy field he was expected to develop into a functioning department and a small greenhouse attached to the laboratory/classroom.

At the time, school farms were far more common than they are now: while Martin's school farm was developing, those around were fast disappearing until at some point in the 1990s, it was the only one left in the Staffordshire state school sector. At this point, Martin discovered the SFN and realized that through this network, he could visit other like-minded teachers and their departments throughout the UK. This showed him what was possible and gave him the impetus to push the development of his own school farm even further.

The farm at Thomas Alleyne School grew and evolved over many years: its first animal house was erected with help from the local NFU and the local Agricultural College; materials were donated from local residents and shops and, thanks to a parent of one of the students, it had a free supply of sawdust for bedding from the workshops of the local prison! Open days were always well supported, with people keen to see what went on behind the walls of the Victorian kitchen garden. The roundabout next to the field, where the Tamworth Pigs were kept, became known locally as 'The Pig Roundabout'.

The farm always tried to maintain links to the town, reporting on significant events in the local press, being part of Open Farm Sunday when everyone was invited, and opening the school farm for assessment during the Britain In Bloom competitions. The farm was always open to visits from the local feeder schools to support their teaching of the curriculum, and it provided a service to many supplying incubators, fertile eggs, and brooders so they could rear chicks within their own classrooms, as well as providing student labor for many of their environmental projects. Supported and enabled by the SFN, Martin learned from other Headteachers that having a farm gave them a competitive edge when parents were choosing the school for their children to attend. The farm's profile was enhanced by winning several prizes, including a greenhouse, tools, cash, and many other resources. Such wins had benefits for the farm but more importantly for the pupils involved, many of whom were not especially academic or good at sport. Their involvement in competitions such as the Royal Shows' Food and Farming Challenges and other competitions organized by the SFN led to impressive changes in pupils' interactions with others. When on several occasions, those same students won at the Royal Show and went on to talk to and shake the hands of various members of the Royal Family, their understanding of what was possible changed beyond all recognition.

The value of the school farm at Thomas Alleyne was recognized during an early Ofsted inspection. The school was awarded Good with five Outstanding Features, one of which was for Art and the other four for the School Farm. A few examples of the text from this report clearly demonstrate the true value of school farms:

> the farm provides excellent opportunities for students' personal development. For example, students learn the importance of routine and the need for commitment when caring for animals; they learn to work in a team. Many regularly appear at lunchtime and after school to deal with feeding and mucking out. Students also develop confidence and self-esteem as they see their plants growing successfully and their animals flourishing. Nor are the benefits merely one-way. These animals are extremely well cared for and therefore very sociable … .
>
> … the importance of the farm to the school extends well beyond the bounds of the curriculum. It provides an opportunity outside lessons for those who wish to work in agriculture and horticulture, or even veterinary science, to practice the skills that will be required.

Discussion: the role of networks and the future

Schools Farms undoubtedly benefit from the existence of a network in terms of connection, sharing good practice, and simply being part of something bigger beyond their own school grounds.

School farms and gardens, as well as other farming and growing activities, provide an important grounding for young people and links into the wider agricultural sector and pathways into employment related to agriculture and horticulture. In the UK, there is currently no clear educational route into agriculture, except for untested new Technical Qualifications (TQ) that City & Guilds and the National Land Based College have developed. Other school-based qualifications that are recognized towards Progress 8 and 'league tables' are small-animal based, such as BTEC Animal Care, and are usually delivered without any contact with farm livestock. School farms together with the School Farms Network help to provide one means of achieving this.

An important question to consider is what the future of school farms in the UK looks like; the network continues to grow from year to year, although we do also see closures associated with cost or the progress towards academization, among other things. The COVID-19 pandemic has also placed considerable additional pressures on school budgets and school staff and pupils. At the time of writing, it is fair to say that many schools are at breaking point.

The future may also lie with the inclusion of more technological advancements in school farm activities. High-tech growth is becoming increasingly practiced in other forms of urban farming and growing and could be a way forward to broaden the scope of a school farm's reach and value. We argue that, although there has been ad-hoc investment into the practice, a major focus by funders and authorities is around high-tech growth in schools. Since 2015, there has been a steady growth of hydroponics and aquaponics in schools, such as the Geodome in Wythenshawe (Real Food Wythenshawe, 2020). A more joined-up approach is required to ensure success across the UK and avoid substantial financial losses, such as with the Wigan UTC example, to ensure that models are sustainable. In doing so, school farm and garden programs can connect more explicitly to the *STEM* agenda, allowing for students to improve their health and wellbeing alongside adding to the curriculum. The SFN has a considerable role to play in these future developments.

The growth of networks and new initiatives to support the links between schools and farm education continues to grow, for example, through LEAF's (Linking Environment and Farming) farm Sunday campaign, the RHS campaign for school gardening, or the Countryside Classroom Website.

Over the last few years, initiatives connecting schools and farming have grown exponentially; all have at their heart a better connection between pupils and the environment, be that agriculture, horticulture, or other areas. Through these initiatives, schools have an increasing availability of resources to use both within the school and better connection with real-life experiences, often away from the school grounds.

In recent times (2020), schools and school farms have been heavily impacted by the COVID-19 pandemic like so many others. Continued change in guidelines and rules, together with the constant need for continual vigilance across the schools for positive cases, have all taken a toll on School Farm Network members. It is likely that as we move through the pandemic, some SFN members may close, but there is a flip side in the increasing recognition of the value that outdoor activity has played in the health and wellbeing of students through the pandemic, in particular, something many practitioners have recognized for a long time.

Despite these pressures, the post-COVID landscape places a greater emphasis on these spaces, particularly those enabling a more local food system (Schoen & Blythe, 2020). During the pandemic, outdoor learning has received more attention due to the ability of children to socially distance themselves and take part in educational activities.. Austin (2021) argues that we may see an increase in school gardens following the pandemic, with models from Denmark and other exemplars replicated in the UK. The social, environmental, and health benefits have been more explicit during the pandemic, with schools and other actors investing in the practice and exploring how to mainstream the concept moving forwards (Austin, 2021).

Conclusion

In the UK, school farms offer an invaluable opportunity for students to get first-hand experience in a way that is much stronger and valuable than simply a visit (or series of visits) to farms away from the school site. Educational attainment has been shown to increase in schools where a farm is in operation. In addition to the strengthening of wellbeing and citizenship that outdoor teamwork generates, the farm can also be used as a hands-on resource for all teachers. This value is expected to increase in the post-COVID world, and with that comes an increase in the value and need for the School Farms Network. The value of the School Farms Network in supporting schools to develop these spaces is clear; teachers running school farms already exceed their contracted hours and have little time to organize and network across the UK. Advocacy is equally difficult for individual schools, although when journalists and the media visit, they are impressed! A forum for exchanging ideas requires managing, stimulating, and access to other organizations that can provide additional support and promotion.

In the future, the School Farms Network plans to continue to support school farms in the UK. As part of this, we make three recommendations for the future:

1. The SFN should continue to develop training resources and courses for school teachers who are new to or are established in school farming. This can be done through the biannual conferences and also through the British Accreditation Council Accreditation that SF&G have recently received.
2. The network should further develop links to policymakers to continue to support the growth of School Farms in the UK.
3. Funders should consider the value of networks and supporting organizations across the whole green sector and ensure that monies support these networks accordingly.

Finally, it is hoped that the school farms movement and the School Farms Network in the UK will continue to grow and develop, providing schoolchildren an opportunity that goes beyond classroom learning.

Acknowledgments

Keeley Smith – Gloverspiece, & Martin Wedgwood for the contribution of case studies.

References

Agricultural Education Magazine. https://www.naae.org/index.cfm (Accessed January 2021).

Austin, S., 2021. The school garden in the primary school: Meeting the challenges and reaping the benefits. *Education 3-13*, 1–15, DOI: 10.1080/03004279.2021.1905017

Burt, K.G., 2016. A Complete History of the Social, Health, and Political Context of the School Gardening Movement in the United States: 1840–2014. *Journal of Hunger & Environmental Nutrition*, 11(3), pp. 297–316, DOI: 10.1080/19320248.2016.1157542 (Accessed 12 August 2021).

Burt, K.G., Lindel, N., Wang, J., Burgermaster, M. & Fera, J., 2019. A nationwide snapshot of the predictors of and barriers to school garden success. *Journal of Nutrition Education and Behaviour*, 51(10), pp.1139–1149.

Christie, P. & Gaganakis, M., 1989. Farm schools in South Africa: The face of rural Apartheid. *Comparative Education Review*, 33(1), pp.77–92. JSTOR, www.jstor.org/stable/1188726 (Accessed 26 Apr. 2021).

Corbett, M., Brett, P. & Hawkins, C., 2017. What we're about out here: The resilience and relevance of school farms in rural Tasmania. *Journal of Research in Rural Education*, 32(4), 1–12.

Egginton-Metters, I., 2019. School Farms Network Conference:2019: Conference Report Overview. Unpublished Report. Bristol, UK: Social Farms & Gardens, 10 pp.

Farm Urban, n.d. *Projects: Greens for Good.* https://farmurban.co.uk/projects/ (Accessed January 2021).

Food Tank, 2019. *16 School Garden Initiatives Revitalising Lunch in the Cafeteria.* https://foodtank.com/news/2019/09/16-school-garden-initiatives-revitalizing-lunches-in-the-cafeteria/ (Accessed November 2020).

Get Oldham Growing, 2021. https://www.oldham.gov.uk/getoldhamgrowing (Accessed January 2021).

Goodson, I., 1993. Rural studies aspects of subject history. In Goodson, I.J (ed.) *School Subjects and Curriculum Change*. London: Routledge, pp 84–102.

Hardman, M. & Larkham, P., 2014. *Informal Urban Agriculture: The Secret Lives of Guerrilla Gardeners.* London: Springer.

Healthy Plymouth, 2021. https://www.healthyplymouth.org/youth-engagement/healthy-plymouth-terra-cura-school-community-gardens (Accessed April 2021).

Howarth, M, Brettle, A, Hardman, M, et al., 2017. *What Evidence is There to Support the Impact if Gardens on Health Outcomes? A Systematic Scoping Review of the Evidence.* Report. SHUSU, University of Salford.

Howarth, M, Brettle, A, Hardman, M, et al., 2020. What is the evidence for the impact of gardens and gardening on health and well-being: A scoping review and evidence-based logic model to guide healthcare strategy decision making on the use of gardening approaches as a social prescription? *BMJ Open*;10, p.e036923. doi:10.1136/bmjopen-2020-036923

Mead B.R., Christiansen P., Davies J.A.C., Falagán N., Kourmpetli S., Liu L., Walsh L. & Hardman C.A., 2021. Is urban growing of fruit and vegetables associated with better diet quality and what mediates this relationship? Evidence from a cross-sectional survey. *Appetite.* https:// doi.org/10.1016/j.appet.2021.105218.

Moore-Colyer, R., 2004. Kids in the corn: School harvest camps and farm labour supply in England, 1940–1950. *The Agricultural History Review*, 52(2), pp.183–206. Retrieved 16 April 2021, from http://www.jstor.org/stable/40275928

National Agriculture in the Classroom, 2013. https://agclassroom.org/ (Accessed 6January 21).

Real Food Wythenshawe, 2020. https://www.realfoodwythenshawe.com/projects/geodome/ (Accessed 6 January 2020).

Saunders, M., Minnett, M. & Daglish, D., 2014. *Improving the Quality of Student Learning through School Farms.* Unpublished Report. University of Lancaster, 77pp.

Schoen, V. & Blythe, C., 2020. COVID-19: A growing opportunity for community gardening in London. RUAF. https://ruaf.org/news/covid-19-a-growing-opportunity-for-community-gardening-in-london/ (Accessed 7 April 2021).

Schreinemachers, P., Baliki, G., Manandhar, R., Dhruba, S., Bhattarai, R., Gautam, I.P., Ghimire, P.L., Subedi, B.P. & Bruck, T., 2020. Nudging children toward healthier food choices: An experiment combining school and home gardens. *Global Food Security*, 26, p.100454, National Association of Environmental Educators. Website: https://www.naae.org/index.cfm (Accessed 10 November 2020).

Smith, D., 2011. The Spade as mighty as the sword. The story of the Dig for Victory Campaign. London: Aurum Press, 250 pp.

Social Farms & Gardens, 2020. *Growing Care Farming, Annual Survey 2020: Full Report.* Unpublished report. Bristol: Social Farms & Gardens.

United States Holocaust Memorial Museum, 2020. https://collections.ushmm.org/search/catalog/irn612681 (Accessed 14 October 2020).

Viljoen, A & Wiskerke, J.S.C., (Eds.), 2012. *Sustainable Food Planning: Evolving Theory & Practice.* Wagenigen: Wageningen Academic Publishers, 598 pp.

Wells, N.M., Myers, B.M & Henderson, C.R., 2014. School gardens and physical activity: A randomized control trial of low-income elementary schools. *Preventive Medicine*, 69(supplement), pp. 527–533.

Wells, N.M., Meyers, B.M, Todd, L.E., Henderson, C.R., Barale, K., Gaolach, B., Ferenz, G., Aitken, M., Tse, C.C., Pattison, K.O., Hendrix, L., Carson, J.B., Taylor, C. & Franz, N.K., 2018. The carry-over effects of school gardens on fruit and vegetable availability at home: A randomized controlled trial with low-income elementary schools. *Preventive Medicine*, 112, pp. 152–159.

5

FOODWAYS, FARMS, AND ECOLOGY

School farms and cultivation of precision agriculture in Bandung upland

Frans Ari Prasetyo

Introduction

The ecological crisis is worsening in the 21st century, which has affected the agricultural and food systems in the world. Since what Friedmann and McMichael (Friedmann, 1989, McMichael, 2009) termed 'the food regime', combined with this thrust of argument from political ecology, food sovereignty similarly emphasizes the social effects of 'neoliberal globalization' (Bernstein, 2014). The historical analysis explains how food production and consumption relations are central to global capitalism's functioning and reproduction. There has also been a pressing need for agricultural countries like Indonesia to reimagine their agriculture. Agriculture is the key element of essential food, biodiversity, and humanity's relations with nature. It is vital to return to practices that are less mass-oriented, less globalized, and more localized. These agricultural movements for food have developed a wealth of historical, political, technical, organizational, and entrepreneurial skills, and advance a wide range of demands. These include land reform and food sovereignty (Desmarais, 2007, Desmarais, 2003), sustainable and agroecological agriculture (Altieri, 1995, Holt-Gime'nez, 2006, Gliessman, 2007), local food (Halweil, 2004), community food security (Winne, 2008), and how food made history (Higman, 2012) in making world food map, origins of domestication and agriculture practice.

The food crisis and persistent social and environmental failures have spurred the formation of social movements concerned with food and agriculture. Many studies have indicated that local food systems are among the solutions to mitigate these impacts (Hinrichs, 2003, Allen, 2003). It is challenging to question ways of occupying the land, treating ecology, and providing food, but how can we reassemble what it means to enact and govern land and agriculture for food and ecology and advocate for agricultural policy in Indonesia, especially Bandung.

DOI: 10.4324/9781003176558-5

As practiced by participants in the food sovereignty movement, agroecology goes beyond production based on ecological principles and local traditional knowledge, placing it within a transformative socio-political project (Holt-Giménez, 2013) and 'people of the land' (Desmarais, 2002). Food sovereignty centered on the collective 'right to produce food', meaning protecting farm sectors from trade 'dumping' and land sovereignty for land users (Borras, 2012).

During the mid-1990s, Indonesia was starting to see declining vitality in the agricultural sector as an amalgamation of environmental problems arose simultaneously with the removal of agricultural subsidies (Gerard, 2001). Indonesia lost 5.1 million farmers between 2003–2013 (Indonesia, 2003, 2013), with their numbers falling to 26 million. The agricultural census in Indonesia is carried out every ten years, decline in 2013 the number of farmers is expected increase in 2023 and to continue in the next few years. At this rate, Indonesia would lose all its farmers by 2063 (Anthony, 2020). As economic agricultural growth stagnates, Indonesia's resources begin to deplete, agricultural land begins to decrease, and farmers' numbers continually decrease. In addition, there are many farmers without land.

In various studies on land in Indonesia, such as those conducted by Booth (2016), Peluso (1992), and White and Wiradi (1989), it was explained that the unequal agrarian structure, tenure of land, and natural resources are at the root of poverty. In progress, land access-ownership is transformed politically on the inside, a new conception of land sovereignty. Refer to La Via Campesina-LVC, it primarily reflects agrarian populist traditions intellectually, and in mobilization, food sovereignty departs from land sovereignty (Martínez-Torres, 2010, McMichael, 2014), as a real example for Indonesia. This is an important aspect that underlies agrarian issues and agriculture (Borras, 2015, McMichael, 2015). Both are closely related to the foodways and ecology and the ongoing or intensified dispossession of the world's peasants or small farmers; 'the literal displacement of millions of families from the land and their rural communities' (Wittman, 2010). Throughout history, the most significant connection between society and nature has been agriculture (Wittman, 2009) and food (Higman, 2012). Inspired by the 'Will to Improve' (2007) by Tania Li, a contextualized theoretical framing of a smaller community group, attempts to see the improved practice of Indonesia's agriculture in the peri-urban, tropical area of Bandung upland – surrounded by mountainous volcanic area – a source of food as well as a city ecological belt with economic and environmental degradation that must be to improved. Also, Redfield (1961) detects a cluster of closely related attitudes concerning small communities and how they relate to farmer society and land and agriculture systems.

This study examines small local communities of farmers with the aim to improve cultivation with precision agriculture practices in school farms in Bandung upland by Odesa and Buruan Manglayang (BM). This offers hope of pulling agriculture out of the crisis of ecological and environmental degradation, the foodways system and nutrition, and social and economic forces, including overcoming the COVID-19 situation. COVID-19 has created significant disruptions, and widespread hunger has reared its head, has been a cataclysmic event for the global system on many levels, and has spilled over into a complex food crisis on a global scale (Clapp, 2020). COVID-19 is forcing us to look at short-term solutions. However, at the same time, the pandemic opens the opportunity to push forward with a long-term, transformational change which merges perspectives from the practice of food ecology farming and small-business practice of precision agriculture, through participatory community work in school farms, to steward long-term social, economic, and environmental viability in Bandung upland.

Bandung upland: agriculture and ecology landscape

Bandung is a colonial city with architectural and educational history at its center; in a peri-urban (upland) area is historically famous for tea, rubber, quinine, coffee, as a source for food, and as a vegetable and fruit producer. As the capital city of the West Java province, Bandung consists of an area of 167.7 km², ranging from 657–1,050 meters above sea level, and trapped within a giant basin that was once an ancient crater. The peri-urban areas in Bandung Regency consist of an area of 1,768 km² with 280 villages, ranging from 500–1,800 meters above sea level (BPS, 2018, 2020, 2021); the Bandung upland area comprises only 20–25 percent of Bandung Regency .

Bandung upland, with the demography, geography, resources (land) access, and historical profiles of the farmer community, contributes to a unique case where agriculture, foodways, and ecological practice are abundant, and yet society is still marginalized and impoverished. It is a systematic rather than an arbitrary process, the hallmark of the geography of capitalism when the process by which the social relations of societies are translated into capitalist of spatial forms. Smith (1990) puts it as uneven development.

The peri-urban fringes of Bandung upland have historically consisted of substantial farms and have been a source for food. Planting habits include crops such as cabbage, lettuce, spinach, tomatoes, potatoes, broccoli, chilies, watercress, choy sum, eggplant, cucumbers, carrots, scallions, and red onions. This area is arable land, with rich volcanic soil and a tropical climate, cool temperatures, and constantly exposed to sunlight so that it is contested for agriculture or settlement. Inadequate policy choices have meant that upland Bandung struggles to reach its potential. Bandung upland experiences structural poverty, a nutrition gap, and social degradation accompanied by ecological degradation. The agricultural sector only contributes around 0.14 percent of total GDP, whereas food provisioning services contribute around 4.63 percent (Jawabarat, 2016).

This is felt by peri-urban Bandung, whose dependence on the agricultural sector has decreased in the last two decades. Traditional agriculture tends to be a monoculture, focusing on vegetables due to changes in land expansion, especially for settlement, according to what Simon (2008) states. By observing the

Bandung peri-urban's upland face be found golf courses, hotels, villas, luxury apartments and restaurants are built alongside poor settlements, where the land is also assigned for agriculture purposes to meet subsistence needs. In peri-urban areas such as Bandung upland, the land has a double meaning, as agriculture and food production space in the perspective of individualism and social spaces whose community benefits from it of the spatial changes that occur in land capital values. Following Morgan's (2013) argument, there is no one-size-fits-all approach in designing a food policy and it all depends on society's local context. Agriculture strategy to achieve sustained agricultural productivity aims to break monoculture structure by designing integrated agriculture/food/ecology systems.

The ecological devastation, food crisis, and land crisis of Bandung upland are caused by uneven land use development and capitalism agriculture due to a top-down development scheme. Its focus has become blinkered, narrow, and its programs partial and susceptible to capitalist overtures. Food politics and land capitalism create the mass alienation of the population from the natural conditions of their existence, food, and land. In order for a combination of food and land access to be relevant in rural or peri-urban society they mostly rely on land as agricultural production spaces. As it changes society's structure and agriculture, then it is about changes in land and food governance.

Bandung upland's agriculture creates foodways and ecology practices in unique ways that lend themselves to the formulation of a specific prescription that can only be applied to specific cases, geographies, and communities. The foodways address not only the issues around availability and accessibility of food but also the sustainability of livelihoods at the local society level, which all relate strongly to an active individual and society's life, especially farmer position and land access in inequality agrarian structure for agriculture. They qualify as capital's other by an ensemble of qualities attributed for land and agriculture, which include their sustainable farming principles and practices (Bernstein, 2014), their capacity for collective stewardship of the environments they inhabit, their vision of autonomy (Wittman, 2010), and their 'peasant frugality' (McMichael, 2010).

Farmers, foods, villages, and policy

In Indonesia generally, including in Bandung upland, agricultural problems are villages problems that have implications for various sectors. Farmers will be trapped in a crisis, inclusion, inequality, and access, back in the trap of capitalism agriculture and environmentally unsustainable resources. That is why local agricultural practice is important socially, ecologically, culturally, and economically as well as its use and meaning in a variety of different contexts. An ecological response to the climate crisis and food crisis would recognize that some regions may be more suited to agriculture and food security/sovereignty with precision agriculture with local ecology determination. It is a radical proposal for substantive change in existing (global/capitalism) agriculture: a food regime based on the right of the farmer and the country to define their own agricultural and food policy.

The community's policy management and movement are increasingly required to address complexities around the alleviation of food shortages and farmer poverty, particularly in agriculture, and maintain the ecological base and multifunctional interactions between land, food, and villages in peri-urban areas, where farmers live. The relationship between three correlated drivers of food demand include: 1) growth of household expenditures, 2) rural/urban differences in household characteristics, and 3) levels of urbanization – and must change in the future (Warr, 2020). Through Sobal et al. (1998), the wide-ranging literature on food systems reveals multiple perspectives and world views. Here, the foodways system is a combination of the conceptual framework of access of land (Ribot, 2003) and food in food security (Maxwell, 1996, Carolan, 2012), food sovereignty (Jarosz, 2014), and food justice (Gottlieb, 2010) as being part of a broader understanding of the food and land. Food systems have usually been conceived of as a set of activities ranging from production through to consumption (Ericksen, 2007). Then, how people's (farmers) in Bandung upland improvised lives and survived life with devise strategies to make their way through the day, coming up against or collaboration done in surprising ways construct a foodways system that can contain interactions and have strategies for agriculture.

Indonesia has 81,616 villages (BPS, 2018) and specific regulations (Village Law No.6/2014), which have the potential to be radically capable of empowering residents/farmers in the villages to refuse the presence of agricultural companies, defend territory, make the government accountable to the people, especially small farmers, and create coalitions of empowered villages and farmers. The favorable situation for farmers in villages, which is also supported by (Food Law No. 18/2012) and (Agricultural Cultivation Systems Law No. 22/2019), a combination of laws for agricultural and food in rural and peri-urban areas.

All villages in Indonesia have a village index such as IDM *Indeks Desa Membangun* (Building Villages Index) and IKL *Indeks Kualitas Lingkungan* (Environmental Quality Index), including villages in Bandung upland. In other words, they are categorized as *Desa Maju* (developed villages) and *Desa Mandiri* (independent villages) by getting a *Dana Desa* (village budget) from the Indonesian government. However, the villages in Bandung upland are underdeveloped villages with residents' income below the regional minimum wage of Bandung Regency: 3.2 million IDR per month (under $220 per month). Twenty percent of the population is poor and receives BLT *Bantuan Langsung Tunai* (the unconditional cash transfer program); most village recipients are farmers. Therefore, it is crucial to improve villages and farmers' living standards and meet their food needs, considering that they are disadvantaged. Accordingly, Warr (2020) calls for projections of future food consumption levels and their commodity composition, making changes in Indonesian households' nutrient intake.

The Indonesian government introduced a food law in 2010 which initiated a program to accelerate the diversification of food consumption (*percepatan penganekaragaman Konsumsi Pangan* p2KP) to reduce dependence on rice consumption and reduce the burden of rice imports, which continue to increase. It was then supported in 2020 by the *Kawasan Rumah Pangan Lestari* KRPL (Sustainable Food Housing Area) program and Local Food Development. However, the implementation is not significant for changes in food governance and farmer welfare, especially in Bandung upland. They are still underdeveloped villages, receiving BLT for poor residents (farmers) and with poor access to nutritious food, even though they own an agricultural system and food production source.

Indonesia underwent reforms in 1998 and experienced democratization which resulted in a change in government policy towards farmers and agriculture, which at that time been controlled. On the other hand, there are also demands to drive towards environmental sustainability to compensate for the degradation of ecology and how to provide food for a growing population of hundreds of millions. The Indonesian government made a dispositive formalized top-down approach to farmers back to 'control era'- new order era before reforms 1998 through the farmer certification policy under the Decree of the Ministry of Agriculture No. 120/2014. This certification is obtained by participating in a program called *Sekolah Lapangan Untuk Petani* (field school for farmers) to standardize capacity and technical skills in farming. The aim of standardization is to control farmers by trapping them advances with achieve access and incentives. New Indonesian farmers control the new age of capitalism. The sovereign/disciplinary/control transition was arguably the result of ongoing contestation between various heterogeneous elements; each attempting to territorialize the agri-food landscape (Dwiartama, 2018).

The most useful description of a food system is a chain of activities from production ('the field') to consumption ('the table'), with particular emphasis on processing and marketing and the multiple transformations of food that these entail (Heller, 2003, Dixon, 1999, Cannon, 2002) and how this is done in the practice of precision agriculture for ecology foodways through the school farm (O'Hara, 2017) by/for the community, in order for the community to obtain sufficient nutrition (Sobal, 1998). This is similar in thought to the idea of agroecology by Altieri (1995), who discussed how to study, design, and manage alternative agroecosystems that address not just environmental/ecological aspects of the crisis of modern agriculture, but the economic, social, and cultural ones. Van der Ploeg (2021) states that agroecology represents and is rooted in many agricultural practices and social relations of production within agriculture.

School farm: movement, practice, and community

Bandung upland has to address land, food, agricultural, ecological, and nutritional challenges. Then, the foodways have to be considered in their entirety to raise the locality's prominence as part of the solution by community base to acknowledge the interdependency between of resources, access and practice. This also illustrates that localism carries political heft in opposition to the globalization of diets (Lang, 1999, Hinrichs, 2000). Kirwan and Maye's (2013) review of the links between food security and local food movements to encourage local and alternative food movements is significant. Given this disequilibrium within food movements, Holt-Giménez (2011) suggests developing strategic alliances between progressive and radical tendencies and building a 'movement of movements' capable of addressing the most immediate problems and promoting structural changes necessary for developing sustainable, equitable, and democratic food systems. Social reality can be changed so that inequality can be reduced and be expected general welfare can increase, as took place in Bandung upland.

Odesa and BM tried to engage in food and agriculture as a little community Redfield,1961) as new social movement Scott1990), and resistance as everyday politics - seeing James Scott's (1989). When communities are fully empowered, they make democratic and participatory decisions on issues that directly affect them, especially on food and nutrition; these communities are sensible local ecology managers, natural resources, and a (transformation/resistance) movement in societies. The importance of mutual agriculture consensus is to see that all farmers in the area express interest in the local food system and to keep ecology in doing agriculture. Based on the idea that people need to interact with each other within a community, community farming initiatives position themselves as the gateway between food and people.

Odesa is located in four villages, while BM is in one village. They identify the specific causes of the ecology crisis and food crisis and address them effectively in a structural sense. The critical transformation with precision agriculture through school farms provides more advantages as a practice of autonomous sufficiency; where everyone (farmer) is fulfilled, especially regarding food, nutrition, the economy, and get the ecological situation sustainable for the future.

Since 2014, Odesa, as a social entrepreneur farming/ecology NGO, has collaborated with local farmers in four villages in Bandung upland, namely *Cimenyan*, *Cikadut*, *Mekarmanik*, and *Mandalamekar* (see Picture 5.1). Odesa began as an effort led by a philanthropist, has shifted its orientation to public participation (farmers), and engaged a broader cross-section of community stakeholders to focus on food, education, health, the economy, and technology/ecology management in grassroots movements. This is through ecological farming procedures on critical land and informal education in school farms with young people and hundreds of farmers in mutual partnerships. Odesa created the *Samin* school as a *Sabtu-Minggu* (Saturday/Sunday) informal school, which takes every Saturday for junior/high-school children aged 10–16 years old, and every Sunday for elementary school children aged 4–10 years old. They use *Samin* as name and spirit duplicate of the *Samin* community as an indigenous farmer community in Java, as being wise and humble fighters for land, and environmental and social-ecological justice against extractivism. Odesa introduced the school farm to the children of farmers and taught them how to farm in their own yard, plant seeds, and how precision agriculture will become the basis for their future agricultural/ecological knowledge.

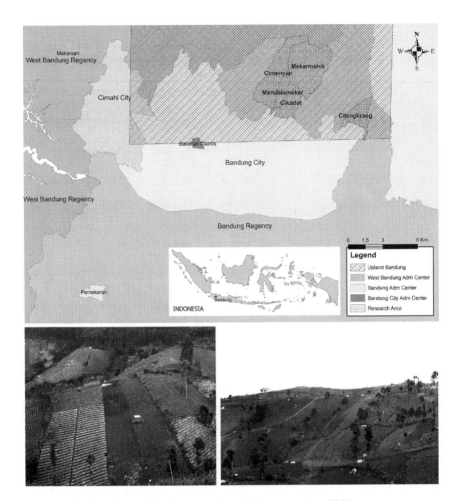

PICTURE 5.1 Bandung upland maps and agriculture practices, 2020.

Moreover, school farms are carried out participatory for farmers in informal and participatory meetings directly in the practice of cultivating precision agriculture. Odesa also created an informal school, routinely conducted directly on the farm and classrooms called *Rumah Literasi* (literacy house) for farmers' children as extra education outside of formal school time .

Odesa has sponsored self-sufficient farming collectives, encompassing hundreds of farmers by providing seeds, and responded to the COVID-19 crisis by issuing free and shared food to farmers and impoverished communities. The school farms are being established for the local community to provide people with training, workshops, knowledge, and informal education for both farmers and their children to understand ecological, economic, and health transformation in the food system by the way of agriculture. In practice, they invite farmers to make changes to their cropping patterns, which were originally dominated by vegetables, to diversify with other crops. Odesa promoted planting Kelor (Drumstick tree/Moringa oleifera), Hanjeli/Jali (Job's tears/Coix lacryma-jobi), and Sorghum. These three crops have high nutrition values, and are high in vitamins and protein, and can replace farmers' dependence on rice as the main food and exclusive way of farming. The farmers also planted sunflowers (Helianthus annuus), which produce vegetable oil and seeds that can be turned into popular snacks such as Guaci/Kuaci. All of these plants are easy to grow, care for, and harvest. They are all also types of herbal medicinal plants. Their uses go beyond food. These plants have an economic value greater than vegetables and rice, and moreover once harvested, they can be used for more nutritious animal feed compared to grass, and provide mutual substitution value – good nutrition's for animal and significant increases farmers income.

The Odesa base camp in the village of Cimenyan has an independent nursery system, called *Taoci-Tanaman Obat Cimenyan* (Cimenyan Medicinal Plant), which provides seeds for farmers in the Bandung upland area where they work and sell them to the wider public. Due to the growing demand for seeds, Odesa collaborated with the farmers who were previously given free seeds and had harvested plants to implement an independent nursery system, which adds additional economic value. Odesa not only promotes these plants as an alternative to crops grown on agricultural land, which are usually vegetables planted in an alternating way, Odesa also promotes planting them in yards where residents can directly consume them as *Pertanian Pekarangan* – yard farming (see Picture 5.2).

PICTURE 5.2 Cultivation of precision agriculture in Bandung upland (top) and yard farming (bottom), 2020.

Farmers use land in their homes to grow the recommended crops and vegetables to be directly consumed, reducing the cost of buying food and resulting in additional household income. A Kelor farm can increase household income by $50 per month on top of the primary income from vegetable farming. Some residents grow vegetables in their yard with an income of $5–10 per week and can also meet their household food needs without buying anything extra. Also, housewives can become influencers by successfully inviting around 40 housewives to become vegetable farmers in their backyards, which generate a household income of around $5 per week and can provide nutritious food for families to grow themselves. Family food security is formed by changing household economic habits.

Odesa's work as an entrepreneurial motivator for farmers to increase their capacity for capital production and social capital. What Odesa does have is a level of vulnerability that is risky by leaving structural and class gaps at the farmer community level and it is seen as working at the grassroots level, autonomously but still adopting top-down developmentalism practices that are packaged in participatory action planning. Farmers do not have authority over their crops, including their land. There is surveillance over how to manage land and determine the types of plants that are considered suitable for farmers' lives, in addition to political interests through agriculture sustainable, community development, ecology, and enhancement of capital farmers. When they do not comply with Odesa's 'orders', farmers can be expelled from this community circle and cannot access seeds, sell crops from the promoted plants, and do not get other assistance for food, infrastructure, and education for their children. The farmers no longer feel part of Odesa, and these farmers will return to their original habits and traditional farming methods by growing vegetables with some improvement due to the help they received from Odesa. This is a common problem in hierarchically developed communities due work top-down structure.

Another community with simpler structural scales and smaller capacities is Buruan Manglayang (BM), which has been active since 2018 and emerged based on the initiative of residents who live around Mount Manglayang in the village of Cilengkrang (see Picture 5.1). They formed a small community and agents of change who practice precision agriculture by inviting residents to engage in household-scale precision agriculture practices in yards through the school farm. The results of this agricultural pattern carried out by BM are only to meet household needs and become a new household-scale economic alternative. Unlike Odesa, BM works on a smaller area and in a smaller capacity, is not farmer based, does not have agricultural land, and consists of various formal and informal professions.

BM runs a school farm in a different way from Odesa. They gather at a resident's house with no fixed schedule, temporarily and randomly share information that focuses on precision agriculture in narrow land or the household yard, and determine the types of plants to be planted and create nursery system, all carried out independently in a school farm scheme by community participants.

They practice precision farming in their yard to supply their household needs and create a small food network. The types of plants grown tend to be food and vegetable crops that are only for household consumption, not for selling. The main objective is to fulfill household food needs with healthy, nutritious, cheap food that is easy to obtain around the home, and to reduce household economic consumption. In the COVID-19 pandemic, people with low incomes are increasingly experiencing food shortages. School farm practices carried out by the BM community help overcome this problem by carrying out household-scale precision agriculture practices by providing seeds and selecting types of food and vegetable crops that are nutritious, easy to grow, and quick to harvest. This can result in a decrease of up to 30 percent in household economic expenditure on buying vegetables.

BM plant vegetables that are quick to harvest and easy to care for, such as spinach, water spinach, and choy sum. This community, together with residents, also grows nutritious and plants with a high economic value that have an attractive and beautiful aesthetic appearance, such as Rosela (roselle/hibiscus sabdariffa), Telang (Asian pigeonwings), and sunflowers (Helianthus annuus). Rosella and Telang can be made into a tea and a syrup that can be consumed or sold at a high price. Telang is a herbal medicine for the eyes and can also be used as a natural blue food coloring. Sunflower seeds can be consumed as snacks or made into vegetable oil, both of which are nutritious and have a high economic value that can help increase household income .

The school farm pattern is also applied to children and young people who live in the area. They routinely engage in household-scale farming scenarios; they learn in informal schools run by this community. What BM did is snowballing and starting to be followed by many residents because they have seen the benefits related to their food, nutrition, and economic needs. They are taught how to farm, plant seeds to protect nature, and independently provide a healthy and nutritious food system by small-scale agricultural products which end up on their dining table. It is proposed criteria to evaluate food systems, including nutrition and health, rights and influence, security, sustainability, equality, and social inclusion. This achievement has come over time. Unlike Odesa, which tends to work systematically, structured with control and supervision even though it is a top-down structure with specific achievement targets within a certain period, BM looks to be more independent and tends to be flexible, temporary, sprawling, and easier to spread in the absence of hierarchical/structural control and engagement.

At present, Odesa and BM are prioritizing building alliances among popular sectors in the countryside and the city for the recovery and (re)construction of local food systems. When assembling local agriculture and ecology practice for food with school farms, they are assembling a new idea of a food system that would fit into a growing and changing society (see Picture 5.3). Autonomous agriculture practices with school farms by a participatory approach provide engagement and social capital transformation practices spread across villages as a

PICTURE 5.3   School farm in Bandung upland, 2019–2020.

settlement model. This model is centrally linked to food production areas with the cultivation of agriculture precision and ecological determination for sustainable foodways systems. They also improve the damaged ecology system resulting from careless farming and the pressure on land and food access, and enhance social solidarity, community building, and participation with social justice in society.

The school farm in ecological agriculture design and foodways systems is an improved for economic, food, and ecological sustainability with proposed local autonomous community management specifically in tune with the local resource base such as land, crops, seeds, and the operational farmers' framework of existing environmental and socio-economic conditions. Farmers in Bandung upland have always held the seeds in their hands: they are taught to grow and harvest all of their food, plant their own land/gardens to feed their families, make their lives better, and the ecological ecosystem of soil is maintained. In addition, Odesa and BM seem to answer the challenge and at the same time carry out the work of the Indonesian government program to accelerate the diversification of food consumption through diversification of various types of plants for eating as well as implementing Sustainable Food House Areas by diversifying food crops that have a high economic value, as well as conducting *Pertanian Pekarangan* (yard farming). Odesa is in a more vulnerable situation to be co-opted and annexed by capitalist system and state claims compared to BM because it has the infrastructure of political/power relations and social capital with structural control. So even though Odesa will still have 'management' or change actors, BM will be very vulnerable to disbanding because there are no structural ties and relationships between the people involved, and there are no actor domination or actor change scenarios, because there is no hierarchical structure. Both would more easily transform from a community into an NGO through top-down political support to become a profit consultant by the state project or corporation for community development program or Corporate Social Responsibility program, made their social and political position an "elite" when dealing with society (farmers), making inclusions.

Conclusion

The documentation of Bandung upland's agricultural initiatives has led to the belief that initiatives are connected, even evolving into a collective grassroots movement, built and transformed to achieve more significant impacts. Odesa and BM's experiences show a school farm with agriculture cultivation, providing answers to the possibilities between political and social trends in the food movement expressed by Giménez (2011) based on its discourse, models, key actors, institutions, and documents. By being inclusive in mapping society, we can observe the dynamics that shape the system. This practice faces challenges. As noted by Mount (2012), opportunities are widely available, but also need to be critically examined when it comes to the governance of alternative food movements, pulling agriculture out of the crisis of ecological and environmental degradation, the food system and nutrition, and social and economic forces, including overcoming the COVID-19 pandemic. An agriculture ecology and foodways system can be worked on and continue to be developed on the inclusive access for food and land, combined with a more radical and democratic vision of organizing production to integrate ecological knowledge and principles in society. The residents/farmers of Bandung upland can conduct a local redevelopment of cultivation of agriculture precision with community participation, which would change the unpredictable pattern of expenditure of (farmers') household food production/consumption and takes explicit account of the effect of land (use), food, and ecology. They are at the grassroots, growing food sources, providing seeds, processing fertilizers, bringing products to market, bridging food networks and social capital, and maintaining the environment, although it will also lead to patron client relationship and hierarchical actors. Furthermore, to an extent, they represent whole other communities that are struggling to build resilient and sustainable solutions to face the global crises within a local context.

The presence of Odesa and BM in upland Bandung is to change cropping patterns through a school farm that aims to establish a food system for the people to be directly implemented autonomously. However, what they advocate and what Ostrom (1990) shows is that local people are best able to put their agriculture, food, and ecological knowledge into practice. Like the argument that farmers are best equipped to govern the conditions and management of their workplace, local communities are best equipped to manage the environments and ecosystem they rely on. They do not try to change the structure and access to the world food system, but try to contribute to the socio-spatial local alternative movement for food and ecology through school farms that carry out precision agriculture which makes a significant contribution to local (farmers') economic wellbeing, health, education, and environment. However, it is pessimistic to expect an improvement in the structure of control over agricultural land and access to large-scale food, let alone changing the world's foodways. Optimistically, school farms can contribute to the promotion of public nutrition and increased household income. However, the changes made by them are also fragile due to the co-optation of groups, government, or more considerable capital, even though it is on behalf of the community and farmers. It presents a local view that can inform, enable, and inspire a new generation of ecologically minded food farms in the world and socialistically minded agroecology, envisaging the day when these identities merge in the local, national, regional, and international levels of political commitment to put the society and nature metabolic relation basis through ecology and food.

Acknowledgment

I am very grateful to all editors and two anonymous reviewers who helped me to improve this chapter. I thank Izzuddin Prawiranegara for their help.

References

Allen, P., Fitzsimmons, M., Goodman, M., & Warner, K. 2003. Shifting plates in the agrifood landscape: The tectonics of alternative agrifood initiatives in California. *Journal of Rural Studies*, 19, pp.61–75.

Altieri, M.A. 1995. *Agroecology: The Science of Sustainable Agriculture*. Boulder, CO: Westview Press.

Anthony, I.M. 2020. A land without farmers: Indonesia's agricultural conundrum. *Jakarta Post*. Accessed 20 Jan 2021 <https://www.thejakartapost.com/longform/2020/08/13/a-land-without-farmers-indonesias-agricultural-conundrum.html>

Bernstein, H. 2014. Food sovereignty via the 'peasant way': A sceptical view. *The Journal of Peasant Studies*. 41(6), pp.1031-1063. doi:10.1080/03066150.2013.852082

Booth, A. 2016. *Economic Change in Modern Indonesia: Colonial and Postcolonial Comparisons*. Cambridge, UK: Cambridge University Press.

Borras, Jr., S.M., Franco, J.C., and Suárez, S.M. 2015. Land and food sovereignty. *Third World Quarterly*, 36, pp.600–617.

Borras, Jr. S.M, and Franco, J.C. 2012. *A 'Land Sovereignty' Alternative? Towards a People's CounterEnclosure*. Discussion Paper Worksheet. TNI Agrarian Justice Programme. Accessed 23 Feb 2021 <https://www.tni.org/en/publication/a-land-sovereignty-a lternative-0>

BPS (ed.) 2018. *Jumlah Desa Menurut Provinsi dan Topografi Wilayah 2011–2018*. Jakarta: BPS Statistic Indonesia.

BPS (ed.) 2020. *Bandung Dalam Angka*. Bandung: BPS Bandung City.

BPS (ed). 2021. *Kabupaten Bandung Dalam Angka 2021*. Bandung: BPS Bandung Regency.

Cannon, T. 2002. Food security, food systems and livelihoods: Competing explanations of hunger. *Die Erde*, 133, pp.345–362.

Carolan, M. 2012. *The Sociology of Food and Agriculture*. London: Routledge.

Clapp, J. and W.G. Moseley 2020. This food crisis is different: COVID-19 and the fragility of the neoliberal food security order. *The Journal of Peasant Studies*, 47, pp.1393–1417.

Desmarais, A.-A. 2002. The Vía Campesina: Consolidating an international peasant and farm movement. *Journal of Peasant Studies*, 29, pp.91–124.

Desmarais, A.A. 2003. Vi'a Campesina: Peasant women at the frontiers of food sovereignty. *Canadian Woman Studies*, 23, pp.140–145.

Desmarais, A.A. 2007. *La Vi'a Campesina: Globalization and the Power of Peasants*. Halifax: Fernwood.

Dixon, J. 1999. A cultural economy model for studying food systems. *Agriculture and Human Values*, 16, pp.151–160.

Dwiartama, A. 2018. From 'disciplinary societies' to 'societies of control': A historical narrative of agri-environmental governance in Indonesia. In J. Forney, C. Rosin and H. Campbell (ed.) *Agri-environmental Governance as an Assemblage*. London: Routledge.

Ericksen, P.J. 2008. Conceptualizing food systems for global environmental change research. *Global Environmental Change.*18(1), pp 234-245.

Friedma, H. and P. McMichael 1989. Agriculture and the state system: The rise and decline of national agricultures, 1870 to the present. *Sociologia Ruralis*, 29, pp.93–117.

Gerard, F., I. Marty and ERWIDODO 2001. The 1998 food crisis: Temporary blip or the end of food security? In Ruf, F. and Gérard, F. (eds.) *Agriculture in Crisis: People, Commodities, and Natural Resources in Indonesia, 1996–2000*. Montpellier: CIRAD.

Giménez, E. H. A. A. S. 2011. Food crises, food regimes and food movements: Rumblings of reform or tides of transformation? *The Journal of Peasant Studies*, 38, pp.109–144.

Gliessman, S. R. 2007. *Agroecology: The Ecology of Sustainable Food Systems*. New York: Taylor and Francis Group.

Gottlieb, R., and A. Joshi 2010. *Food Justice*. Cambridge, MA: The MIT Press.

Halweil, B. 2004. *Eat Here: Reclaiming Homegrown Pleasures in a Global Supermarket*. New York: Norton.

Heller, M. C., Keoleian, G.A 2003. Assessing the sustainability of the US food system: A life cycle perspective. *Agricultural Systems*, 76, pp.1007–1041.

Higman, B. W. 2012. *How Food Made History*. Hoboken, NJ: Wiley-Blackwell.

Hinrichs, C. C. 2000. Embeddedness and local food systems: Notes on two types of direct agricultural market. *Journal of Rural Studies*, 16, pp.295–303.

Hinrichs, C. C. J. 2003. The practice and politics of food system localization. *Journal of Rural Studies*, 19, pp.33–45.

Holt-Gime'nez, E. 2006. *Campesino a Campesino: Voices from Latin America's Farmer to Farmer Movement for Sustainable Agriculture*, Oakland, CA: Food First Books.

Holt-Giménez, E., & Altieri, M 2013. Agroecology, food sovereignty and the new green revolution. *Journal of Sustainable Agriculture*, 37, pp.90–102.

Holt-Giménez, E., & Shattuck, A 2011. Food crises, food regimes and food movements: Rumblings of reform or tides of transformation? *Journal of Peasant Studies*, 38, pp.109–144.

Indonesian Statistic, BPS. 2003. *Sensus Pertanian*. Jakarta: BPS - Statistic Indonesia.

Indonesia Statistic, BPS. 2013. *Sensus Pertanian*. Jakarta: BPS – Statistic Indonesia.

Jarosz, L. 2014. Comparing food security and food sovereignty discourses. *Dialogues in Human Geography*, 4, pp.168–181.

Jawa Barat, BPS. 2016. *Statistik Kependudukan JawaBarat*. Bandung: BPS Jawa Barat.

Kirwan, J., and D. Maye 2013. Food security framings within the UK and the integration of local food systems. *Journal of Rural Studies* 29, pp.91–100.

Lang, T. 1999. The complexities of globalization: The UK as a case study of tensions within the food system and the challenge to food policy. *Agriculture and Human Values*, 16, pp.169–185.

Li, T. M. 2007. *The Will to Improve: Governmentality, Development and the Practice of Politics*. Durham: Duke University Press.

Martínez-Torres, M. E., & Rosset, P. M 2010. La Vía Campesina: The birth and evolution of a transnational social movement. *The Journal of Peasant Studies*, 37, pp.149–175.

Maxwell, S. 1996. Food security: A post-modern perspective. *Food Policy* 21, pp.155–170.

Mcmichael, P. 2009. A food regime genealogy. *The Journal of Peasant Studies*, 36, pp.139–169.

Mcmichael, P. 2010. Food sovereignty in movement: Addressing the triple crisis. In Hannah Kay Wittman, Annette Aurelie Desmarais, and Nettie Wiebe (Eds.). *Food Sovereignty. Reconnecting Food, Nature and Community*. Canada: Fernwood.

Mcmichael, P. 2014. Historicizing food sovereignty. *The Journal of Peasant Studies*, 41, pp.933–957.

Mcmichael, P. 2015. The land question in the food sovereignty project. *Globalizations*, 12, pp.434–451.

Morgan, K. 2013. *Urban Food Governance: The Dunedin City Council Community Resilience Forum Public Lecture*. Dunedin City Council; Dunedin, NZ.

Mount, P. 2012. Growing local food: Scale and local food systems governance. *Agriculture and Human Values*, 29, pp.107–121.

O'hara, J. K., and M. C. Benson 2017. *The Impact of Local Agricultural Production on Farm to School Expenditures*. Cambridge, UK: Cambridge University Press.

Ostrom, E. 1990. *Governing the Commons: The Evolution of Institutions for Collective Action*. Cambridge, UK: Cambridge University Press.

Peluso, N. L. 1992. *Rich Forests, Poor People: Resource Control and Resistance in Java*. Berkeley, CA: University of California Press.

Redfield, R. 1961. *The Little Community and Peasant Society and Culture*. Chicago, IL: Chicago University Press.

Ribot, J. C., and Peluso, N. L 2003. A theory of access. *Rural Sociology*, 68, pp.153–181.

Scott, A. 1990. *Ideology and the New Social Movements*. London: Routledge.

Scott, J. C. 1989. Everyday forms of resistance. Copenhagen Papers 4.

Simon, D. 2008. Urban environments: Issues on the peri-urban fringe. *Annual Review of Environment and Resources*, 33, pp.167–185.

Smith, N. 1990. *Uneven Development: Nature, Capital, and the Production of Space*. Athens, GA: University of Georgia Press.

Sobal, J., Khan, L.K., Bisogni, C. 1998. A conceptual model of the food and nutrition system. *Social Science & Medicine*, 47, pp.853–863.

Van Der Ploeg, J. D. 2021. The political economy of agroecology. *The Journal of Peasant Studies*, 48, pp.274–297.

Warr, P. 2020. Urbanisation and the demand for food. *Bulletin of Indonesian Economic Studies*, 56, pp.43–86.

White, B., and Wiradi, G 1989. Agrarian and non-agrarian bases of inequality in nine Javanese villages. In G.P. Hart, A. Turton, and B. White(eds.) *Agrarian Transformations: Local Processes and the State in Southeast Asia*. Berkeley, CA: University of California Press.

Winne, M. 2008. *Closing the Food Gap*. Boston, MA: Beacon Press.

Wittman, H. 2009. Reworking the metabolic rift: La Vía Campesina, agrarian citizenship, and food sovereignty. *The Journal of Peasant Studies*, 36, pp.805–826.

Wittman, H., A.A. Desmarais and N. Wiebe 2010. *Food Sovereignty. Reconnecting Food, Nature and Community*, Oakland, CA: Food First.

6

PSYCHOLOGICAL BENEFITS OF SCHOOL FARMS TO STUDENTS

Kathryn R. Terzano

Nature and psychological restorativeness

Environmental psychologists and design professionals, such as landscape architects, have looked to nature for its aesthetic value as well as its psychologically restorative effect on people. They have long studied the benefits of nature, from spending time in nature to simply having a view of nature, and argued for improved mental health through exposure to nature. This exposure to nature does not need to involve any great time or expense; these positive benefits to mental health may be evident after as little as ten minutes spent in nature, according to a recent scoping review of published articles and books on the mental health of US university students (Meredith et al., 2020). This quality was inherently understood and expressed as early as the middle of the 19th century when famed American landscape architect Frederick Law Olmsted wrote about his perception of the restorative character of nature (Olmsted, 1865).

Early academic studies of these psychological benefits often focused on either the stress-reduction qualities of nature (Ulrich, 1983) or the recovery of the ability to focus and maintain attention (Kaplan & Talbot, 1983; Kaplan & Kaplan, 1989). In a seminal study, Kaplan (1995) found that, in addition to sleep, people look for other ways to help regain the ability to focus. In this study, Kaplan (1995) examined the ways in which nature can help people to recover from stress and regain focus, arguing that time spent in nature helps to mitigate stress as well as recover the ability to maintain directed attention. Hartig, Evans, Jamner, Davis, and Garling (2003) also experimented with the effects of nature on stress recovery. In their study, all participants received a pre-test and a post-test. Half the participants completed mental tasks that were designed to increase stress. All participants, immediately after arrival or immediately after completing the tasks, were subjected to one of two treatment conditions: 1) sitting in a room

DOI: 10.4324/9781003176558-6

with a tree view and then taking a nature walk, or 2) sitting in a room without a view and then taking an urban walk. The study found a greater decline in blood pressure, an improvement in an attentional task, better emotional affect, and less anger in the participants who took part in the nature treatment compared to those participants who took part in the urban treatment (Hartig et al., 2008). Ulrich et al. (1991) also investigated the stress-relieving effects of natural environments compared to urban environments. In this study, participants viewed a stress-inducing film and then watched a video of one of six natural or urban settings (Ulrich et al., 1991). Participants were monitored for physiological measures of stress, and participants also provided self-ratings of their stress levels. Ulrich et al. (1991) found that participants exposed to the nature treatment recovered from the stressful movie faster and to a greater degree than participants who watched the urban video.

Other researchers have looked at whether nature needs to be natural, which has implications for human-made 'natural' environments like farms. Although people may label any environment of plants and animals as 'nature', farms and parks are generally places that are created and cultivated through human intervention. Does it matter, then, whether the 'nature' that one experiences is truly nature or is the result of the work of humans? Krieger (1973) argued that it does not matter, and he used Niagara Falls as an example since Niagara Falls is reinforced with concrete, thus making it partly manmade. Krieger even suggested that the creation of artificial environments might be desirable. Ittis (1973), on the other hand, strenuously disagreed with Krieger's assertion that artificial environments can be substitutes for nature. Ittis (1973) furthermore argued that planners should be dedicated to the preservation of nature. Wilson (1984) agreed with Ittis (1973) that artificial, plastic environments are undesirable, but only for the purpose of emphasizing that the larger goal should be on conservation and preservation – not because artificially created environments lack psychological benefits.

Still, other researchers have examined people's preferences for natural versus urban scenes. Kaplan, Kaplan, and Wendt (1972) asked participants to view slides of natural and urban scenes and then to rate the scenes for preference and complexity. They found a strong preference for nature scenes to urban scenes, that complexity was related to preference for both types of scenes, and that complexity did not; however, they explain the preference for nature scenes. Another study (Nasar & Terzano, 2010) found that people find daytime nature photographs to be restorative, but that in some cases, nighttime scenes of urban skylines were more desirable.

How people respond to scenes of nature and urban settings is important for planners to understand. This kind of knowledge can influence the way that buildings are sited, provide support for sidewalk improvements (e.g., trees and planters), and encourage the development of school farms, urban farms, parks, and other 'natural' places. Further applications concern placing natural environments near hospitals and other stressful places to help patients and visitors find stress relief. The evidence is strong that people find nature to be restorative, but the value of urban scenes (especially night skylines) is still emerging research.

Psychological benefits of school farms and greenspace

School farms offer the opportunity to bring 'nature' to the schools, giving students exposure to plants and sometimes animals (e.g., bees and chickens) in a controlled setting. School farms may be especially important in areas where children have little access to parks or recreational activities in nature. Reviewing the literature on school farms demonstrates that there is a significant amount of evidence, over the course of years, pointing toward such farms having positive impacts on students of varying ages. A caveat around too much of the research surrounding school farms specifically is that critics find the research methods less rigorous than desirable (Blair, 2009; Williams & Dixon, 2013). However, given the number of studies that find evidence of positive influences, it seems reasonable to believe that school farms can be used as a tool to provide some psychological well-being for students and potentially to increase academic performance. The popularity of school farms indicates that there could be good opportunities in future research for longitudinal studies. There may especially be robust opportunities for additional empirical research on the psychological benefits of school farms, as the literature tends to look at such benefits through greenspace more generally, which will also be reviewed here.

Beginning with the academic benefits of school gardening, Blair (2009) undertook a review of 12 quantitative and seven qualitative studies of the impacts of school farms, with a specific aim of seeing if such farms could improve both academic achievement and classroom behavior in students. In nine of the 12 quantitative studies, the review demonstrated statistically significant *positive* differences in academic testing measures between students who had access to school farms in their curriculum and those who did not (Blair, 2009). For science scores, school farms appear particularly helpful, with an increase in these scores in all 12 of the quantitative studies under review (Blair, 2009). Blair's (2009) review of qualitative studies that focused on K-6 students (that is, students aged five to 12 years old) 'Uniformly [...] showed [...] positive behavioral and social outcomes', including 'heightened motivation and enthusiasm, improved sense of self, teamwork, community, and parental involvement' (p. 35). Williams and Dixon (2013) reviewed and synthesized results from 20 years' worth of quantitative and qualitative studies on academic outcomes in schools, culminating in 48 studies that met their criteria for review. They found that in measuring direct learning outcomes, the vast majority of studies (33 of the 40 studies) resulted in positive outcomes, with six studies reporting non-significant results and only one study reporting negative outcomes. Supportive of Blair's findings that school farms are particularly beneficial to science scores, Williams and Dixon (2013) found that 14 of the 15 studies that looked specifically at science outcomes showed benefits due to school farms. Williams and Dixon (2013) concluded that 'the results of the studies show overwhelmingly that garden-based learning had a positive impact on students' grades, knowledge, attitudes, and behavior. These positive impacts prevailed for nearly every outcome group, including the elementary, middle, and high school levels' (p. 225).

Blair's (2009) and Williams and Dixon's (2013) results are substantiated by a six-year study that took place in Spain centered on students who were considered at-risk for dropping out of secondary school (Ruiz-Gallardo, Verde, & Valdés, 2013). In this study, Ruiz-Gallardo, Verde, and Valdés (2013) assisted the school faculty with creating a garden-based learning program, enrolling a total of 63 at-risk students into the two-year learning program over the course of the study. The gardening space that was created for the program included a greenhouse and an area for crops, as well as an area for a work table and blackboard (Ruiz-Gallardo, Verde, & Valdés, 2013). Of the students recruited into the program, prior to their introduction to garden-based learning, 87.3% of students had been failing at least five subjects, but after becoming involved in the garden-based learning program, 93% of the students failed two subjects or fewer (Ruiz-Gallardo, Verde, & Valdés, 2013). The researchers also gathered qualitative information from the students' teachers and parents, finding that the students' attitudes toward school had improved and that they were taking on more responsibility (Ruiz-Gallardo, Verde, & Valdés, 2013). This study also assessed patterns of disruptive behavior in the classroom and found that over the six years of the study, school gardens had a statistically significant effect on reducing such behaviors, including in individual students who had exhibited disrupted behavior (Ruiz-Gallardo, Verde, & Valdés, 2013). The researchers defined disruptive behavior as 'failure to comply with teacher request within 5 seconds; use of obscene vocabulary; disturbance of other peers; taking a different direction from that of teacher or assignment; and a number of class expulsions' (Ruiz-Gallardo, Verde & Valdés, 2013, p. 262). Even though this was just one study completed with a relatively small sample size, it is helpful to have evidence of school farms positively influencing student behavior. Furthermore, studies such as this one can be placed into the larger context of the research that is being conducted on the psychological benefits of school farms and greenspace.

Engemann et al. (2019) undertook a longitudinal study in Denmark to see if the amount and duration of greenspace to which children are exposed mitigate their risks of psychiatric disorders. Although this particular study was descriptive rather than explanatory, the results show that exposure to greenspace during childhood was correlated with better mental health and that this protective aspect of exposure to greenspace accumulates over time (Engemann et al., 2019). Overall, their findings point to 'high levels of childhood green space [being] associated with a lower risk of developing any of a spectrum of the adolescent into adult psychiatric disorders' (Engemann et al., 2019, p. 5190). Since children spend much of their time at school, the results of this study could bolster the need for greater amounts of greenspace on school grounds, including having school farms. The bulk of the existing literature shows that researchers have been more engaged with understanding the well-being effects of what is termed 'green schoolyards' rather than studying outcomes associated with the integration of school farms. A popular definition of green schoolyards is grounds that 'are multi-purpose, environmentally beneficial spaces that incorporate natural elements, such as gardens, wooded areas, and greenspaces, with traditional play features, and often include outdoor classrooms or learning components as well' (Plovnik & Strongin, 2015; Healthy Schools Campaign & Openlands, 2016, cited in Bates, Bohnert, & Gerstein, 2018, p. 2). Although many of the studies reviewed in this chapter focused on these green schoolyards, the main theme is an attempt to understand how nature is psychologically beneficial to schoolchildren. As school farms are a way to expose children to plants – 'nature' in a similar way that designed parks can be considered to be nature – the results from these studies could suggest that school farms would have similar effects.

Chawla et al. (2014) undertook a qualitative study that investigated various types of green schoolyards on the grounds of elementary schools (that is, students aged nine to 12 years old), as well as high school students (students aged 14 to 18 years old) taking part in farming either at their school or in an after-school gardening program. Researchers aimed to see if such spaces resulted in a measurable reduction of stress in students and an increase in their emotional resilience. However, they were careful not to directly ask their participants about their stress, anxiety, or perceived resilience or to characterize nature as a refuge. However, such wording and themes arose unprompted in conversations with administrators and teachers. Specifically, at their study sites with high school gardeners, an analysis of keyword and frequency counts from interviews showed that, among the 52 participants, words such as calm, peaceful, relax, and relaxed were used 186 times. The frequency of words related to reduced stress was not related to the students' demographics, whether age, ethnic origin, or socioeconomic status, nor was the frequency of stress-reduction words related to whether gardens were new or mature or whether the student participation in gardening was by choice or as a curricular requirement. Furthermore, 50 of the high school gardeners reported that they were better able to focus after being in the garden. At one study site that allowed fourth through sixth graders (that is, children aged nine to 12 years old) access to a naturalized habitat, the researchers recorded more than 700 hours of observation in the habitat; in that time, there were zero occurrences of disruptive or inappropriate behavior (e.g., rudeness) (Chawla et al., 2014). This is similar to results shown by Ruiz-Gallardo, Verde, and Valdés (2013) that garden-based learning reduces disruptive behavior, though this particular set of Chawla et al.'s participants was not in a garden or farm.

Positive impacts for high school students engaged in school farming were also reported in a small photovoice project conducted by Lam, Romses, and Renwick (2019). They engaged a total of 16 high school-aged students in a project wherein participants could take photographs of the farms and gardens in which they worked and then wrote about their experiences (Lam, Ramses, & Renwick, 2019). Not all of the sites engaged with the study were on school grounds, but given the themes of respect and relaxation that came up during the project, this study adds qualitative evidence to the benefits that such farms and gardens can provide to students. Participants described their experiences with gardening as 'rewarding' and '[feeling] good about yourself in the end' (Lam, Ramses, & Renwick, 2019, p. 4). One participant stated that 'It calms me and allows me to think, not negatively, but logically' (Lam, Ramses, & Renwick, 2019, p. 6). Although this study had too small of a sample size to be generalizable, the evidence continues to lend support to the idea that school farms and gardens can offer a reprieve from stress.

A further study on green schoolyards lends support to improved psychological and behavioral outcomes. Bates, Bohnert, and Gerstein (2018) conducted a study on the effects of green schoolyards at three public elementary schools in Chicago – all of which had recently been renovated to have such schoolyards – observing student behavior and physical activity at two different points in time. During the second round of observations, they found that 'a greater percentage of children were interacting with others on the schoolyard [...] with increases in positive and neutral interactions' (Bates, Bohnert, & Gerstein, 2018, p. 6). However, in this study, they observed 'higher rates of negative social interactions among African-American and White students' when compared to Latino students (Bates, Bohnert, & Gerstein, 2018, p. 7). The researchers speculated this might have been driven by the difference in schoolyard activities, with a greater percentage of Latino students taking part in recreational activities that involved structure and cooperation, such as ball games, than their African-American and White peers (Bates, Bohnert, & Gerstein, 2018). Although such a difference would need to be researched further, integrating a school farm, which would likely have more structured elements, could be beneficial to students regardless of ethnicity, as seen in Chawla et al. (2014).

Psychological and behavioral changes associated with greenspace have also been studied in younger children. Taylor and Butts-Wilmsmeyer (2020) found an effect of frequency of greenspace exposure on kindergarten (aged five to six years old) children's self-regulation in a quasi-experimental study. They define self-regulation as 'a multidimensional construct that includes aspects of emotion, cognition, and behavior' (Schmitte et al., 2015, cited in Taylor & Butts-Wilmsmeyer, 2020, p. 1) and undertook the study at two public schools in Toronto that had recently been updated with green schoolyards (Taylor & Butts-Wilmsmeyer, 2020). The experimental manipulation placed students into one of two categories: low frequency or high frequency of the curriculum taught in the greenspace. The effect showed an interaction with gender, with the increased frequency being more impactful among girls (Taylor & Butts-Wilmsmeyer, 2020). They also found that observed time spent in greenspaces – whether that was through a structured school curriculum or during unstructured playtime – had a positive impact on children's self-regulation for both genders (Taylor & Butts-Wilmsmeyer, 2020). In a large study in the Netherlands with an approximate sample size of 700 students, Van Dijk-Wesselius et al. (2018) conducted a longitudinal prospective intervention study to measure various impacts of green schoolyards on children aged seven to 11 years old. Similar to Taylor and Butts-Wilmsmeyer's (2020) study, there was one difference attributed to gender, with green schoolyards' positive effect on an increase in physical activity but only for girls (Van Dijk-Wesselius et al., 2018). Otherwise, they found that after schoolyards were converted to having greenspace, there was 'a positive impact on children's appreciation of the schoolyard, attentional restoration after recess and social well-being' and that this was true regardless of gender (Van Dijk-Wesselius et al., 2018, p. 24). However, they did not find that there was any positive impact of green schoolyards on the emotional functioning of children in the study (Van Dijk-Wesselius et al., 2018) and that attentional restoration appeared to be most influential after a significant period of time had elapsed since the schoolyard was converted to greenspace (Van Dijk-Wesselius et al., 2018).

From this review of the literature on the benefits of both school gardens and greenspaces on school grounds, impacts are widely reported as positive, although there is obviously a need to continue investigating all possible interactions among the variables present in such spaces. While much of the literature that is focused on psychological benefits does not apply directly to school gardens, evidence still points to the reintroduction of nature into the curriculum – as well as playtime at school – as a positive influence on students' well-being and school farms are no doubt a part of the natural system. Future research should investigate if school farms that are not otherwise part of a green schoolyard have similar effects, clearing up the possibility that such a link is merely tangential. As this research area remains exploratory, the following case study is meant to illustrate an example of how farming and gardening can work within a school setting. It continues to explore benefits that the primary instructor has observed over years of running a school gardening program.

Case study: Granville Schools' Sustainability Project

Granville is a village and township in central Ohio, a state in the Midwest region of the United States. Located about 30 miles (48 kilometers) northeast of the state's capital city, it is a small suburban community of about 9,000 residents with a median income above the state's average (U.S. Census Bureau, 2019). Approximately 2,500 students in grades kindergarten through 12th grade (aged 5 through 18 years old) are enrolled in the Granville public schools (NCES, 2020). The affluence of the community is important because 73% of the school district's funding is generated through local property taxes, which are greater when the property values are higher, and through local fundraising; the other 27% of funding comes from state and federal sources (NCES, 2020). With above-average property values compared to the state, Granville Schools' students benefit from a well-funded school system when compared to less affluent communities in the state.

Granville Schools have both a school farm, located behind the middle and high school buildings and also the Granville Land Lab, a 100-acre (approximately 40.5-hectare) outdoor educational space for students of all ages in the school district that is located a half-mile (0.8 kilometers) from the schools (Land Lab, 2020). Since around 2005, both the farm and Land Lab have been used to produce food for the school cafeteria during the academic year and for a community farmers' market during the summer months. The school garden includes raised vegetable beds, a greenhouse, a hoop house (a variation on a greenhouse), chicken coops, and an aquaponics system, while the Land Lab has a bee apiary, fruit trees, and nut trees. Students also participate in tapping maple trees to produce maple syrup to be used in the school cafeteria.

The school farm is a very student-driven project, originally created in a class on sustainable agriculture taught by environmental science and ecology teacher, Jim Reding. In an interview conducted on September 30, 2020, Mr. Reding reported how students had wanted more than simply having a school garden or farm – they wanted to practice the sustainability concepts they learned in class, and they worked for two days coming up with ideas for how their garden could take shape. However, with school budgets determined ahead of each school year and each dollar carefully allocated, finding adequate funding was an issue, and 12 students took it upon themselves to write a grant proposal. The proposal was rejected at first due to practical concerns regarding keeping deer out of the farm and also keeping the garden running during the summer months when students generally are not enrolled in classes. Students addressed these issues themselves, contacting construction professionals for estimates for fencing to keep deer out of the farm, as well as proposing that Mr. Reding teach a summer class on sustainable agriculture, which would take care of any staffing concerns over the summer, and students in the class would provide much of the labor in the farm. Over time, people from the community have also volunteered to assist with the farm during the summer months.

The goals of the school farm are to produce food, increase biodiversity, and provide an outdoor laboratory setting where different academic classes can use the space to engage their students. The farm has been used for lessons in physics, fine arts, and industrial technology, in addition to environmental science. Beyond teaching school subjects, though, the farm has been instrumental in reaching out to other community members who do not have students in the school system, including elderly community members. Mr. Reding also feels that the school farm has been instrumental in teaching students problem-solving skills and communication skills through gardening-related activities as well as community activities such as presenting to the town council. The farm provides important lessons for learning how to fail as well, since, unlike in a controlled laboratory setting, the results of the students' efforts – whether there will be a successful harvest – cannot be as easily predicted.

In terms of mental health or therapeutic benefits from the farm, Mr. Reding believes these become evident when realizing that he often sees students spending time in the farm when they do not have to be there, whether actively working in the farm or simply sitting on a bench in the farm, and he describes it as an oasis for the students. Students not enrolled in Mr. Reding's classes have also worked in the farm, and during the summer months, Granville Schools allow students from other districts to be involved with the project. Mr. Reding also relayed that in making the argument to the town council that chickens should be allowed to be part of the farm, part of the argument was that holding or petting a chicken could have therapeutic benefits, as with any other therapy animal, such as a dog. Notably, the chickens are raised for their eggs, not as a meat source.

Although Granville Schools do not keep records of their graduates' future career paths or university degree choices, Mr. Reding remains in contact with some of his former students and believes that more students are pursuing environmental sciences as a career option. One such student is Dustin Braden, who graduated from Granville High School in May 2017 and then from Ohio Wesleyan University in December 2020 with a double major in Environmental Studies and Geography. He is currently enrolled in postgraduate work in Geography at the University of Delaware. Mr. Braden worked in the Granville Schools farm as a student in AP Environmental Science and volunteered several summers in the farm after that class and during college. In personal communication with Mr. Braden via email on the February 5, 2021, Mr. Braden stated,

> My time in the farm really influenced my college experience. I was actually able to work with Dr. Ashley Allen (Ohio Wesleyan University) on an undergraduate research project studying urban gardens in Columbus, Ohio – and since then, I have been working on a food access mapping project with her. I also had the chance to work on several sustainable food projects at Ohio Wesleyan University (including vermiculture – worm composting!). Working in the farm with Mr. Reding gave me the confidence to pursue these projects as an undergrad and inspired my interest in food.

When asked about the mental health benefits of gardening, Mr. Braden commented about the farm as a place to relieve some of the stress and anxiety that accompany being in school. He perceived other benefits for himself as well, stating,

> The other therapeutic benefits I see in school farms are tied to the value they provide: feeling more confident in myself and my work and having strong social connections with the rest of the farm students.

Mr. Reding hears of more and more students putting gardens in their own yards and providing garden beds for neighbors. Mr. Reding also finds it telling that, although there are no locks on the farm or its accompanying sheds or greenhouse, there has not once been a case of vandalism, demonstrating the value of this place for those in the community. Students – even those not directly involved with the farm project – are aware that they are allowed to take any produce or flowers for free, as they or their classmates are responsible for putting in the labor, although he will often find a goodwill offering left behind.

Recommendations and implications

The Granville case study suggests some of the benefits of interactive, applied learning through engagement with nature and agriculture. This case study gives researchers a reason to believe that this subject should be pursued further, but a gap in the research remains, where more than suggestive results are needed. A pre-test and post-test procedure with psychological questionnaires would help to establish whether any improvement, for example, in rates of depression or ability to focus, actually took place. An alternate way to measure these psychological benefits would be random sorting of students into a control group, which would not participate in the school farm activities or lessons, and an experimental group, which would participate in the Sustainability Project. Finally, I recommend a comparison of measured psychological benefits across several different school farms for a comparison of data with students from different backgrounds and geographic areas.

Conclusion

The benefits of spending time around plants and animals have been known since at least the 19th century and have been examined through research for several decades. With time spent in nature or natural-like surroundings offering stress reduction and restoration of the ability to focus, school farms make sense as a means of giving this same opportunity to students, who may not have access to greenspace or gardening at home or elsewhere in their community. Whether they choose to passively spend time in a school farm, perhaps by strolling through a greenhouse or reading a book on a bench outdoors or actively spend time by participating in the growing, caretaking, and harvesting of food, students may reap important benefits. Although the psychological benefits of school farms on students have not been directly measured, qualitative evidence from school farms such as Jim Reding's suggests that the benefits exist.

References

Bates, C.R., Bohnert, A.M. and Gerstein, D.E., 2018. Green schoolyards in low-income urban neighborhoods: Natural spaces for positive youth development outcomes. *Frontiers in Psychology*, 9, p. 805.

Blair, D., 2009. The child in the garden: An evaluative review of the benefits of school gardening. *The Journal of Environmental Education*, 40(2), pp.15–38.

Chawla, L., Keena, K., Pevec, I. and Stanley, E., 2014. Green schoolyards as havens from stress and resources for resilience in childhood and adolescence. *Health & Place*, 28, pp.1–13.

Engemann, K., Pedersen, C.B., Arge, L., Tsirogiannis, C., Mortensen, P.B. and Svenning, J.C., 2019. Residential green space in childhood is associated with lower risk of psychiatric disorders from adolescence into adulthood. *Proceedings of the National Academy of Sciences*, 116(11), pp.5188–5193.

Hartig T., Evans G.W., Jamner, L.D., Davis, D.S. and Garling, T., 2003. Tracking restoration in natural and urban field settings. *Journal of Environmental Psychology*, 23, pp.109–123.

Ittis, H., 1973. Can one love a plastic tree? *Bulletin of the Ecological Society of America*, 54, pp.5–7.

Kaplan, R. and Kaplan, S., 1989. *The Experience of Nature: A Psychological Perspective*. New York: Cambridge University Press.

Kaplan, S., 1995. The restorative benefits of nature: Toward an integrative framework. *Journal of Environmental Psychology*, 15, pp.169–182.

Kaplan, S. and Talbot, J.F., 1983. Psychological benefits of a wilderness experience. In Altman, I. & Wohlwill, J.F. (Eds.), *Behavior and the Natural Environment*. New York: Plenum, pp.163–203.

Kaplan, S., Kaplan, R. and Wendt, J.S., 1972. Rated preference and complexity for natural and urban visual material. *Perception and Psychophysics*, 12, pp.354–356.

Krieger, H., 1973. What's wrong with plastic trees? *Science*, 179, pp.446–455.

Lam, V., Romses, K. and Renwick, K., 2019. Exploring the relationship between school gardens, food literacy and mental well-being in youth using photovoice. *Nutrients*, 11(6), p.1354.

The Land Lab, 2020. Who we are? The Land Lab: Granville, OH. Retrieved from https://thelandlab.wordpress.com/who-we-are/

Meredith, G.R., Rakow, D.A., Eldermire, E.R., Madsen, C.G., Shelley, S.P. and Sachs, N.A., 2020. Minimum time dose in nature to positively impact the mental health of college-aged students, and how to measure it: A scoping review. *Frontiers in Psychology*, 10, p.2942.

Nasar, J.L. and Terzano, K., 2010. The desirability of views of city skylines after dark. *Journal of Environmental Psychology*, 30(2), pp.215–225.

National Center for Education Statistics (NCES), 2020. Granville exempted district details. Retrieved from https://nces.ed.gov/ccd/districtsearch/district_detail.asp?ID2=3904539

Olmsted, F.L., 1865. The value and care of parks. Reprinted in Nash, R. (Ed.) 1968, *The American Environment: Readings in the History of Conservation*, Reading, MA: Addison-Wesley, pp.18–24.

Ruiz-Gallardo, J.R., Verde, A. and Valdés, A., 2013. Garden-based learning: An experience with 'at risk' secondary education students. *The Journal of Environmental Education*, 44(4), pp.252–270.

Taylor, A.F. and Butts-Wilmsmeyer, C., 2020. Self-regulation gains in kindergarten related to frequency of green schoolyard use. *Journal of Environmental Psychology*, 70, p.101440.

Ulrich, R.S., 1983. Aesthetic and affective response to natural environment. In Altman, I. & Wohlwill, J.F. (Eds.), *Human Behavior and Environment: Advances in Theory and Research* (Vol. 6). New York: Plenum, pp.85–125.

Ulrich, R.S., Simons, R.F., Losito, B.D., Fiorito, E., Miles, M.A. and Zelson, M., 1991. Stress recovery during exposure to natural and urban environments. *Journal of Environmental Psychology*, 11(3), pp.201–230.

U.S. Census Bureau, 2019. Quick facts. Granville village, OH. Retrieved from https://www.census.gov/quickfacts/fact/table/granvillevillageohio/BZA115218

Van Dijk-Wesselius, J.E., Maas, J., Hovinga, D., Van Vugt, M.V.D.B.A. and Van den Berg, A.E., 2018. The impact of greening schoolyards on the appreciation, and physical, cognitive and social-emotional well-being of schoolchildren: A prospective intervention study. *Landscape and Urban Planning*, 180, pp.15–26.

Williams, D.R. and Dixon, P.S., 2013. Impact of garden-based learning on academic outcomes in schools: Synthesis of research between 1990 and 2010. *Review of Educational Research*, 83(2), pp.211–235.

Wilson, E.O., 1984. *The Right Place, in Biophilia*. Cambridge, MA: Harvard University Press.

7

HARITHALAYAM CAMPUS FARMING MISSION

A case study in Kerala, India

Divya Chandrasenan, Ramshad Khan Rawther, and Jayapraveen J

Introduction and purpose

Calhoun and Cortese (2005) stated that:

> The educational experience of students is a function of what they are taught, how they are taught, and to some extent by how the university manages, conducts research, operates, purchases, designs facilities, invests, and interacts with local communities …. All parts of the university are critical in helping to create transformative change in the individual and collective mindset. Everything that happens at a university and every impact, positive or negative, of university activities, shapes the knowledge, skills, and values of students.
>
> *(p. 7)*

Following the spread of the COVID-19 pandemic and the consecutive floods which occurred in the state of Kerala, India, the Government recommended greening missions around the state. In response to the recommendation, the University of Kerala, the oldest of the state, initiated the 'Harithalayam Project' at the university campus representing the sustainable food initiative of the university. It also included the intention to revive farming on its campus at Karyavattom, which was once an agricultural hub, where rice was extensively cultivated in the region until the fields were cleared to set up the campus in 1967. Since its inception, the 'Harithalayam Project' has remained an entirely student-driven initiative. The major objective behind the mission for the university was to take the lead in encouraging students to become active partners in the greening mission and hence develop sustainable development literacy among them. A monitoring committee was given the responsibility for program oversight and made all

DOI: 10.4324/9781003176558-7

the core decisions surrounding its administration. The 'Harithalayam Project' at Kerala University's Karyavattom campus was started through a Monitoring Committee Meeting, which took place over the 'Google Meet' application due to COVID-19 restrictions. Later, the Kerala University Greenery Project was inaugurated by the Honorable Chief Minister of Kerala on World Environment Day (June 5, 2020). The farm was started with the support of the State Forest Department. About 16,495 saplings were planted on approximately 27 acres (11 hectares) of the campus.

The 'Harithalayam Project' was founded with the following three-fold mission:

1. To ensure self-sufficiency and healthy food that support people's wellbeing and the environment at the University of Kerala and beyond.
2. To develop sustainable development literacy and responsible citizens and leaders through formal and informal education.
3. To transform the campus into a green campus through collaborative programming and outreach.

About the campus farming project, Harithalayam

In line with the mission stated above, farming at the campus has flourished since the planting of the pilot plot on June 5, 2020. The tree saplings included many indigenous varieties. Thousands of coconut saplings and more than 500 banana seedlings were planted in the vicinity of Haimavathi Pond on the campus and near various departments. The farm was extended to the Department of Environmental Science, Haimavathi Pond, Engineering wing, and near the A-type quarters. Vegetable cultivation also became a part of the project and was started in the North Block area of the campus. The cultivation included varieties of tapioca, tomatoes, sweet potato, brinjal, chili, and fruit like pineapple and banana.

Paddy was cultivated in about 12.5 acres of land with the help of technical assistance from the State Department of Agriculture.

Fish farming is also in progress in the Haimavathi Pond area. The nursery cage was set up in July 2020 with help from fisherman from the Perumathura area, and the nursery cage produces about 2,000 tilapia of the Chitralatha variety and 1,000 monosex tilapia.

The project is progressing with the aim of converting the dry campus into a wet campus. While 20 acres of the campus would be utilized for paddy farming, five acres would be used for vegetable and tuber crop cultivation. In addition, 5,000 fruit saplings and 1,000 coconut saplings are being planted. A plot of five acres is earmarked to create a garden to cultivate rare plant species indigenous to the Andaman and Nicobar Islands. The academic community dedicates up to two hours every day after class hours to nurture the fields. The university has initiated 'Karshika' (agriculture) scholarships to student farmers, the first of its kind

PICTURE 7.1 Land preparation for vegetable cultivation and harvest. Recourse: Prof. (Dr.) A. Gangaprasad, Chief Coordinator, Harithalayam Project, University of Kerala.

PICTURE 7.2 Transplantation of paddy seedlings to prepared land and paddy field ready for harvest. Recourse: Prof. (Dr.) A. Gangaprasad, Chief Coordinator, Harithalayam Project, University of Kerala.

in India. The Student Agriculture Fellowship is being set up with the aim of instilling in students an interest in farming. It is hoped that with the implementation of the 'Harithalayam Project', the university campus will be transformed into an innovative role model park Picture 7.1 an Picture 7.2.

Experiential learning through campus farming

The word campus includes all open and closed spaces, and open green spaces within the boundaries of the university (Keles & Uzun, 2016). In addition to the various educational activities, campuses provide opportunities for the students to improve their social and cultural development and benefit from the community's behavior and communication skills (Yilmaaz et al., 2012). Karyavattom campus is the main campus of the University of Kerala, which is about 15 kilometers from the state's capital city. It houses the various teaching departments at the University of Kerala. The campus covers about 359 acres of land. There are 41 departments at the university, of which 32 are located at the picturesque Karyavattom campus. Figure 7.1 shows the Karyavattom campus map.

The overarching goal of student involvement in campus farming is to create awareness and make students literate on food sustainability issues. It is concluded that the knowledge of the issues and action strategies, locus of control, attitudes, verbal commitment, social norms, personal efficacy, and individual sense of responsibility are significant variables that motivate an individual to be proactive about environmental issues (Hines, Hungerford & Tomera, 1987). Learning facts & descriptive knowledge will encourage individual involvement to gain procedural knowledge and social support networks . The students' combined efforts will help to build the agricultural capacity of the community by encouraging responsible citizens and leaders through informal education.

Campus farming at the Karyavattom campus follows a participatory method through an experiential learning approach. It adheres to experiential learning principles, which are essential to students' understanding of the forces and implications of a sustainable food system. Providing students with concrete experiences in which they can act in accordance with their newly acquired knowledge regarding the food system is of the utmost importance as it raises the probability of students taking meaningful action in the future (Hines, Hungerford & Tomera, 1987). This is possible at a time when students have expressed a strong desire to engage in solution- and action-based opportunities to help mitigate environmental problems. Across the world, especially because of the COVID-19 pandemic, higher education institutions are restructuring their teaching approach and moving towards a more applied, experiential-based pedagogy. Here at the University of Kerala, the 'Harithalayam Project' is a student-led initiative that follows an experiential learning approach. The project tries to expand the reach of the campus farm into student and community service, inquiry, hands-on research, and experiential learning opportunities. The campus farm creates an atmosphere to foster a unique and experience-based awareness of sustainable agriculture. The fundamental goal of the Campus Farm is empowering students around food through hands-on interaction; along with discussion and research that bridges multiple disciplines across campus . Many research studies show that students' learning and behavioral changes are enhanced when integrated into campus environmental initiatives and are place based. These campus farms can provide students with educational experiences that tangibly link campus operations, the curriculum, and academic research.

FIGURE 7.1 University of Kerala – map of Karyavattom campus.

Methodology of the research study

The campus farm under the broad title of 'Harithalayam' is a novel initiative in the entire state. Considering its significance, we thought of carrying out research on the campus farming initiative. Prior to starting the research study, we had several research questions, especially about the extent of sustainable literacy among students engaged in the campus farming program. With research questions in hand, we endeavored to determine the best way to answer them. We were primarily concerned with the educational aspects of the campus farm. We used observation, interviews, and surveys for data collection. We followed a mixed methodology where quantitative data were collected using a survey questionnaire, and qualitative data were collected through observation and interview. The study employed semi-structured interviews with students of the Karyavattom campus to investigate sustainability perceptions and personal attitudes towards campus farming. It was designed to complement the sustainability literacy assessments of students. A survey questionnaire related to sustainable literacy was used to assess the students' levels of knowledge, attitudes, and behaviors concerning sustainability. Due to COVID-19 restrictions, it was not possible to collect the data personally; hence, we hosted our survey questionnaire online rather than distributing paper-and-pencil forms. The 'Google Form' online survey software was used for the study. A link to the survey was sent out to the students engaged in the campus farming initiative. The researcher has adopted a convenient sampling method for the primary data collection. A convenient sample of 250 students was included in the study. Also, a focus group discussion among the students was conducted. Invited participants included students who had participated in the 'Harithalayam Project' at the Karyavattom campus.

Student interview

Interview questions were developed from the questions to be included in the student sustainability literacy survey and questions derived from the literature review of student assessment tools used at other universities that were designed to get participants to self-describe attitudes towards campus farming. Interview questions and coding schemes were re-designed throughout the process as data were simultaneously collected and analyzed. Sub-questions were identified and asked to gather more information regarding the participants' involvement in campus farming. A purposive sampling technique was used to figure out the sample students for the interview. Further students were identified through snowball sampling, which involved asking each participant to identify other potential participants but were subject to the same qualification criteria. Though the target sample size was between 15 and 20 participants, the sample included ten individuals due to issues to do with the pandemic. Interviews were conducted individually through the 'Google Meet' application due to COVID-19 restrictions and were recorded and then transcribed.

Sustainability literacy scale

From the extensive review of related literature, the questionnaire developed by Fransisco Borges (2019) was selected and adapted to measure the levels of knowledge, attitudes, and behaviors concerning sustainability among the students involved in campus farming.

The questionnaire selected was a translated version of the sustainability literacy scale developed by Michalos et al. (2011), which was used in an exploratory study with adults in the Canadian province of Manitoba. The sustainability literacy scale was given to a small group of sample students of the Karyavattom campus. This preliminary study resulted in several changes affecting the items included in the knowledge, attitude, and behaviors dimensions, namely, the exclusion of some items and the addition of others.

Content validity was established through the opinion of a panel of experts. The questionnaire was a five-point Likert scale having both knowledge and attitude dimensions ranging from Strongly Disagree (coded 1), that is corresponding to the least favorable answer, through Disagree (coded 2), Neither Agree nor Disagree (coded 3), and Agree (coded 4) to Strongly Agree (coded 5), corresponding to the most favorable answer. Regarding the behavior dimension, the Likert scale ranges from Never (coded 1), that is corresponding to the least favorable response, Rarely (coded 2), Often (coded 3) Very Often (coded 4), and Regularly (coded 5), corresponding to the most favorable answer.

Factor analysis was conducted to assess the instrument's factor structure and the internal consistency of the items in each dimension (De Vellis, 2012).

Figure 7.2 shows a display of scree plot is the explanation for total variance explained in graphic form. The scree plot diagram shows how the downward trend eigenvalue is used to determine the number of factors used subjectively.

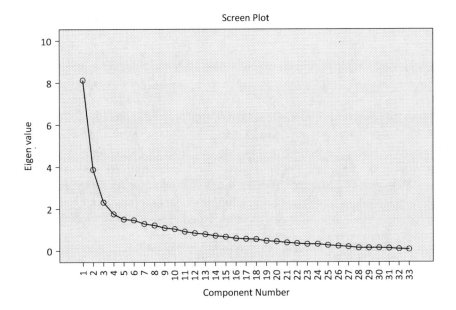

FIGURE 7.2 Scree plot diagram.

Table 7.1 of the rotated matrix component shows no item passing through the charge factor 'cut off point' <0.30. The highest factor loads are in item 14 of 0.800, and the smallest point 12 is 0.409. One item is excluded from further analysis because the factor load is <0.3. Thus, the number of items in the instrument for sustainability literacy scale is 32 items.

According to Table 7.1, it is evident that the questionnaire maintained its three-dimensional structure. The three factors were distributed as factor 1 (Attitude), Factor 2 (Behavior), and Factor 3 (Knowledge).

Again, the items associated with each factor were subjected to an internal consistency and reliability assessment, based on Cronbach's alpha coefficient (Table 7.2).

Results

Findings based on Sustainability Literacy Scale

Administration of the Sustainability Literacy Scale was executed among 250 students engaged in campus farming. Due to the COVID-19 pandemic, we were unable to collect data from a good number of samples. We received 219 responses to our survey.

a. *Knowledge regarding sustainability*

Table 7.3 shows, in percentage form, the distribution of students' responses to the eight items pertaining to the knowledge dimension. The responses correspond to a three-point Likert scale. The first column refers to 'Agree', the second column corresponds to 'Not decided', and the third column refers to 'Disagree'.

Close examination of the table reveals that except for two, all other items have an agreement level of 85%, which is consistent with the mean scale value obtained earlier. Item K2 'Sustainable development emphasizes respect for human rights' has the highest agreement level of 94.5%. About 19.2% of students are not quite sure that sustainable development emphasizes gender equality. More than 80% of the students believe that farming education is an important component for sustainability, and hence it is to be included in the curriculum. Moreover, more than 80% of students believe that it is insignificant to estimate the monetary value of the ecosystem while considering sustainable development. They do not want to compromise sustainable development for monetary gain.

b. *Attitudes regarding sustainability*

Table 7.4 summarizes, in percentage form, the distribution of respondents' responses to the 12 items constituting the attitude scale.

The table shows that most of the respondents have a positive attitude towards sustainability. More than 95% of the students believe that we need stricter laws

TABLE 7.1 Rotated component matrix

Items		Component	
	Factor 1	Factor 2	Factor 3
A3	Overuse of our natural resources is a serious threat to the health and welfare of future generations.	.793		
A8	Adopting sustainable development as a national priority is key to maintaining India's status as one of the most livable countries in the world.	.715		.306
A2	The present generation should ensure that the next generation inherits a community at least as healthy, diverse and productive as it is today.	.663		
A6	The teaching of sustainability principles should be integrated into the curriculum in all disciplines and at all levels of education.	.652		
A4	Farming will give less scope for higher education accessibility to future generations.	.640		
A14	For highly educated youth it is unwise to do farming.	.638		
A1	Every girl or boy should receive education that teaches the knowledge, perspectives, values, issues and skills for sustainable living in a community.	.609		
A5	We need stricter laws and regulations to protect the environment.	.552		
A9	Poverty alleviation is an important topic in education for sustainable development.	.527		
A10	Taxes on polluters should be increased to pay for damage to communities and the environment.	.495		
A11	I am willing to seek for further knowledge and skills in farming.	.493	.478	
A7	Governments should encourage greater use of fuel-efficient vehicles.	.409		.308
K1	Helping people out of poverty is an essential condition for India to become more sustainable.			
B7	I participate in activities related to environmental sustainability.		.800	
B2	I attend courses on sustainable development.		.668	

B9	I look up information about the environment or sustainability of the university on the respective website.	.654		
B6	I volunteer to work with local charities.	.641		
B8	I look at problems from different angles.	.640		
B3	I talk to others about how to help people living in poverty.	.607		
B10	I look up information about the new sustainable development goals of the United Nations.	.584		
B12	Farming leads to increase in standard of living.	.509	.437	
B5	I look for signs of ecosystem deterioration.	.483		
B4	I think about what it means to live in a sustainable manner.	.482		
B1	I walk or ride a bicycle to places instead of going by car.	.452		
B13	I enjoy the relationship with nature through farming.	.390	.305	
K4	Sustainable development requires quality education for all.			.798
K6	Sustainable development entails a reflection on the meaning of quality of life.			.769
K9	Farming education is an important component of education for sustainable development.			.662
K5	Sustainable development emphasizes gender equality.			.653
K3	Ensuring a long and healthy life for all contributes to sustainable development.		.309	.608
K8	Estimating the monetary value of the service our ecosystems provide is important for sustainable development.			-.603
K2	Sustainable development emphasizes respect for human rights.			.552
K7	Food safety is one aim of sustainable development.			.501

TABLE 7.2 Cronbach's alpha reliability coefficient for each factor, scale mean, and standard deviation

Factor 1 Attitude Cronbach's Alpha 0.832 Scale means 51.51 ± 5.89		*Factor 2 Behavior* Cronbach's Alpha 0.837 Scale means 42.62 ± 8.03		*Factor 3 Knowledge* Cronbach's Alpha 0.705 Scale means 31.74 ± 3.85	
Items	*Item-Total Correlation*	*Items*	*Item-Total Correlation*	*Items*	*Item-Total Correlation*
K9[a]	.488	**A12**[a]	.497	**K1**[b]	
A1	.539	**A13**[a]	.352	**K2**	.474
A2	.591	**B1**	.354	**K3**	.505
A3	.657	**B2**	.579	**K4**	.615
A4	.514	**B3**	.516	**K5**	.610
A5	.464	**B4**	.478	**K6**	.679
A6	.562	**B5**	.410	**K7**	.421
A7	.375	**B6**	.535	**K8**	.484
A8	.667	**B7**	.727	**A9**[a]	.529
A10	.495	**B8**	.528		
A11	.480	**B9**	.536		
A14	.556	**B10**	.505		

[a] item added to the scale; [b] item eliminated from the scale.

TABLE 7.3 Knowledge regarding sustainability. Agreement, disagreement, and indecision with regard to the content of items expressed in percentage form

Items	*Agreement %*	*Undecided %*	*Disagreement %*
K4 Sustainable development requires quality education for all.	87.7	8.2	4.1
K6 Sustainable development entails a reflection on the meaning of quality of life.	89	6.8	4.1
K9 Farming education is an important component of education for sustainable development.	86.3	9.6	4.1
K5 Sustainable development emphasizes gender equality.	72.6	19.2	8.2
K3 Ensuring a long and healthy life for all contributes to sustainable development.	87.7	8.2	4.1
K8 Estimating the monetary value of the service our ecosystems provide is important for sustainable development.	2.7	13.7	83.6
K2 Sustainable development emphasizes respect for human rights.	94.5	4.1	1.4
K7 Food safety is one aim of sustainable development.	83.6	9.6	6.8

TABLE 7.4 Attitudes towards sustainability. Agreement, disagreement, and indecision with regard to attitude towards items expressed in percentage form

Items	Agreement %	Undecided %	Disagreement %
A3 Overuse of our natural resources is a serious threat to the health and welfare of future generations.	97.3	2.7	0
A8 Adopting sustainable development as a national priority is key to maintaining India's status as one of the most livable countries in the world.	87.7	11.0	1.4
A2 The present generation should ensure that the next generation inherits a community at least as healthy, diverse and productive as it is today.	93.2	5.5	1.4
A6 The teaching of sustainability principles should be integrated into the curriculum in all disciplines and at all levels of education.	98.6	1.4	0
A4 Farming will give less scope for higher education accessibility to future generations.	67.1	12.3	20.5
A14 For highly educated youth it is unwise to do farming.	56.2	9.6	34.2
A1 Every girl or boy should receive education that teaches the knowledge, perspectives, values, issues and skills for sustainable living in a community.	97.3	2.7	0
A5 We need stricter laws and regulations to protect the environment.	95.9	4.1	0
A9 Poverty alleviation is an important topic in education for sustainable development.	87.7	11.0	1.4
A10 Taxes on polluters should be increased to pay for damage to communities and the environment.	83.6	16.4	0
A11 I am willing to seek for further knowledge and skills in farming.	89.0	9.6	1.4
A7 Governments should encourage greater use of fuel-efficient vehicles.	83.6	9.6	6.8

and regulations to protect the environment. Though more than 80% of the student population is willing to seek further knowledge and skills in farming, around 20% believe that farming will not give less scope for higher education's accessibility to future generations. More than 50% of students believe that it is unwise to farm if they are highly educated. This reveals their perception of farming as a job. They do not consider farming as a profession. This reflects the need for revamping the attitude of students towards farming as a profession. Almost all students (98.6%) are of the opinion that the sustainability principles are to be integrated into the curriculum of all disciplines and at all levels of education.

c. *Behavior regarding sustainability*

Table 7.5 summarizes, in percentage form, the distribution of respondents' responses to the 12 items constituting the behavior scale.

The table shows that the responses for items B12 and B13 show a high level of commitment towards sustainability. Most of the responses show an average level of commitment. It is to be noted that only 27% of the students attend courses on sustainable development. Around 96% of students enjoy the relationship with nature through farming which reveals their interest in farming. However, almost 25% of students were not able to decide with respect to sustainability behavior.

TABLE 7.5 Behavior towards sustainability. Agreement, disagreement, and indecision with regard to behavior towards items expressed in percentage form

Items	Agreement %	Undecided %	Disagreement %
B7 I participate in activities related to environmental sustainability.	43.8	35.6	20.5
B2 I attend courses on sustainable development.	27.4	35.6	37.0
B9 I look up information about the environment or sustainability of the university on the respective website.	45.2	26.0	28.8
B6 I volunteer to work with local charities.	50.7	28.8	20.5
B8 I look at problems from different angles.	65.8	26.0	8.2
B3 I talk to others about how to help people living in poverty.	47.9	38.4	13.7
B10 I look up information about the new sustainable development goals of the United Nations.	35.6	24.7	39.7
B12 Farming leads to increase in standard of living.	80.8	15.1	4.1
B5 I look for signs of ecosystem deterioration.	45.2	32.9	21.9
B4 I think about what it means to live in a sustainable manner.	54.8	35.6	9.6
B1 I walk or ride a bicycle to places instead of going by car.	39.7	30.1	30.1
B13 I enjoy the relationship with nature through farming.	95.9	4.1	0

Findings based on interview

The students opined their concern on farming that motivates them to develop their sustainable literacy. Interested students in farming are selected without any external compulsion but through self-initiation from various departments and are awarded fellowships. The participating students' attendance is mandatory, and taken by the department's staff. The fellowship is provided based on this. They stated that upland paddy cultivation, vegetable plants, and banana plantations are the major items of cultivation. Varieties of coconut plantations are another major highlight to this. Students, research scholars, teachers, and staff work with great enthusiasm and togetherness for the success of this project. They face many challenges during their work, such as pest and insect attacks, lack of quality seeds and saplings, and climatic changes. They reckon that proper care and scientific measurements were taken to lessen these challenges. These activities equipped them to create a pro-environment attitude and sustainability behavior . Proper sustainable living is enlightened in the minds of the staff and students by implementing this kind of entity. They also point out certain suggestions for the implementation and accomplishment of this farming . They enunciate that more land area must be utilized for cultivation, effective techniques must be adopted to improve crop production, fertilizers and bio-pesticides should be used moderately, and hybrid varieties of crops must be used. Mixed crop cultivation should be encouraged. All these show their persuasion towards a sustainable environment and sustainable farming.

The analysis suggests that, overall, students were able to identify and express their attitudes and conceptions of sustainable development. During the interview, the sustainable literacy dimensions identified during the literature review were mentioned by many of the students.

Discussion

The present study dealt with the assessment of sustainability literacy level of students of Karyavattom campus at the University of Kerala, with respect to three dimensions: knowledge, attitude, and behavior. The Sustainability Literacy Scale used for the study shows a three-dimensional structure allowing measurement of knowledge, attitudes, and behaviors related to various sustainability themes. The study shows that though the students have a high level of agreement towards knowledge and attitude dimensions, the level of agreement with respect to behavior dimension was average. According to the findings, sustainability knowledge of campus students is at a high level, but their approach or behavior to the environment and environmental issues is at a low level. In addition, they have a positive attitude about sustainable development. This clearly focuses on the significance of introducing an experiential learning approach towards sustainable education. Our students of today are the teachers or the academics of the future. Therefore, these students' knowledge, attitudes, and behavior towards sustainability significantly impact sustainable development. Lugg (2007) studied how outdoor experiential pedagogy might contribute to the current sustainability education agenda. He discussed possibilities and issues arising from a review of outdoor, environmental, and sustainability education. Similarly, the project discussed in the study also reveals the significance of informal outdoor education in developing sustainability literacy among campus students.

Despite that students expressed some concerns during the interview, the investigators found that the program was pioneering new expectations and commitments to food security and sustainability literacy. In addition, the 'Harithalayam Project' addresses local priorities and takes into consideration the local environment, society, and economy. The initiative engages the student community of the Karyavttom campus in formal and non-formal education throughout the process, and is a sustained effort that constantly reinvents itself to meet the needs of the community. A similar program in Costa Rica found significant intergenerational learning in that information was disseminated from the classrooms to the broader community (Vaughan et al., 1999). Also, other evidence that educational institutions act as agents for environmental learning and are factors that contribute to intergenerational learning include actively involving parents in student activities and focusing on local environmental issues (Duvall & Zint, 2007). Orr (1992), Smith-Sabasto (1997), and Theobald and Nachtigal (1995) focused on the need for students to know about their community, its environment, history, economy, interactions of culture, and ecology. The more they become sustainably literate, the more they will be concerned about their community's health and welfare. Healthy sustainable communities that perceive their interdependence can define their economic roles and connect efficiently with other communities. Thus, one of the most critical needs of today's society at both global and local levels is to redesign education for the purpose of creating ecologically sustainable communities (Lock, Ruso & Monteyo, 2013).

The 'Harithalayam Project' was implemented at the campus as part of the statewide initiative taken by the Government of Kerala to make use of barren lands, schools, colleges, universities, and even residential premises for farming to ensure food security in the state. The state was badly affected by the successive floods which occurred in the state in 2018 and 2019. Though the initiative was started as a remedy for food security, the University of Kerala implemented the 'Harithalayam Project' as a step to develop sustainable development literacy among the students at the campus. The COVID-19 pandemic affected the project to a considerable extent as the campus was locked down and students were away from the campus. Though they actively participated in the land preparation and transplantation of seedlings, due to the COVID-19 pandemic, together they could not put their hands to work during harvest.

In his article, Amel et al. (2017) has mentioned that information alone will not change behavior. According to behavioral science theories, certain interventions can bring a behavioral change towards sustainable development (Michie et al., 2011, p. 1), and such interventions help to increase or maintain such behaviors (Morra Imas & Rist, 2009). The 'Harithalayam Project' would, in the long run, enable our students to develop behavioral changes towards sustainability.

Conclusion

For the last two years, severe floods have affected the south Indian state of Kerala due to unusually high rainfall during the monsoon season. It was the worst flood in Kerala in nearly a century. Declining environmental quality and agricultural production in the region as well as the whole state, which is a challenge due to several reasons, has forced the University of Kerala to consider an alternative approach towards sustainability through campus farming. Within this context, the University of Kerala launched the 'Harithalayam Program', which used the principles of both campus farming and environmental education to enhance sustainable literacy among the students at the campus. Results from a quantitative survey and qualitative interview among the students indicate that the program has been successful to a great extent.

The 'Harithalayam Program' has offered a unique opportunity to examine and evaluate how the dimensions of sustainability literacy are enhanced through a campus farming initiative. By using experiential learning theory, this study examined how students engage in campus farming initiatives that can improve their sustainability literacy and behaviors. It also explores their motivations and aspirations and research towards farming. The study tries to exhibit a campus initiative that may help educators design learning activities for sustainable living. The study's findings reveal that though students developed knowledge and an attitude towards sustainable development, the behavioral change towards sustainable development among the students remained low. The present study was done during the first year of implementation of the project. The investigator believes that the project, in the long term, will bring a considerable change in the behavior of students towards sustainability. Also, the university is planning to integrate farming into the curriculum by giving credits to students during their final assessment of academics every semester. It will be made mandatory that students must engage themselves with farming every week in line with their curriculum. The University of Kerala is undergoing a revision of the curriculum with respect to transforming it into an outcome-based curriculum. One of the program outcomes put forward by the University of Kerala is the development of sustainable behavior among the students. The vision and mission of the University of Kerala are also moving in this direction.

References

Amel, E. et al. 2017. 'Beyond the roots of human inaction: Fostering collective effort toward ecosystem conservation', *Science*, 356(6335), pp.275–279, https://doi.org/10.1126/science.aal1931.

Burt, K.G. 2016. 'A complete history of the social, health and political context of the school gardening movement in the United States', *Journal of Hunger & Environmental Nutrition*, 11(3), pp.297–316.

Calhoun, T. and Cortese, A.D.. 2005. 'We rise to play a greater part: Students, faculty, staff, and community converge in search of leadership from the top'. http://www.scup.org/csd/3/pdf/SCUP-CSD-101705.pdf

Duvall, J. and Zint, M. 2007. 'A review of research on the effectiveness of environmental education in promoting intergenerational learning', *The Journal of Environmental Education*, 38, pp.14–24.

Gul, A., Keles, E. and Uzun, O.F. 2016. 'Recreational demand and trends in the campus students and lecturers of Süleyman Demirel university', *Journal of Architecture Sciences and Applications*, 1(1), pp.26–43.

Hall, R.O. 1985. 'Environmental education in Costa Rica', *Prospects*, 15, pp.583–591.

Hines, J.M., Hungerford, H.R. and Tomera, A.N. 1987. 'Analysis and synthesis of research on responsible environmental behaviour: A meta-analysis', *The Journal of Environmental Education*, 18(2), pp.1–8.

Lock, S., Ruso, R. and Monteyo, C. 2013. 'Environmental education and eco-literacy as tools of education for sustainable development', *Journal of Sustainability Education*, 4(1), pp.97–110.

Lugg, A. 2007. 'Developing sustainability-literate citizens through outdoor learning: Possibilities for outdoor education in Higher Education', *Journal of Adventure Education and Outdoor Learning*, 7(2), pp.97–112, https://doi.org/10.1080/14729670701609456.

Michie, S., van Stralen, M.M. and West, R., 2011. 'The behaviour change wheel: A new method for characterising and designing behaviour change interventions', *Implementation Science*, 6, p.42, https://doi.org/10.1186/1748-5908-6-42

Morra Imas, L.G. and Rist, R.C. 2009. *The Road to Results: Designing and Conducting Effective Development Evaluations*. World Bank. © World Bank. https://openknowledge.worldbank.org/handle/10986/2699 License: CC BY 3.0 IGO, http://hdl.handle.net/10986/2699

Orr, D.W. 1992. *Ecological Literacy: Education and the Transitions to a Postmodern World*. Albany, NY: SUNY.

Smith-Sebasto, N.J. 1997. 'Education for ecological literacy' in P.J. Thompson (ed.) *Environmental Education for the 21st Century: International and Interdisciplinary Perspectives*. New York: Peter Lang, pp.279–288.

Theobald, P. and Nachtigal, P. 1995. *Culture, Community, and the Promise of Rural Education*. Bloomigton: Phi Delta Kappan, pp.132–135.

Yilmaz, T., Gokce, D., Savkli, F. and Cesmeci, S. 2012. 'A research on the use of the common locations by the disabled people within the university campuses: An example of the Olbia culture center of Akdeniz university', *The Journal of Tekirdag Agricultural Faculty*, 9(3), pp.1–10.

PART 3

Process-focused perspective

8

HOW DO CHILDREN AND YOUTH LEARN THROUGH FARMING AND GARDENING ACTIVITIES?

Linda Jolly and Erling Krogh

Introduction

During the summer of 2010, 22-year-old orphan Bosco Paulo in the village of Nyandira in the Uluguru Mountains in Tanzania received one young goat as a loan. Bosco's father was dead and his mother mentally ill. In addition, Bosco had the responsibility for his younger brother at the family's small farm. He was several years behind the other pupils and was on the way to give up junior high school. Like the other 15 orphans in the village who also received a kid as a loan, one year later, Bosco had learned to feed and care for the goat. The goat had produced a new kid, and Bosco built a little barn for the goats. This summer, it was not the teacher and advisor Solomon Nicholaus who taught the next year's group of orphan apprentices about nutrition in the different fodder plants and the feeding of the goats according to different nutritional requirements. It was Bosco.

The teachers from the local secondary schools also heard Bosco teach, and the science teacher was amazed at Bosco's knowledge of the fodder qualities of plants. They knew the local flora, but what they now heard was something they had neither read nor been told before. Two years later, Bosco gave a female kid back to the goat project so that a new orphan would have the same chance. In that way, he repaid the loan he received. In 2014, Bosco graduated from the national secondary school. After two more years, he finished his agricultural vocational education. His initial dream was to become a doctor or science researcher. Still, his current agricultural knowledge and skills can contribute to improving his own family's and his fellow villagers' livelihoods.

When Bosco and the other orphaned youth talk about what the goat and the learning process have meant for them, most of them emphasize that their attitude has changed. We can explain the change in several ways. The orphans can contribute to the household in which they live with the money made from the

DOI: 10.4324/9781003176558-8

sale of goat milk, a household usually comprised of grandparents and uncles and aunts and their children. In addition, they have acquired knowledge and skills in goat keeping. Gradually, the farmers in the villages treat the orphan dairy goat farmers with respect. The local inhabitants consider the youth as competent goat farmers. The youth can also pay for school fees and textbooks.

The orphans have organized themselves in local groups where they support each other and learn from each other's experiences. They tell us that they increasingly see possibilities to create a future according to their own wishes. Therefore, they claim that their relationships with family and friends, they themselves, and their possibilities to create a future of their own choice have changed. In addition, they also experience the wish and capacity to contribute to their local community. Of the first 16 youth, only two wanted to be teachers before they received a goat, but one year later, there were eight aspiring to be teachers. The reason? They wanted other orphans and youth in difficult situations to have access to the positive development they themselves had experienced.

What we have seen in Tanzania is very similar to the experience we have had in guiding student teachers and in the cooperative projects between farms and schools over the last 20 years in Norway. When learning through practical outdoor work, students connect to animals and plants, fellow students and farmers, instructors and teachers, tools and machines, and harvesting of agricultural commodities and making them into market products or meals. In short, the students connect to the agricultural activities and orient their attention and will towards completing the tasks. During the process and after the result, it is usually possible to observe how the students master the tasks. When they connect to the activity or task, their willpower awakens. When mastering occurs, the students change their posture and body movements. In addition, we hear related comments or exclamations and see the consequences in their cooperation with others and often a new glow in the students' eyes. These moments of change are valuable for the student to reflect upon. It is not until the student has experienced or done a task that they feel is valuable that they think about whether it is meaningful to reflect on the relationship between themselves and the process and result of their work. The execution of the task leads to self-understanding, not only as an inward process but also in relation to the work, arena, and local community.

The theory of relationship-based experiential learning

This is the essence of what we call 'relationship-based experiential learning'. The theory builds upon certain pre-conditions, which we will explain in this chapter. We include the example from Tanzania because we want to emphasize that our intention goes further than giving input to the flora of learning theory. For us, there is more at stake than discussing the ordinary meaning of learning. Learning is about daring to see what a human being is or can be, also in a spiritual sense, and which conditions are necessary in order to learn and transform their behavior and self-understanding. Therefore, we also consider what humans search for and how each person can realize more of their human potential. Furthermore, we are of the opinion that society needs learners who develop engagement, willpower, and the ability to transcend outdated patterns and solutions so that they as adults can meet and cope with the challenges of sustainability which the coming generation will face. This is our motivation for developing a theory on relationship-based experiential learning.

In the following text, we will initially focus on the central characteristics of school learning in our own society and the experiences we have gathered through many years as teachers and advisors in work using agriculture and horticulture as arenas for learning. This gives a societal and empirical background for our theory of learning. Furthermore, we try to define the concept of learning as an inner process of change triggered by outer circumstances. With the point of departure in this definition, we discuss essential attributes that characterize the changing and learning human being. Finally, we present our theory of learning with practical examples.

The theory of relationship-based experiential learning also builds upon experience with teacher education in natural science and agriculture as well as on the Norwegian national project *Living School* (1995–2000). As an integral part of the education of our teachers, we participate in classroom lessons regularly in many high schools and junior high schools throughout the country. In *Living School*, school gardens and partner farms became learning arenas for students who do practical tasks such as cultivating plants and caring for animals.

Classroom lessons reflect the politics of education in Norway and Europe, which focus increasingly on measurable learning results in separate subjects such as mathematics, natural science, languages, and social studies. Artistic and practical subjects receive less attention and even fewer resources in the daily school routine. The goals in the curriculum in these subjects have also become more theoretical and cognitively oriented. This contributes to increased theorizing of education. For example, former 'cooking' lessons are now 'food and nutrition'. The current curricula increasingly connect nutritional facts to measurable results, with less emphasis on cooking and the human capacities and social competencies developed through the shared work tasks. *Living School* arose as a counter-reaction to both theorization and increasing distance between pupils and basic life processes. The growing degree of abstraction in school subjects also widens the gap between the local community and the school. *Living School* oriented learning activities and practical skills towards the food's path from the field to the table. In Norway, less than 2% of the working force are farmers, and today, even the farmers' children often have little knowledge about the production which goes on at the home farm.

In the span between the classroom and the practical learning arenas, we have arrived at the conclusion that the educational system in Norway needs revision, but preferably revolution. In the classrooms, we meet a large group of students who show signs of increasing learning fatigue on their way from kindergarten to high school. Compared with the lively activity we witness in the school garden and on the farm, the classroom situations often appear pale and lacking in energy. 'Reason is a gun for hire', maintained the philosopher of science, Paul Feyerabend. The coming generation undoubtedly needs both common sense and a broad spectrum of theoretical knowledge to be able to meet the challenges of the future, but they also need the ability to translate theory into solutions for practical problems in a complex world. We need people who have experiential knowledge of life processes and who can and will cultivate and harvest from nature in a skillful, cautious, and caring manner. The society also needs people who can exhibit concern for each other as a balance to a fragmented and individualized societal organization. Thus, the global community needs people who are connected to each other and to basic life processes, who have the empathy, willpower, engagement, and ability to meet challenges and find new, and so far, unthinkable, solutions to future scenarios. The world needs education for sustainable development. The education of actors for sustainable development presupposes practical and meaningful learning arenas such as the garden and farm (Krogh & Jolly 2012).

Thus, education needs a new theory of learning. The cognitive-oriented school divided into segregated subjects with an overall focus on measurable learning results corresponds with theories of learning, which restrict learning to the construction of meaning. These current theories vary from emphasis on mental constructivism to a focus on the construction of meaning as an interplay between social and cultural processes and mental learning. The emphasis on mental learning downplays the undiscussable fact that a brain resides in a living body and that the body, not the isolated brain, is the acting subject in every encounter with the world. Focusing on mental construction, therefore, usually leads to a de-prioritizing of physical skills and practical and esthetic activities. The learning theory of constructivism also casts a shadow over the human ability to connect to the world and develop the will to act. The energy in the practical arenas for learning seems to relate precisely to the fact that the student trains and develops their ability to connect to activities and each other. Also, in addition, their own will and commitment to finding new solutions to concrete challenges are ignited. The practical arenas for learning have given us many examples and stories about how students can learn in ways that create energy directed towards the future. We want to share our conceptual extraction of these stories with you.

We begin with a consideration of three basic attributes or founding capacities of the intertwined physical and spiritual human being that our work with outdoor education on the farm and in the garden has shown us. These basic capacities or abilities, the ability to connect and build relationships, the ability to act with a directed intention, and the ability to think creatively and find new solutions, serve as a foundation for our model of relationship-based experiential learning, which we will present at the conclusion of this chapter.

Learning – connecting the inner human being with the outer world

Edward Deci and Richard Ryan have developed and refined their theory of self-determination since the early 1970s (Deci 1975, Deci & Ryan 2012). Their understanding of the human being builds upon a synthesis of theoretical discussions and more than 100 empirical studies:

> The starting point for SDT (Self-determination theory) is the postulate that humans are active, growth-oriented organisms who are naturally inclined toward integration of their psychic elements into a unified sense of self and integration of themselves into larger social structures.
>
> *(Deci & Ryan 2000: 229)*

The self-determination theory further claims that inner motivation is the foundation for being able to learn and, in a wider context, develop oneself, express one's human potential and connect to the outside world. Through a meta-analysis of 128 studies over three decades, Deci, Koestner, and Ryan (1999) documented that external reward systematically weakens inner motivation. In addition, some of the field studies document that especially creativity, problem-solving abilities, and the ability to work through concepts are weakened through external reward or control (Amabile 1982, Grolnick & Ryan 1987, McGraw & McCullers 1979). These findings question and challenge the effects of the widespread use of testing and standardized evaluations in school subjects. The main result seems to be more a regurgitation, copying of learning, that is adapted to this kind of evaluation but simultaneously impairs motivation and gives meager learning results.

Our concern is how learning situations, learning tasks, and forms of cooperation between the teacher/instructor and student can strengthen the student's inner motivation and thus promote learning. We need to clarify our understanding of the relationship between internal motivation and learning. We maintain that intrinsic (internal) motivation, as the basis for learning, is an inner human movement, but that the interaction with outer social, cultural, and physical circumstances in which the learner participates, awakens, stimulates, and promotes the learner's internal learning activity. Therefore, the choice of learning activity and the relationship between the teacher/instructor and the student is decisive, both for inner motivation and for learning. Learning, as we define the concept, implies an enduring confirmation, expansion, or change of former understanding and behavior. However, it is necessary to emphasize that such a movement of behavior is intricately bound to experience in the physical world. Current or former physical experiences are necessary conditions for learning, thus the name of our theory of learning – relationship-based experiential learning.

Learning means change of understanding and behavior, often characterized by alteration and transition, and we see the inner human being as the active motivator in learning. In the following, we will deal with essential and universal human attributes that, according to our experience and our theoretical considerations, characterize the inner human being. We do not rely on defining inner psychological needs, such as in the theory of self-determination. Instead, we derive three essential and unmeasurable but still observable human attributes, intertwined as the driving force of human life and as the founding characteristic of humans as incarnated spiritual beings. Human activities open for observability of the lived expression of human attributes such as empathy and different qualities and nuances of willpower, such as perseverance, endurance, and patience.

In our opinion, the acceptance of unmeasurable but observable and spiritual human attributes is commensurable with approval and endorsement of physical mechanisms underlying evolutionary biology, but not with ontological materialism.[1]

Still, the main scientific question is not if an observation of a phenomenon is commensurable with an existing theory, but according to pragmatism (James 1912, Dewey 1916), if the theory gives a satisfactory and useful explanation of an observed phenomenon. We have not found that ontological materialism offers a satisfactory explanation of emotions and willpower or a useful differentiation and nuancing of the qualities of emotions and willpower. Therefore, we will introduce a preliminary sketch of the core human attributes, but first, describe the characteristics of what we see as the essence of being human.

The human being – in dynamic change and choice

The developing human being has a distinctive and continual ability to initiate change internally, bodily, and in their surroundings. The ability to cause change and development relies on the human capacity to think and reflect to affect the surroundings physically with the limbs (such as the hand) and tools, as well as the ability to cooperate. The human being is unique in the animal kingdom due to their ability to choose and change ways of understanding. The ability to choose is possible because the human being is conscious, conscious of themselves, as well of their capacity to choose and to change.

The ability and opportunity to choose rests on some fundamental prerequisites.

The first to be recognized is that choice presupposes that the human being is not omniscient. If human beings had been omniscient, every choice would be given or impossible. Limited knowledge is a prerequisite for making a choice. In the same way, equilibrium is both an unimaginable condition and an impossible final goal for the human being. Temporary balancing of disequilibrium is possible, but the continuous dynamism will re-instate unbalance and continually new situations of choice.

The second aspect is that the existence of time and space makes a choice possible and, in our opinion, inevitable for intentional human activity. The time dimension implies two prerequisite conditions for choice. Past occurrences provide a necessary basis for choice in the present, and choice is necessary to realize goals for desired future situations. In addition, decision-making processes are dependent on the experience of continuity and duration (Bergson 1889/1990). Space establishes an anchor in a fluctuating life and defines concrete choice alternatives. Human embodiment in physical space within a limited time span, together with the ability to determine the presence in the span between the past and the future, creates the necessary conditions for being able to choose.

The third aspect is that choice is dependent on the co-existence of three core human attributes:

- *Connecting*: the capacity to connect oneself to something else, to build relationships.
- *Intending*: the purposeful orientation in the form of directed intention.
- *Transcending*: the capacity to go beyond earlier understandings and modes of action.

Without the ability to connect oneself to the physical world, the choice would be of no interest. Intention gives both the possibility for orientation and the necessary drive to choose. Transcendence of earlier understandings and modes of action bursts the frames of routines and automation and is a necessary condition that enables the choice to lead to development.

If we cut to the bone, the essence of human existence is the possibility and capacity to choose. The human being is in the world, and in the world, human essence is transition: one who is continuously choosing and changing.

Connecting: building relationships

> The farmer led the class of 14–15-year-olds around the farm the first morning, showing them all the tasks that awaited them. The biggest boy in the class was busy putting hay down the t-shirts of his classmates, demonstrating an obvious indifference to what the farmer said and the farming activities. His heaviness and problems with concentration had made school garden lessons a trial for both student and teacher. On the farm, his motivation did not seem to be any better. He had told me, the teacher, many times that he didn't need this 'stuff' because he was going to be a computer expert like his father. After some days, he came to me, obviously shocked and disturbed about something he had discovered. 'Do you know what they get paid on this farm?' he asked. 'Not even the farmer gets a decent salary!', was his comment. We took up the topic in the lesson later that day, food prices from the field to the table, what it means for producers of food that we can have 'cheap' food, millionaires who own the supermarkets, and that we use only 11% of our income on food. There was a marked change in both his attitude and effort for the rest of the agricultural excursion.

This boy's conversations with farm workers laid the path to an extended understanding of and increased engagement with agriculture and food production.

He connected with them through working side-by-side and asking questions about why they were at the farm. No lesson could have hoped to give him such motivation and interest. Other students have connected to certain tasks, like the journalist, who, ten years after participating in the work at the farm, wrote, 'I yearn to be back at the farm working with the compost and seeing how it transforms through the different stages'. Or the girl who could not be persuaded to go through the door of the barn on the first day because of the smell, but she refused to leave the barn and the cows she had learned to love on the last day. Caring for animals, working with soil, repairing machines, harvesting fruit and vegetables, and cooking meals while getting to know the people on the farm are all examples of connection, of building relationships.

This basic ability of connecting, essential for learning, is given from birth. Comprehensive research shows that the infant has both the ability to connect and to feel empathy, being open towards others and the world, without being I-centered, such as Piaget assumed (Ferrucci 1990, Bråten & Gallese 2004). The physical body and senses constitute the entrance and access to any meeting with the world. The human being is in the world through and in their body and is, according to Merleau-Ponty (1945/1962), a bodily subject. The basic ability of connection must therefore have a physical capability to express itself through the human body. The mirror neurons constitute the physical basis for the human ability to connect immediately with the surroundings (Rizzolatti & Sinigaglia 2008).

Connecting closely relates to the human ability to *feel*. While connecting constitutes humanity, the human ability to feel and the different feelings essentially express and influence human relations. Therefore, feelings are also the foundation for learning. Cognitive learning theory tends to neglect this self-evident fact. We will not underestimate the significance of cognitive learning but rather stress how different feelings influence learning. Anxiety can potentially block any learning, while the happiness of mastering to a larger degree will facilitate learning.

Intending

During the last days at the farm, the teacher noticed a group of students that hardly had time to eat lunch. The curious teacher went to see what was more important than food for 14/15-year-old youths. She found the students working with the firewood. They had had their turn, as everyone in the class, collecting logs felled in the farm forest. The students had sawed, cleaved and stacked the wood, which would heat the greenhouses in the spring and fall. Long rows of woodpiles witnessed to many hours of intensive work done by the class. Still, there remained two large piles of timber. On their own, these students had decided to finish cutting up all the wood before they left the farm. Considering the two days left on the farm, the teacher told them that they had already done a very good job, but that it was impossible to finish all of it. Two days later the students had transformed the remaining logs into firewood. When asked what they had learned on the last day, one of the boys wrote: 'I have learned an incredible amount! We have learned to work effectively, eat healthy and be happy'.

While connecting and building relationships occurs in the present, intending to engage or engaging in goal-oriented activity looks towards the future. The intending, willing human being awakes when they meet a real need and tasks that ask for their action. As is the case with the cutting of firewood, students might choose to sacrifice some needs (like a lunch break) to fulfill other needs and intentional goals. The intention has costs. There is often resistance, but also rewards, as the young man's own evaluation clearly illustrates.

Human experience and learning are connected to active participation. Merleau-Ponty (1945/1962) argued that Descartes was wrong in his famous statement, 'I think, therefore I am' and instead postulated 'I can' precedes 'I think that'. In our experience, as in the story above, when a pupil chooses to throw themselves into a task, the work is often accompanied by shouts or an expression as they cleave a log, pull up a fish over the railing of the boat, or when the milk squirts from the udder into the cup. A positive 'I connect' to something often leads to 'I will/I want to' act to take care of this. The mastering of the action creates the experience of 'I can'. The experience of mastering can become even stronger through the resistance the task has presented. This strengthens, in turn, self-confidence and contributes to forming of character.

Intending relates to *willpower*. Connecting precedes intending, and connecting might release different feelings, from engaged interest to disgust. Obviously, disgust rather fosters a repulsion, while engaged interest most likely fosters attraction. The direction and the strength of human willpower rely on the feelings released by the experience of connecting. In addition, Assagioli (1974) distinguishes between different qualities of willpower (see below: The second phase: execution of the task).

Intending through willpower is another core condition for learning. Therefore, it is important to conceptualize and be conscious about both direction, strength, and different qualities of willpower.

Transcending

Bosco, the orphan dairy goat farmer in Tanzania, had learned how to care for his goat and had shown that he could also teach others. He learned to know the plants and their qualities from the older farmers. In addition, he tested the feeding of his milk goats with root tubers from a plant that was treated as a weed. Instead of pulling up the weeds and disposing of them like the other farmers, he harvested the root tubers, dried them and gave them to his goats. The yield of milk from Bosco's goats doubled through feeding the wild tubers. Currently, Sokoine University of Agriculture is analyzing the nutritional content of the tubers.

Much of the current school teaching focuses on learners' acquisition of patterns of thought, systems for organizing knowledge, and logical reflection. Within this cognitive learning tradition, there is room for inquiry by applying scientifically accepted theories and methods and for the appliance of known patterns and systems to new situations. The latter trains the ability to transfer modes of thinking to unfamiliar territory, such as applying mathematical formulas to hypothetical situations. These paths of learning and routines for thinking are safe, predictable, and easy to evaluate. The application of knowledge and skills might be satisfactory and efficient for problem-solving in societies and environments with well-known and predictable characteristics. However, such approaches may not be adequate in meeting the needs of a changing and challenging world. They might also fall short of giving students confidence in their capacity to contribute to change in the world and with themselves.

Transcending implies forming new contexts that consciously allow for challenging well-proven patterns and solutions. The creation of a radically different organization of elements in an original solution often requires a leap from the known and an intuitive recognition of the new – like seeing the potential in the root of a weed! Scharmer (2018) maintains that access to the source of creation or intuitive recognition demands an inner movement where the learner gets the opportunity to meet learning situations or activities with an open heart, open will, and open mind.

Still, within an existing mind-set, both transcending and a refining of patterns of thought and action are possible. However, inevitably the core assumptions underlying a mind-set or a worldview limit transcending of the same assumptions. Ontological materialism assumes that all human experiences have a physical cause. According to the worldview that currently dominates natural sciences, there is no spiritual dimension independent of physical reality. Furthermore, popular science literature in this field often stresses and elaborates how the human brain and humanity's evolutionary heritage monitors feelings and willpower, for example, the mechanisms for the physical release of endorphins, as explanations for joyful experiences (Baumeister & Tierney 2012, Duhigg 2014, Johnston & Olson 2015). From this point of view, an open heart and open mind seem to be poetical, non-scientific concepts because feelings and willpower derive from physical causes.

However, there is no necessity to equate natural sciences with ontological materialism and no necessary ontological opposition between the understanding of human beings as incarnated spiritual beings and acceptance, interest, and application of a natural scientific approach on physical causes and effects in and on human beings. Leaving ontological materialism, scientific investigations of feelings and willpower can focus on these phenomena as they occur in human activities and experiences. Based on our investigations, we assume that connecting, intending, and transcending constitute three interdependent core attributes of the 'choosing' human being. We also assume that transcending is possible. Still, what Bourdieu (1977) calls 'Doxa', the taken-for-granted assumptions underlying any worldview, science, unconscious psychological patterns, and societal and cultural understandings, norms, and values, might occur as insurmountable barriers for transcending.

Through revealing, not rejecting, what is taken-for-granted, open heart, will, and mind might be achievable. Furthermore, the realization of characteristics and elaboration of qualities of the core attributes connecting and intending will strengthen the understanding of human motivation. Transcending also presupposes the acquisition of an independent relation to core assumptions underlying what is taken-for-granted. According to Bergson (1946), letting go of familiar thoughts and ways of acting and establishment of new and different understandings demand intuitive leaps in the form of conscious opening and liberating activity. A rapid reorganizing of the thought follows the leap and behavior patterns in accord with the new insight such as what Piaget (1952) called accommodation. In this way, the human being can further develop or even transcend patterns in an intuitive and creative process, which can meet hitherto unknown problems. Such as with Bosco, the accompanying experience of empowerment can open new horizons for personal development and future tasks!

Our choice of connecting, intending, and transcending as core human attributes relates to a long history of philosophy, pedagogy, psychology, and sociology. Johann Heinrich Pestalozzi, relying on the ancient philosophers Plato and Aristotle, developed his pedagogy around Hand, Heart, and Head as the main concepts (Brühlmeier 2010). In accordance with Pestalozzi, Rudolf Steiner built the Waldorf pedagogy on willpower, feelings, and thought (Steiner 1907/1996). 'Liberty Hyde Bailey', the founder of the 4-H movement, added Health to Hand, Heart, and Head (Bailey 1903, 1905). Within psychological motivation theory, Edward Deci and Richard Ryan (2000) found that the fulfillment of competence, belonging, and self-determination releases inner motivation. The health sociologist Antonovsky (1987) identified manageability, emotional meaningfulness, and comprehensibility as the three main components of the sense of coherence and humans' ability to manage stressors. These common perspectives rely on empirical studies and experiences of active human beings followed by the

TABLE 8.1 The connecting, intending, and transcending human being

Attribute modes	Initial condition	Developed capacity	Possible refinement
Connecting	Feeling, emotion	Interest	Insight/empathy
Intending	Willpower	Drive	Character
Transcending	Thought	Acquirement of patterns/ logical reasoning	Intuition

formulation of a few similar human attributes, needs, capacities, or relations to others .

The connecting, intending, and transcending human being

In summary, we have described what we see as observable, core attributes of the inner human being attribute that provide a basis for understanding our theory of learning. We maintain that these inner, active attributes are the driving forces for learning. At the same time, learning requires a relation to the external world. The setting, content, and process of learning are crucial not only for learning but also for the students' inner development and for their relationship to themselves, their environment, and their contribution to the challenges of our time. These attributes are not clearly divided and independent of each other but are developed together through confrontation with real-life situations. Our assumption is that the path of learning for sustainable development moves from the upper left attribute of connection towards the refined abilities on the right to be able to transcend common patterns and dare to trust intuitive understandings that can bring new and hitherto unconceivable solutions.

Relationship-based experiential learning

The founder of experiential learning, John Dewey, focused on the concept of education, not on the concept of learning. Still, he maintained that human survival depends on the ability to learn and that active learning processes presuppose experience (Dewey 1916: 4 and 390). Unlike David Kolb's model for experiential learning, Dewey's model for inquiry did not assert abstract conceptualization as any necessary component or step before testing and experimentation .

Dewey, for his part, meant that the development of abstractions, for example, concepts and theoretical models and perspectives, might be a *possible* side effect or by-product of inquiry (Dewey 1916: 22). According to Dewey, unrest or

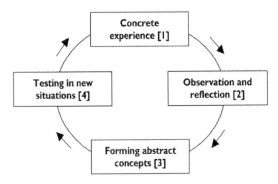

FIGURE 8.1 David Kolb's model for experiential learning (1984).

disturbance caused by the experience of dysfunctions, problems, or crises during habitual acts motivate inquiry. Therefore, inquiry aims at extending beyond the power of habit by deducing improvement of earlier routinized actions from logical analyses of specific experiences.

During the inquiry, tentative working hypotheses and concepts are tools for the development of action plans (Ibid.: 312). Furthermore, Dewey states that only the practical testing of the hypothesis in material activity makes it possible to draw conclusions of its validity (Miettinen 2000: 67). Therefore, in 1894, Dewey, together with his wife, established the University of Chicago Laboratory School to test out and evaluate his contextualized theories of schooling and teaching. According to Dewey, reasoning, as well as the solution of problems, relates to action and specific situations. Afterward, it is possible to transfer, explore, and test out developed procedures for the solution of problems in other situations. Dewey asserts that concepts are primarily generalizations of relations between human beings and between humans and their environment. In his opinion, concepts comprise more than mental constructions .

Just like the pragmatist John Dewey and a range of sociocultural learning theorists, we believe that social and physical relations and activities substantiate human learning processes. Contrary to Dewey (1916, 1938), Piaget (1952), and Jarvis (2012), we do not maintain that human beings' experience of mental unrest or discrepancies needs to be the overarching driving force and condition for the initialization of learning processes. Experience of unrest or discrepancies is one of many possible motivations for learning. We see the three core attributes as the basic driving forces behind any learning and development. The kindling of these driving forces occurs in relation to others, to the human environment.

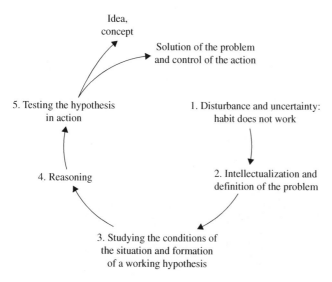

FIGURE 8.2   John Dewey's model for inquiry interpreted by Miettinen (2000: 65).

We agree with Frankl (1959), who claims that the will for meaning is the main, unifying, and connecting the human driving force in any relation and situation.

Like Dewey, we find relationships to be the point of departure for human activity and human sciences. Learning is connecting. It is relationship based because long-lasting confirmation, extension, or change of previous understanding and behavior presuppose that human beings, with their core attributes as driving forces, meet and experience the physical and social world. The assumption of the inner human driving forces is the main feature separating relation-based experiential learning from Dewey's pragmatism and sociocultural learning theories.

The learning activity is a part of a vocation (farmer/gardener) or necessary activity; for example, feeding cows which is a task in dairy farming. We consider learning to be an inner movement or change accompanied by the learner's participation in physical activities, in some way using their body or senses. The white arrows in Figure 8.3 form a cycle and illustrate the four phases of the learning process. Outside the arrows, we have named each of the phases of the physical learning activity. Between the arrows, the boxes mark turning points in the learning process.

According to our experience, the learners continually experience tension between orienting their attention and interest towards the learning activity or being distracted by other circumstances. In the figure below, within each of the white arrows, the red-colored statements separated vertically by double-sided black arrows characterize the opposite poles in relation to the learning activity (Figure 8.4).

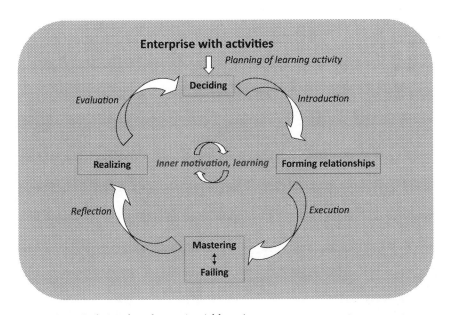

FIGURE 8.3 Relation-based experiential learning.

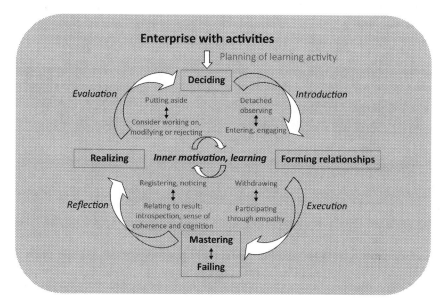

FIGURE 8.4   The tension between engaging and withdrawing.

The tension between two extremes, between being detached, absent, with-drawing, distracted, and uninterested in the activity, and the opposite, being present, focused, engaged, interested, and participative, is a challenge for learning.

A weak connection to the task often leads to a lack of inner motivation for learning with a lower probability of achieving results that lead to reflection, realization, and evaluation. The opposite pole, active engagement and participation tend to activate the learner's inner motivation and increase learning outcome as well as reflection, realization, and evaluation of the task. In accordance with the self-determination theorists Edward Deci and Richard Ryan, we assume that inner (intrinsic) motivation both initiates learning and development and opens up for liberation and expression of the human potential. In addition, inner motivation seems to be a gateway for social integration.

> Humans are active, growth-oriented organisms who are naturally inclined toward integration of their psychic elements into a unified sense of self and integration of themselves into larger social structures.
>
> *(Deci & Ryan 2000: 229)*

Through attentively observing the learning activity, the teacher can facilitate a change in the student from being detached and mentally absent to becoming a vigilant participant throughout the learning process. During the *introduction* phase, the teacher can invite the students to connect with each other and the execution phase by showing the purpose of the activity and application of necessary tools to perform the execution. Throughout *execution*, the teacher can apply strategies for supervision and guidance to prevent students from withdrawing. Likewise, through observing the students throughout their execution phase, the teacher's wise application of observations and the result can facilitate and engage the students' *reflection*, their later realization, and *evaluation*, either the student chooses to reject, continues, or improves the activity .

The teacher, coach, or instructor is the key facilitator and conductor of relation-based experiential learning. Although the students' core attributes are driving forces for their learning, the kindling and maintenance of these forces throughout learning processes presupposes a relation between the learner and their environment. Thus, students' exposure to or meetings with others and the environment can arouse, inspire, and activate their driving forces for learning, but, contrarily, in other situations, even impair, undermine, and impede the same driving forces.

Considering the characteristics of the core attributes, students' prerequisites for learning, content and composition of the learning activity, and situational conditions framing the execution of the activity, the teacher's role, and complex task, is to facilitate the students' learning. The facilitation requires the teacher's mastery of the execution of the learning activity, and, simultaneously, during all phases of the learning process, the attentive ability to observe different students and, on this basis, adjust, assist, support, and guide the students to promote their engagement, participation, reflection, and evaluation throughout the activity. The art of teaching is difficult to generalize due to

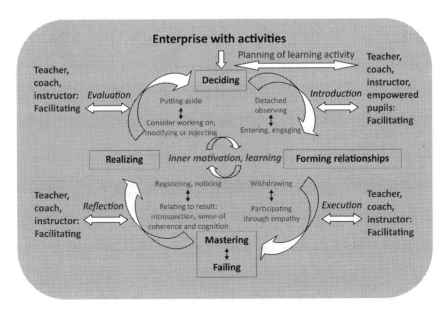

FIGURE 8.5 The teacher as the key in relationship–based experiential learning.

the requirement of situational awareness and contextual sensibility. Therefore, facilitation demands the ability to adjust teaching to the unpredictability that characterizes everyday situations and life in general (Biesta 2013, Sæverot 2013).

The core attributes continuously intertwine and interact in human consciousness and actions. Still, the significance and roles of each attribute differ in the four phases of the learning process. During the introduction phase, the teacher's facilitation of students' motivation to enter and join the learning activity is crucial. According to Antonovsky (1987), the experience of comprehensibility and manageability is a gateway for the choice of entering and joining an activity. Still, Antonovsky maintains that emotional meaningfulness is the major driving force or call for people to participate actively in any situation. This can occur when the student experiences that they have something to contribute or can be useful in doing the task. Our experience is that the feeling of contributing to a social community releases a strong drive for learning and opens for self-realization (Gjøtterud et al. 2015, Gjøtterud & Krogh 2017).

The better the quality of connections and relationships to the task, other actors, and teacher, the greater the chance will be that the student takes the challenge and engages themselves in the work at hand. The connecting, relationship-building human attribute is therefore in focus at the beginning of the learning process. Through forming relationships at the start, the students orient themselves even more towards fulfilling the task. Even though the comprehensibility and manageability of the task have a strong influence on entering the learning situation, meaningfulness is the most important factor for deciding to partake in the task.

The *execution phase* gives the student a chance to practice skills and use different qualities of the will. The act of doing a task primarily trains the attribute of intention (will). As one says, iron is hardened in the fire. Resistance experienced while doing the task can increase training of the will. The teacher may arrange the task to practice certain specific qualities of the will according to the nature of the task and the needs and qualifications of the student. Some students might have too rigid a focus and goal and need to train the capacity to find alternative solutions, while others need to focus on organizing or endurance to complete the task. The teacher can help the development of skills and willpower through observation, imitation, and identification with role models and other students as guiding assistants (Bandura 1986, Vygotsky 1962). With practical tasks, the teacher can facilitate step-by-step development of competency as described by Dreyfus and Dreyfus (1986). In doing tasks that encourage the use of several senses, the student can get a broader perspective and further develop their own sense perception (Clemetsen, Krogh & Thorèn 2011: 223).

It is important to facilitate room for reflection before reaching a conclusion. The motivation for thinking through and finding better solutions is stronger underway than when the result is reached. The execution phase of the task is crowned with success or failure, where failing can be just as valuable for learning as mastering the task if the failure does not threaten the student's self-respect. Failure also opens for a new and improved execution of the task.

Mastering the task helps to develop an expectation of mastering, an inner belief in one's own ability to act and reach a goal (Bandura 1986). The concept differs from the concept of coping (Lazarus & Folkman 1984) that refers to strategies for adjusting to and handling stress. Mastering the task leads to resonance in the student and opens for reflection on the achievement in at least three different ways. The first is that the execution, mastering, and experience of the result can strengthen the students' self-understanding and self-efficacy. The second lesson is what the task means for the whole undertaking at the farm or garden so that the student can see both the local and societal context and view the benefit of their contribution in a wider perspective. In addition, the personal and societal importance can trigger the student's curiosity and interest in understanding the principles and procedures behind the successful execution of the task, and perhaps even how ways of working are applicable and transferable to other tasks.

In the reflection phase, the teacher can facilitate the students' experience of coherence (Antonovsky 1987). Potentially, the first two phases in the learning process can lead to a feeling of meaningful participation and manageability. Thereafter, the experience of mastering might create transparency through the student's own development and experience of coherence. Learning occurs in the interaction between the inner motivation and meeting with a physical, social, and cultural world. The experience of coherence develops when the learners see the result in connection to what it can mean for others and the community. Seeing what one's own participation has contributed affects the student's self-understanding in relation to their surroundings. In this way, Antonovsky's concept of coherence expands the qualities of our earlier definition of learning.

Realization and reflection provide the students with the basis for evaluating what they will change, continue with, or reject concerning the task. In this way, realization and reflection are the foundation for choice and decisions. During the evaluation phase, it is important to stimulate the student's own reflections to prevent them from just rushing onto a new task. If the student chooses to continue or change the task and the way of doing it, the reflection will promote both remembering and eventual improvements. At the same time, reflection simplifies the conveyance of acquired knowledge and skills as instruction. Conveying to others often requires concepts and examples. Reflection is also important for the development of a deeper understanding and for implementing use of more curriculum-oriented learning. Risku-Norja and Korpela (2009) found that pupils often remember knowledge and skills from their execution of practical learning tasks better than knowledge from ordinary classroom teaching. In addition, the teachers' use of experiences with the farm/garden work later at school seemed to improve pupils' performance.

International research shows that learning tasks connected to relevant local activities strengthen the learning of school subjects and, in addition, result in wider recognition and understanding among students. A large research project in the United States, 'Closing the Achievement Gap' (Lieberman & Hoody 1998), concluded that local projects where the students themselves take the initiative to concrete practical measures under the direction of capable teachers/advisors resulted in a better learning environment, increased motivation for learning, and significantly better results in language, science, and math tests. Haubenhofer and colleagues (2008) documented achievement of learning goals and effects of learning on an organic farm in three cases in the Netherlands: 1) a one-day visit, 2) a week's stay on the farm, and 3) 20 participatory visits over the course of one year. The research showed a gradual and significant increase in learning achievement from the first to the third case. In addition, a survey of the parents concluded that the students in case 3 became driving forces in changing family practice at home towards a more sustainable way of living.

The four phases of the model: narratives, theory, and use

Before we discuss the model for relationship-based experiential learning in detail, teachers should consider some aspects in the planning phase:

- *Learning arenas*: our experience comes mostly from relatively small, diversified family farms as well as school gardens. On a small farm, the family, often several generations, are instructors and role models.
- *Societal relevance*: a working farm lives from its production. Learning tasks are thus immediately relevant as a part of the farm's production. In addition, cooking and preparing meals during the work periods also have obvious relevance. Where there is more specialization, cooperation with different farms can give a wider spectrum of relevant tasks.
- *Joint planning*: the teacher knows the students, as well as the themes that connect to tasks at the farm, but the farmer (or gardener) knows which tasks are necessary and possible. Joint planning can facilitate the matching of tasks to students and their special needs and to learning specific subjects. The aspects of connecting, exercising the will, and developing thinking and knowledge should be under consideration during the planning phase.
- *Investigation and initiative*: the learning tasks have potential as opportunities for finding solutions and taking independent initiatives. As one farmer says, 'We know they are engaged when the students start suggesting other ways of doing things'.

The first phase of learning: introduction

The students and the helpers on Solli farm stand in a circle in the barnyard. The farmer wishes them welcome to the farm as his dog makes the rounds, joyfully greeting each child with a lick and a wagging tail. The farmer asks them to tell a little about what they did the last time they were at the farm. He remarks about the good work that they did and what it meant for the farm. Then he brings them up to date about what has happened since. He also tells them about the tasks that require their help today. The students divide-up in groups and receive the tools they need as well as initial instructions. Before they go to their tasks, the farmer reminds them about when they meet for lunch and that they will return to the circle at the end of the day.

The farmer is a role model from the moment the students arrive at the farm. He is a clear leader and authority as he makes the rounds and greets each and everyone. No one is left out or forgotten. Reminding them of what they have achieved earlier inspires them to want to do their best. Their connection with the farm/garden is strengthened. The farmer's enthusiasm about the tasks is contagious, and the students become eager to choose from the palette of tasks for the day.

As a role model, the students observe the farmer/gardener, to begin with, and in doing the tasks. They will mimic their movements and ways of working. This is a path that Bandura (1986) described as a method for the acquisition of skills and knowledge. Bandura points out that the pupils do not just identify with the teacher's technical performance and instruction but also with the teacher as a person. Therefore, it is important that the instructor/teacher/farmer/gardener connects, inspires, and reflects on what they are doing together with the students.

Considerations for the first phase

- *A focus for gathering.* A place to gather, preferably in a circle and close to the working arenas.
- *Including.* Be sure that each pupil gets eye contact and even a handshake. Show interest and ask short questions as to anything special that can influence students' participation in the work tasks of the day. Bring in an animal or something else which can inspire them to caretaking.
- *Inspire.* There are many ways to inspire students at the start. Meaningfulness and context are important aspects.
  - o *Goal orientation.* The students can be inspired by a clear understanding of the purpose of the task and the results which are expected.
  - o *Show/describe.* Show examples of results from earlier tasks.
  - o *Usefulness.* Explain/illustrate the use of the results and process, both in relationship to skills and to product or service. Take practical function, insight, and esthetic value (for example in clearing an overgrown area) into consideration.
  - o *Mastery.* Show how students can acquire skills and knowledge by doing the task.
  - o *Process motivation.* There are many ways to motivate during the process with the tasks. Sometimes competition between groups can inspire. Problem-solving is both motivation and learning. Switching roles

in a group and trying different work techniques and organization is possible.

- *Instruct*
    - o *Clarity.* Short, concise description of the work process in different steps.
    - o *Tools.* Show and demonstrate important tools. If necessary, the students can try, observe again, and try once more.
    - o *Safety precautions.* Clear instruction as to safety.
    - o *Attention to roles.* What is the role of the teacher/instructor and the role of the students at different steps in the process?
    - o *Allotted time.* How long the work should continue, breaks, and enough time to sum up at the end. The time schedule should be clear before the work starts.

The second phase: execution of the task

One teenage girl in the group that was to cleave logs was very negative and began by saying, 'I have tried to cleave already, but I have never been able to do it'. The instructor assured her that this time she would succeed and proceeded to select the logs that were easiest to cleave. After a couple of tries, the girl cleaved first one log and then several more. 'I can do it!' she exclaimed.

In the second quarter of the model, the focus is on the execution of tasks. The students do the task with instruction and advice from the teacher/farmer. The connection to the tools, plants/animals, work process, and other workers continues to be developed. In order to achieve a result, the student needs the ability to endure and apply their will.

The girl in the story above demonstrates an attitude that many have from earlier experience. She did not believe she could master the task. However, when the task was prepared according to her level of skill and strength, she managed well. Vygotsky (1939/1962) emphasized that the human being has a potential for learning or a proximal development zone that stretches beyond what we can manage alone. Social cooperation through learning from others, for example, through instruction and guidance, might trigger and expand the pupil's proximal zone of development. Skilled teachers vary between instruction and following closely, but also keep a certain distance so that the one who is doing the task can participate actively and experience the acquirement of skills and mastery.

After many years of research, especially on a woman who had survived the concentration camps of the Holocaust, Antonovsky (1987) concluded, as we have described earlier, that comprehensibility, manageability, and meaningfulness are the basis for building good health and characteristics for good learning processes. The girl in the story understood why the logs needed to be cloven, but the task was not meaningful since she did not believe that she could handle it. When she could both understand and manage the task, it also became meaningful for her.

Many students are characterized by a stable and often very low degree of belief as to what they can learn in certain areas. The stable and poor mental attitude often connects to earlier failures, such as the girl had experienced with cleaving. Through experiences of mastering, students can change a stable mental attitude to an attitude of mental growth (Dweck 2012). The positive belief of one's capacity to grow and learn can open up further development of problem-solving skills.

> The students are going to sow seeds. The gardening teacher shows them with her fingers how they should press the soil around the seeds and how deep they should sow the seeds. Afterwards she holds her fingers over theirs so that they can feel how lightly they should press the soil. As she goes from the one to the other, she talks with them about how the seeds need protection, but also air, light and water to be able to germinate.

Schön (1983) discusses how the learning of practical skills can occur through reflection during the process. The pupil or learner must learn to feel how to put the right pressure on the soil when sowing seeds.. By creating room for a conversation during and around the sowing, the students can understand and learn the consequences and grounds for each step. Reflections can and should occur during the process of doing the task, especially reflections which naturally connect to the different steps in the process.

Considerations for the second phase

- *Starting, progressing, ending.* The teacher/farmer is the director for the process of doing the task. They should conduct an analysis and divide the process into clear steps. Step by step, the students complete the task under the direction of the instructor. When the students obtain skills in the process, they can take over the role of instructor themselves.
- *Transforming the steps of the task to steps in learning through stimulating senses and will.*
  o *The training of qualities of the will.* There will always be a connection to thought processes during the practical work, but here we want to emphasize the exertion of will. An analysis of qualities demanded of the participants at each stage of the task can show which aspects of will the pupil can exercise and train. Assagioli (1974) distinguishes between seven qualities of will. We have added flexibility as an eighth quality:
  o Strength (energy, dynamic power, intensity).
  o Regulation (mastery, control, discipline).
  o Directedness (concentration, goal orientation, attention).
  o Flexibility (uncertainty combined with problem-solving creativity).
  o Courage (initiative, fighting spirit, daring – also to be different).

- ○ Implementation (decisiveness, determination, resoluteness, promptness).
- ○ Toughness (persistence, endurance, patience).
- ○ Binding together (organization, integration, synthesis).
- ○ *Use of different senses and discerning through sense experience.*
  - ○ *Sound*: the messenger for depth of space, movement, rhythm, and occurrences. An underestimated sense, perhaps more important than sight.
  - ○ *Smell*: messenger for memories and feelings.
  - ○ *Sight*: messenger for an overview, gives a possibility for dividing up.
  - ○ *Touch*: messenger and establisher of connection, awakens feelings.
- *Learning- and process-oriented guidance*: vigilant flexibility throughout the process is necessary to be able to facilitate a continuous connection between execution and outer occurrences and the learning process among the pupils and individual learners. Use of the proximal development zone and cooperative learning, Antonovsky's three principles, and Schön's reflection during the process can be of help.

The third phase: obtaining the results

> The youths at an institution for child welfare who were learning to ride horses write down what they have done after each lesson on cards that the therapist collects and puts into a book for each pupil. Dennis had practiced equestrian vaulting on the horse for the second time and had some problems seeing anything new that he could write on the card for the day. What had he mastered today? 'I did exactly the same things as last time' he began with saying. Then he was quiet for a moment and smiled broadly as he commented that this time, he sat with his arms out in gallop, but the first time it was only in trot. 'And we were two on one horse', he concluded with an eager voice.

The experience of mastering creates a space for a resonance in the learner, which in turn opens up for reflection and afterthought in several areas, both in relation to the students' self-image and self-understanding. As in the story above, the resonance of mastering showed itself in bodily gestures, smiles, and exclamation. Mastery can also influence attitudes in relation to the development of knowledge and skills and being able to see the task in a societal context. In addition, the resonance created by doing the task can stimulate the students to express their own experience of mastery and evaluate their execution of the task (Bråthen & Gallese 2004). The words can contribute to anchoring the experience in the pupil. The youngsters in the example above also received a book in which their stories of mastery were collected. It documented the youths' own development and reinforced their mental attitude on growth potential (Dweck 2012).

However, mastery does not always need to be reflected in words. It can give a clear echo and be obvious without verbal formulation. How the teacher/instructor works with the student and their results depends on the goal and the way the pupil worked with the task.

Considerations for the third phase

- *Schedule time and plan the appropriate frame around the reflection on doing the task.* The task often takes so long that the teacher and students often omit reflection or do it very briefly. This can decrease the dividends that the students can reap from the experience.
- *Let the students sum up their experience!* The goal is that the students themselves formulate what has happened and come up with their own thoughts about the process and the result. The students can formulate their experiences in several ways, for example, by writing a log, telling each other, and sitting in groups to discuss. The teacher can help by drawing together their thoughts, which can create a clearer picture of the work.
- *Open up a diverse reflection.* Not only are knowledge and concrete results important, but also how the students' experience has affected their understanding and how they have changed through the process. This is important for further goals and new tasks (fourth phase).
- *Choose what to reflect on verbally and what you do not need to force into shared words.*

The fourth phase: going on or trying again

One of the youngsters in the junior high school class looked very tough. His earring, leather jacket and smart phone constantly outside of his pocket were signs that spoke a clear language. He had a side-kick, a yes-man who re-enforced the tough image. These two were assigned a job in the garden that spring morning, digging and planting a bed. There was more swearing than digging, but somehow, they completed the task, not meticulously, but enough to say they could choose another task to fill the time until lunch. Their vocabulary about the garden work gave no doubt as to their attitude. They would never ever be caught doing such a thing again. Off they went to the woods to collect some spring flowers for the table – part of a botany lesson on local plants. After each work session on this farm, the pupils receive grades according to a scale they created together with the farmer/teacher: 0 – not being where you are supposed to be, 1 – being there but doing nothing, 2 – being there, doing a little when the leader nags, 3 – being there, working alright with lots of pauses, 4 – being there, working continually together with the others, 5 – being there, working very well, cooperating with the others, 6 – working exceptionally well without supervision and taking responsibility.

When the turn came to these two boys, they got a 3 for the work in the garden. This was a higher grade level than what they usually achieved at school. After lunch, it was their turn to wash the dishes. To the great surprise of the instructor, they came rushing out of the house an hour before the workday was finished, went right to the garden and proclaimed that they wanted a new bed to dig! Now there was more digging than swearing.

Recognition and realization of the results of the preceding process are the foundation for the learners to consider and decide what they wish to do with what they have learned. The process, experience, and mastery of the task Facilitates an experience of *empowerment* to be able to go further as a participant, initiator, and eventually an instructor – or use the experience and knowledge to increase insight into different areas and do other tasks where the new insight can be used (see igure 8.5).

Although this is a spiral that hopefully propels the learner into further tasks and goals and can be seen as a long process, it is important for us to emphasize how powerfully this sort of experience can influence students in their own development and in acquiring skills and knowledge in the course of a short period of time. The small spirals can lead rapidly to large consequences. As in the teenagers in the story above, getting positive feedback, seeing concrete results, and knowing that you can do even better next time is sometimes like a centrifuge. They are propelled into further action. The teachers are often astonished to see how students who show no signs of initiative or will at school transform in front of their eyes into learners who are eager to contribute. Even such 'trivial' tasks as making waffles for the other workers can have a huge effect on the one who serves their own product and can see that what they have done is important for others.

Relationship-based experiential learning on farms: a summary

We hope that we have taken the reader on a journey where they might view learning in a different manner than is common in schools in most industrialized countries today. Our point of departure has not been in theory on learning but in the concrete experience and observation that we have done in farm-school projects, both in Norway and now in Tanzania. This experience has led us to reconsider how we learn, which in turn led to the question of what it is in each human being that learns, changes, connects, and creates.

What we have not discussed in this chapter is the importance of farm and garden work in relation to cultivating a caretaker role for nature in the coming generation. The largest environmental crisis might not be the climate, pollution, or desertification, but the fact that children and youth have extremely little contact and experience with nature. This has been a leading motivation behind the work between farms and schools in Norway from the beginning.

Through the contact with plants, animals, soil, and the people who produce our food, relationship-based experiential learning is not just a model for learning that engages the whole human being, but also a model for learning for sustainable development, empowerment, and self-efficacy that is necessary if we are to find solutions. Our research has shown that such learning makes a difference. Students who learn in this way are often inspired to engage actively in issues of sustainability; connected, intentionally motivated, and hopefully transcending the inadequate practices of our time.

Learning theories often avoid the question about what motivates people to desire and make a change. Relationship-based experiential learning recognizes human vitality and the enormous capacity for altruism and empathy and ventures to describe how these human attributes can be stimulated and cultivated in systematically adapted learning processes. Cautious, compassionate, and dedicated care for our natural resources can build a bridge between the potential strength of children and youth and concrete, meaningful tasks. This gives hope for the future.

Note

1 In 1859, Charles Darwin received a paper from the young researcher and biologist Alfred Russel Wallace, who had, based on relatively short fieldwork, developed a theory and concepts about evolutionary development similar to Darwin's own. This incident pushed Darwin to publish 'On the Origin of Species', based on long-lasting fieldwork and theoretical considerations for decades, together with Wallace's paper. Wallace, who up to his death was a highly reputed proponent of evolutionary biology, simultaneously was an active and open proponent of spirituality and one of the founders of the British Society for Psychical Research.

References

Amabile, T.M. 1982. Social psychology of creativity: A consensual assessment technique. *Journal of Personality and Social Psychology*, 43, pp.997–1013.
Antonovsky, A. 1987. *Unravelling the Mystery of Health: How People Manage Stress and Stay Well*. San Francisco: Jossey-Bass.
Assagioli, R. 1974. *The Act of Will*. New York: Penguin.
Bailey, L.H. 1903. *The Nature Study Idea: Being an Interpretation of the New School-Movement to Put the Child in Sympathy with Nature*. New York: Doubleday, Page & Co.
Bailey, L.H. 1905. *Outlook to Nature*. New York: Macmillan.
Bandura, A. 1986. *The Social Foundations of Thought and Action: A Social Cognitive Theory*. Engelwood Cliffs, NJ: Prentice-Hall.
Baumeister, R.F. & Tierney, J. 2012. *Willpower: Rediscovering the Greatest Human Strength*. New York: Penguin Press.
Bergson, H. 1889/1910. *Time and Free Will: An Essay on the Immediate Data of Consciousness*. London: George Allen and Unwin.

Bergson, H. 1946. *The Creative Mind: An Introduction to Metaphysics*. New York: Philosophical Library.

Biesta, G.J.J. 2013. *The Beautiful Risk of Education*. Boulder: Paradigm Publishers.

Bourdieu, P. 1977. *Outline of a Theory of Practice*. Cambridge, UK: Cambridge University Press.

Bråten, S. & Gallese, V. 2004. Stein Bråten and Vittorio Gallese on mirror neurons systems implications for social cognition and intersubjectivity. *Impuls*, 58 (3), pp.97–107.

Brühlmeier, A. 2010. *Head, Heart and Hand. Education in the Spirit of Pestalozzi*. Mcallen: Sophia Books.

Clemetsen, M., Krogh, E. & Thorèn, A.K.H. 2011. Landscape analysis in local planning processes in Norway. In Jones, M. & M. Stenseke (eds.) *The European Landscape Convention: Challenges of Participation*. London: Springer Landscape Series, pp. 219–237

Deci, E.L. 1975. *Intrinsic Motivation*. New York: Plenum.

Deci, E.L. & Ryan, R.M. 2000. The 'what' and 'why' of goal pursuits: Human needs and the self-determination of behavior. *Psychological Inquiry*, 11, pp.227–268.

Deci, E.L. & Ryan, R.M. 2012. Self-determination theory. In P.A.M. Van Lange, A.W. Kruglanski, & E.T. Higgins (eds.) *Handbook of Theories of Social Psychology: Vol. 1*. Thousand Oaks, CA: Sage, pp. 416–437.

Deci, E.L., Koestner, R. & Ryan, R.M. 1999. A meta-analytic review of experiments examining the effects of extrinsic rewards on intrinsic motivation. *Psychological Bulletin*, 125, pp.627–668.

Dewey, J. 1916. *Democracy and Education: An Introduction to the Philosophy of Education*. New York: Macmillan

Dewey, J. 1938. *Experience and Education*. New York: Collier Books.

Dreyfus, H. & Dreyfus, S. 1986. *Mind Over Machine: The Power of Human Intuition and Expertise in the Era of the Computer*. New York: Free Press.

Duhigg, C. 2014. *The Power of Habit: Why We Do What We Do in Life and Business*. New York: Random House.

Dweck, C.S. 2012. *Mindset: How You Can Fulfill Your Potential*. Constable and Robinson Limited. New York: Ballantine Books.

Ferrucci, P. 1990. *Inevitable Grace: Breakthroughs in the Lives of Great Men & Women: Guides to Your Self-Realization*. New York: Jeremy P. Tarcher/Perigee books, The Putnam Publishing Group.

Frankl, V. 1959. *Man's Search for Meaning*. London: Rider.

Gjøtterud, S., Krogh, E., Dyngeland, C., & Mwakasumba, N.S. 2015. Orphans as agents for change. *International Journal for Transformative Research,* 3(1), pp. 3–15.

Gjøtterud, S.M. & Krogh, E. 2017. The power of belonging. *International Journal for Transformative Research*, 4(1), pp. 8–17. 10.1515/ijtr-2017-0002

Grolnick, W. S., & Ryan, R. M. 1987. Autonomy in children's learning: An experimental and individual difference investigation. *Journal of Educational Psychology*, 52, pp. 508–517.

Haubenhofer, D., Hassink, J. & Kragt, I. 2008. Inventarisatie Jeugdboerderijen. Report 174 Planning Research Internationally. Wageningen: Wageningen University.

James, W. 1912. *Essays in Radical Empiricism*. New York: Longmans, Green and Company.

Jarvis, P. 2012. *Adult Education and Lifelong Learning: Theory and Practice*. London: Routledge.

Johnston, E. & Olson, L. 2015. *The Feeling Brain: The Biology and Psychology of Emotions*. New York: W. W. Norton & Company.

Kolb, D.A. 1984. *Experiential Learning: Experience as the Source of Learning and Development*. Englewood Cliffs, NJ: Prentice Hall.

Krogh, E. & Jolly, L. 2012. Relation-based experiential learning in practical outdoor tasks. In Wals, A.E.J. & Corcoran, P.B. (eds.) *Learning for Sustainability in Times of Accelerating Change.* Wageningen: Wageningen Academic Publishers, pp. 213–225.

Lazarus, R.S. & Folkman, S. 1984. *Stress, Appraisal and Coping.* New York: Springer.

Lieberman, G.A. & Hoody, L.L. 1998. *Closing the Achievement Gap. Using the Environment as an Integrated Context for Learning.* San Diego, CA: State Education and Education Roundtable.

McGraw, K.O. & McCullers, J.C. 1979. Evidence of a detrimental effect of extrinsic incentives on breaking a mental set. *Journal of Experimental Social Psychology*, 15, pp.285–294.

Merleau-Ponty, M. 1945/1962. *Phenomenology of Perception: An Introduction. [Original title: Phénoménologie de la perception, 1945].* New York: Humanities Press.

Miettinen, R. 2000. The concept of experiential learning and John Dewey's theory of reflective thought and action. *International Journal of Lifelong Education*, 19(1), pp. 54–72.

Piaget, J. 1952. *The Origins of Intelligence in Children.* New York: W.W. Norton and Company.

Risku-Norja, H. & Korpela, E. 2009. School goes to the farm: Conceptualisation of rural-based sustainability education. In Çakmakcki, G. & Taşar, M.F. (eds.) *Contemporary Science Education Research: Scientific Literacy and Social Aspects of Science.* Istanbul: ESERA, pp. 175–184.

Rizzolatti, G. & Sinigaglia, C. 2008. *Mirrors in the Brain. How our Minds Share Actions and Emotions.* New York: Oxford University Press.

Scharmer, O. 2018. *The Essentials of Theory U: Core Principles and Applications.* San Francisco, CA: Berrett-Koehler Publishers.

Schön, D. 1983. *The Reflective Practitioner. How Professionals Think in Action.* London: Temple Smith.

Steiner, R. 1907/1996. *The Education of the Child and Early Lectures on Education.* Hudson, NY: Anthroposophic Press.

Sæverot, H. 2013. *Indirect Pedagogy: Some Lessons in Existential Education.* Boston & Rotterdam: Sense Publishers.

Vygotsky, L.S. 1934/1962. *Thought and Language.* Cambridge MA: MIT Press.

9

USING THE OUTDOORS TO ENHANCE LEARNING EXPERIENCES AT SECONDARY SCHOOL

Donna Ashlee and Robyn Fuller

Introduction

'Outdoor learning' is a term that has been interpreted in many ways and has seen a shift from the more supervisory role of a teacher of children who is playing in an unorganized manner outdoors to a more recently established ideology that outdoor learning is structured; aiming to contextualize a student's learning through outdoor experiences (Williams and Scott, 2019). It has also been viewed differently between primary and secondary education, with primary education taking a leading role in establishing outdoor learning into their curriculum (Williams and Scott, 2019; Harvey et al., 2020); agreeing with the evidence that suggests structure, careful planning, and regularity of activities within the environment are key aspects to developing successful outdoor learning experiences. This has led to Brockhill Park Performing Arts College's implementation of the Rural Dimension style learning strategies within the school. Not only is there a need to understand that careful planning is required but also that outdoor learning sessions deserve the same application and attention to planning as traditional indoor learning. Attention also needs to be paid by teachers to understand and observe the benefits it can bring by being outside (Williams and Scott, 2019). Findings by Williams and Scott (2019) during their research included a common trend that outdoor learning improved behavior in terms of confidence, resilience, and engagement, which is in line with the findings of the Natural Connections Demonstration Project (2016). Both projects and others alike continue to further cement Brockhill's belief in outdoor learning (Williams and Scott, 2019; Waite et al., 2016) for many benefits to both learner and teacher.

Never has it been so important to engage young people with the countryside. Our work with Linking Environment and Farming Education (LEAF Education, 2018) on teenager engagement highlights this. While most teenagers surveyed

DOI: 10.4324/9781003176558-9

agreed that young people should be more interested in how food is produced, overall, it appears that they have a very limited view of what food production and farming specifically involve.

This chapter explores how we attempt to combat the contemporary challenge of how teenagers understand where food comes from, food security, and sustainability. We do this through our ethos of outdoor learning, the full integration of the whole school curriculum with the school farm, and have developed and delivered our very own practically applied level 1 and 2 accredited courses, the 'Great Outdoors' in which all year 7 and 8 students participate.

This chapter is written collaboratively by two colleagues from Brockhill Park Performing Arts College in Kent, UK: Donna Ashlee and Robyn Fuller. The Farm Team is headed by Donna and Robyn but supported by two other teaching colleagues and a small team of Site Staff who look after the livestock's feeding throughout the school holidays. A wider teaching team delivers the Great Outdoors curriculum.

Both colleagues have been extensively involved in the development of the school farm and its use within the school as well as outreach programs within the community. Both are also Teacher Leaders of the school's large Young Farmers' Club.

The following chapter brings together Brockhill Park Performing Arts College's outdoor learning strategies as a case study to demonstrate how these can be applied to engage students and become an integral part of the school ethos and culture. A large amount is related to the on-site school farm, but many projects do not require vast amounts of outdoor space but simply access to the outdoors.

Brockhill Park Performing Arts College's farm as a case study for outdoor learning

Brockhill Park Performing Arts College is a large Academy secondary school situated above the historic town of Hythe, Kent, overlooking the English Channel. It is home to one of the largest school farms in the UK, stocked with native and continental cattle, commercial sheep, rare breed pigs, free-range hens, and a variety of small animals. It is also equipped with a walled garden, glasshouses, and a farm shop.

The farm sits adjacent to the school's Mansion building, built in 1611, and is likely to have been linked to Saltwood Castle to provide meat and wood in Norman times. More recently, the Tourney family held the estate seat, and eventually, the Brockhill house and land were purchased in 1949 by Kent County Council for use as a school. Brockhill is a mixed comprehensive school for students between the ages of 11–18 with a roll of 1400 students, including a Sixth Form. The school is a specialist in Performing Arts and has a Rural Dimension. The school sits in the Folkestone and Hythe district of Kent, and the school population is predominantly White British. The area's demographic is above the national average for free school meals[1], special educational needs,[2,] and the Index

PICTURE 9.1   The traditional-style farmyard at Brockhill built in the 1960s.

of Multiple Deprivation[3] (Kent County Council, 2020). Brockhill is a coastal school.

The Farm Team at Brockhill is passionate about the need to engage young people with the countryside and is uniquely placed to do so. We became frustrated that much work has been focused on embedding the teaching of where food comes from into the Primary curriculum in the UK but, until more recently, the Secondary sector had been substantially overlooked. Brockhill students are extremely fortunate to enjoy extensive outdoor space and the on-site farm, but the Farm Team also wanted to enable students who are not lucky enough to have this provision at their own primary or secondary school to enjoy and learn from Brockhill's facilities.

Having the opportunity to reflect upon the process that Brockhill went through to integrate the whole school's curriculum fully with the school farm has provided valuable insights into the journey and contemporary challenge of engaging teenagers with understanding where food comes from, food security, and environmental sustainability.

Brockhill's Farm is on the school site and easily accessible to students, being open before and after school, at break time, and lunchtime for students. One classroom overlooks the traditional farmyard, and another is upstairs in the main farm building itself. The farm is a working farm with beef, pork, and lamb supplying the school's canteen and its own Farm Shop .

The farm has always been a valuable part of Brockhill student life, but real change has occurred over the past 20 years in developing the Farm Fortnight, the Great Outdoors course, and Farming School. Changes in the National Curriculum and government policy have not emphasized rural studies, but the school has had the foresight to see beyond short-term change and formulated a plan based around the whole school ethos of 'Shaping the Future through Creative Learning'. Integral to this is the support from the Senior Leadership Team and their commitment to the farm's longevity. Brockhill has a positive culture of risk-taking and flexibility within school life and a school curriculum that has allowed staff to create their own outdoor framework. The financial undertaking alone takes planning and commitment, and, as a result, the staff are careful to ensure that both animal welfare and curriculum needs are met.

Back in 2009, the school farm was not being utilized by teaching staff across the whole school curriculum, despite there being a successful Young Farmers' Club with a track record of successful livestock showing and breeding its own high-quality beef cattle. The farm appeared quite insular, reaching only a fraction of students, and only delivering one subject. This situation was not a financially sustainable model, which had to change, and a 'use it or lose it' approach was quickly adopted and a strategy put forward. A team was developed to build on the vision of the Senior Leadership to rejuvenate interest across the whole school staff. The change was instigated initially by a survey carried out into

PICTURE 9.2   The site of Brockhill Park Performing Arts College's farm. Key to Picture 9.2: A Farm classroom. B Main farm building housing farrowing pens, fattening pens, grooming room, feed store, and Sixth Form classroom. C Outdoor pig pen. D Rabbit and guinea pig enclosures. E Cattle barns. F Lambing barn. G Outdoor pig enclosure. H Backfield for grazing. I Walled garden and glasshouses. J Farm Shop. K Lean-to cattle pen. L GO bulb growing area. M GO flower corridor area. N GO tree planting zone.

the school farm usage, which found that, due to staff changes and curriculum pressure, most teachers were no longer using the farm as a teaching resource. Interestingly, but sadly, some staff were unaware of the available facilities or how to utilize them to complement their lessons.

New strategies implemented

The action group delivered a new strategy that teaching staff from across the curriculum embraced. This strategy can also be used in settings with a more limited outdoor space and farming provision, in which most actions are easily adaptable. The actions taken include 1. Farm Fortnight, 2. Farming School, 3. Great Outdoors (GO) course, 4. Young Farmers' Club, 5. Outdoor Teacher Training, and 6. Collaboration with like-minded organizations.

1. The instigation of Farm Fortnight

To ensure that every curriculum area used the on-site farm's services, Farm Fortnight was launched and has run for over ten years. The concept is that every curriculum area teaches at least one lesson using the school farm as a stimulus. The Farm Team makes sure that the Fortnight coincides with seasonal interest, and lambing time is the most popular. Lessons have included Mathematics trails that study feed quantities and stocking density; Art students draw animals from life; Drama students use the setting as a location for a play; Dance develops choreography within the setting; and Design Technology students design and make products such as bird feeders. It was important to get staff on board and positive about the project from the outset, and we were conscious that it was there to add value to their teaching rather than simply be another thing added to an already long to-do list! Farm Fortnight was launched during a staff-training session, and we were upbeat, positive, and excited about engaging fellow professionals. Students helped with tours of the farm, and many staff remarked on how confident, articulate, and passionate the students were. This allowed easy demonstration of the farm as a vehicle for change.

At first, staff needed assistance to plan and deliver sessions but quickly became more confident. Most curriculum areas wrote the lessons into schemes of work which helped to embed the rural dimension within Brockhill further. Farm Fortnight probably does not need to run anymore, but it is a positive way of welcoming new staff, and often Subject Leaders pass on opportunities to younger or new staff to get them to experience and think about the outdoors within a supportive framework.

2. The beginning of Farming School

Brockhill's Farm has always welcomed feeder primary schools to visit the farm and for pupils to gain some hands-on experience with animals. However, this was limited to a basic farm tour which, although enjoyable for the pupils, was somewhat limited educationally. In 2011 thoughts turned to what more we could do with such a wonderful facility. Indeed, the school farm, in addition to its intrinsic educational value, is a unique selling point for the Academy. Also, we were very aware that schools were beginning to run themselves much more like businesses in this neoliberal climate. Therefore, encouraging positive visits from feeder primaries was increasingly important to safeguard the future secondary school role. Local research was completed, and contact was made with feeder primary schools about what would encourage them to visit us. The key result was specific links to their curriculum, which made complete sense. The experience alone was out of this world for some children who had never stepped foot on a farm or even seen a cow, but to reinforce their learning, using these animals appeared to be the next logical step. On-going conversations enabled the development of six differentiated curriculum sessions, which could be rolled out to primary schools, aiming at different key stages and yearly topics.

Ensuring that the sessions were well resourced was necessary for the pupil experience to be high quality; grants were applied for the Farming School and the space was successfully furnished. Most grants came from within the local community as people could see the value of our aims, which gave us growing confidence in our venture.

After testing out sessions with a local primary school, Farming School was launched in 2012 and offered six different sessions to Key Stage 1 (KS1)[4] and Key Stage 2 (KS2)[5]. The different sessions included:

- **Moo and Make**: investigates variation and species of farm animals and how they have adapted for survival. This is aimed at Key Stage 1 and is an excellent introduction to our school farm. An animal mask-making activity allows pupils to focus upon animal characteristics and serves as a take-home reminder of the day .
- **Farmyard Finding**: discusses variation between and within species, along with the animal's development over time; this is also aimed at KS1.
- **Chicken Run**: considers materials and their thermal properties and how we use these to house our animals at Brockhill Farm; this is aimed at KS1 and KS2. The pupils thoroughly enjoy hunting for our free-range chicken eggs and meeting our hens.
- **Happy Habitats**: delivery gives pupils an understanding of healthy green spaces by having tours of the farm and fields, allowing discussions about CO_2 and O_2 exchange, then undertaking a science-based experiment. Finally, the health of small animals is checked, and other influences on happy living for domesticated animals are considered; this is aimed at KS2.
- **Farm to Fork** is our most popular session, which looks at animal uses, primary and secondary products, food groups, supporting British farmers, and sustainability. Following the interactive farm tour, the pupils embed the knowledge in the classroom. A butter-making challenge makes for an

PICTURE 9.3   Proud pupils thoroughly enjoying the Moo and Make farming school session.

exciting group task to end with and serves as a tangible reminder of the session.

- **A Journey of a Jumper** develops an understanding of the farming year, seasons, and their effects on farming; how we benefit from the seasons as we follow the journey from breeding sheep to a finished jumper. The popular wool dyeing and weaving activity results in a wall-hanging created by the pupils, which they take back to their own classroom.

All these topics involve outdoor time with the animals and collaborative learning activities indoors or outdoors, which embed and then extend the previous learning.

Since developing Farming School, visits have been regular with lots of repeat sessions, a small sum per pupil is charged to cover costs essentially, but this has also enabled the funding of future projects such as the development of our own course for Key Stage 3 (KS3)[6] students. Visiting teachers have evaluated sessions to ensure the sessions stay relevant. The large number of pupils who have never been to a farm before is shocking, as are the numbers who have a limited understanding of where food comes from or have only ever seen some farm animals in a book – Farming School hopes to redress the balance.

3. **Great Outdoors (GO) course**

Ernst and Monroe undertook a study, and later, Dillon concluded that there are significant benefits to outdoor learning, not only for wellbeing but also for understanding (Ernst and Monroe, 2004; Dillon, 2006). Although this may be contested by others such as Daniel Willingham, who feels that learning with exciting stimulus may detract from the actual acquisition of knowledge (Willingham, 2009), Brockhill senior leaders and teachers routinely testify to the benefits in Brockhill students, whether it be emotional, behavioral, or a feeling of achievement. We cannot lay claim to academic enhancement having taken place solely due to outdoor learning, but we do believe that everyone's interpretation of success is different, and achievement is on a sliding scale.

The Great Outdoors (GO) course has been written by Brockhill staff as an enrichment course for all Key Stage 3 students. The aim of this course is to teach the core values of where food comes from, food security issues, and environmental sustainability. Today every student in year 7 and year 8 has one timetabled lesson of GO per week. This is a real investment of time and resources into our school farm and is an integral part of tying our school farm into the whole school curriculum.

Teaching of GO encourages the use of outdoor spaces and alternative activities to provide novel stimuli to aid a student's work across the school as well as igniting their passion for learning. GO encourages students to learn through revolutionary methods, which remove them from the traditional book and teacher-led learning styles by encouraging a hands-on practical aspect. It aids the learning of students who may achieve through these different learning methods and has helped to engage students not only in GO but across the curriculum. GO has been developed in line with the Ofsted manifesto on outdoor learning, which discusses the need to inspire students through simple yet engaging and preferably outdoor learning opportunities. By addressing issues around repetitive, 'safe', and old-fashioned classroom-based activities and aiming to provide a range of different topics which are both current and important in today's economy, the staff at Brockhill feel that every student should be supported in their journey towards achievement. In 2017, the Natural Connections Demonstration Project's findings further cemented our ideology around outdoor learning by concluding that such learning events had a positive effect on students' wellbeing and, in turn, their academic progress. Not only did they have a positive impact on the students but also on the teachers who benefited from delivering outdoors as well.

A favorite GO topic is Chicken Run. This topic examines food security and the production of eggs through different production systems. Students explore Brockhill's free-range system, complete chicken health checks and accommodation evaluations linked to the Five Freedoms of welfare. The course ends with developing omelet recipes and every student cooking an omelet using Brockhill's own eggs. Some students have not tasted an omelet before, and it is positive to see how they embrace this, and many continue this at home, showing this via their homework projects or have keenly reported back independently what they have been doing. The effect of students encouraging parents to make simple changes to food at home can be very powerful.

The topic focusing on creating a Bug Hotel is always well received; habitats are examined, insects are classified, and a Bug Hunt is completed! The Bug Hotel is designed and evaluated before being created for real.

Students also enjoy the other food-production-focused units. The burger-making unit examines different methods of beef production internationally before focusing upon our own semi-intensive system. We investigate different breeds of cattle, traceability, and slaughter. We do not shy away from significant and controversial topics; we teach the facts. The topic ends with creating our own burger recipes by the students using our very own beef mince produced on our school farm. The unit end is celebrated with a barbecue.

PICTURE 9.4   One of the students is proudly showing off the class creation.

Like Farming School, GO needed resourcing well, and we were fortunate to receive funding for equipment to help maintain our chickens, allowing the delivery of topics about food provenance and cooking skills, a 'smoothie bike' to encourage students to consider healthy eating, and donations of trees for planting projects.

GO is taught by a wide range of teaching staff, and while it is essential to keep the team tight, it is also important to include staff from a range of subject areas as this brings different qualities to the team and the teaching. This further embeds cross-curricular links, which also embellish creative learning. Currently, staff from Science, Geography, Mathematics, English, Drama, and Information Technology curricula deliver the course.

During the Farming School development, it was crucial to reassure outside educators that we were qualified to deliver farm visits. To facilitate as many Farming School visits as possible, some of our support staff run some sessions with our Sixth Form students assisting. It was, therefore, necessary to become a CEVAS (Countryside Educational Visits Accreditation Scheme) accredited school farm with CEVAS accredited staff. Undertaking the training was inspiring and gave us further ideas for developing GO into an accredited course in itself. Students were enjoying the course so much and were feeling immense pride in achieving in ways that were outside the norm of what was expected in school that we wanted to reward this. We set about researching the CEVAS course and how it was structured to see if the principles could be applied to GO. In 2015, we became accredited with OCN Credit for Learning after creating our own bespoke course, and in 2016, we celebrated the first achievers in our level 1 course.

It was a huge success, with students showing an increased engagement and desire to achieve the certificate, and so we began holding awards ceremonies for those students, the first of which was held on Open Farm Sunday in 2016 with awards presented by the Mayor. We feel that it is vital to celebrate students' achievements, and this gives us an opportunity to showcase our work to the broader community, thank funders, and extend our passion for where food comes from to our students' families.

Following this, we were determined to emphasize learning outside the classroom and alternative ways for our students to feel successful; and GO was accredited to not just level 1 but now level 2. Since 2016 we have had over 200 students achieve awards in our Great Outdoors accredited course, something of which we are incredibly proud. GO is an ever-evolving course within our school and the main aim is to engage students with their world, environment, farming, and where food comes from. A yearly strategy team comes together to plan, evaluate, and assess the topics' delivery. This strategy group activity continues throughout the year, and topics are edited and sometimes completely changed depending on current world issues. This supports students' understanding and engagement with current affairs, such as carbon emissions, climate change, food provenance, and supporting British farmers. GO strives to increase student's

Personal, Learning, and Thinking Skills (PLTS), including teamwork, communication, and research, through engaging in further aspects of curriculum topics such as climate change, food production, food security, and healthy eating. Currently, we run a topic looking specifically at the 'Wonder of Trees' where students are engaged in tree-planting projects to help offset the school-farm emissions and aid the effort to help reduce climate change. Students are required to consider feelings and emotions, learn about democracy, garden design, and planting. Students also learn about different aspects of farming (beef, pig, sheep, and chicken production) and consider how far farming has come in terms of animal welfare, and even consider the positives and negatives of veganism, meat farming, and the effects on the environment. At Brockhill, we feel it is a duty to educate students about the importance of balance in the world to ensure its longevity; and GO gives us the opportunity to do so. Thanks to the help and encouragement we have received, we are also able to deliver key concepts of the national curriculum focus such as literacy, numeracy, and oracy within the subject, meaning that important transferable skills are learned, and the students sometimes do not even realize the academic skills they are gaining, on top of the fun!

We are excited to be developing topics including the impact of bees, and we aim to create a bee and butterfly corridor running the length of our school site linking the local village with the neighboring Country Park. This is to be rolled out in 2021.

GO has enabled us to assess how aware of the environment our students really are. It is no longer shocking how little students know about where their food comes from; instead, we expect this and use our topics as a springboard. Activities encouraged are making a meal at home with ingredients that can only be bought from within ten miles of your house; some students really engage in this and, for instance, have taken trips with their family to the local mill to get flour. It is exciting for us to see how they develop and *want* to engage in their own learning about food, taking on board the environmental implications. This helps inform our discussions about food miles in class.

In 2019, we completed a student survey asking a range of questions to year 8 students who were finishing their Great Outdoors journey. The questions included: what do you like about GO? What skills have you learned? Do you enjoy GO? The responses were incredibly warming. Students felt they had developed social, personal, emotional, and democratic skills as well as empathy and responsibility. Some students even went as far as to say they enjoyed receiving their weekly homework as interesting topics. This confirms to us that our engagement in this area continues to be valid and a worthy cause.

We have found that the Great Outdoors course gives students who are less academically able to feel as though they are achieving in school. Students have volunteered to promote the course at parents' evening and have made promotional videos for sharing with others the benefits of GO as they feel it is imperative to the development and understanding of our world.

Following the development of GO, we have held seminars about outdoor learning in collaboration with FACE (Farming and Countryside Education now LEAF Education) and hosted visits from other schools to share good practices and how to use different spaces. We actively encourage schools to share resources and continue to be determined to help others deliver similar content and tailor the course to suit their own surroundings.

4. **Young Farmers' Club**

At Brockhill, we run a Young Farmers' Club, affiliated to the UK National Federation of Young Farmers' Clubs. This is a safe place for young people from our school to come together and learn more about the skills of animal husbandry. Members can prepare and train livestock to show in agricultural shows across the South East of England. We are regulars at the Kent County Show, where our students camp out for show week caring for our livestock and showing them over the three show days in a full program of events. It is a real accolade to be a member of the Show Team, where camaraderie is high. Members continue to build upon PLTS, particularly teamwork, organization, and communication, and for some, it is their first time away from home. The BBC television show *Countryfile* was interested in interviewing our team and showcasing our school farm in prime time. The Young Farmers' Club runs a small public event program for our local community to share our work. Public engagement with agriculture is needed now more than ever, particularly to stem the disconnect between young people and agriculture which is concerning. We participate in LEAF's popular Open Farm Sunday event, welcoming visitors onto our school farm annually. On the day, we run a schedule of talks which include our own students speaking of their experiences on our school farm.

5. **Outdoor teacher training**

It was clear that new staff are initially nervous about taking students out of the classroom and into a potentially dangerous workplace. Some have not visited a farm before, and others are concerned about behavior management outside the 'safe' environment indoors. We run our own training program to help staff overcome these fears and encourage the use of the outdoors, not just the farm, in their teaching. During the Covid-19 period, having an outdoor facility at school has become even more important, not only for mental health but also for ventilation and social distancing. It has been positive to see many more lessons being taken outside.

6. **Collaboration**

We are proud to work with LEAF (Linking Environment and Farming) Education. Having previously run seminars with FACE (Farming and Countryside Education), we understood the value and power of collaboration, and making changes with like-minded people and organizations often has a

PICTURE 9.5   Members of our Young Farmers' Club enjoy calf rearing and haltering training.

more significant impact. We took an integral role with the LEAF commissioned Teenager Research Project, supported by Rothamsted Research, which examined the relationship between teenagers and food and farming. This includes how the industry could work better with young people and encourage them to make more informed choices about where food comes from and, perhaps, even consider a career in an industry that previously has not always communicated well with young people. We have been concerned for some time with the apparent disconnect between young people, not knowing where food comes from.

One thousand teenagers were surveyed with key findings revealing a limited understanding of food production and a lack of information on careers in the sector. Two-thirds of those surveyed thought farming was just long hours and hard work, while only a quarter thought it rewarding. Unsurprisingly, most students surveyed believed farmers should consider the environment and that farming practices should be sustainable (LEAF, 2018). Our students' responses to the questions were strikingly different and pleasing to see given the work we do. Our role was to help analyze the research findings and facilitate focus groups at a 'Teenager Engagement Day' organized by LEAF Education and hosted by The Farm School in Harpenden, Hertfordshire. The event aimed to empower young people, enable them to have direct input into how the relationship between teenagers and the food and farming industry could be improved, as well as to develop five collaborative projects to make changes following the key research findings. Our Sixth Form students stepped up to the challenge and ran focus groups with other teenagers. We were delighted that HRH, the Countess of Wessex, joined the day and participated in the conversations with the students in her role as LEAF Hon. President.

Encouragingly, research findings found that one in five young people wanted to find out more about the sector, and to do so, they would turn to social media (LEAF, June 2018).

As a direct response, a national Farming Fortnight was developed as one of the five projects. This was established in June 2019. Farming Fortnight is now an annual national online campaign in the UK to encourage schools to participate in a wide range of national curriculum-linked farming topics with resources freely available for educators to download. Each day has its own hashtag developed by our school farm, and participants are encouraged to use these on social media channels. We filmed some of the video blogs that focus on the different topics, including a focus on farm to fork with our own beef production, free-range chickens, and lambing season at Brockhill. We are also members of the School Farms Network, which empowers staff from school farms all over the UK in sharing expertise and providing valuable professional development.

Emotional and social development of students

The school farm and Young Farmers' Club have become a lifeline for some of our students, particularly those who are unable to cope emotionally or socially and find it a haven to share interests and build bonds with other like-minded students. For example, Student A said, "before I began my Animal Management A-Level, I had no friends and was a bit of a loner, now I have a big group of friends and feel like I belong." Student B shared that the School Farm "gives me a feeling of ownership," others explained that "working with the chickens is calming when I often get stressed and, in my head," and our favorite quote, "I feel like I achieve when I work with the animals in GO and I'm learning responsibility, but I wouldn't feel like this in other subjects." For us, the teachers and staff who work in this area of our school, it is a privilege to facilitate these emotional and social developments and feelings of success. In 2020, while one member of staff was undertaking their Master's in education, a research question was asked, and a study carried out: does attending Cattle Club affect attendance? The project looked at a small group of students who chose to attend Cattle Club, and a comparison was made between Cattle Club day attendance and non-Cattle Club days. The results were very encouraging, and although the sample group was small, the research showed that particularly those more vulnerable students, for example, young carers, were 50% more likely to attend school on a Cattle Club day than a day they weren't having any interactions with animals. The results also provided two common themes throughout – these being 1. Happiness and 2. Social Inclusivity (Fuller, 2020). As shown by Finning and Kearny, a common belief is that school itself is not necessarily the initial cause for non-attendance, but home life and individual situations may also lead to attendance irregularities. These outside causes could include situations such as being a young carer (such as student A), in a low-income family, a child in care, or otherwise disadvantaged (Fuller, 2020). Therefore, Brockhill staff continue to try and make the farm feel like a family to allow students a sense of belonging, which they may or may not have in their personal lives. In the future, we would like to run a further research project on outdoor learning in general to see the potential impacts on a student's ability to learn.

A place of wellbeing

In 2008, the Labour government launched their Learning Outside the Classroom manifesto, which talked positively about the social and emotional benefits of outdoor learning, with the aim of this becoming a more proactive part across the curriculum. This followed positively on from the DfES's stated aim in 2003 to improve student prospects by tackling social skills development (DfES, 2003). This shows that the development of a school purpose to include wellbeing has been at the forefront of government discussion for a substantial period. When the Natural Connections Demonstration Project launched their specific project to assess the merit of outdoor learning on emotional and academic success, the findings endorsed our own beliefs. That outdoor learning made students and teachers have a feeling of success and development both emotionally and academically – 92% of students claimed to have improved health and wellbeing in addition to 93% having improved social skills. The next obvious stage was to engage with our nurture and counseling team to create a link for students and the farm animals to help aid their mental health development. This was welcomed by the team, and together we began building a nurturing area in the farm buildings. This involved welcoming and comfortable furniture, students using art to express feelings by creating a mural to decorate the area and providing lots of easy access to the small animals during their session times. Unfortunately, this project has still not come to fruition due to the Covid-19 pandemic and school's closure. However, since the pandemic, the need for this space has become more evident following reports of a sharp increase in demand for counseling sessions currently being provided for young people during lockdown (Weale, 2020).

Challenges we faced

The journey of embedding outdoor learning into the curriculum at Brockhill continues. Although we are well supported in our workplace, we have faced challenges. The constraints of time and funding being the two most obvious.

Teachers are notoriously time-poor; the pressures of the curriculum and managing our everyday teaching jobs alongside our commitment to outdoor learning have proved a juggling act at times. Having a trusted team was crucial to our success; we kept each other motivated when things got tough, challenged each other, and celebrated together.

Financial challenges are well documented in education; our school does not get extra funding because of the farm; therefore, financial management is vital to enable a special but expensive resource to run. Grant funding and fundraising are done in addition to the day-to-day workload. Once again, teamwork, building community contacts, and raising awareness of what the School Farm offers enable success.

We also found that collaborating with like-minded individuals and organizations is important; for example, the School Farms Network in the UK provides help and support, professional development, and perhaps the most important of all, networking. Being part of a supportive group of people whom you can call on for help and advice can help to feel less isolated and more supported with the school farm project.

Conclusion

In conclusion, promoting understanding of the world and encouraging students to embrace a relationship with it is a critical priority for educating young students. Brockhill's action plan grew from its simple beginnings in Farm Fortnight to include Farming School, the Great Outdoors course, and the collaborative work that has taken the educational experience to a national platform to champion outdoor learning. The key driver behind this has been a Farm Team that is truly passionate and the support from the Senior Leadership Team in providing financially for the school farm as well as investing professionally in the school's staff. This support has been crucial to the development of the school farm and is a starting point for others wishing to pursue a similar facility. Given the significant benefits of applying for the Great Outdoors course in a school farm, we believe that all schools, regardless of location and outdoor space, can and should be offering outdoor learning. We understand that not all schools have a satisfying area of outdoor space that others have, but with care, an adaptable plan, and GO units that can be cherry-picked, this will suit a range of school settings. Online opportunities are also available such as #FarmerTime, run by LEAF Education which pairs farmers and teachers together with farmers using technology to video call into classrooms regularly, something else that the Farm Team at Brockhill endorses and takes part in. In today's era of Covid-19, being outdoors has become even more important, and now is the time to ring the changes – we believe that all schools should be in the vanguard of this development. If we embrace the outdoors through learning, we know the benefits for students and the community, and our world could be incredible.

Glossary of terms

1. Free school meals are provided by the UK Government on an income-related benefits eligibility criterion. Eligibility differs slightly between England, Scotland, Wales, and Northern Ireland.

2. Special educational needs are a legal term used to describe learning problems or disabilities that make it harder for children to learn than most children their age.
3. The Multiple Deprivation Index is a measure of relative deprivation (essentially poverty) at a small-scale local level. Factors include: Income Deprivation, Employment Deprivation, Education, Skills, and Training Deprivation, Health Deprivation and Disability, Crime, Barriers to Housing and Services, and Living Environment Deprivation.
4. Key Stage 1 is Early Years Foundation Stage, ages 5–7 (years 1 and 2).
5. Key Stage 2 is Early Years Foundation Stage, ages 7–11 (years 3–6).
6. Key Stage 3 is the legal term given to the first three years of schooling in England and Wales, commonly known as years 7, 8, and 9. Brockhill runs a two-year KS3. The students are between 11 and 13 years old.

References

Department for Education, 2003. *Every Child Matters.* Norwich: The Stationary Office.

Dillon, J., Rickinson, M., Teamey, K., Morris, M., Choi, M.Y., Sanders, D. and Benefield, P., 2006. The value of outdoor learning: Evidence from research in the UK and elsewhere. *School Science Review*, 87(320), p.107.

Ernst, J. and Monroe, M., 2004. The effects of environment-based education on students' critical thinking skills and disposition toward critical thinking. *Environmental Education Research*, 10(4), pp.507–522.

Fuller, R., 2020. *Does Attending Cattle Club Affect Attendance?* Unpublished manuscript, 1 May 2020. Typescript

Harvey, D.J., Montgomery, L.N., Harvey, H., Hall, F., Gange, A.C. and Watling, D., 2020. Psychological benefits of a biodiversity-focussed outdoor learning program for primary school children. *Journal of Environmental Psychology*, 67, p.101381.

Kearney, C.A., 2008. School absenteeism and school refusal behavior in youth: A contemporary review. *Clinical Psychology Review*, 28(3), pp.451–471.

Kent County Council, 2020. *Facts and Figures.* https://www.kelsi.org.uk/__data/assets/pdf_file/0009/108738/Facts-and-Figures-Booklet-2020.pdf (Accessed 19 January 2021).

Linking Environment & Farming, 2018. *LEAF Teenage Years Engagement Survey Summary of Findings.* Warwickshire: LEAF, October 2018.

Ofsted, 2021. Learning outside the classroom, LOTC. *Microsoft Word.* lrningoutsdetheclssrm.doc (lotc.org.uk) Accessed 26 February 2021.

Waite, S., Passy, R., Gilchrist, M., Hunt, A. and Blackwell, I., 2016. *Natural Connections Demonstration Project, 2012–2016.* Final Report.

Weale, S., 2020. Sharp rise in number of calls to childline over coronavirus. *The Guardian.* https://www.theguardian.com/world/2020/mar/27/sharp-rise-in-number-of-calls-to-childline-over-coronavirus (Accessed 15 October 2020).

Williams, Ryan Thomas, and Carla Daniella Scott, 2019. The current state of outdoor learning in a U.K secondary setting: Exploring the benefits, drawbacks and recommendations. *ABC Journal of Advanced Research*, 8(2), pp.109–122. doi:10.18034/abcjar.v8i2.537.

Willingham, D.T., 2009. *Why Don't Students Like School?: A Cognitive Scientist Answers Questions about How the Mind Works and What It Means for the Classroom.* Hoboken, NJ: Wiley.

10

WORKING TOWARDS THE GARDEN

A case study of Middle East agricultural preservation, school farming, and alternative horticultural programs

Kholoud Jamal Moumani and Amani Jamal Momani

An overview of farm-to-school and alternative horticulture programs

In a modern world continuing its reach towards globalization, many regions have discovered a common concern in the growing health of its youth (Moss et al., 2013). This response is often seen with efforts in increasing physical activity using school and afterschool sports programs, nutritional health with govern-ment-funded balanced meal plans, and health education conducted throughout a student's life in public school. These programs are incredibly effective for the student and have been shown to provide a wide range of benefits to both students and their environment. Of the many programs that have been used to benefit the student, farm-to-school and alternative horticulture farming programs present a holistic approach that can benefit the students in both mind and body.

Its practice having been recently increased across the Middle East, farm-to-school programs seek to incorporate public schooling with the effort of local farms, the goal of practice in physical interaction with the production of healthy, natural foods, education in balanced nutrition, and application of healthy eating (Vallianatos et al., 2004). These farm-to-school programs take a wide variety of approaches in achieving these goals.

Some programs involve monthly outings to local farms to incorporate physical interaction with the production of healthy foods. During these outings, students are able to physically interact with foods in the environments through which those foods are produced. This offers a very kinesthetic approach to learning that is able to holistically involve the students (Joshi et al., 2008). Another approach to physically incorporating students is the use of farm-to-school programs in allowing students to also interact with the healthy foods in their daily lives. This is done by taking foods from local farms and including them in the meals offered

DOI: 10.4324/9781003176558-10

through school cafeterias. This encourages students to apply what they learned at the farms in a comfortable and familiar setting that will also likely follow them inside the household. This method is also effective in the sense that it connects what students learned in a foreign setting to their daily lives, which will provide them a foundational connection in applying what lessons in nutrition and physical fitness they are taught (Berlin et al., 2013).

It is also important to incorporate education in balanced nutrition both within and outside the traditional classroom environment. Farm-to-school programs plan to achieve this by classroom lecture plans that parallel the lessons taught by the programs' physical portions. These lessons in balanced nutrition offer students a correct model of healthy daily living that will comprise yet another part of their holistic education. This portion of farm-to-school programs has also been shown to add a local familiarity for students that encourages them to become more active in their community, which presents the potential for farm-to-school programs to increase the safety and wellbeing of their communities through the communal synergy the programs foster (Izumi et al., 2010). This portion continues the ability of farm-to-school programs to be 'very effective at enhancing academic performance, physical activity, language arts, and healthful eating habits' (Graham and Zidenberg-Cherr, 2005).

As farm-to-school programs continue their approach towards a complete holistic education, many make good-faith efforts in incorporating the actualized application of healthy eating (Botkins and Roe, 2018). This is the final piece in ensuring the student receives a holistic education, and it has been achieved in a diverse set of ways. An example of these methods is the inclusion of a cafeteria salad bar sourced by the farms visited and aided by the students. This is a fun method of encouraging students to actualize their education and apply their lessons and physical work for the community in the form of changing their diet in new and dynamic ways (Joshi et al., 2008).

Similar to farm-to-school programs, alternative horticultural programs have a goal to combine public schooling with the effort of local farms to encourage healthy practices for students. Both types of programs take a holistic approach to education, making sure to use the three main foundations of holistic farming education: practice in physical interaction with the production of healthy, natural foods, education in balanced nutrition, and the application of healthy eating. Alternative horticultural programs, however, take a more non-traditional and economical approach to the objective. These programs outline a very intentional goal to also economically benefit both the schools and farms that are participating. This is done in many ways throughout the world. These programs have also found a particular synergy with the Middle Eastern region (Bagdonis et al., 2009).

To briefly explain how alternative horticultural programs differ from farm-to-school programs, it is necessary to delineate the nuances for each type of program and how those nuances are seen in the application. While both carry the same goal of holistic education for students, alternative horticultural programs divide the focus more evenly between both students and local farms. This introduces an interesting parallel between farms and schools that offers a unique synergy between the two clients of the change. These farms are able to take advantage of the holistic education taking place and fasten their brand to be the perfect conduit for lesson application. Alternative horticultural programs ensure that this is the case (Allen and Guthman, 2006).

Another nuance that differentiates alternative horticultural programs from school-to-farm programs is its economic angle causing programs to take a non-traditional approach to education. This means alternative horticultural programs often take efforts similar to that of non-profit organizations and local businesses when approaching education. For example, many alternative horticultural programs involve sponsoring an event where students volunteer to host a market for selling local natural foods to the community. This allows the students to apply their education to a real-life situation while the local farm is given an opportunity to provide and sell its product.

In the following, the essay will review the effects and benefits of different programs oriented towards socially conscious agricultural efforts in the Middle East and how they can be adjusted to become farm-to-school alternative horticultural programs that have risen in the last decade throughout the Middle East. This qualitative study will then review a diverse set of programs in several regions of the Middle East that are already farm-to-school and alternative horticultural programs and touch on how they are improved to provide a more holistic education that encourages health and communal improvement and how their costs may be minimized. The research is designed to offer insight into how the following questions might be answered:

- Who should be responsible for covering all costs? Should parents be charged for healthy school meals?
- Should outside sponsors be part of this community program? Should such programs be tax-exempt to reduce costs?
- Should the government support local farmers and schools with low-income students and provide better accommodations, funds, or grants?

Thorough research and a correct diagramming of current farm-to-school and alternative horticultural programs across the Middle East will show the diverse set of benefits that are provided by such programs. No matter the community's demographics, these programs have created a community with an increased value on mind and body. These benefits should guide the future provision of important decisions involved with the standards of nutrition and nutrition education, physical education, health implementation, communal health, and the close relationship between the financial, physical, and mental health of a school's environment.

The following programs were selected by a number of criteria granting them validity in this research. Firstly, all programs qualify by region, as all directly impact the Middle Eastern region's farming economy and education practices. Secondly, all were deemed to be effective in the betterment of affected regions. Thirdly, the following programs were considered to be created as a result of their area of effect. This is to say, these programs uniquely adapted to the needs of their community and, in turn, aided the surrounding community positively.

Socially conscious programs oriented towards agriculture throughout the Middle East

The Ark of Taste foundation is an agriculturally oriented program dedicated to preserving foods and products that are at risk of disappearing within the next generation. The program takes a particular focus on African and Middle Eastern cultures, as environmental circumstances put many agricultural products of the two regions at risk. For the Middle East, some of these foods include the Begawi chickens of Egypt, the Midad olive oil of Jordan, the cedar honey of Lebanon, and the Noo'ah Loof of Palestine. The Ark of Taste fights to preserve these foods and will often communicate with governments, local communities, and community farms to achieve this goal. The socially conscious aspect of this foundation is clear: the preservation of culturally significant foods and produce will work to the benefit of local communities in a diverse set of ways (Ark of Taste, 2020).

This foundation could easily be reoriented to become an alternative horticultural program dedicated to the physical health and nutritional education of Middle Eastern youth. The preservation of culturally significant foods and produce creates a massive opportunity for education. These foods could be used as a conduit for education on how students are able to incorporate healthy eating into their lives. This would also help students learn how to practice healthy nutrition within their culture's foods, as the education given by Ark of Taste is focused on local cultural values and practices. The physical fitness aspect of these farm-to-school and alternative horticultural programs could also be easily inserted within the cultural education through simple sports and physical exercises that are taught in parallel to the subject of healthy nutrition. The application of healthy eating can be made through the common method of incorporating local foods into school cafeterias. The foods that are given a spotlight during lessons on nutrition can be featured for students in the meals offered by the cafeteria. For the alternative horticultural aspect of Ark of Taste, the foundation would be able to work towards the economic benefit of farms by offering to host organized events in which local farms are able to sell food to the community. These foods would be the same as those discussed in students' classes, and this will provide another environment in which students are able to apply the lessons they are taught.

Food Not Bombs is a protest organization with operating chapters in Jordan, Israel, Turkey, and Iran. The organization protests the amount of money spent by countries on war efforts and asks that money be dedicated instead to combating hunger and malnutrition both in local communities and around the world. Food Not Bombs hosts free events, offers reading material, and organizes protests that all advocate for the organization's cause. Recent events include hosting food drives to donate unneeded foods that will later be given to impoverished community members and local distributor-sponsored protests against hunger and malnutrition (Food Not Bombs, 2013). The socially conscious aspect of Food Not Bombs that can be utilized as a farm-to-school or alternative agricultural program is its use of food and local food distributors as a method to benefit each chapter's community.

The reorientation of the Food Not Bombs protest organization can occur in several ways. The best method made apparent by the organization's tradition of hosting events is creating an event-oriented specifically to a community's local youth. This event will be able to incorporate all the necessary aspects of farm-to-school alternative horticultural programs: advocation of physical fitness, nutritional education, application of healthy eating, and development for the economic development of local farms and schools. These events will likely be on school grounds or in local park areas, allowing students to have a significant amount of space to practice sports and exercise. The events organized by Food Not Bombs will also be able to create activities designed to encourage and educate on physical fitness for students. These same activities will also supplement the nutritional education component, which will be done mostly through in-school lessons before and after such events. At these events, local farms can be hosted to offer activities, lessons, and produce for students. This will allow students to fulfill the application of the education component of farm-to-school programming while also fulfilling the economic development for the local farm component of alternative horticultural programs. These events will all provide a complete and holistic education for students on the subjects of healthy nutrition and physical fitness.

The La Vie Café in Palestine takes a perspective of community enrichment in its goal to aid the agricultural standing of Ramallah. This café makes use of a personal urban garden that was created for both the use of the café and the local community. These fresh grown foods are a key part of La Vie Café and its role in the agricultural development of its community. Along with this, La Vie Café also hosts the work of local artists and provides a method through which local artists are able to sell their work. This is an aspect of the café that already speaks to the foundational component of alternative horticultural programs contributing to the economic development of the local community. The café also donates a portion of its proceeds to the effort of planting trees in Ramallah. With all of this, the café even regularly posts educational videos on the subject of nutrition and local produce to social media (Saleh, 2020).

If used as a place of education and activity, La Vie Café can easily be oriented to function to serve the same purposes of farm-to-school programs and alternative horticultural programs. This would best be done through regular events where the café hosts students and fosters physical fitness, nutritional education, the application of healthy eating, and participation within the community. It is possible for this to be done in a similar method to that of the Food Not Bombs organization. Activities will be created that are designed to encourage and educate on physical fitness and supplement the component of nutritional education. Similar to the urban garden of La Vie Café, other local farms can be hosted during these events that will also offer activities, lessons, and produce for students. Like with the Food Not Bombs events, this will fulfill the application of the education component of farm-to-school programming while also fulfilling the economic development for the local farm component of alternative horticultural programs.

Farm-to-school programs throughout the Middle East

The Food Heritage Foundation based in Lebanon is a program hosted by the American University of Beirut, and the foundation is dedicated to the cultural preservation of Lebanon's culinary traditions. The foundation consists of an incredibly wide range of events and objectives that are in support of this effort. These events include Souk aal Souk, a farmer's market that

> aims at promoting organic and healthy food of local farmers and small producers from different Lebanese areas. It intends to build and strengthen linkages between urban residents and rural producers by offering city residents access to healthy traditional food, and direct contact with the producers
>
> *(The Food Heritage Foundation, 2020)*

This market is one that encourages the participation of local youth in its activities, allowing for a place of participation and education where students can apply the nutritional health they are taught in the school environment. The foundation also hosts lessons on cooking regional foods that are very accessible to the local community.

Along with this, schools are often encouraged to take their students to the events hosted by the Food Heritage Foundation, such as Souk aal Souk, food tourism events, culinary lessons, and more (The Food Heritage Foundation, 2020). These programs all address the foundational components of farm-to-school alternative horticultural programs. They encourage physical fitness, educate students on healthy nutrition, offer students an environment in which they can apply their education in their daily lives, and provide local farms and schools opportunities for economic development.

The My Arabian Almanakh initiative provides a one-on-one opportunity for the student to learn and apply physical fitness, nutritional health, and how to benefit their community. The initiative has an online and physical presence that is accessible to be used by anybody in the Middle East, but it is designed specifically for Middle Eastern students to apply in their local schools and communities. My Arabian Almanakh initially began exclusively online, and the journal was dedicated to educating students on how to incorporate gardening into their daily lives for the benefit of themselves, their schools, and their communities. The journal is now also published as a complete guide for students to carry with them as they go about their daily lives (Laura 14Allias et al., 2017).

This journal presents many benefits, as it serves as a conduit for students to create themselves farm-to-school and alternative horticultural programs that will benefit their schools and communities. This is the best example of an application that can be offered to a student, as they would be the ones ensuring that all the components of these programs are addressed. The planning will also serve to address the components of physical activity and interaction with the community. The programs made with the My Arabian Almanakh journal all have the capacity to create excellent programs that will foster community excellence and ensure students and their communities all receive the full amount of benefits that are offered by farm-to-school and alternative horticultural programs.

Based in Kuwait, Re:Food focuses on creating and maintaining a network that redistributes food waste that is still fresh and edible. This organization differs from others in this review in a sense. Re:Food is an organization created by the youth of Kuwait. In the vein of the guidelines advocated by the My Arabian Almanakh journal, students have worked to create this farm-to-school program from the ground up. The program subsists on student volunteers who gather excess food products from local farms and distributors, re-package the items into healthy meals, and offer the new meals to the impoverished members of the local community (Aleisa, 2020).

Like the aforementioned farm-to-school and alternative horticultural programs, the methods in which Re:Food accomplishes its goal of benefiting the local community also fulfill the foundational components of such school-oriented programs. The act of students' volunteering addresses the need for exercising physical fitness, and this specific exercise will be in working towards the benefit of the community. The creation of nutritionally balanced meals will require the education of healthy nutritional eating for all volunteers. This will ensure all students are given an adequate background that they will be able to practice both in school and their daily lives at home. Volunteering at the Re:Food organization is also an excellent example of applying a student's education to real-life situations that directly benefit the community. The volunteering work done by students will also advocate for the economic development of schools and local farms as the work will sustain and enrich the community as a whole.

Mashjar Juthour is an organization dedicated to environmental activism. The Palestine-based organization consists primarily of a two-and-a-half acre park and arboretum that advocates for the country's natural preservation. The park resides in Thahr al Okda, on the outskirts of Ramallah, and has been enriched to become a home for 'traditional terraces and ancient olive trees surrounded by wild oaks, hawthorns, and more' (Juthour, 2015).

The park completes its role as a farm-to-school program by hosting volunteering and education events for the local youth both inside the park and within the local school system. Several different volunteering roles are able to be fulfilled by students. Many students assist in the planting of trees that further advocate for the enrichment of the park. Other volunteering opportunities for students involve the use of peer-to-peer education, a method of teaching that asks students to learn the material together and educate each other, hosting exercise programs for all ages within the park, creating lesson plans and activities for younger students to participate in, and more (Juthour, 2015).

The events and volunteering opportunities that are hosted by Mashjar Juthour all clearly and well address the foundation aspects of farm-to-school and alternative horticultural programs in the Middle East. The park provides a very natural and encouraging environment for the practice of physical fitness, and the programs and volunteering opportunities geared towards physical fitness that are offered only serve this purpose further. Educational events hosted both inside the park and inside local school systems fulfill the critical component of such programs to offer nutritional education, while the use of peer-to-peer education is a clever and effective way to ensure that such lessons are understood as best as possible and are maintained within the lives and communities of students targeted by the lessons. Offering an actualized and well-kept environment for students to apply their learning addresses the third component of farm-to-school and alternative horticultural programs. The use of a park also contributes to local economic development as the organization directly plays the role of agricultural maintenance and advocates for local enrichment of nature, economic development, education for students in physical fitness, nutrition, and the application of healthy living.

Alternative horticultural programs throughout the Middle East

With a unique economic perspective towards educating students and connecting local farming and produce to schools, the following alternative horticultural programs take a strong push towards effectively filling out the essential components of what makes these programs so beneficial towards their local communities. The Jordan-based Al Hima organization, for example, focuses on the economic development of local farms and increasing their connections within the community. The organization takes its name from the rangelands of Jordan and emphasizes the importance of land management and enrichment (Klos, 2018).

Regarding the education efforts of Al Hima, the organization has a key focus in raising awareness for local farms and the importance of their support. This focus is also the component through which the alternative horticultural program is enacted. These awareness efforts are often directed towards schools, where students are encouraged to participate in the local community and learn more about local farms and produce. This accomplishes all the goals of farm-to-school and alternative horticultural programs. Physical fitness and the application of learning are encouraged by increased participation in the community, nutritional education is achieved through students' communication with local farms, and the local farms are benefited economically through more robust connections with the community.

Cewas Middle East is a non-profit organization focused on improving the local community and economy of several regions throughout the Middle East by funding, educating, and hosting select programs designed to educate on the importance of sanitation and clean water. The mission statement lists four primary components to their goal: ecosystem development, entrepreneurship support, finance support, and knowledge and training (Cewas Middle East, 2020). These four components also parallel that of effective farm-to-school and alternative horticultural programs. The knowledge and training component is often directed towards local students, and these lessons all focus on physical fitness, balanced nutrition, and how students can apply what they have learned. The finance and entrepreneurship support component coincides perfectly with the unique aspect of alternative horticultural methods: economic development of local farms and schools. Finally, the emphasis on ecosystem development is a strong motivator for farms to connect with their local community and reap the benefits of a new population of educated students and families that now understand the importance of supporting local farms and eating local healthy products.

Results & discussion

Who should be responsible for covering all costs?

In the reviewed programs, we have seen independent, government, and community funding plans that are all able to adequately fund and sustain fully operational and beneficial farm-to-school and alternative horticultural programs. This means all funding methods are technically capable of being used to create a solid and effective program that involves students, schools, and local farms. However, this does not answer which method would be the best or most appropriate for most models. Considering it is crucial that such programs maintain a strong connection with both the public community and public schools, it would make sense that these projects should be government-funded. This will also ensure a productive synergy between organizations and programs with that of school staff and administration. Several examples were discussed in the review that would not best fit a government funding plan.

For example, the La Vie Café of Palestine works best as a privately and independently owned business supported by customers and, resultingly, the local community. There is also a beneficial synergy here, as advertising for other efforts towards creating farm-to-school and alternative horticultural programs in the Middle East will be able to apply with the work of independent profit-oriented businesses naturally.

Because of the diverse plans used effectively in the review, there does not seem to be a perfect answer to how such programs should be funded. All methods have been proven to be effective. However, there may be added benefits to federal funding to which other types of funding do not have a claim. Because these programs should ideally be oriented towards the local community and public schools, federal funding will be able to ensure programs keep schools and students' wellbeing in focus. Additional requirements could be set in place to regulate farm-to-school and alternative horticultural programs that other methods such as independent funding and crowdsourcing will be unable to create or enforce.

Should parents be charged for healthy school meals?

The question of whether or not parents should be charged for healthy school meals can be answered in the same manner that the previous question has been: federal funding will be able to adequately enforce such regulations on successful farm-to-school and alternative horticultural programs. Considering the principle that the communities most in need of such programs are communities with increased needs, it is crucial that the physical and nutritional health of students not be inhibited due to their families' financial situations. This presents an added obstacle to the creation of farm-to-school programs, and that obstacle's difficulty is worsened when considering it is necessary for alternative horticultural programs to also present an economic benefit for both participating schools and farms. Federal funding will be able to navigate these obstacles as best as possible. Independent funding will not be adequate, as this funding method is singularly profit-oriented, and paying for healthy school meals will be counterintuitive. Crowdsourcing is also unlikely because this type of funding is often very limited and unable to cover the costs of consistent and widespread costs such as providing all students with healthy school meals. The review of farm-to-school and alternative horticultural programs across the Middle East shows that parents should not be charged for healthy school meals, and the best way to achieve this is through federally funded farm-to-school programs.

Should outside sponsors be part of this community program?

The review has given many examples of outside sponsors that have presented incredible benefits to community programs. La Vie Café is an outside sponsor that has sponsored local education and community enrichment for the students and continues to do so. Another example of this is the Food Heritage Foundation, based in Lebanon. This foundation is an outside sponsor that has hosted incredible events that are effective in delivering all the components necessary for farm-to-school and alternative horticultural programs. The foundation's lessons on cooking traditional and accessible foods for the local community can be seen as an outside sponsorship to a farm-to-school program, but these lessons encourage physical fitness, teach balanced nutrition, and provide an opportunity to apply what is learned by students.

Should such programs be tax-exempt to reduce costs?

With the rapid increase in farm-to-school and alternative horticultural programs, many have asked if these programs should be tax-exempt so that the programs may be more cost-effective. As discussed, these programs all present massive advantages to local communities and, eventually, the regions those communities reside in. These programs should then be seen as a reasonable and responsible investment that should not be taxed. These federally funded programs are not profit-oriented, and they are instead dedicated to benefiting the community. This should earn these programs the same status as traditional non-profit organizations, meaning that they are tax-exempt so that they are able to better focus on and implement the essential components of farm-to-school and alternative horticultural programs.

Should the government support local farmers and schools with low-income students and provide better accommodations, funds, or grants?

Considering the principle that the support of local farms, public schools, and students are all foundational aspects of these programs, it is reasonable to ask that they are heavily supported by the government. The methods in which the government should support local farms, schools, and students have already been discussed in the answers to previous questions. The creation of federally funded farm-to-school and alternative horticultural programs that holistically benefit the student, local farms, and the local community is a substantial investment that should be made as soon as possible.

Conclusion

The modern world continues its reach towards globalization and, as a result, continues to notice common trends that occur on a global scale. One of these noticed issues is that of children's health. Many regions have made efforts to ensure that the good health of children is maintained. These efforts take the form of encouraging physical activity through school programming, the education of nutritional health in the traditional school environment, the offering of situations where lessons in physical fitness and nutritional health can be applied, and the development of local farms and communities. A comprehensive review of these efforts in the Middle East has shown that these efforts are incredibly positive for students, their families, communities, the Middle East, and the world as a whole.

The goal of farm-to-school programs to incorporate public schooling with the effort of local farms has been shown to be worthwhile. The opportunity for physical interaction with the production of healthy, natural foods, education in balanced nutrition, and the application of healthy eating are all incredibly beneficial to the student and become an integral motivating factor to the students' positive health, the betterment of the community, the economic development of local farms, and the preservation of local produce and culture. These are the diverse set of benefits provided by farm-to-school and alternative horticultural programs across the Middle East. This review presents that these programs substantially assist communities in having an increased value on mind and body. The answers that have been provided through the review of examples across of these programs across the Middle East should be followed to best ensure the success and effectiveness of these programs.

References

Aleisa, M., 2020. Re:food. [Online] Available at: https://www.refoodkuwait.org/jobs [Accessed 1st October 2020].

Allen, P. and Guthman, J., 2006. From "old school" to "farm-to-school": Neoliberalization from the ground up. Agriculture and Human Values, 23(4), pp.401–415.

Allias, L., Talathi, P., Coughlan, L. and Fernandez,C., 2017. My Arabian Almanakh: A Gardening Journal for Arabia. The Dreamwork Collective.

Ark of Taste, 2020. Ark of Taste. [Online] Available at: https://www.fondazioneslowfood.com/en/what-we-do/the-ark-of-taste/ [Accessed 1 October 2020].

Bagdonis, J.M., Hinrichs, C.C. and Schafft, K.A., 2009. The emergence and framing of farm-to-school initiatives: Civic engagement, health and local agriculture. Agriculture and Human Values, 26(1), pp.107–119.

Berlin, L., Norris, K., Kolodinsky, J. and Nelson, A., 2013. The role of social cognitive theory in farm-to-school-related activities: Implications for child nutrition. Journal of School Health, 83(8), pp.589–595.

Botkins, E.R. and Roe, B.E., 2018. Understanding participation in farm to school programs: Results integrating school and supply-side factors. Food Policy, 74, pp.126–137.

Cewas Middle East, 2020. Our Story. [Online] Available at: https://www.cewasmiddleeast.org/our-story [Accessed 1st October 2020].

Food Not Bombs, 2013. Groups in Africa & the Middle East. [Online] Available at: https://www.foodnotbombs.net/middle_east.html [Accessed 1st October 2020].

Graham, H. and Zidenberg-Cherr, S., 2005. California teachers perceive school gardens as an effective nutritional tool to promote healthful eating habits. Journal of the American Dietetic Association, 105(11), pp.1797–1800.

Izumi, B.T., Alaimo, K. and Hamm, M.W., 2010. Farm-to-school programs: Perspectives of school food service professionals. Journal of Nutrition Education and Behavior, 42(2), pp.83–91.

Joshi, A., Azuma, A.M. and Feenstra, G., 2008. Do farm-to-school programs make a difference? Findings and future research needs. Journal of Hunger & Environmental Nutrition, 3(2–3), pp.229–246.

Juthour, M., 2015. Our Story. [Online] Available at: http://juthour.org/About/ [Accessed 1st October 2020].

Klos, S., 2018. The Concept of Al Hima. [Online] Available at: http://wanainstitute.org/sites/default/files/fact_sheets/HIMA.pdf [Accessed 1st October 2020].

Moss, A., Smith, S., Null, D., Long Roth, S. and Tragoudas, U., 2013. Farm to school and nutrition education: Positively affecting elementary school-aged children's nutrition knowledge and consumption behavior. Childhood Obesity, 9(1), pp.51–56.

Saleh, M., 2020. Our Story. [Online] Available at: https://www.lavieramallah.com/our-story [Accessed 1st October 2020].

The Food Heritage Foundation, 2020. The Food Heritage Foundation. [Online] Available at: https://food-heritage.org/ [Accessed 1 October 2020].

Vallianatos, M., Gottlieb, R. and Haase, M.A., 2004. Farm-to-school: Strategies for urban health, combating sprawl, and establishing a community food systems approach. Journal of Planning Education and Research, 23(4), pp.414–423.

PART 4

Place-focused perspective

11

THE SCHOOL AS A POTENTIAL RESOURCE FOR THE TRANSFORMATION OF THE TERRITORY

Elisabetta Antonucci

Introduction

This chapter is set in a contemporary urban context, a setting witnessing the growing pressure put on its public sector by multiple contemporary social challenges. It analyzes the search for tools and intervention methods capable of adapting and relating to the setting's fragmented and variable reality.

In this framework, the study identifies a potential for transformation in the educational context, starting from the assumption that any change in the configuration of a city is also determined by the modification of cultural paradigms that define it and the development of cognitive tools and skills that make this modification possible (Castoriadis, 1990).

This potential for transformation comes from the interweaving of energies, actions, and relations inside the school and between the school and the community outside; it comes from the school being an educational community and being active in and penetrated by multiple spheres of society (urban, relational, socio-educational, cultural). This chapter looks at the school as a potential activator of the transformation of values and cultural attitudes and the dynamics underlying the territory's configuration that define the way resources and services are accessed.

In light of this, this study refers to an educational experience interweaving school and territory, started in 2015 at the Lido of Venice, and still continuing in the San Basilio area, see Figure 11.1.

This educational experience has been studied and actively supported through innovation in the shapes and spaces of learning. This was achieved by developing socio-educational practices that can interact with the territory by building spaces for collaboration, exchange, and sharing of intentions, thus starting a change in its spatial and relational assets.

DOI: 10.4324/9781003176558-11

Participant observation is an approach that requires the active presence of the researcher in an investigation. As a process of 'cultural immersion' built on the interaction between the observer and the subjects being observed (Semi, 2010), it has involved interaction between organizations and those managing studies, projects, and interventions, following from inside the transformation processes initiated.

In the context of participant observation, this study focuses on a process of recovery and preservation of depleted or underused green areas, a process where local schools acted as activators. This process was implemented through plans of study and intervention on the territory and nurtured new learning styles based on an active approach.

The process is observed along with its phases of evolution: from identifying and recovering the areas involved to creating a network of cultivated areas suitable for widespread urban agriculture and self-production. Throughout these phases, the school created new partnerships in the community, and to a certain extent, transformed it while bringing forth its trajectory of fieldwork research in innovative learning spaces and styles.

The plans of study and intervention have been observed to contribute towards protecting the territory against the logic of gentrification and progressive over-tourism in the city and as a resource for the emancipation/redemption from decisions given from above. These forms of resistance develop through the creation and dissemination of observation and analysis tools and the growth in the territory's knowledge.

As a whole, the process of recovery and preservation of green areas has been observed as a form of re-appropriation of the territory that we should defend it for the right to use and produce in the city (Sassen, 2008; Lefebvre, 1976). These multiply in the contemporary urban context and turn to urban space as a resource of opposition (Signorelli, 1996), a land of experimentation and transformation.

These are multifaceted, capillary realities that highlight the need for a more accessible and inclusive city, the need to regain a social and political space in which to express oneself, exercise choices, and act and initiate practices of change. In Venice, these realities can be identified in the diversity of committees, associations, and informal groups that move around different territorial issues searching for possible answers, using them as an opportunity to introduce new interpretations of the territory and ideas for change.

As a path towards the rediscovery and activation of the transformation potential of which the school is the bearer, the process of restoring green areas has constituted an ideal observation field of the conditions that make the activation possible, as well as of the effects of this change on the territory and styles of learning: the progressive shaping of an 'educating territory'. A territory where the places of residence, free time, and culture, including marginal and depleted urban areas, all become learning settings and educating spaces.

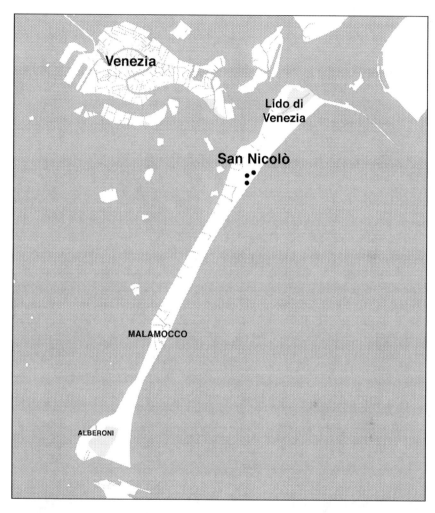

FIGURE 11.1   A map of the San Nicolò–Lido di Venezia area where the teaching experience was born and the San Basilio area where it has continued since 2017.

Territorial context

Venice represents an illustrative context concerning the diffusion and effects of the logic of gentrification and the emergence and multiplication of experiments to protect the right to the collective creation and use of the urban space.

In this sense, Venice appeared to be an ideal observation field regarding the complexity of the contemporary urban setting in which the school is located and of educational experimentation paths that, as in other territories, are taking shape. These experiments turn to the urban context as a place of learning as they

194 Elisabetta Antonucci

cross the boundaries between education and transformative intervention, the direct practice of change (Paba, 2003).

The experience to which this study refers takes shape initially in the Lido area and continues in a second phase in the San Basilio area. These two contexts experience unresolved issues and fragility linked to the problematic coexistence between the precarious balance of territory management and the pervasiveness of commercial opportunism's logic. In Venice, the latter is becoming increasingly evident in the escalation of the environmental risk, progressive erosion of historical and architectural heritage, public space, and opportunities for collective life and participation. The Lido of Venice is an island presently lamenting the lack of a comprehensive vision. It presents itself as an inorganic composition of landscapes inherited from an agricultural past, and depleted or underused areas awaiting redefinition. This is the case of the frame around which the didactic experiment in the object has taken shape.

The neighborhood of San Basilio, between the main railway station and the island of Giudecca, was, until the mid-20th century, one of the main manufacturing districts of the city, now converted for tourist, or, in some cases, academic purposes. Its social structure comprises three separate contexts (and uses of the city) that barely communicate: mostly elderly long-term residents, university students, and tourists. Like the rest of the city, it is experiencing a critical emergency in employment and housing opportunities, skyrocketing lease and real estate costs, and scarcity of services. Factors are driving an increasing exodus of the resident population. In recent years, in response to these challenges, variegated

PICTURE 11.1 Former hospital al Mare-Lido in Venice. One of the 33 buildings that were once wards and are now abandoned. Photo by Margherita Boccali.

geography of committees, informal groups, and collectives have emerged. They promote community activism in the city, trying to develop new intervention trajectories, looking at public and social spaces as a resource for change.

Between 2009 and 2012, Venice saw the occupation of a wing of Palazzo Tron, a historic building on the Grand Canal which was destined for alienation, as the seat of the faculty of urban planning. Its creation was to serve as a forum of associations for the reopening of the Arsenale[1] to citizens, as a committee for the protection of the island of Poveglia from its proposed alienation and privatization, and as a committee for the defense of Venice against the increasing risks posed by mega cruises. It is against this background of social and civic activism that, since 2015, the experiences of in-field learning innovation developed, conceived as an opportunity for learning, change, and action, on which this study will focus.

Origin of the teaching experience between school and territory

The didactic experience observed in the San Basilio area originates from the attempt to preserve and recover the vast abandoned area of the former Ospedale[2] al Mare on the Lido of Venice, a cultural heritage site now destined for tourist conversion. The attempt launched in 2011 by a committee of residents was based on a vision of 'urban voids' as a potential platform for the experimentation with styles of shared planning and management of the city. In this case, the depleted area also became a space of experimentation in didactic practices and learning-oriented styles towards in-field observation research work.

Beginning in 2014, the recovery promoting committee started involving schools of different levels in study plans focused around the area. The study plans looked at the area according to environmental, historical, and architectural points of view, as a way of activating the territory and as an opportunity to extend relationships and resources around the territory's protection and the definition of its possible future directions of use. From this perspective, the committee identified and proposed topics of analysis that could produce thought, frameworks of knowledge, and useful data to support the attempt to recover and enrich the wealth of reasoning and experiences. The committee has been a constant interlocutor along with the evolution of the study plans. It accompanied the students in the stages of discovery/knowledge of the area and subsequent re-processing of the recorded observations. In this way, it represented for schools the opportunity to present a wealth of knowledge about the area, the island, and the city, rooted in an active presence in the territory and deeply intertwined with the personal experiences and biographies of the people involved in the committee.

In the implementation of the study plans, teachers have used their wealth of experience and knowledge in playing the role of mediator between the context of regeneration and its language and the school context, adapting and integrating the plans to the structure, contents, and purposes of the institutional study curricula. This immersion in the context and the direct approach with an unre-solved territorial issue has placed the schools involved in a condition of active participation in a collective process, of co-responsibility in protecting an impor-tant part of the territory, and in the dissemination of frameworks of knowledge on it.

Under these conditions, the study plans have to a certain extent incorporated some characters of the collective efforts to protect the depleted area: the daily groundwork on the territory and the participated planning of the actions to be carried out, translating them into didactic practices and styles of experience-based learning. The learning processes initiated by the study plans took shape in this contingency of a situation, starting by determining the problems entailed, through the search for possible strategies and solutions, in a dimension of field-work, in which the teacher has taken on the role of guide and facilitator of an experience..

The abandoned area in itself, as part of a geography of marginal spaces, left to the dynamics of nature and spontaneous use, rich in experiences of plural mem-ory (Turpino, 2012, p. 212) and continuous transformation, has oriented schools towards a working style in which knowledge is not acquired by transmission but is deposited over the course of experience.

An example of this way of working comes from the process of drawing on pos-sible future uses of one of the 33 abandoned buildings that are part of the hospital complex, see Pictures 11.1, 11.2, and 11.3. The schools involved in the process went through a wide-ranging exploratory phase, in-field observation activities, and discussion with the resident committee members and their wealth of knowl-edge about the area. This was a phase in which the students immersed them-selves in the history, landscape, and architecture of the area and learned about the system of processes, factors, and inter-dependencies behind the origin of its abandonment. The combination of theoretical reflection and comparison with the knowledge produced in other parallel study plans[3] and fieldwork has shaped a multi-layered approach to the context in its three-dimensionality, with a primary focus on comprehension by life experience. Overall, the study plans were there-fore configured as spaces for experience-based analysis, reflection, and re-elabo-ration in the constant relationship of exchange between schools and the collective learning process generated in the community by the efforts to protect the al Mare hospital area. The knowledge arising from the realization of the study plans is action-based and oriented, and in this light, it has contributed to the protection of an area otherwise left alone and has kept attention on it even after the end of the recovery. This aim is pursued with the publication of documentation on its historical and environmental value, potential, and condition of abandonment.

Examples of this documentation include a short film about the landscape on the stretch of coastline in front of the disused health facility, research on the plant species that populate it, and publications of some of the study plans about the historical and landscape characteristics of the area. The experience of the Lido context formed the foundation from which the experience, still underway, in

PICTURE 11.2   The Marinoni theater inside the seaside hospital. It was a place where
medical conferences and performances were held for patients and staff.
Photo by Margherita Boccali.

the San Basilio area took shape, initiated by one of the schools, the Vendramin
Corner Institute, which was involved in the study plans around the abandoned
area. Since 2016, the institute has dealt with the classification of plant species that
populate the stretch of coast[4] in front of the former al Mare hospital, which until
the 1970s was dedicated to the treatment of bone diseases.

Itineraries between study and intervention, between school and territory in San Basilio

The progressive limitation of access to the disused area of the former Ospedale
al Mare, caused by the consolidation of the prospect of tourist conversion, led to
an abrupt ending of the recovery and preservation projects. The didactic experience started there continued in a different form in the San Basilio area, where the
Vendramin Corner institute is located.

Since 2017, the institute has promoted educational experimentation, developed from three study plans based on the experience shaped in the Lido context.

The study plans, in this case, concerning the San Basilio area, analyzed the area
from an environmental and social point of view, in line with the didactic direction
that characterizes the institute. They were conceived as an opportunity to acquire
tools for reading and to understand the territory, oriented to action/intervention
on the area, and more broadly concerning the environmental and social frailties

PICTURE 11.3   Itineraries of exploration and study in the building of the Marinoni theater. Photo by Elisabetta Antonucci.

affecting the city, an example being the pursuit of the activity of classification of plant species on the stretch of coast in front of the former hospital, Picture 11.1.

Specifically, the environmental study plans concerned the identification of depleted green areas adjacent to the school, their botanical classification, recovery, and preservation in order to facilitate their accessibility and the introduction and dissemination of urban agriculture practices, and the study and recovery of the lagoon's traditional agricultural plants that are being gradually replaced by intensive industrial production.

Over three years, they involved the students of the institute and the adjacent primary school. They were organized into survey trips in the area, interventions on the territory, and in-depth sessions at schools under the guidance of teachers, and the collaboration of experts and associations active around the city's environmental protection.

The study plans have been organized in their structures, contents, and timing by the shared planning of teachers and the community actors (organizations, informal groups) involved in the area, thus building the first field of collaboration between the school and the surrounding community.

As in the case of the Lido area, also in this context, the study plans were conceived in a form that could be continuously remodeled in their making, adaptable to the times and spaces to which they relate. They developed by combining the needs that emerged from the observation phase and the directions provided by the curricular programs. The plans took the shape of learning and training spaces and trajectories to act and experience a process of transformation of the area driven by premises that are an alternative to those of gentrification.

They have embodied this direction through 'proximity micro-actions' to recover the urban and social fabric, eroded by the processes of subordination of the community needs to mass tourism. With 'proximity micro-actions' we mean the activities of study exploration, recovery and preservation, and urban agriculture that are implemented. Practices have entered into relation with the territory by acting on a minimal level, as small impulses to build a progressively wider transformation scenario.

The first effect of those practices is observed in the area around the institute in the relations between initially non-communicating neighboring contexts and the definition of a core -community of interest around the care of the identified green areas. Today part of this process includes a primary school, retirement home, art high school, and vegetable garden for elderly people where a socially based regeneration project is underway, aiming to give life to spaces of inclusion for fragile people. Care practices have played a fundamental role in defining and extending this first nucleus as well as in building networks of relationships in which the most consolidated ties are an element of cohesion and facilitation for the intertwining of new connections (Uzzi, 1996). The recovered areas and the projects that are gradually defined around them, starting from the study plans, are also valuable resources to create a community of interest.

The primary school park adjacent to the Vendramin Corner Institute has become, first through the shared construction of a greenhouse with recycled materials and then through the launch of educational paths around the thematic axes of plants/sowing and nutrition, a device to involve teachers, parents, and students to enlarge the school community. In the garden, which is dedicated to elderly people, the occasions of joint work with the school classes and the yield of that shared work between the elderly people and the students became a resource to strengthen an inter-generational dimension of 'sharing'. This project currently involves elderly people and high school and primary school students. The students support the daily care and management of the garden which offers an opportunity for relationships, exchange, and debate. At the same time, the garden context represents for the students an opportunity for experience, encounters, and growth that the context of daily life does not offer to everyone.

The launching and stratification of practices and experiences, as well as the aspect of sharing and collaboration, are transforming the recovered areas into spaces for the re-appropriation and reconstruction of communities, conceived in terms of co-responsibility in the care of the territory and of education about its value.

Taking care of a space, cleaning and cultivating it are actions that transform spaces and relationships and are at the same time practices that have 'the power to increase an individual grip and extension on the territory' (Mumford, p. 236), which facilitate a process of rediscovery of the relationship with the territory. In this sense, they represent for the students involved in the study plans in-field learning styles that are defined in direct relation with the territory, by going out and living it.

Styles that focus on an artisanal dimension interpreted as a 'process that combines physiological effort and the acquisition of skills' start from the assumption that the material on which we work in turn works us (Deleuze, 1997).

The direct manipulation, contact, and practice of the territory are meant as a physical and emotional experience; they nourish an aptitude for exploration, push teaching beyond the styles and times of the classroom towards experience-based learning, which moves in a social dimension of interaction (Gherardi and Nicolini, 2004), through a regime of gradual participation in common work practices with a combination of actors (Wenger, 2000). The observation of the areas identified is conducted, and the relationship of the populations with the territory takes place daily by exploring and experiencing the place and relating to those who live there through the cooperation in the daily activity of care and preservation. This modality initiates learning forms that proceed by the sedimentation of experiences rather than by transmission/assimilation of information. In this learning context, the teacher plays the role of mediator and facilitator, and the recovered areas, as an archive of varied and interconnected knowledge, become, as in the case of the abandoned area of the former Ospedale al Mare, a significant learning environment.

The vegetable garden, elementary school park, the Vendramin Corner Institute garden, and other green areas in recovery facilitate the rediscovery of links between portions of the territory, its management issues still left unresolved, and its unexpressed potential of resources that can be activated. They are spaces that facilitate the 'learning-by-doing' style by taking responsibility and making choices. The garden adjacent to the Vendramin Corner Institute is observed and studied by students through plant care, soil preparation, sowing, and by relating to the elderly people who care for it. Over the course of studying and working in the field, students make choices about the organization of the times and methods of intervention in an increasingly autonomous way and constantly collaborate with teachers, elderly users, and operators. In this way, they come to assume an increasingly conscious and responsible attitude and a supporting role, also in the preparation of convivial occasions of exchange between the context of the garden and the residents of the area, and discover in themselves unexplored resources and potential.

Rediscovering and recovering pieces of territory in a state of neglect or under-utilization is, therefore, a practice that helps to remodel territorial knowledge, nurture opportunities to experience the territory, and become aware of its value (Magnaghi, 2013). These practices are similar to what Magnaghi defines as a 'territorial approach' (Magnaghi, 2013) which places at its center 'the reconquest by the inhabitants of the knowledge of the production of environmental and territorial quality' (Magnaghi, 2013, p. 75). This is a practice which is based on the awareness that both the society and the individual in their actions contribute to the territory's construction.

Green areas as a space for social re-weaving

The definition of synergies between educational interventions and the territory, the stratification of experiences and practices, gives life to a broader project: the study of the lagoon's traditional agricultural plants, nowadays rarely seen or entirely replaced by agri-food production, and the effects of their disappearance on the territory. This project is broadening to new subjects, placing them in the broader perspective of self-production and strengthening local agricultural sources as an alternative to intensive agriculture and its effects. The network of subjects initially involved is expanding to include a public library on the island of Giudecca, not far from the San Basilio area. It is a large building, with only some parts being used, adjacent to primary and secondary schools with which it has a fairly consolidated relationship, also used by various associations active in the area and involved every year in the island's arts festival – a potential social and cultural reference space that is not adequately valued. The Vendramin Corner Institute is starting a collaboration with some schools nearby to recover part of an external terrace of the building and an adjacent garden, both unused, to include them in the system of green areas that are slowly emerging in the neighborhood of San Basilio. The idea is to connect them to other similar elements of the territory, recovered by subjects engaged in Venice around the theme of promoting urban agriculture.

Specifically, this concerns the Spazi Verdi association which promotes synergistic farming systems in the garden of a retirement home on the island and some grassroots agricultural experiences started by private citizens on the island of Vignole. The evolutionary trajectory of this process, currently interrupted by the health emergency, is to create a network of diffuse urban gardens, existing local markets, and related supply networks of agricultural products, also involving proximity shops within the perspective of support and recovery of the dimension of cultural exchange inherent in the nature of the market – a dimension that has always belonged to the history, identity, and evolution of this city.

The launch of the recovery process of the green area adjacent to the library and the terrace is facilitating the emergence of a nucleus of social and cultural reference that consists of the library, neighboring schools, and green areas adjacent to them. A nucleus that, together with that defined in the San Basilio area, opens up the possibility of building a network of schools that can assume the role of units/references spread over the urban territory. It enhances the potential of a structure of this type in educational terms and in terms of relations, intervention, and transformation on the territory.

Being a part of a relations system enables the schools to access a dimension of constant circularity of knowledge and resources and absorb experiences from different contexts, giving them a new meaning (Cottino, 2009). Each green area is a micro-context with a history, a wealth of experiences, habits, and relations. The recovery intervention in these areas opens up to the interaction with a repertoire of different knowledge and experiences that are partly reused and adapted in the encounter and relationship with new micro-contexts. A dynamic in which the subjects involved experience a generative style of action (Lanzara, 1993), considered as the ability to think and operate through different contexts, and to recognize and compose resources and differences.

By moving in a system of relations, these experiences are fueling mutual learning processes, in which students and residents have the opportunity to develop shared skills and tools for observation, analysis, and planning of the territory. It initiates learning styles based on constant circulation, transfer, and adaptation of knowledge, visions, and experiences (Gherardi and Nicolini, 2004) through contact and encounter as defined by Deleuze (1997).

The school as a trigger of a territorial rewriting process

The Vendramin Corner Institute moves through didactic/educational practices that are slowly but steadily activating resources and subjects around the mending of an eroded urban and social fabric. It does so by developing relation and collaboration networks, starting a process of gradual transformation of the territory. The action dimension is pivotal in this process, which unfolds by relating different contexts and combining repertoires of knowledge and experience.

The setting of synergies between the educational intervention and the territory starts from an area of proximity. For this area, the school acts as a trigger and resource for the development of geography of new connections, meanings, forms of use, and housing, becoming in a certain sense the generative element of an urban project.

In this process, the recovered areas function as an element of a transformation that proceeds by 'small changes that, by structuring themselves in a network, can affect the social and physical organization of the territory ... starting with people, considered for their potential, their ability to act' (Paba, 2003, p. 125). These areas act as platforms for experimentation, discovery, and re-elaboration. Thanks to their flexibility, they become incubators and disseminators of alternative territorial organization models, questioning established configurations and structures. They are capable of involving and reactivating resources, generating relationships, and promoting the cooperation of different components of society.

The areas are becoming territories of social aggregation, co-managed and co-designed spaces in which shared learning practices, new forms of social life, and production are experimented and integrated. Re-inhabiting spaces, changing their layout, re-imagining and adapting uses with a view to multi-functionality, including them in a network of connections are all educational practices and forms of intervention that are fueling a process of transformation of the area. It is similar to the process that Mumford defines as insurgent urbanism, a process that sees its subjects' gradual involvement in a dimension of sharing and choral construction, mutual learning, and collaboration towards a common goal. It opens up opportunities for decision and action against the erosion of the vital fabric of the city.

The recovery process is gradually involving new types of space, as in the case of some commercial establishments in the San Basilio area and around Campo Santa Margherita (one of the historic squares of the area) and an exhibition space used in February 2020 for the public presentation of the results of the observation/study phase of the area. The expansion of the outlined panorama of spaces, relationships, and practices reveals the school's ability to relate to unused or underused spaces and help initiate their transformation.

The school activates a process of reconfiguration of the area's spatial and relational assets by recovering little-used pieces of territory, placing them at the center of new trajectories of meaning and use and new populations related to them. In this process, the sharing of care practices and the collaboration in the construction of projects nourish a dimension of shared responsibility between school and territory. Starting from taking charge of territorially fragile situations, the school is slowly building terrain of shared educational responsibility.

In this dimension, the school is beginning to experiment itself as a social laboratory that is born and defined in the constant relationship with the specificity of its territorial context, as a place crossed and lived by different populations, an environment capable of stimulating the construction of bridges between generations, a territorial presence capable of accommodating the potential of society in the making, and a point of reference for the associations operating in the city.

What has been described can help to understand how the construction of a synergic relationship between school and territory can help to activate a reorganization of the urban fabric and access/usability of spaces and services, start improvements in urban quality, and in parallel facilitate the acquisition of planning and observation/analysis skills of the territory by students and residents.

Conclusion

The experience observed in its different phases highlights how the direct relation with the territory constitutes a favorable condition for the emergence and activation of the transformative potential inherent in the school. The relation with the context of the disused area at the Lido of Venice has given the schools involved the opportunity to experience in-field work and to develop study plans aimed at the acquisition of tools of observation/interpretation rooted in the experience of the territory, to experiment educational practices capable of entering into synergy with the territory by modifying it and forms of learning anchored to experience. In the context of San Basilio, the school is becoming the impetus for a transformation of the physical and relational configuration of the neighboring territory by launching study trajectories that unfold through micro-interventions, and by building relationships, identifying and connecting resources, which have given rise to the first community of interest around the recovery of unused green areas.

The school is slowly becoming the activating core of a process of rewriting its surroundings, moving through educational practices conceived as forms of intervention for the recovery and protection of a physical and relational land-scape of the area. It is a complex process characterized by slow evolution times, which sees its transformative potential in the relational dimension, in the deep immersion in the urban fabric. A process in which the school is experimenting itself as a laboratory open to the territory, a potential reference for the territory, a space for civic action/participation, and an impetus for the dissemination of similar experiments in other areas of the city.

The experience underway in the San Basilio area is progressively transform-ing the relationship between school and territory, orienting it towards a dimen-sion of 'educating territory'. A dimension in which the school is going beyond its normal frames of times and operational and communication styles that find their reference in the school building and the classroom, and relates to the territory identifying it as a learning environment, an opportunity for discovery and expe-rience. Thanks to the sharing of repertoires of knowledge, experiences, and rela-tions, a dimension can facilitate the start of a path of emancipation/redemption from predefined choices and conditions of inequality in access to local resources.

The experience of the San Basilio area encountered obstacles along its way posed by the school's bureaucracy, an educational vision that still tends to be limited to the dimension of the classroom, and the lack of recognition and insti-tutional support. In response to these issues, the network of subjects involved in the projects is being structured into a stable work nucleus made up of teachers, students, and external coordinators with a monitoring and mediation role.

This passage testifies to the achievement of a deeper awareness of the mean-ing, effects, and future prospects of what has been started. Building and formal-izing an organizational structure aims to restore more recognizable contours to the current path in terms of assumptions, objectives, and methods of action and facilitate relationship collaboration with the territory.

Notes

1 The compound of the Arsenale occupies the north-eastern edge of Venice, extend-ing for about 48 hectares and is currently used by the Ministry of Infrastructures and Transport for safeguarding the lagoon in order to complete the works for the realiza-tion of the MOSE System, by A.C.T.V. Municipal Transport Company, by THETIS S.P.A., a civil and environmental engineering company.
2 The former Ospedale al Mare-Lido di Venezia was established in the late 19th cen-tury as a marine hospice for poor children with tuberculosis. During the 20th cen-tury it became a modern hospital, a reference point of excellence. It specialized in climatic therapy that focused on sun, air, and physical movement. The hospital had a concept of care that was not limited to drug therapy but included the patient's quality of life, attention to physical and mental activity, and the quality of spaces. For this reason, among the 33 buildings that made up the hospital there was also a library and a theater.
3 Studies about the history and memory of the area produced by other schools were part of a stock of knowledge useful regarding the course of future development.
4 The stretch of coastline in front of the disused health facility, following the end of its care function in the seventies and decommissioning of the entire complex in the

early 2000s, has gradually become a habitat that hosts rare species of flora and fauna. The committee, together with LIPU-Venice, on the basis of a study on the plant and animal species present, had requested their inclusion among the SIC areas, sites of community interest; the request was not approved. Currently, it is among the few freely accessible areas on the island but in the future it is expected to be a tourist destination that is very likely to erase its prospect as a valuable landscape.

References

Castoriadis, C. 1990. *La Rivoluzione democratica. Teoria e progetto dell'autogoverno*, Elèuthera: Milano.

Cottino, P. 2009. *Competenze possibili, sfera pubblica e potenziali sociali nella città*, Jaca Book: Milano.

Deleuze, G., Guattari, F. 1997. *Rizoma*, Castelvecchi: Roma.

Gherardi, S. & Nicolini, D. 2004. *Apprendimento e conoscenza nelle organizzazioni*, Carocci: Roma.

Lanzara, G. F. 1993. *Capacità negativa. Competenza progettuale e modelli di intervento nelle organizzazioni*, Il Mulino: Bologna.

Lefebvre, H. 1976. *La produzione sociale dello spazio*, Moizzi: Milano.

Magnaghi, A. 2013. *Il progetto locale. Verso la coscienza di un luogo*, Bollati Boringhieri: Torino.

Paba, G. 2003. *Movimenti urbani. Pratiche di costruzione sociale della città*, Franco Angeli: Milano.

Sassen, S. 2008. *Territorio, autorità, diritti. Assemblaggi dal Medio Evo alle età globale*, Mondadori: Milano.

Semi, G. 2010. *L'osservazione partecipante*, Il Mulino: Bologna.

Signorelli, A. 1996. *Antropologia urbana*, Guerini: Milano.

Turpino, A. 2012. *Spaesati. Luoghi dell'Italia in abbandono tra memoria e futuro*, Einaudi: Torino.

Uzzi, B. 1996. The Sources and Consequences of Embeddedness for the Economic Performance of Organizations: The Network Effect, *American Sociological Review*, Vol. 61, pp. 674–698.

Wenger, E.. 2000. *Comunità di pratica e sistemi sociali di apprendimento in Studi organizzativi*, Vol. 1, pp. 7–29, Franco Angeli: Milano.

12

SCHOOL ROOF FARMS

Challenges and success pillars

Samaa R. Badawi

Introduction

Hunger is a serious threat to public health; according to The State of Food Security and Nutrition in the World 2019, approximately 821 million people suffered from hunger in 2018 (The United Nations, 2020). Besides, each day, 25,000 people die from starvation (Holmes, 2009). One of the essential groups affected by the food shortage problem is children. It is well known that children are a crucial agent in shaping a better world. Raising healthy and well-educated children is the way to a sustainable future.

Nevertheless, around 10,000 children worldwide die from hunger each day. Malnutrition remains one of the major obstacles affecting all areas of a child's growth, including performance in the classroom (Chinyoka, 2014). Relationships between nutrition and brain function have been the focus of much research. Growden and Wurtman (1980) have shown the impact of dietary foundations on normal brain functions. Other studies have been done with school-aged children and point to a direct correlation between poor nutrition and lowered school performance (Wood, 2001; Taras, 2005). For example, Lahey and Rosen (2010) assessed the impact of school feeding programs on pupils' academic performance in Mlunduz, Tanzania. They found that learners got better grades in an examination during the school feeding program (Maijo, 2018). Another study emphasized the same result. At a middle school in Northern California, which analyzed how the amount of food supplied by the school and consumed by students at the school sites impacts academic performance, those that receive food at school more frequently have better educational results (Wood, 2001).

Moreover, it was found that children who eat breakfast and lunch at school rely on school meals for half of their daily energy intake (Weber & Chen, 2017). It was also proved that school meals are healthier than meals brought from home

DOI: 10.4324/9781003176558-12

or elsewhere (Minaya & Rainville, 2016; Ptomey et al., 2016). It is a pity to say the problem of food scarcity is continuously increasing. It is expected that by 2050, global food production will drop by more than 50%. In contrast, the population is estimated to reach 9 billion (United Nations, 2018).

On the other hand, agricultural land per person is shrinking. It decreased from 0.38 ha in 1970 to 0.23 ha in 2000, with a projected decline to 0.15 ha per person by 2050 (Bruinsma, 2003). The accelerated rates of urbanization had a significant impact on reducing agricultural lands, and thus food production. The United Nations clarifies that by 2030 urban areas are projected to house 60% of people globally (United Nations, 2018), resulting in increased demand for land for housing and other uses (Asamoah, 2010). Accordingly, land-use conversion from agricultural land to urban land use is becoming more frequent (Pramanik & Sarkar, 2010).

Furthermore, urbanization contributes to climate change (Azam & Khan, 2016), which has been identified as the greatest threat to human life (Scharf & Kraus, 2019). Among all aspects affected by climate change are agriculture and food supply. The effects of climate change have affected optimal environmental growing conditions through rising temperatures and changes in rainfall patterns (Germer et al., 2011; Hatfield et al., 2011).

One of the solutions that has become evident in recent times as a practical measure to improve climate resilience, and at the same time provide fresh food, is Urban Agriculture (UA) (Hardman & Larkham, 2014; Martellozzo et al., 2014; Baldock et al., 2019). Urban Agriculture (UA) is defined as a localized food system, which means the production, processing, distribution, consumption, and recycling of food occur in the city for feeding local populations (Hendrickson & Porth, 2012). It has increased in popularity over the last few years, especially after lockdowns and the COVID-19 pandemic (Ketchell, 2018).

Many examples of Urban Agriculture exist worldwide, such as community gardens, vegetable gardens, and roof farms. However, such greening activities face a problematic situation because of disordered urbanization, escalation in land prices, intense competition among the various land uses, and increasing population (Kumar et al., 2019; Ibáñez Gutiérrez & Ramos-Mejía, 2019). Such challenges have reduced the applicability of green surfaces, increased pressure on farmers, and made it more costly and difficult to farm in the traditional way (Iheke & Ihuoma, 2016).

Green roofs have become an auspicious choice for densely populated urban areas (Hui, 2011). As building roof surfaces cover 20–25% of urban areas, many countries started to utilize their roofs and transform them into roof farms that tackle sustainable design issues and provide fresh food (Arabi et al., 2015; Poptaniand Bandyopadhyay 2014).

Children are among the groups most affected by the food shortage problem. Because children are the mainstays of the future, many countries have paid attention to the importance of using school roofs as farms that provide healthy food to students and help them in their academic performance and support the educational process.

Accordingly, this chapter aims to present the experiences of various school roof farms because of their significance regarding raising the younger generation to be aware of sustainability. Besides, this chapter explores the challenges these projects faced, the pillars of their success, and the benefits that schools and local communities accrue from the roof farm projects.

Literature review

Green roofs are living vegetation installed on the top of buildings (Breuning & Yanders, 2008). They make cities more livable by providing green spaces (Luckett, 2009) and mitigating several environmental problems (Weiler & Scholz-Barth, 2009). The concept of green roofs is not a new one, and it was incorporated into designs in the late 1940s because of land scarcity issues. Due to the development of roof technology, Germany was the first country in the world to adopt green roofs in its buildings (Snodgrass and Snodgrass, 2007). It was followed by Northern Europe and North America, and a few countries in Asia (Abass et al., 2020).

Purely recreational green roofs that comprise little or no edible vegetation have limited benefits compared to roof farms (Design for London, 2008). Therefore, it is possible to promote more useful green roof functions by adding roof farms (Brown et al., 2003). Roof farms are a strategy for intensifying Urban Agriculture activities, improving nutrition and food security, and other environmental and social benefits (Hui, 2011). Many countries have set up roof farms on their buildings, such as Germany, which incorporated roof farms into many administrative buildings. In Athens, a great roof farm was built on the station building of trolley in Athens, which is the biggest in Greece. Many examples are found in Canada, such as the roof farm of the Roulant building in Montreal. In the United States, one notable project is the Eagle Street Rooftop Farm in New York City (Rooftop Farms, 2020). Despite the harsh climate in the UK, supermarkets convert their roof spaces into vegetable gardens (Hui, 2011) to sell the crops in the supermarkets below. In Japan, a roof garden rental space offers 16 small plots for rent that turns wasted space into a profitable business (Rooftop Farms, 2020).

Believing in the importance of roof farms and the significant role they can provide for children, the concept has extended to schools and other educational buildings. Schools play a vital role in preparing and sustaining students' health; besides, they participate effectively in solving food scarcity problems. It is well known that nutrition is a tool to increase equity among all students for academic success (Wood, 2001). Schools' rooftops are wasted spaces that have the potential to be transformed into gardens to produce fresh food for students (Ross & Anderson, 2010). Many children growing up today in urban cities are detached from nature and have no relationship with farming. Schools are a place where kids can learn about nature and where their food comes from. Farm-based education has been shown to foster awareness about the environment and a sustainable future (Selzer, 2019). Engaging children in growing, harvesting, and cooking their food is urgent nowadays. Studies have revealed that healthy school meals, food literacy, and fostering healthy habits early on can positively affect children's health (Schwartz et al., 2015). Promoting healthy eating in schools has proven short-term success in behavioral change towards healthy food choices. Research conducted over a two-year period at a selected middle school in western New York demonstrated that providing students with two lessons on nutrition by community members has a positive impact on the knowledge and awareness of healthy food choices among students (Border, 2019).

Many schools use roof farms as classrooms where children can learn about food and the food system besides host other lessons. Farm-based education is a newly emerging field; it uses farms as a real learning environment. Farm-based education combines academic study with a farming context. Previous studies revealed that students showed better learning results when allowed to study in farms compared to classrooms. Farm education supports students with different learning abilities. It supports students with moderate learning difficulties, as well as talented pupils. Moreover, it increases long-term retention of what has been learned and improves understanding (Smeds et al., 2015).

Many types of research have well documented the benefits associated with farming in schools. A study conducted by Mary Selzer in 2019 about the roof farm of the Fifth Street public school complex clarifies that the roof farm provides students with a living classroom to learn about sustainable agriculture and nutrition. Also, teachers have incorporated the space into science, math, and humanities lessons. The same situation existed in Rothenberg School in Cincinnati, Ohio, where roof farms promote positive educational outcomes and make students active and engaged with their community. Besides, roof farms connect children raised in the city to food growing practices for a greener future (Selzer, 2019). A study was done by Onwumere, Modebelu, & Chukwuka (2016) in senior secondary schools in Ikwuano, Abia State, Nigeria, which revealed that time spent learning outdoors engages pupils who may have become disengaged and encourages them to feel included and motivated to become a part of their group (Onwumere et al., 2016).

School roof farm project case studies

1. Vo Trong Nghia's Farming Kindergarten roof farm – Vietnam

a. *Introduction to the project*

Vo Trong Nghia kindergarten is located in Donghai, Vietnam; it was built in 2013. The school is situated beside a shoe factory and is intended for children of the factory workers and other low-income children and serves up to 500 pupils

(Architects, 2020). Vietnam was historically an agricultural country, and then it moved to a manufacturing-based economy. The rapid urbanization deprived children of green lands, and thus a relationship with nature. The Farming Kindergarten arose as a solution to those issues (Wang, 2016).

b. *The project description*

The kindergarten building encompasses a 200 sqm green roof, which provides children with a large vegetable garden and playground. The building's form enables the students to reach the green roof easily as it is composed of a triple ring spiral that creates three courtyards. The access to the green roof is at the start of the spiral, where the roof begins to rise from the yard.

c. *The project benefits*

Environmental benefits: the green roof reduces the ecological impact and minimizes the carbon footprint of the school. It acts as an insulator to the classrooms and saves them from the heat island effect and urban flooding. The building depends mainly on natural ventilation and lighting; the kindergarten is operated without air conditioners in the classrooms, despite being located in a harsh tropical climate. The building is covered by vertical louvers, which provide shading and are utilized as a vertical garden for creepers such as bitter gourd and cucumber (Community, 2020). Local and recycled materials used in construction minimize the carbon footprint and environmental impact (Livinspaces, 2020).

Other sustainability strategies are used. Recycled wastewater from the factory is used to irrigate the green roof and flush toilets. Moreover, all rainwater falling in the Farming Kindergarten is collected eventually in water tanks and then pumped up to the green roof. The kindergarten also uses solar power to heat water. Previous studies reveal that 48% of energy consumption (Livinspaces, 2020) and 40% of freshwater were saved, thus significantly reducing its overall running costs (Editors, 2014).

The kindergarten's sustainable design received a Silver Provisional Certificate as a LOTUS pilot project, a green rating system by the Vietnam Green Building Council (Wang, 2016). Children educated in the Farming Kindergarten will become Green People. In the future, the goal is that they will convey their experience to the next generation (Livinspaces, 2020).

Social benefits: the roof farm gathers students, their parents, community members, and teachers together to collaborate in planting, harvesting, and exchanging agricultural knowledge among them (Wang, 2016).

Educational benefits: the essence of the design approach was to educate students about sustainability and the importance of agriculture and to recover their connection to nature. The kindergarten provides an experimental learning space for a sustainable lifestyle. The green roof presents an opportunity for active learning and provides an agriculture experience. The green roof is not the only tool to teach students about sustainability; the building's whole design and operation serves this goal and minimizes the environmental impact by applying many sustainable features. These features are designed visibly for children to support sustainable education and teach them about energy-saving processes (Wang, 2016).

Economic benefits: in addition to the learning experience, the farm produces five different vegetables (Livinspaces, 2020). The edibles harvested by the children are used for school-day lunches, with the rest distributed to their families, helping out families with a relatively small budget. The young learners are inculcated in the joys of wholesome organic food while being proud of contributing to their households (Medina, 2015). The classes below the green roof don't use air conditioning; hence the cost of electricity is minimized because the green roof insulates the classes from heat gain. The use of a combination of cost-efficient local materials, recycled materials, and low-tech solutions In the construction process respond to the project's tight budget. applied to construction and respond to the project's tight budget (Community, 2020).

d. *The project challenges & success pillars*

In conclusion, Vo Trong Nghia kindergarten, as a building dedicated to serving low-income children, has become an honorable international project model in developing countries for its sustainable design and educational program. Although the project faced many problems it succeeded in creating a beneficial roof farm. Below is a summary of the challenges and success pillars of this project.

The economic challenges: the tight budget was the main challenge that faced the project.

The success pillars:

People: the collaboration between teachers and students and the active involvement of parents and volunteers from the community was the central pillar of success. All of them collaborated in constructing, planting, harvesting, and managing the farm. Parents and other volunteers helped in teaching activities to transfer knowledge among generations. The management of the Farming Kindergarten depends on involving parents, volunteers, and the management team. The educators also include teachers, parents, and volunteers from the neighborhood to convey their agriculture experience to the next generation.

Sustainable construction techniques: the designer of the farm depended on many sustainable construction techniques. He used local materials and traditional building techniques. The roof farm is part of a more extensive design that serves the environment, using solar panels, recycling processes, greywater from the factory, and rainfall for irrigation.

2. **St. Simon Stock R.C. elementary school roof farm – United States**

a. *Introduction to the project*

The school is located in St. Simon Stock, Bronx, New York. It was installed in 2005.

b. *The project description*

The area of the roof is about 3500 square feet. It is divided into plots for both elementary and graduate school research. Nearly half of the roof was planted with native plants, and the other half was planted with edible crops. Recycled materials were used in the construction process of the roof farm. Besides, the safety criteria were applied carefully. A high fence was installed on the top of the parapet walls and planted with vine plants to attract hummingbirds and butterflies (Greenroofs, 2018).

c. *The project benefits*

Environmental benefits: the green roof of the building helps clean the air, stormwater retention, provide the students with a healthy park where they can grow fresh vegetables, and find a place of peace.

Educational benefits: the school faculty developed a curriculum that utilizes plants, soil, and animal life as a tool for interdisciplinary education as students can conduct science experiments. Moreover, students take an ongoing role in planting and harvesting various fruits and vegetables, collecting and analyzing data, and writing papers in the green classroom. Monitoring equipment, including a weather station, thermo-couples, and soil moisture probes, have been installed. The kit serves educational goals and monitors how much water is held and used by the soil and plants under varying climatic conditions.

Economic benefits: about half of the roof was planted with edible crops, producing organic food for the students and providing fresh school meals.

d. *The project challenges & success pillars*

The project faced two main obstacles: the roof's limited weight, which required a lightweight growing medium, and the second one was the construction cost (Roofs, 2020).

The success pillars:

People: community members, parents, teachers, and students provided many of the required equipment. The fence, plantings, and technical and weather monitoring equipment were all provided and constructed by them, which helped overcome the second obstacle, the construction cost.

Institutional support: the Bronx Initiative for Energy and the Environment and GRHC Corporate Member Barrett Company provided grants to the school for the construction which helped in reducing the construction cost (Roofs, 2020).

Sustainable construction techniques:

A new lightweight growing medium developed by the Gaia Institute was used. This growing medium is 75% lighter than other growing media (Gleason, 2006).

3. **Harringay primary school roof farm – London, England**

a. *Introduction to the project*

Harringay school is located on Falkland Road, London. Due to the school's expansion work, the new building took up the existing garden space. Accordingly, in 2005 the school built a new green roof.

b. *The project description*

A green roof was installed on top of the gymnasium building with an approximate area of 190 sqm. This green roof aimed to create an international roof garden that celebrated Harringay's diverse communities and displayed food and medicinal plants from around the world (Ronaldson, 2005). The roof contains a tropical bed, native English bed, and vegetable beds. It also includes a wormery to make compost.

c. *The project benefits*

Social benefits: the roof provides a unique space for students, their families, and the community to grow kitchen herbal remedies. The green roof offers facilities for events such as concerts and social gatherings.

Educational benefits: the green roof also contains an outdoor classroom that provides a flexible facility for learning and researching the environment and sustainable building techniques. Moreover, the green roof has been developed as a valuable curriculum resource. Besides, there are regular workshops for various members of the community to learn about plants. At other times the children have engaged in conversations about horticultural subjects. Occasionally, it has been a chance for children struggling with English to involve themselves in lessons (Ronaldson, 2005).

d. *The project challenges & success pillars*

The economic challenges: the principal barrier to this project was funding (Design for London, 2008).

The success pillars:

People: involving the community was one of the primary reasons behind this project's success. Parents, grandparents, and other community members have been involved in the design, construction, management, accountability, and support of the roof garden project. Besides, they were the primary source of funding for the project.

Institutional support:

Despite the funding problem, Haringey Council was able to provide the budget to proceed with the project (Design for London, 2008).

Sustainable construction techniques:

The outdoor classroom is made using sustainable materials, utilizing local craftsmen's skills and expertise (Ronaldson, 2005).

Precise process:

The green roof construction went through a precise process. Starting with a Structural Engineer's report assessing the roof's load-bearing capacity, the removal of roof tiles, adding a waterproof layer, designing the garden, constructing a perimeter fence around the roof, and finally constructing the hard and landscape elements. The children have been involved in the roof garden work from the outset. Initially, they were encouraged to submit designs and ideas. Some excellent submissions were rewarded with prizes. Accordingly, the children's feeling of enthusiasm and belonging kept the project's momentum going (Ronaldson, 2005).

4. **Ng Yuk secondary school roof farm – China**

a. *Introduction to the project*

Ng Yuk school is located in Shatian, Hong Kong, China. In 2006, the biology teacher Chan Chai-yuen, the laboratory technician, and the school's students raised three rooftop gardens with their own hands.

b. *The project description*

The roof farm was constructed by using disused equipment and 470 sqm of the school roof was turned into an environmentally friendly ecosystem.

Herbs, vegetables, fruits, green walls, and various types of plants in addition to a fish pond and fountain became home to a variety of animals, including several generations of fish, turtles, and flocks of migratory birds, who like to stop by to drink from the pond and snack on the fish (Journal, 2014).

c. *The project benefits*

Environmental benefits: the roof gardens cool down rooms beneath them by three to five degrees Celsius. Besides, many other sustainable techniques are used to save energy and at the same time maintain a comfortable environment. Solar window film has been applied to classroom windows. Moreover, solar panels and wind turbines are installed (Journal, 2014).

Social benefits: the green roofs offer students more space to relax or take part in activities and enjoy their time. The residents from the surrounding high-rise buildings also complimented the school on the pretty garden added to their view.

Educational benefits: the roof gardens provided a chance to create a bird watching station that enables students to study the migratory patterns of the various species that pass through. It can be said that the green roof acts as a showcase of the sustainability concept (WeCan, 2020). As a result, students understand renewable energy principles, and they have a good grasp of plant knowledge.

d. *The project challenges & success pillars*

The economic challenges: like many other projects, funding was the main challenge of the project.

The success pillars:

People: the distinctive point in this example is that one person believed in the importance of roof farms, and he was then able to transmit his passion to his students, their parents, and the school. They were able to succeed in the project and overcome all the obstacles they encountered.

Institutional support:

The HK Electric Clean Energy Fund and the Energy Innovation Competition provided the project with grants used in the construction process and provided the required equipment.

Sustainable construction techniques:

The roof farm was constructed by using disused equipment. The innovative ideas and application techniques used in Ng Yuk roof gardens resulted in the project being awarded many awards. In 2014, the Hong Kong Green Building Council selected Ng Yuk roof gardens as the winner of the Chairman's Award and the Grand Award Winner in Hong Kong (Journal, 2014). The project was also rewarded with the Hanson Outstanding Award. Moreover, the school has long been participating in local and overseas competitions. Awards have been received for their original design concepts and energy conservation prototypes. Besides, the students are invited to serve the school and community as energy-saving ambassadors. These innovations have earned a silver medal in the Skyrise Greenery Awards 2012 (Greening, 2012).

5. Jože Plečnik high school roof farm – Slovenia

a. *Introduction to the project*

Jože Plečnik high school is a public school in the center of Ljubljana, Slovenia. The school has no open space of its own.

b. *The project description*

A 50 sqm roof garden on a terrace was designed to act as a vegetable garden. The roof garden attracts bees, butterflies, and other insects, increasing biodiversity and creating a laboratory for discovering nature. The roof garden also acts as an outdoor classroom and a place for socializing (Trbižan, 2020).

c. *The project benefits*

Social benefits: the roof is a big success and is much visited during lessons and school breaks by students. Various events and workshops take place in the roof garden. Besides, building the garden has strengthened the bond between participants.

Educational benefits: the vegetable garden helped students learn about plants and agriculture. Moreover, it led to mutual understanding and increased awareness and responsibility towards the environment.

d. *The project challenges & success pillars*

The economic challenges: the main challenge of this project was the lack of funds.

The success pillars:

People: the collaboration among teachers, students, and volunteers was a central pillar of this project's success. The lack of funds was significantly compensated by voluntary work. 25% of the project's total value was paid for by voluntary work, while the school paid 20%.

Institutional support: different companies supported the project as 55% of the project's total value was paid for by donations. Without dedicated individuals and the expert help of an NGO, the project would have been hard to realize.

Sustainable construction techniques: all the construction and planting was carried out by students themselves, with the help of expert mentors.

Precise process: this project followed a precise process, which represents one of its success pillars. Those process steps can be summarized as follows: the project's idea was clear and presented to as many stakeholders as possible; decision-makers supported the first step (e.g., a school principal or other institution); an action plan was set up by experts who offered technical and aesthetic guidance that made the implementation more comfortable; various experts were involved which helped in gaining new knowledge; many users were included in the process (Trbižan, 2020).

6. **Jackman school roof farm – Canada**

a. *Introduction to the project*

Jackman school is a junior public school located in the east end of Toronto (Conservation Council of New Brunswick, 2020).

b. *The project description*

The green roof area is 90 sqm (Iswm, 2020). The green roof was built as a part of greening projects the school has been working on since 1999 (Green Schools, 2020).

c. *The project benefits*

Environmental benefits: the school had a heat problem, so the green roofs are used to cool the building in summer and warm it in winter (Feeley, 2019). The roof conserves energy, filters and captures stormwater, and purifies the air. It also provides a habitat for insects and birds (TDSB, 2020).

Educational benefits: unlike most other green roofs, Jackman's green roof has an indoor observation deck, and the students, staff, and parents are always looking to educate others (TDSB, 2020).

The project challenges & success pillars

The economic challenges: the project fund was the main challenge.

The success pillars:

People: the students, staff, parents, and community have worked together to green the school and carry out the green roof.

From the previous analysis of the selected schools, it became evident that the challenges that their roof farms faced, the success pillars for these projects, as well as the benefits accrued by the schools and local communities were similar and can be summarized as follows.

Challenges and success pillars of schools' roof farms

Reviewing the school roof farm projects in the previous six cases shows that all cases share common challenges and success pillars that arise in the application of the projects. Nevertheless, the rooftops farm projects have brought many benefits in return. The following section highlights the significant challenges that the selected schools faced while constructing their roof farms, the success pillars, and benefits of roof farms for both the schools and the community.

1. The challenges of schools' roof farm projects

The selected schools faced some similar challenges while creating their roof farms. The first challenge was the project cost. This problem was solved through the funds received from various governmental and non-governmental organizations, the volunteering work and participation of many schools and community members, and recycling unused materials in the school to construct the gardens. All of these factors reduced the cost of the projects. The second challenge was the buildings' construction system and the roofs' bearing weight which limited the soil and infrastructure needed for planting. However, this problem was solved by new technologies offered by specialized companies, which provided a lightweight growing medium to suit the roofs' bearing weights. The environmental conditions were also one of the challenges. High wind speeds and direct sun exposure for long periods affect plants. Still, profound studies and advice from experts about suitable types of plants that bear such environmental conditions enabled this problem to be overcome.

2. The success pillars

The success of the studied cases was built on common pillars. They are People, Institutional support, Sustainable construction techniques, and Precise process. What follows is the explanation of the four pillars.

a. *People*

Of course, people are always the primary driver of any project. The spark of the idea starts with the imagination of a person or a group of people. Then the idea moves to larger groups and so on to follow its specified path until it becomes a successful project in the end, as in the case of Ng Yuk school in China. The biology teacher believed in the importance of roof farms and transmitted his passion to his students, colleagues, directors, and the community. Finally, they have created one of the most successful school roof farm projects in China, which is the recipient of many excellence awards.

Another aspect of how people influence the success of projects is the principle of participation, which involves sharing ideas and work among students, teachers, administrators, parents, and various community groups. It is this participation that works to overcome the difficulties facing the implementation of the project. Volunteer work and the transfer of experiences between everyone make work successful, as in the case of Vo Trong Nghia's Farming Kindergarten in Vietnam. The process of establishing the farm and teaching children about agriculture, and managing and maintaining the project involved the participation of teachers, parents, and diverse community members, which led to the transfer of experiences from one generation to the next.

Another positive outcome of the participation process comes from a sense of belonging and responsibility. Every individual feels that they belong to this project and have a duty to preserve and make it successful. In many cases, graduate students return to visit their roof farm project in Ng Yuk school in which they worked diligently, and sometimes they take their wedding photos in the roof garden, as Chan Chai-yuen explained in some interviews.

b. *Institutional support*

The second important factor for the success of roof farm projects in schools is institutional support at various levels. Whether it is government agencies, private institutions, non-profit organizations, or the institutions that aim to achieve sustainability, this support is represented in many ways, including providing the necessary funds, as in the case of Jože Plečnik school in Slovenia. The school obtained 50% of the project's value through donations. The same goes for Harringay school in England; it received grants from the Big Lottery Fund, Awards for All, the Scarman Trust, the City Bridge Trust, and the Community Fund. They were even able to convince the council to help in construction work and repair. One of the various bodies' methods of support is to create incentive prizes to reward successful projects, as happened in Ng Yuk school. The Hong Kong Green Building Council selected Ng Yuk roof gardens as the winner of the Chairman's Award.

c. *Sustainable construction techniques*

Roof farms are one of the projects that aim to achieve sustainability in all areas. Therefore, relying on sustainable building materials helps achieve project goals. At Ng Yuk school, the project made use of recycled materials to construct the roof farm. Banners were used as waterproofing. The planters and fish ponds were made of bricks and banners.

Also, at Nghia's Farming Kindergarten, Vietnam, the roof farm and entire school building are based on local materials, saving on the project and transportation costs and emissions resulting from transportation. The school's design also relied on natural lighting and ventilation, which reduced the electrical energy needed to operate the building. Utilizing companies' new techniques is also essential, as in St. Simon Stock school in the United States, where a lightweight growing medium developed by the Gaia Institute was used.

d. *Precise process*

Following a straightforward process for constructing a school roof farm guarantees the project's success. The construction of a roof farm goes through various stages. The first step is creating a Structural Engineer's report assessing the load-bearing capacity of the roof. Then, the removal of the roof tiles and adding a waterproof layer take place. After that come designing the garden and finally constructing the complex and landscape elements. While designing and constructing the roof farm, the students' safety is a significant factor. Building a high fence surrounding the whole roof is a priority. Those fences can also be utilized to support climbing plants. The use of non-slipping materials should be used for creating walkways. Providing a suitable number of access points to the roof in addition to fire systems is also essential. The use of recycled materials and utilizing unused school equipment in construction reduces construction costs. After constructing the roof farms, maintenance and monitoring are an essential factor for preserving them.

The school roof farm provides many benefits to the school and local community, as explained briefly below.

3. **The benefits of roof farms**

Despite the obstacles which face any roof farm project, many benefits can result from creating roof farms. They can be classified into four categories: environmental, social, educational, and economic benefits.

a. *Environmental benefits*

The roof farm's vegetation system reduces heat gain and is used to cool the building in summer and make it warm in winter. As a result, it reduces CO_2 emissions resulting from heating or cooling the building. Because roof farms produce food, they reduce food transportation accordingly, the CO_2 emissions from transportation are decreased, and waste is reduced by generating less packaging. Besides, plants help clean the air by absorbing harmful particulates. Roof farms also improve urban stormwater management. The composting system used in fertilizing the plants recycles organic wastes. The vegetation acts as sound insulation and noise absorption. The vegetables and fruits planted in the roof attract birds and insects, increasing biodiversity and providing a chance to create a laboratory for discovering nature.

b. *Social benefits*

Roof farms play an essential role in increasing nutrition awareness, inspiring healthy lifestyles, providing fresh food, and improving students' food choices. Besides, farming increases children's self-esteem, fosters relationships with other students and staff, and enhances parental involvement. The roof farm can reflect the community's variety and celebrate the diverse communities where plants are planted worldwide. The roof also provides the students with a green open space to sit, play, and enjoy their time, and as a place where they can grow fresh vegetables. The social role of roof farms extends to assist the local community; they provide gathering spaces and offer facilities for concerts and performances that foster social relationship. Roof farms enhance the aesthetic value and bring nature back to urban areas. They also provide a good view for neighbors overlooking the roof.

c. *Educational benefits*

Roof farms provide an opportunity for active learning. They educate students about sustainability, the importance of agriculture, and enable them to discover their connection to nature. They also act as an outdoor classroom to offer varied teaching methods for many courses. Roof farms help teachers develop a sustainable curriculum and help students conducting science experiments. Making the green roof a part of a comprehensive sustainable system can effectively teach students the various sustainability aspects. Roof farms also help in holding regular workshops for the community members to learn about plants.

d. *Economic benefits*

The crops harvested from the roof farm are used for school lunches. In some cases, the rest of the crops can be distributed to the students' families. The roof farm crops increase local food production. Roof farms can be a practical arena for developing small businesses, especially in low-income areas.

Conclusion

The rates of hunger and undernutrition in the world are accelerating dramatically. Children are one of the essential groups affected by hunger. It is well known that malnutrition affects all areas of a child's growth, including learning abilities. This problem has prompted many countries to pursue urgent solutions. Due to the dense urbanization and limited space in cities, utilizing the buildings' roofs as productive farms has become a promising solution. Many countries started to transform the roofs of their buildings into roof farms. Schools' buildings are one of the prominent examples of creating roof farms.

This chapter reviewed six successful cases of schools that utilized their roofs as roof farm projects to explore the challenges that faced the projects, the success pillars shared among the studied cases, and the benefits of roof farms to schools and broader communities. This chapter can guide schools that wish to start their journey towards transforming their roofs into productive roof farms.

By reviewing the six case studies from Vietnam, the United States, England, China, Slovenia, and Canada, it was evident that all projects faced problems related to project cost, buildings' construction, and environmental conditions. Nevertheless, all cases succeeded in solving these problems and shared four main pillars of success. The first pillar was people who initiated the idea and collaborated during the whole journey of constructing the roof farm until the idea became a tangible project. The second pillar was institutional support of governmental and non-governmental bodies by providing grants, helping in the construction process, and initiating rewards for the distinct projects. The third pillar was sustainable construction techniques; using available materials and recycling equipment and using environmentally friendly materials reduce the project cost and achieve sustainability. The fourth pillar was the precise process, following a straightforward process for constructing the projects from the beginning that guarantees the project's success. Of course, while designing and constructing the roof farm, the students' and users' safety is a significant factor to be considered.

The roof farm projects benefit both the schools and the broader community at different levels. At the environmental level, they reduce heat gain, manage stormwater, and purify the air. They provide fresh food and green open spaces for enjoyment and social communication on the social level. On the educational level, roof farms provide active learning and educate students about sustainability and agriculture. On the economic level, the roof farms increase local food production and reduce food transportation and processing costs. Roof farming practices in schools are easy to be applied and can be created with little resources and much engagement.

References

Abass, F., Ismail, L.H., Wahab, I.A. and Elgadi, A.A., 2020. A review of green roof: definition, history, evolution and functions. *IOP Conference Series: Materials Science and Engineering*, 713(1), p. 012048. IOP Publishing.

Arabi, R., Shahidan, M.F., Kamal, M.M., Jaafar, M.F.Z.B. and Rakhshandehroo, M., 2015. Mitigating urban heat island through green roofs. *Current World Environment*, 10(1), pp.918–927.

Architects, V. 2020. Farming kindergarten. Retrieved 2020, from *VTN Architects*: https://www.vtnarchitects.net/institutional-properties/farming-kindergarten

Asamoah, B., 2010. *Urbanisation and Changing Patterns of Urban Land Use in Ghana: Policy and Planning Implications for Residential Land Use in Kumasi* (Doctoral dissertation).

Azam, M. and Khan, A.Q., 2016. Urbanization and environmental degradation: Evidence from four SAARC countries: Bangladesh, India, Pakistan, and Sri Lanka. *Environmental Progress & Sustainable Energy*, 35(3), pp.823–832.

Baldock, K.C., Goddard, M.A., Hicks, D.M., Kunin, W.E., Mitschunas, N., Morse, H., Osgathorpe, L.M., Potts, S.G., Robertson, K.M., Scott, A.V. and Staniczenko, P.P., 2019. A systems approach reveals urban pollinator hotspots and conservation opportunities. *Nature Ecology & Evolution*, 3(3), pp.363–373.

Border, K.M., 2019. Implementing a farm to school nutrition education program in a large urban school. *Journal of Nutrition and Dietetic Practice*, 3(1), pp. 1–6.

Breuning, J. and Yanders, A., 2008. *Introduction to the FLL Guidelines for the Planning, Construction and Maintenance of Green Roofing*. Baltimore, Maryland: Green Roofing Guideline.

Brown, K.H., Carter, A. and Bailkey, M., 2003. *Urban Agriculture and Community Food Security in the United States: Farming from the City Center to the Urban Fringe*. Community Food Security Coalition.

Bruinsma, J. ed., 2003. *World Agriculture: Towards 2015/2030: An FAO Perspective*. London: Earthscan.

Chinyoka, K., 2014. Impact of poor nutrition on the academic performance of grade seven learners: a case of Zimbabwe. *International Journal of Learning & Development*, 4(3), pp. 73–84.

Community, W.A., 2020. Farming kindergarten. Retrieved 2020, from *World Architecture Community*: https://worldarchitecture.org/architecture-projects/hfnfc/farming-kidergarten-project-pages.html

Conservation Council of New Brunswick, 2020. Design ideas for green school grounds. Retrieved 2020, from *Learning Outside*: https://www.learningoutside.ca/green-school-grounds/

Design for London, 2008. *Living Roofs and Walls: Technical Report: Supporting London Plan Policy*.

Editors, A., 2014. Farming kindergarten in Vietnam by Vo Trong Nghia architects. Retrieved November 2020, from *The Architectural Review*: https://www.architectural-review.com/awards/ar-emerging-architecture/farming-kindergarten-in-vietnam-by-vo-trong-nghia-architects

Feeley, D., 2019. Cool roofs. Retrieved December 2020, from *Eriesd*: https://www.eriesd
.org/cms/lib/PA01001942/Centricity/Domain/872/Cool%20Roofs.pdf

Germer, J., Sauerborn, J., Asch, F., de Boer, J., Schreiber, J., Weber, G. and Müller, J.,
2011. Skyfarming an ecological innovation to enhance global food security. *Journal für
Verbraucherschutz und Lebensmittelsicherheit*, 6(2), pp.237–251.

Gleason, P., 2006. Learning from green roofs: a Bronx School's lesson in saving energy.
Retrieved November 2020, from *The Environmental Magazine*: https://emagazine.co
m/learning-from-green-roofs/

Green Schools, 2020. *Resource Guide: A Practical Resource for Planning and Building Green
Schools in Ontario*. Ontario, Canada: Green Schools.

Greening, 2012. *Paving Hong Kong's Roofs in Green*. Hong Kong: Development Bureau
The Government of the Hong Kong Special Administrative Region.

Greenroofs.com, 2018. ST. Simon Stock R.C. elementary school. Retrieved November
2020, from *Greenroofs.com*: https://www.greenroofs.com/projects/st-simon-stock-r
-c-elementary-school/

Growdon, J.H. and Wurtman, R.J., 1980. Contemporary nutrition: nutrients and
neurotransmitters. *New York State Journal of Medicine*, 57.

Hardman, M. and Larkham, P.J., 2014. The rise of the 'food charter': a mechanism to
increase urban agriculture. *Land Use Policy*, 39, pp.400–402.

Hatfield, J.L., Boote, K.J., Kimball, B.A., Ziska, L.H., Izaurralde, R.C., Ort, D.,
Thomson, A.M. and Wolfe, D., 2011. Climate impacts on agriculture: implications
for crop production. *Agronomy Journal*, 103(2), pp.351–370.

Hendrickson, M.K. and Porth, M., 2012. *Urban Agriculture: Best Practices and Possibilities*.
Columbia, MO: University of Missouri, pp.1–52.

Holmes, J., 2009. Losing 25,000 to hunger every day. *UN Chronicle*, 45(3), pp.14–20.

Hui, S.C., 2011. Green roof urban farming for buildings in high-density urban cities. In
The Hainan China World Green Roof Conference 2011, 18–21 March 2011, Hainan
(Haikuo, Boao and Sanya), China.

Ibáñez Gutiérrez, R.A. and Ramos-Mejía, M., 2019. Function-based and multi-scale
approach to green roof guidelines for urban sustainability transitions: the case of
Bogota. *Buildings*, 9(6), p.151.

Iheke, O.R. and Ihuoma, U., 2016. Effect of urbanization on agricultural production
in Abia State. *International Journal of Agricultural Science, Research and Technology in
Extension and Education Systems*, 5(2), pp.83–89.

Iswm, 2020. Green Roofs. Retrieved December 2020, from *Innovative Stormwater
Management Practice*: http://iswm.ca/details.php?id=201.0

Journal, B., 2014. Ng Yuk roof garden received the highest honour at GBA 2014. Retrieved
November 2020, from *NYSS*: https://www.nyss.edu.hk/nygreen/2014gba.pdf

Ketchell, M., 2018. Urban farming: four reasons it should flourish post-pandemic.
Retrieved 2020, from: https://theconversation.com/urban-farming-four-reasons-it
-should-flourish-post-pandemic-144133

Kumar, Vikash, et al., 2019. Rooftop vegetable garden: a new concept of urban
agriculture. *Agriculture & Food: e-Newsletter*, 109–112.

Lahey, M. and Rosen, S., 2010. Dietary factors affection learning behavior. Retrieved
November 2020 from http://childrensdisabilities.info.

Livinspaces, 2020. Learning curve: farming kindergarten in Vietnam by Vo Trong Nghia
Architects. Retrieved November 2020, from *LIVINSPACES*: https://www.livinspa
ces.net/projects/architecture/learning-curve-farming-kindergarten-in-vietnam-by-
vo-trong-nghia-architects/

Luckett, K., 2009. *Green Roof Construction and Maintenance*. New York: McGraw-Hill Education.

Maijo, S.N., 2018. Impact of school feeding programme on learners' academic performance in Mlunduzi Ward, Tanzania. *International Journal of Educational Studies*, 5(3), pp.125–130.

Martellozzo, F., Landry, J.S., Plouffe, D., Seufert, V., Rowhani, P. and Ramankutty, N., 2014. Urban agriculture: a global analysis of the space constraint to meet urban vegetable demand. *Environmental Research Letters*, 9(6), p.064025.

Medina, S., 2015. Students grow their own food at this experimental kindergarten. Retrieved November 2020, from *METROPOLIS*: https://www.metropolismag .com/architecture/educational-architecture/students-plant-their-own-food-ex perimental-kindergarten/

Minaya, S. and Rainville, A.J., 2016. How nutritious are children's packed school lunches? A comparison of lunches brought from home and school lunches. *The Journal of Child Nutrition and Management*, 40, pp.1–7.

Onwumere, M., Modebelu, M.N. and Chukwuka, I.E., 2016. Influence of school farm on teaching of agricultural science in Senior Secondary Schools in Ikwuano Local Government Area, Abia State. *Open Access Library Journal*, 3(6), pp.1–6.

Poptani, H. and Bandyopadhyay, A., 2014. Extensive green roofs: potential for thermal and energy benefits in buildings in central India. In 30th International PLEA Conference (pp. 1–8), Ahmedabad, Gujarat, India.

Pramanik, C., Dey, S.K. and Sarkar, A., 2010. Effect of urbanization on agriculture: a special scenario on Andhra Pradesh. *Indian International Journal of Applied Science and Computations*, 17(2), pp.121–128.

Ptomey, L.T., Steger, F.L., Schubert, M.M., Lee, J., Willis, E.A., Sullivan, D.K., Szabo-Reed, A.N., Washburn, R.A. and Donnelly, J.E., 2016. Breakfast intake and composition is associated with superior academic achievement in elementary schoolchildren. *Journal of the American College of Nutrition*, 35(4), pp.326–333.

Ronaldson, M., 2005. News half term report December 2004. Retrieved November 2020, from *lcherbalists*: http://www.lcherbalists.co.uk/roofgarden/news/halfterm.html

Roofs, B., 2020. St. Simon Stock R.C. Elementary School | Bronx, NY. Retrieved November 2020, from *Between the World and the Weather Since 1928*: https://www.bar rettroofs.com/project/st-simon-stock-r-c-elementary-school-bronx-ny/

Rooftop Farms, 2020. Eagle street rooftop farm. Retrieved December 2020, from: http://rooftopfarms.org/

Ross, A. and Anderson, D.L., 2010. *Nutrition and Its Effects on Academic Performance How Can Our Schools Improve*. Michigan: Northern Michigan University.

Scharf, B., and Kraus, F., 2019. Green roofs and green pass. *Buildings*, 9(9), p.205.

Schwartz, M.B., Henderson, K.E., Read, M., Danna, N. and Ickovics, J.R., 2015. New school meal regulations increase fruit consumption and do not increase total plate waste. *Childhood Obesity*, 11(3), pp.242–247.

Selzer, M., 2019. *Rooftop Garden-Based Education: Cultivating a Healthy and Environmentally Aware Urban Youth*. Senior Honors Thesis at University of North Carolina at Chapel Hill.

Smeds, P., Jeronen, E. and Kurppa, S., 2015. Farm education and the value of learning in an authentic learning environment. *International Journal of Environmental and Science Education*, 10(3), pp.381–404.

Snodgrass, E.C. and Snodgrass, L.L., 2007. *Green Roof Plants: A Resource and Planting Guide* (No. 04; SB419. 5, S5.). Portland, OR: Timber Press.

Taras, H., 2005. Nutrition and student performance at school. *Journal of School Health*, 75(6), pp.199–213.

TDSB, 2020. Jackman avenue junior public school. Retrieved 2020, from *School Web*: https://schoolweb.tdsb.on.ca/jackman/Eco-School

The United Nations, 2020. *The State of Food Security and Nutrition in the World Report*, Rome.

Trbižan, G., 2020. Good practice: little terrace roof garden. Retrieved December 2020, from *Interreg Europe*: https://www.interregeurope.eu/policylearning/good-practices/item/3297/little terrace-roof-garden/

United Nations, Department of Economic and Social Affairs, Population Division, 2018. *World Urbanization Prospects: The 2018 Revision*. New York: United Nations.

Wang, L., 2016. Green-roofed farming kindergarten teaches 500 Vietnamese children how to grow their own food. Retrieved December 2020, from *INHABITAT* https://inhabitat.com/green-roofed-farming-kindergarten-teaches-500-vietnamese-children-how-to-grow-their-own-food/.

Weber Cullen, K. and Chen, T., 2017. The contribution of the USDA school breakfast and lunch program meals to student daily dietary intake. *Preventive Medicine Reports*, 5, 82–85.

WeCan, P., 2020. NYSS on winning the green building award. Retrieved November 2020, from *Project WeCan*: http://www.projectwecan.com/2014/11/21/nyss-on-winning-the-green-building-award/

Weiler, S. and Scholz-Barth, K., 2009. Green Roof Systems: A Guide to the Planning, Design, and Construction of Landscapes over Structure. Hoboken, NJ: Wiley.

Wood, M., 2001. Studies probe role of minerals in brain function. *Agricultural Research*, 49(10), p.4.

13

BUILDING COMMUNITY RESILIENCE

The synergy between school farms and neglected urban open spaces

Ali Fouad Bakr and Nehad Abd Gawad

Introduction

Notably, urban growth and overpopulation have significantly contributed to weakening community resilience. Community resilience (CR) refers to the interconnected relationships of various systems that can directly impact human society at the community level, including the socio-economic, ecological, and built environments. In 2012, the Torrens Resilience Institute launched a report entitled *Developing a model and tool to measure community disaster resilience*, which described the community as resilient when

> members of the population are connected to one another and work together, so that they are able to function and sustain critical systems, even under stress; adapt to changes in the physical, social or economic environment; be self-reliant if external resources are limited or cut off, and learn from experience to improve itself over time.
>
> *(Fitzpatrick, 2016, p. 58)*

Nevertheless, contemporary cities are confronting environmental challenges such as climate change, global warming, and an energy shortage, as well as global pandemics like the Covid-19 virus. Among these challenges, food security became a critical issue, making political leaders and national actors aware of this dilemma. They have been forced to develop policies of food governance and search for new initiatives of agriculture to enhance food security (Pimbert, 2009).

Additionally, the Covid-19 pandemic has highlighted the necessity of delivering nutritious food to the public, particularly the youth, representing a market value to food producers (NIPN et al., 2020; Cleveland Clinic, 2020). Thus, food is a significant element of various sectors, public health, social justice, energy,

DOI: 10.4324/9781003176558-13

water, transportation, and economic development to achieve CR. To cope with these environmental and urban crises, the paradigm trends of urban revitalization should be more oriented towards green urban development through strategies of sustainable urban planning and landscape. Accordingly, urban areas are offered as solutions to achieve sustainable food security in addition to the revitalization of the neighborhoods.

On the one hand, contemporary cities are riddled with neglected urban open spaces (NUOS), which attract illicit activity (e.g., robbery, littering, and homelessness) and negatively impact the environment. NUOS are mainly generated because of the major decentralization process in cities, particularly in metropolitan regions, in the form of changing activities, which generate unused spaces. The evolution of new infrastructure projects has played a major role in creating marginal spaces aligned to railways and/or highways, for instance (Jacobs, 1961;; Monclús, 2018; Abd El Gawad, 2020). Equally important are zoning mechanisms and various land policies which generate vacant land with different forms between districts and neighborhoods (Kim, 2016). So, NUOS are defined as vacant lots, residual spaces, in-between landscapes, brownfields, and forgotten spaces (Abd El Gawad et al., 2019;

Recently, urban developers have recognized NUOS in creating sustainable communities in healthy, environmental, economic, and sociocultural aspects (Monclús & Medina, 2018; Abd El Gawad et al., 2019). These dimensions reflect the relationship between man and the built environment in the form of functional, social, perceptual, visual, environmental, and morphological dimensions. Urban design has used functional, social, and environmental dimensions collectively to integrate NUOS with the urban fabric by the urban agriculture (UA) approach to develop green vegetated spaces like community gardens (CG). Often, CG are constructed in abandoned spaces within low-income neighborhoods to strengthen their access to fresh fruit and vegetables.

On the other hand, the school farm (SF) is one of the UA forms across communities aiming to improve the quality of food. Scientifically, schools play a crucial role in improving dietary habits towards healthy food by developing healthy choices that reach the majority of the community. Although school food is facing a market failure due to poor accessibility and limited financial resources, the SF can achieve several benefits, in terms of health, society, environment, and education (Izumi et al., 2010).

From here, the argument is based on the applicability of NUOS to create new models of the SF for pumping new resources into the urban food system and meeting the self need of the school for organic food. To achieve this plan, this chapter is methodically constructed into as follows. Firstly, explains the emergence of NUOS within the urban fabric, then it turns to demonstrate the global contributions to investigating NUOS. Secondly, presents new comprehensive classifications of NUOS to be a referential model in the revitalization process. Thirdly examines how NUOS would be converted to active urban spaces. Fourthly, explains the concept of the SF to investigate both sectors, objectives, barriers, importance, and benefits of the SF. Finally, presents the synergy between the SF and NUOS by efficient planning and implementation of the SF.

In sum, NUOS could play a fundamental role in delivering sustainable school farm concepts by developing new models, which act as a catalyst in the resilience equation, by tackling different communities' problems as insufficient, and/or poor nutritious food systems. Furthermore, by also presenting a self-sustained schooling system. The hypothesized model will enrich the community with a healthy interactive environment and social equality, promoting community engagement.

Emergency of NUOS

The urban fabric of cities reflects the components of the urban environment: urban spaces and urban solids Historically, urban open spaces (UOS) were the essential components in city planning, which plays a vital role in urban life (Khatibi & Habib, 2015). Unfortunately, they become NUOS as a result of transforming the primary types of UOS into marginalized spaces. The urban development has added new exotic forms of UOS to the urban fabric (Jacobs, 1961; Ghotb, 2014).

Primary forms of NUOS

Urban space has been defined as a dimensionally specified space, which is carved out of the urban solids to enhance functional and visual continuity of the urban environment (Abraham, 2009; Ghotb, 2014). The traditional integrated system of urban open spaces of the city consists of five types: entry foyers, inner-block voids, networks of streets and squares, parks and gardens, and a linear open-space system The development of cities from *industrial* to *post-industrial* and/or *modern* to *post-modern* features has converted the traditional urban spaces into NUOS (Cybriwsky, 1999), see Figure 13.1. For instance, networks of streets and squares are converted from strategic spaces into a vicious mobility cycle ignoring the pedestrian movement (Zafarivahid & Shieh, 2016). Nevertheless, as a result of poor urban management, these networks suffer from physical deterioration similar to the public spaces of parks (Jansson, 2014; Beqaj, 2016; Sameeh et al., 2019). Likewise, the waterfront areas are converted into unused urban spaces of informal green spaces, inactive promenades, or even polluted industrial ports.

Exotic forms of NUOS

The emergence of NUOS is a cumulative process where it is synchronized with the continuous development of a city. Hence, a lot of NUOS are developing and permeating the city's fabric with different typologies. According to Roger

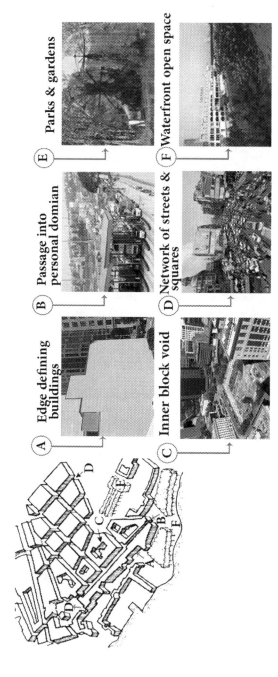

FIGURE 13.1 The traditional conversion of traditional UOS to NUOS (Authors, 2020).

Trancik, who brought NUOS to the urban design realm, NUOS exist due to these rooted causes: the automobile, modern movement in design, urban renewal policies, and privatization of public space (Tranick, 1986). Other causes that contribute to NUOS are lack of attractive activities and amenities within urban spaces (Gehl, 2010; Beqaj, 2016) and lack of regulations defining property rights or ownerships (Haas & Kopanyi, 2017). All of these root causes of the social, economic, and environmental aspects of NUOS underline the negative side of NUOS

Generally, NUOS are thoroughly discussed earlier, conveying several perceptions and viewpoints (Lynch, 1960; Gehl, 2010;; Jacobs, 1961; Pagano & Bowman, 2001). However, within the intended scope of this study, Roger (1986) has defined NUOS as undesirable urban areas that need to be redesigned to impact surroundings positively.

Classification of NUOS

The classification of NUOS includes three main components: vacant land, social unfamiliar space, and transport infrastructure leftover space.

NUOS as vacant land (VL)

Vacancy is the most-known feature of NUOS, which is related to ownership and development (Sinn, 1986Therefore, VL involves numerous types of unutilized lots in the fringes of cities and may involve abandoned structures, which may vary between being totally or partially destroyed (Kivell, 1993; Pagano & Bowman, 2001). VL could comprise small or irregularly shaped parcels (De Biasi, 2017), making the city fabric scattered As a result of development, VL comes in two forms: permanent vacant land and temporary vacant land

Permanent vacant land (PVL) involves previously developed and undeveloped land (Kim, 2016). The previously developed land refers to the previous activity, that is industrial, commercial, and residential activity that is currently absent This VL comes with an environmental cost of contaminated VL (Kim, 2016), which demands more financial resources for remediation and removal of the contaminates (Mohamed, 2012).

The previously undeveloped land refers to land with random green growth, which has never involved any construction or activity (i.e., social, environmental, or economic) More importantly, this type exists in cities on two levels: city scale and neighborhood scale according to various features of scale, ownership, and location. Consequently, this type has much ecological and social potential after development (Hamil & Lucas, 2013For instance, small vacant lots can be revitalized as an active public space for residents as in Philadelphia, where the state has converted vacant lots into community gardens (Kim, 2016)

The previously undeveloped land at the city scale includes remnant parcels, corporate reserve parcels, and VL for speculation (Najjar & Ghadban, 2015). Remnant parcels are always small and irregular spaces without beneficial use, formed by building and regulation laws LI et al., In contrast, corporate reserve parcels are large-sized spaces (e.g., tens of hectares) and owned by local authorities for upcoming investment projects in the city (Haas & Kopanyi, 2017). Finally, VL for speculation is privately owned by citizens to avoid raising land values and the city's growth (Belete, 2010). The previously undeveloped land at the neighborhood scale also involves four types according to their location to the surrounding buildings. They are vacant corner lot, vacant block, suburban yards, and VL system The vacant corner lot is located at the corner of the block, where buildings surround it from the two sides. The vacant block is larger than the vacant corner lot (e.g., an acre) and is surrounded by three sides. The suburban yards are differentiated by undefined shapes and would combine corner lots and vacant block system. Finally, the VL system comprises much VL within a big area and of different shapes (Belete, 2010).

Temporary vacant land (TVL) refers to dual and single-use spaces at specific times, converted to VL eventually It includes two forms: the first relates to the building block, and the other relates to the community (Jacobs, 1961; Shaftoe, 2008). Unfortunately, the sidewalks of contemporary cities have become passive paths as landscape architects have neglected the environmental and social benefits of sidewalks (Ehrenfeucht & Sideris, 2007The second type related to the community scale involves surfaces of parking lots, which often interrupt the pedestrian movement in cities (Jacobs, 1961; Arnott, 2006).

NUOS as a social unfamiliar space (SUS)

SUS is simply a public space with a lost social value, particularly in modern cities (Jacobs, 1961; Dover & Massengale, 2014). The scope of an SUS is composed of neglected paths, nodes, and green spaces, which are all defined as NUOS of the contemporary city (NACTO, 2016).

Urban designers have designed the most recent paths as oversized spaces only for traffic movements (Shukla & Navratra, 2017; Kamel et al., 2017). The hierarchical structure of a boulevard, main street, and arterial roads has contributed to the formation of NUOS by propagating vacant and underutilized spaces. Despite this, they can represent complete streets designed to enhance safety and accessibility by strengthening the sustainability concept by applying green stormwater infrastructure of the streetscape and buildings (Scott et al., 2011). Neighboring streets and pedestrian streets have significantly featured within active building facades (Davies, 2000). These blank walls can be revitalized as green facades, adding a greening style to the neighborhoods (Miller et al., 2013).

Nodes are converted to NUOS by strengthening the sense of insecurity due to the dominance of random plants (Moughtin, 2003; Zucker, 2003). Other forms of nodes have emerged by developing mobility and building regulations, such as *amorphous squares* and *traffic squares* (NACTO, 2016). In 2003, Paul Zucker described the *amorphous square* as an unorganized and formless space with no specific shape (Zucker, 2003). Any neglected *amorphous* square either comes as a sporadic square part of the connected building (NACTO, 2016) or as a convergence point of intersection between two streets of different orientations (Zucker, 2003), jeopardizing pedestrian accessibility. Although urban green spaces are expected to improve the quality of life of the cities' inhabitants (Burgess et al., 1988), they were converted to NUOS with poor management and limited maintenance (Cohen et al., 2016; Salmón et al., 2014).

Classifications of NUOS as a transport infrastructure leftover space (TILS)

Transport infrastructure (TI) indicates the means and elements of transporting people and goods (Kopieca et al., 2019; Baker, 2016). Halprin (1966) classified the physical system of TI based on the street level into four categories: at grade, depressed, elevated stacked, and elevated side by side. Urban planners have named NUOS of transport infrastructure as a residual or leftover space (LS), which is generally neglected due to the oddity of shape and location (Najjar & Ghadban, 2015). Since depressed TILS is explained earlier as remnant parcels, the focus will be directed towards at grade and elevated TILS.

At grade TILS is vacant sideways, which are narrow spaces compared to their length (Irizarry, 2003). Elevated TILS is described as ambivalent landscapes located adjacent, along, and beneath flyovers of highway structures (Zaman et al., 2012). Despite the fact that TILS consists of publicly owned abandoned spaces, it has the potential for non-productive or illegal activities (Franck & Stevens, 2007). By applying the greening approach, TILS can serve as an ecological lung for the community like the Highline Park in New York City Traditionally, urban developers aim at revitalizing TILS by considering adjacent and underneath TILS as curtilage LS (Chapman & Collins, 2012). This curtilage LS is composed of scattered spaces according to the physical complexity of the flyover. Another crucial factor of classifying TILS is the flyover location, which varies between the waterfront and residential territories. Therefore, Table 13.1 illustrates the relationship between the spatial form of LS and the location of the flyover to extract different typologies of LS.[1]

As illustrated in Table 13.1, the spatial form of LS of the waterfront varies between adjacent LS, underneath linear LS, and curtilage LS. Likewise, LS between neighborhoods takes three forms: penetrating LS, integrating LS, and outside neighborhood LS.

From NUOS to active urban spaces

With the limitless challenges of the 21st century, the urban revitalization strategy (URS) had to be involved simultaneously to include environmental risk management, heritage preservation, and maximizing the societal returnsAfter that, the scope of the NUOS application has to deliver economic, social, environmental, and cultural outcomes

TABLE 13.1 All forms of LS of elevated flyover within the urban form

The spatial form of LS	LS of waterfront		LS between neighborhoods		
	Complex	Single	penetrating	Integrating	Outside
Adjacent LS		Waterfront Park		Illinois Institute	
Underneath linear LS		Chicago's River-walk	Colonnade Bike Park	Queensboro Bridge market	Bent way Park
Curtilage LS.	Sabine promenade source		Underground Park	Chicano Park	Muharram Bih flyover

Within the scope of the URS, NUOS can be revitalized according to three main tactics: urban infill development (UID), adaptive development reuse (ADR), and place-making (Archer, 2015;; Thwaites et al., 2007; Sameeh et al., 2019). Urban developers mention that both UID and ADR are mainly used for promoting investments in cities to attract the private sector (Amiri & Lukumwena, 2019). In comparison, place-making is a multifunctional and peo-ple-centered tactic, which seeks to transform NUOS into productive spaces to create community resilience from the economic, social, and environmental side; Sulaiman et al., 2016

NUOS open up new business opportunities from the economic side by tar-geting skilled workers, such as farmers and artists, to generate new activities like local markets and investment farms Also, NUOS like TILS can be attrac-tive public spaces by the innovative design of activities and landscape As for the environmental side, NUOS can be a new source of urban green lungs to provide the communities with healthy environments and a comfortable climate These lungs would be productive green space by the UA approach as a form of commu-nity initiatives, which provide the communities with a wide range of ecosystem services. For example, these services involve developing the urban food system of communities with new food sources (;). For instance, brownfield sites can be redeveloped as farms or community gardens, but that requires adding certain forms of gardening for soil amendments to reduce contamination risks (EPA,

2018). Among these community initiatives, the SF is considered a significant strategy of the UA approach, enhancing the significance of healthy food (Lovell, 2010; Krishnan et al., 2016).

What is the school farm (SF)?

The school farm (SF) is a community food system in the form of urban agriculture (Krishnan et al., 2016). In 1990, the SF was originated in the United States as a concept before it became globally recognized (Braun et al., 2006). It aims to increase the production and distribution of healthy food by enhancing the capacity of both the supply and demand sides (Vallianatos et al., 2004; Korani, 2012). Ultimately, the SF addresses the hunger problem at the school level by enhancing availability, utilization, and accessibility of healthy local food); Adebayo & Mudaly, 2019). Moreover, it is considered a tool to provide students with learning experiences to produce organic food and adopt healthy behavior (Canaris, 1995; Lineberger & Zajicek, 2000; Social Farms & Gardens, 2018).

The SF can serve as either farm-to-school and/or school gardens. These sectors include several activities to connect children with local farming (Foeken et al., 2010; Roche et al., 2012). Farm-to-school is a program that aims at increasing the integration of fresh food from local and regional farms into school meals (New York Department of Agriculture and Markets, 2015), including other activities of harvest festivals, field trips, and educational visits from farmers (Vallianatos et al., 2004; Izumi et al., 2010). For instance, the New York State Farm-to-School Program was created to connect schools with local farmers and food producers to strengthen local agriculture, improve student health, and promote awareness of regional food systems (Must et al., 1999). In this sense, schools would become a new and institutional-scale market for local farmers and food distributors by delivering their crops to the schools (Izumi et al., 2010). The ownership of this sector varies between publicly, privately, and commercially owned, or run for defined missions like charities (Krishnan et al., 2016).

The school garden (SG) refers to a wide range of farm activities according to the scale and category of schools (Bonannoa & Mendis, 2021). These gardens involve chicken coops and beehives, as well as green gardens and aquaculture facilities. The form of the SG varies from windowsill boxes, a few containers in a side alley, to a full garden in unused space (Social Farms & Gardens, 2018). The SG aims at enhancing 'learning by doing' to explore the entire food ecosystem (Savoie-Roskos et al., 2017; Berezowitz et al., 2015). As a result, students capture the real-life experience of the farming industry. The education authorities own almost all SGs (Savoie-Roskos et al., 2017).

Barriers and objectives

As an innovative approach, the SF addresses the root cause of childhood obesity and chronic diseases which can be helped by acquiring healthy behavior (Must et al., 1999; Khan et al., 2009). This gain is centered around the production of sustainable, local, and nutritious meals to enhance students' healthy growth and mental development (Berezowitz et al., 2015). The application of the SF enhances school-community integration by strengthening the local urban food system and shortening the food delivery system (Viljoen, et al., 2005; The SF is a chance to create a new alliance with farmers supporting local agriculture and enhancing farmland preservation (Vallianatos et al., 2004).

There are some challenges to overcome to achieve these objectives, such as regulation, financial resources, and market due to the limited government support and rise in food costs (; New York Department of Agriculture and Markets, 2015). Also, several schools are reluctant to invest in practical agriculture (Must et al., 1999). From a practical perspective, schools tend to generate revenue by offering junk meals to students to the extent that they cannot meet the demand for kitchen facilities (Vallianatos et al., 2004). Therefore, the school has become a staunch opponent against changing students' food culture and eating habits towards fresh food (Kloppenburg, 2007).

In 2018, The Guardian published the article 'How poor policy implementation, loss of land frustrate agric in schools', discussing other challenges of constructing the SF, which include the encroachment of land by developers for other non-agriculture-related projects; the lack of adequate infrastructure in schools for greening spaces; the un-affordability of farm inputs by schools; deforestation that leads to a reduction in the fertility of the soil; as well as the negative impacts of climate change and erosion in the environment (Abasi et al., 2018; Debru & Brand, 2019). From another perspective, the communication between farmers, producers, and schools is another challenge. Where farmers and producers exploit the schools' need for organic resources by increasing food overpricing, this leads to defining specific types of fresh food products according to the financial ability of schools (Korani, 2012; New York Department of Agriculture and Markets, 2015). Moreover, the food accessibility from farms and food markets to schools would be a challenge because of urban discontinuity and poor transportation logistics (Vallianatos et al., 2004).

Importance and benefits of the SF

The importance of the SF goes beyond growing food; it includes multifunctional areas and a learning arena (Blair, 2009; Berezowitz et al., 2015; Ighakpe, 2018). With early development of agriculture skills, crop rotation, mixed cropping, and inter-cropping (Shafer, 2018), the SF results in a student who values the production cycle of food rather than simply considering the supermarket as the primary food source (Callau et al., 2017). Consequently, it emphasizes agriculture as an essential part of a learning culture by engaging youth in growing, harvesting, and cooking food (Vallianatos et al., 2004), leading to a sustainable generation of students adopting a healthy lifestyle (Social Farms & Gardens, 2018).

Regarding the benefits, the SF can achieve social, economic, environmental, and health outcomes in addition to what we have discussed earlier on the health impacts of the SF for communities and individuals (Lovell, 2010; Krishnan et al., 2016; Vallianatos et al., 2004).

Several urban planners have discussed the correlation between student eating habits and wholesaler accessibility. For instance, the more accessible the wholesaler or supermarket, the more youth consume processed or fast food (Krishnan et al., 2016; Shafer, 2018). With these findings, the necessity of food literacy becomes a necessity for a healthy generation (Callau et al., 2017; Ighakpe, 2018). Furthermore, the SF depends on organic waste as fertilizers, which generate food safety. Hence, the food is free of food-borne contaminants and pesticide residues (Vallianatos et al., 2004). Also, the spread of the SF within communities can improve the visual quality of the neighborhoods, which leads to an enhanced sense of well-being and human healthSouth et al., 2018).

In terms of education, the SF serves as a real-life laboratory, where students gain the hands-on experience of cultivation (Blair, 2009; Ighakpe, 2018). In an observational study, the cognitive behavior of students increased by implementing the concept of school farming. In this sense, the researchers identified that the SF in the UK could achieve mental development for students by increasing their scientific skills (Ambusaidi et al., 2019; Costanigro et al., 2020). This finding could be justified by improving the nutritional content of food, which helps students focus, and the ability to learn effectively (Berezowitz et al., 2015). Alternatively, learning by applying and collaborating between students and rural farmers helped them boost their critical thinking and leadership skills (Bellows et al., 2003).

On the social scale, the SF is a new social movement that brings various participants together: farmers, farmworkers, community residents, or students, parents, teachers, and school food staff (Social Farms & Gardens, 2018). It builds a strong sense of place and ownership towards the community as well as a sense of responsibility to preserve the agricultural heritage (Canaris, 1995; Ighakpe, 2018). Another significant benefit is the collective responsibility, which improves students' behavior and attitude and empowers a sense of collaborative engagement (Hoffman et al., 2007). Speaking of the economic benefits, the SF can strengthen the local and regional food economies, particularly the Farm-to-School Program, by promoting their nutritious food in schools (Vallianatos et al., 2004). Therefore, farmers can attain significant sales and open up new markets, leading to a creation of new jobs (Kim, 2016; Somerset & Bossard, 2009; Department of Agriculture and Markets, 2015). Accordingly, farmers can rid themselves of the pressures of real estate developers to sell their land for development projects For instance, many trusts are established in New York to strengthen the economic security of US farmers by building the network between the farm and institutions (Libman et al., 2016).

Regarding the health benefits, the SF is a chance to decrease exposure to different diseases like diabetes and obesity (Krishnan et al., 2016). Besides, the

SF enhances food safety by growing food based on organic fertilizer and fewer pesticides (Vallianatos et al., 2004). Since childhood, establishing healthy diets is a relevant determinant for lifelong well-being and a high fitness level (Shafer, 2018).

On the community level, the SF preserves the green open space of the cities and strengthens the natural environment in communities (Hamil & Lucas, 2013; South et al., 2018). Some urban planners consider the SF as an opportunity to change the urban dweller's perspectives towards farming. And the result is several job opportunities for youth (Hightower, 2011). Hence, the SF is a vital model of urban development that can enhance social capital, community well-being, and civic engagement with the food system In this sense, integrating healthy food and farming experience into the curriculum creates a positive atmosphere impacting the lifestyles of both teachers and families (Bellows et al., 2003; Hightower, 2011). Engaging parents with their children in greening activities can change their shopping pattern behaviors towards healthy and local food choices (Bellows et al., 2003). Moreover, the SF offers a precious chance to improve the land use and activities of the built environment

The synergy between SF and NUOS

Although there are clear benefits to the SF, the application of the SF is not yet noticeable. By adding new landfills, the SF provides a quick solution to ill-planned land use, which led to a downgrade in the value of farmland (Thorpe, 2017). One of the market failures of the current food system is the distance between producer and consumer, encouraging farmers to give up on their land due to a low-profit margin as a result of expanding the supply chain (Thomaier et al., 2014; Hawkes & Halliday, 2017). Expanding the food supply chain comes with an environmental cost; the longer the distance, the higher the volume of CO_2 emissions (Paxton, 2005).

Enhancing the urban food system of communities provides a new approach to deliver a sustainable system able to face its challenges (Krishnan et al., 2016; Coulsona & Sonnino, 2019). This approach foresees urban spaces as an essential framework for a sustainable food system (Maćkiewicz et al., 2018). Here, the applicability of the UA approach is crucial to fill in the need for the SF, where converting NUOS to SFs can provide communities with multiple features of a resilient system (Callau et al., 2017;

Transformation of NUOS to SFs offers a solution to soil loss 'erosion' and increases the community production of organic food (Viljoen et al., 2005; Battersby & Haysom, 2020). The sustainable impact of NUOS, as illustrated in Figure 13.2, offers productive urban spaces of economic, sociological, and environmental perspectives as new components of the continuous productive urban landscapes in a city.

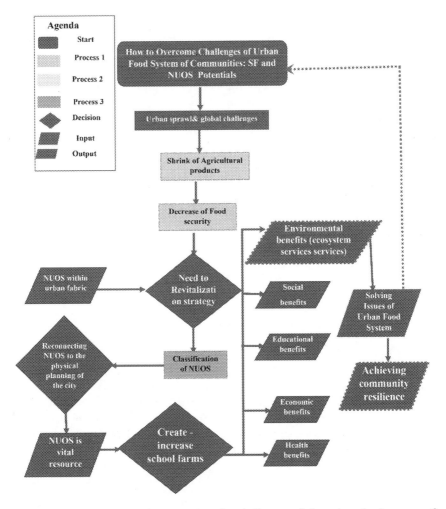

FIGURE 13.2 The vision of overcoming the challenges of the urban food system of communities with the potential of NUOS and SF (Authors, 2020).

Planning and implementation of the SF by NUOS approach

The concept of NUOS revitalization depends to a certain degree on using place-making tactics within three strategies: place-based, people-based, and organization-based strategies, as shown in Figure 13.3.

The place-based strategy is represented by improving the physical attributes of NUOS, while the people-based strategy refers to enhancing food justice by providing local, autonomous, and healthy food (Pimbert, 2009). The third strategy involves integrating NUOS into the high-density communities by growing local food. To clearly understand the dynamics of NUOS revitalization, the following

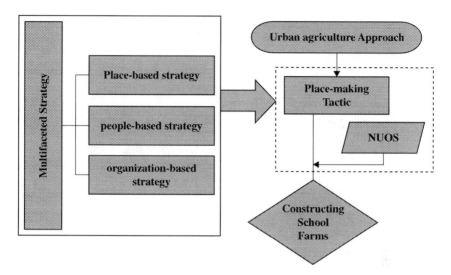

FIGURE 13.3   Strategies of transforming NUOS to the SF (Authors, 2020).

flow chart (Figure 13.4) illustrates the sequence of the proposed planning system of converting NUOS to three scales: macro, meso, and micro of the SF on the urban space scale and built environment scale.

After passing through the step of the NUOS inventory, the next stage is defining the appropriate regulations and laws of creating the SF. The planning system of NUOS revitalization should use land-use planning (LUP) to help urban planners to reallocate them within the physical urban environment Therefore, urban planners must use the fundamental theories of urban design, figure-ground, and linkage to reconnect the SF as a revitalized space with the surrounding area (Lak & Hakimian, 2018). First, use figure-ground to investigate the spatial patterns of the surrounding built environment, particularly educational institutions. Consequently, a geographic information system (GIS) would be a fundamental tool for urban planners. Then, linkage is used to increase the physical connectivity with the networks of streets, squares, and transit systems.

Regarding mechanisms of the planning system, the following points should be addressed:

1. The two sectors of the SF, farm-to-school and school gardens: investigate the different typologies of activities, which vary between growing, holding festivals, and organizing visiting farmers as mentioned before.
2. The classifications of NUOS: to include NUOS as VL, SUS, and TILS.
3. The scale of the SF: to provide a lot of green spaces related to the built environment and urban spaces; involving micro-scale (backyard, balcony, courtyards, wall's structure, patio pots, street verges, and green roof of buildings), meso-scale (urban farms and farmscrapers), macro-scale (urban food forest,

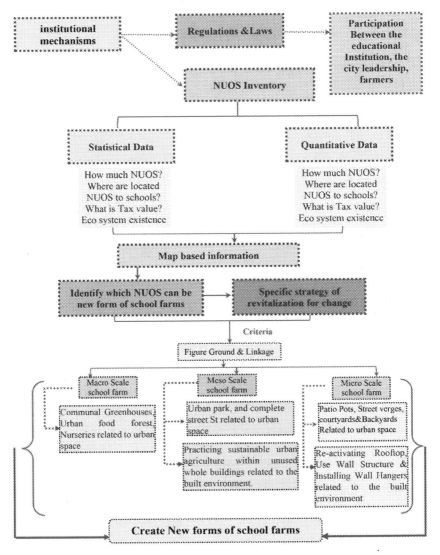

FIGURE 13.4 The sequence of the proposed planning system of converting NUOS to three scales of the SF: macro, meso, and micro (Authors, 2020).

and plant nurseries)The impacts associated with the SF (community scale and individuals scale): achieve social, educational, and health benefits.

Each form of the new model of the SF by revitalizing NUOS will have specific goals according to Five main categories of strategic orientations:

a) Sustainable food production is of high strategic importance to create various models of a sustainable food supply chain (Poppendieck, 2011).

b) The education of students is of high strategic importance to emphasize the significance of hands-on gardening and cooking experiences.

c) Local food economies are of high strategic importance to build a new market for local and regional farmers through the SF (Nestle, 2013).

d) Social commitment is of medium strategic importance to enhance the value of nutritious and fresh food as a lifestyle. Also, it reflects the social bonds between parents and their children.

e) Urban requalification is of low strategic importance to improve the environmental and psychological aspects.

As to effectively implement the SF, there are three challenges: financial, marketing, and legal issues need to be solved.

Financial challenges are the main obstacle to constructing the SF. Hence, the sources of finance could be one of the following:

- On the macro scale of the SF: encourage partnership between the private sector and urban developers.
- Redirect the public funds towards more community-oriented projects (Bonannoa & Mendis, 2021).
- Apply for financial grants to address the problems and needs of the local communities (Amirtahmasebi et al., 2016).
- Increase the social capital of trust by enhancing the voluntary work between inhabitants and city investors (Venn, 2019).
- Encourage the concept of co-financing between farmers and school districts (Thomaier et al., 2014).

Marketing challenges concern empowering the local urban market by:

- Increasing the capital of small farmers by offering on-site selling at faraway sites, where the consumer can purchase directly from the producer.
- Developing new supply chains where direct distribution from farmers to local restaurants and supermarkets can be done (Fattibene et al., 2020).
- Increasing the profitability by an alliance with the regional farmers, which expands the market size by raising new financial resources (New York Department of Agriculture and Markets, 2015).
- Orienting food accessibility to schools according to the distance food travels (Thomaier et al., 2014; Callau et al., 2017).

Legal challenges aim to plan and propose the legislative provisions to control the creation of the SF and institutionalizing them.

- Develop a legal agency to organize planning and management NUOS as SFs. This entity contains all stakeholders involved in the SF and NUOS: local farmers, farmworkers, community inhabitants, students, parents, volunteers,

consumers, developers, investors, owners, school staff, food producers, sup-
porters, and landlords of different types of NUOS (Vallianatos et al., 2004).

- Propose a legal framework of partnerships between farmers to enhance the
SF strategy and exchange knowledge (Korani, 2012).
- Define the legal ownership of the allocated premises, which are available
spaces for growing and weight-bearing capacity and accessibility.
- Create a bottom-up management stream to include volunteers and residents
who can have ownership of the SF development within buildings and rooftop spaces (Pearson, et al., 2010).
- Pay attention to integrate the inhabitants of disadvantaged layers of societies within NUOS (i.e., infrastructure leftover space) in greening the school
farm as new farmers by keeping or constructing their housing facilities
(Nestle, 2013). So, NUOS will be converted to become the source of livelihood and housing.
- Empower local authorities of municipalities to purchase or transfer NUOS
development rights and to release farmers and owners from property tax
(Vallianatos et al., 2004).
- Develop a legal framework to maintain and integrate the SF within public amenities, by stormwater control programs, maintaining vegetation and
plants, and reusing waste disposal.

Conclusion

Within this chapter, a strategy of developing emerging school farms from
neglected urban open spaces (NUOS) was discussed to enrich communities with
the new possibility of a sustainable food system. This strategy aims to facilitate the production, accessibility, and sustainability of local food by empowering
communities to tackle inequalities and limited urban capacities. It aims to curb
poverty and improve food security by maximizing the utility of NUOS to produce a sustainable food system and preserve farmland to achieve economic and
sociocultural gains. Moreover, this strategy highlights various aspects of developing the concept of the school farm from financial, economic, social, educational, and behavioral aspects. Hence, NUOS are a promising opportunity to
overcome the barriers of school farm development within the urban fabric.

The chapter has presented the SF thoroughly by discussing the elements, challenges, and importance of the SF. The SF is an innovative strategy with multiple
urban development-related objectives, aiming to reimagine the quality of education based on accessible nutritious meals with interactive educational activities
without an economic burden. Therefore, the SF can achieve a wide range of
educational, social, economic, and health benefits for communities and individuals. Moreover, this strategy aspires to convert the unpleasant image of NUOS,
vacant land, social unfamiliar space, and transport infrastructure leftover spaces
to a sustainable society. Within the hypothesized process, the transition of vacant
land as a form of NUOS to several constructive models of the SF was discussed.

By combining the elements of the SF, classifications of NUOS, and forms of new gardens related to the scale of urban agriculture, several applications of NUOS can emerge to serve the community, with various forms of agricultural products according to the scale of the school farm including green roofs, sidewalks, and grand urban forests. Then, within this strategy solutions to the challenges of implementing the SF related to financial, marketing, and legal issues were proposed.

In the end, the concept of a resilient community should be tailored based on the specific values of each community. To foster community resilience using this transformational vision, the synergy between NUOS and the school farm should be further elaborated within a community context under the direct supervision of political leadership.

Note

1 N.B: This analysis depends on studying some global examples of LS of elevated flyover according to landscape architects' contributions, due to the lack of data for this type of NUOS.

Bibliography

Abasi, E. et al., 2018. How poor policy implementation, loss of land frustrate agric in schools. [Online], Available at: https://guardian.ng/saturday-magazine/cover/how-poor-policy-implementation-loss-of-land-frustrate-agric-in-schools/, [Accessed 3 January 2021].

Abd El Gawad, N. E. S., 2020. Urban Revitalization of Neglected Urban Open Spaces (NUOS): Place-Making as an Approach, Unpublished Master Thesis, Faculty of Engineering, Department of Architecture, Alexandria University, Egypt.

Abd El Gawad, N. E. S., Al-Hagla, K. S. & Nassara, D. M., 2019. Placemaking as an approach to revitalize Neglected Urban Open Spaces (NUOS): A case study on Rod El Farag flyover in Shoubra, Cairo. *Alexandria Engineering Journal*, 58(3): 967–976.

Abraham, A., 2009. Urban void and the deconstruction of neo-platonic city-form. *Ethics, Place and Environment*, 12(2): 205–218.

Adebayo, O. & Mudaly, R., 2019. Creating a decolonised curriculum to address food insecurity among university students. *Problems of Education in the 21st Century*, 77(2):179–194.

Ambusaidi, A., Al-Yahyai, R., Taylor, S. & Taylor, N., 2019. School gardening in early childhood education in Oman: A pilot project with grade 2 students. *Science Education International*, 30(1): 45–55.

Amiri, B. A. & Lukumwena, N., 2019. Suitability analysis for infill (Re) development within informal context of the city: A case study of Hothkhel, Kabul City. *Urban and Transit Planning*, 247–259.

Amirtahmasebi, R., Orloff, M., Wahba, S. & Altman, A., 2016. *Regenerating Urban Land, A Practitioner's Guide to Leveraging Private Investment*. Washington, DC: International Bank for Reconstruction and Development / The World Bank.

Anderson, E. & Minor, E., 2016. Vacant lots: An underexplored resource for ecological and social benefits in cities. *Urban Forestry & Urban Greening*, 21(January): 146–152.

Archer, E.V. (2015). Improving shared spaces with a placemaking approach: Lessons from Adelaide. Master Thesis, Master of Planning, University of Otago. retrieved from http://hdl.handle.net/10523/5637

Arnott, R., 2006. Spatial competition between parking garages and downtown parking policy. *Transport Policy*, 13(6), November 2006: 458–469.

Baker, M., 2016. *Under the Bridge: Utilizing Covered Liminal Spaces for Sanctioned Homeless Encampments in the City of Seattle*. Unpublished Master of Urban Planning, University of Washington. [Online] Available at: https://digital.lib.washington.edu.

Battersby, J. & Haysom, G., 2020. Urban food security. In: R. Massey, A. Gunter, eds. *Urban Geography in South Africa Perspectives and Theory*. Switzerland: Springer.

Belete, T., 2010. *Development of Urban Vacant Land (The Case of Addis Ababa: Along Ring Road from Bole Square to Megenaga Square)*. Addis Ababa, Ethiopia. Addis Ababauniversity, http://etd.aau.edu.et/handle/123456789/3452?show=full

Bellows, B. C., Dufour, R., Bachmann, J. & NCAT Agriculture Specialists, 2003. *Bringing Local Food to Local Institutions: A Resource Guide for Farm to Institution Programs: NCAT Program Specialists*. NCAT, https://attra.ncat.org/

Beqaj, B., 2016. Public Space, public interest, and Challenges of Urban Transformation. *IFAC-Papers OnLine*, 49 (29): 320–324.

Berezowitz, C. K., Yoder, A. B. B. & Schoeller, D. A., 2015 . School gardens enhance academic performance and dietary outcomes in children. *The Journal of School Health*, 85 (8): 508–518.

Blair, D., 2009. The child in the garden: An evaluative review of the benefits of school gardening. *The Journal of Environmental Education*, 40 (2): 15–38.

Bonannoa, A., & Mendis, S. S. (2021). Too cool for farm to school? Analyzing the determinants of farm to school programming continuation. *Food Policy*, In Press, Corrected Proof, Available online 15 March 2021.

Braun, A. et al., 2006. *A Global Survey and Review of Farmer Field School Experiences: Global Forum for Rural Advisory Services*. Report prepared for the International Livestock Research Institute (ILRI).

Burgess, J., Harrison, C. & Limb, M., 1988. People, parks, and the urban green: A study of popular meanings and values for open spaces in the city. *Urban Studies*, 25 (6): 455–473.

Callau, S., Montasell, J. & Vila, A., 2017. Food cells and food nodes. Two new concepts for rethinking traditional urban and food planning practices. The case of Barcelona's Metropolitan region. In: C. T. Soulard, C. Perrin & E. Valette, eds. *Toward Sustainable Relations Between Agriculture and the City*. New York: Springer: 111–128.

Canaris, I., 1995. Growing foods for growing minds: Integrating gardening and nutrition education into the total curriculum. *Children's Environments*, 12 (2): 264–270.

Chapman, R. & Collins, G., 2012. Bridge aesthetics: Design guidelines to improve the appearance of bridges in New South Wales, Sydney. [Online], Available at: file:///C:/Users/aliba/Downloads/2011_Bridge_Collins.pdf .

Cleveland Clinic, 2020. Navigating nutrition during COVID-19 [Interview] (6 May 2020).

Cohen, D. et al., 2016. The paradox of parks in low-income areas: Park use and perceived threats. *Environment and Behavior*, 48(1): 230–245.

Costanigro, M., Jablonski, B. & Long, A., 2020. Farm to school activities and student outcomes: A systematic review. *Advances in Nutrition*, Mar 1, 11(2): 357–374.

Coulsona, H. & Sonnino, R., 2019. Re-scaling the politics of food: Place-based urban food governance in the UK. *Geoforum*, 98 (January): 170–179.

Cybriwsky, R., 1999. Changing patterns of urban public space: Observations and assessments from the Tokyo and New York metropolitan area. *Cities*, 16 (4): 223–231.

Davies, I., 2000. Urban design compendium. [Online], Available at: Urban Design Compendium.pdf - Google Drive.

De Biasi, A., 2017. Transforming vacant lots: Investigating an alternative approach to reducing fear of crime. *Journal of Environmental Psychology*, 50 (June): 125–137.

Debru, J. & Brand, C., 2019. Theoretical approaches for effective sustainable urban food policymaking. In: C. Brand, et al. eds. *Designing Urban Food Policies*. New York: Springer: 75–105.

Department of Agriculture and Markets, 2015. Farm-to-School. [Online], Available at: https://agriculture.ny.gov/farming/farm-school, [Accessed 12 January 2021].

Dover, V., & Massengale, J. 2014. *Street Design: The Secret to Great Cities and Towns*. Hoboken, NJ: Wiley.

Ehrenfeucht, R. & Sideris, A. L., 2007. Constructing the sidewalks: Municipal government and the production of public space in Los Angeles, California, 1880–1920. *Journal of Historical Geography*, 33: 104–124.

EPA, 2018. Turning Brownfields into community-supported and Urban agriculture. [Online], Available at: https://www.epa.gov/brownfields/turning-brownfields-community-supported-and-urban-agriculture, [Accessed 4 January 2020].

Fattibene, D., Recanati, F., Dembska, K. & Antonelli, M., 2020. Urban food waste: A framework to analyse policies and initiatives. *Resources*, 9 (99).9:99

Fitzpatrick, T., 2016. Community disaster resilience. In: *Disasters and Public Health*. Second Edition ed. s.l.:Butterworth-Heinemann: 57–85.

Foeken, D., Owuor, S. O. & Mwangi, A. M., 2010. School farming for school feeding: Experiences from Nakuru, Kenya. *The Journal of Field Actions*20 (1). https://journals.openedition.org/factsreports/563.

Franck, K. & Stevens, Q., 2007. *Loose Space Possibility and Diversity in Urban Life*. London: Routledge.

Gehl, J., 2010. *Cities for People*. Washington, DC: Island Press.

Ghotb, K., 2014. *Evaluation of the Lost Spaces in Karakol and Sakarya Districts of Famagusta, North Cyprus*. Gazimağusa, North Cyprus: Eastern Mediterranean University.

Gottlieb, R., and Hasse, M. 2004. Farm-to-school. *Journal of Planning Education and Research*, 23 (4): 414–423.

Haas, A. & Kopanyi, M., 2017. *Taxation of Vacant Urban Land: From Theory to Practice*. London: International Growth Center.

Halprin, L., 1966. Freeways. New York: Reinhold.

Hawkes, C. & Halliday, J., 2017. What makes urban food policy happen? insights from five case studies. iPES Food. [Online]. Available at: Cities_execsummary.pdf (ipes-food.org).

Hermann, J. R. et al., 2006. After-school gardening improves children's reported vegetable intake and physical activity. *The Journal of Nutrition Education and Behavior*, 38(3): 201–202.

Hightower, M. W. 2011. Why education researchers should take school food seriously. *Educational Researcher*, 40 (1): 15–21.

Hoffman, A. J., Knight, L. M. & Wallach, J., 2007. Gardening Activities, Education, and Self-Esteem Learning Outside the Classroom. *Urban Education*, 42 (5): 403–411.

Ighakpe, D., 2018. The importance of school farms. [Online], Available at: https://guardian.ng/opinion/the-importance-of-school-farms/, [Accessed 28 9 2020].

Irizarry, R., 2003. *Restructuring the Spaces under Elevated Expressways: A Case Study of the Spaces below the Interstate-10 Overpass at Perkins Road in Baton Rouge, Louisiana*.

Unpublished Mater Thesis, Master of Landscape Architecture in the School of Landscape Architecture, Louisiana State University.

Izumi, B. T., Alaimo, K. & Hamm, M. W., 2010. Farm-to-school programs: Perspectives of school food service professionals. *Journal of Nutrition Education and Behavior*, 42 (2): 83–91.

Jacobs, J., 1961. *The Death and Life of the Great American Cities*. New York: Random House.

Jansson, M., 2014. Green space in compact cities: The benefits and values of urban ecosystem services in planning. *Nordic Journal of Architectural Research*, 2: 139–160.

Kamel, B., Wahba, S., Kandil, A. & Fadda, N., 2017. Reclaiming streets as public spaces for people: Promoting pedestrianization schemes in Al-Shawarbi commercial street-downtown Cairo. In 1st International Conference on Towards a Better Quality of Life, 24–26 November 2017, Technische Universität Berlin Campus El Gouna, Egypt. Available at: https://ssrn.com/abstract=3170365.

Khan, L. K. et al., 2009. Recommended community strategies and measurements to prevent obesity in the United States. *MMWR Recommendations and Reports*, July 24, 58 (RR07): 1–26.

Khatibi, S. . M. & Habib, F., 2015. Defining a structural model for the revitalization of the lost urban spaces (city entrances) in contemporary urban design case study: Entrance of Sanandaj. *Space Ontology International Journal*, 1 (1): 55–62.

Kim, G., 2016. The public value of urban vacant land: Social responses and ecological value. *Sustainability*, 8 (5): 486. Available at: https://doi.org/10.3390/su8050486.

Kivell, P., 1993. *Land and the City: Patterns and Processes of Urban Change*. London: Routledge.

Kloppenburg, J., 2007. *Farm-to-School Program Provides Learning Experience*. Madison, WI: College of Agricultural and Life Sciences, University of Wisconsin-Madison.

Kopieca, A. C., Siguenciaa, L. O., Szostakb, Z. G. & Marzano, G., 2019. Transport infrastructures expenditures and costs analysis: The case of Poland. *Procedia Computer Science*, 149: 508–514.

Korani, Z., 2012. Application of teaching methods, promoting integrated pest management on the farm school in Order to achieve sustainable agriculture. *Procedia: Social and Behavioral Sciences*, 47: 2187–2191.

Krishnan, S., Nandwani, D., Smith, G. & Kankarta, V., 2016. Sustainable urban agriculture: A growing solution to urban food deserts. In: D. Nandwani, ed. *Organic Farming for Sustainable Agriculture*. Switzerland: Springer: 325–340.

Lak, A. & Hakimian, P., 2018. A new morphological approach to Iranian bazaar: The application of urban spatial design theories to Shiraz and Kerman bazaars. *Journal of Architectural Conservation*, 24 (3): 1–17.

Libman, K., Li, A. & Grace, C., 2016. *The Public Plate in New York State: Growing Health, Farms and Jobs with Local Food*. New York: The New York Academy of Medicine.

Lineberger, S. E. & Zajicek, J. M., 2000. School gardens: can a hands-on teaching tool affect students' attitudes and behaviors regarding fruit and vegetables? *HortTechnology*, 10 (3): 593–597.

Lovell, S. T., 2010. Multifunctional urban agriculture for sustainable land use planning in the United States. *Sustainability*, 2(8), 2499–2522.

Lynch, K., 1960. *The Image of City*. Cambridge, MA, London: MIT.

Maćkiewicz, B., Asuero, R. P. & Pawlak, K., 2018. Reclaiming urban space: A study of community gardens in Poznań. *Quaestiones Geographicae* 37 (4):131–150.

Miller, H., Witlox, F. & Tribby, C., 2013. Developing context-sensitive livability indicators for transportation planning: A measurement framework. *Journal of Transport Geography*, 26 (January): 51–64.

Mohamed, A. A., 2012. *Brown Fields from Abandonment to Engagement-transforming Derelict Ruins from Deteriorating to Revitalizing Elements in Cities Scape Analytical Case Studies.* Emscher Park, Germany, Azhar Park, Egypt: The Housing and Building National Research Center-High Institute for Engineering and Technology.

Monclús, J., 2018. Urban transport and technological urbanism. In: C. Díez-Medina, and J. Monclús, Eds. *Urban Visions: from urban planning to Landscape.* New York: Springer: 187–196.

Monclús, J. & Medina, C. D., 2018. Urban voids and 'in-between' landscapes. In: C. D. Medina & J. Monclús, eds. *Urban Visions from Planning Culture to Landscape Urbanism.* New York: Springer.

Moughtin, C., 2003. *Urban Design: Street and Square.* Amsterdam: Cliff Moughtin.

Must, A. et al., 1999. The disease burden associated with overweight and obesity. *JAMA*, 282 (16): 1523–1529.

NACTO, 2016. *Global Designing Cities Initiative.* New York: National Association of City Transportation Officials.

Najjar, L. & Ghadban, S. S., 2015. In-between forgotten spaces in Palestinian cities: The twin cities of Ramallah and Al-Bireh as a case study. *WIT Transactions on Ecology and The Environment*, 193: 811–822.

Nestle, M., 2013. *Food politics: How the food industry influences nutrition and health.* Revised and expanded ed. Berkeley, CA: University of California Press.

New York Department of Agriculture and Markets, 2015. Getting local food into New York State schools: A local procurement toolkit to bring together producers and schools in New York State. [online], Available at: https://www.agriculture.ny.gov/f2s/index.html.

NIPN, EPHI & IFPRI, 2020. *COVID-19 and its Impacts on Childhood Malnutrition and Nutrition-related Mortality* [Interview] (23 September 2020).

Pagano, M. & Bowman, A. O., 2001. Vacant land in cities: An urban resource, Washington, DC: https://www.brookings.edu.

Paxton, A., 2005. Food Miles. In: A. Viljoen, K. Bohn & J. Howe, eds. *Continuous Productive Urban Landscape (CPUL): Essential Infrastructure and Edible Ornament.* Amsterdam, Architectural Press.

Pearson, L., Pearson, L. & Pearson, C., 2010. Sustainable urban agriculture: Stocktake and opportunities. *International Journal of Agricultural Sustainability*, 8 (1–2): 7–19.

Pimbert, M., 2009. *Towards Food Sovereignty: Reclaiming Autonomous Food Systems*, London: International Institute for Environment and Development.

Poppendieck, J., 2011. *Free for All: Fixing School Food in America.* 1 ed. Berkeley, CA: University of California Press.

Roche, E. et al., 2012. Social cognitive theory as a framework for considering farm to school programming. *Childhood Obesity*, 8 (4): 357–363.

Salmón, P. et al., 2014. The identification and classification of green areas for urban planning using multispectral images at Baja California, Mexico. *WIT Transactions on Ecology and The Environment*, 191: 611–621.

Sameeh, R., Gabr, M. & Sherine, A., 2019. Reusing lost urban space. In: S. Attia, Z. Shafik & A. Ibrahim, eds. *New Cities and Community Extensions in Egypt and the Middle East.* Springer: 181–198.

Savoie-Roskos, M. R., Wengreen, H. & Durward, C., 2017. Increasing fruit and vegetable intake among children and youth through gardening-based interventions: A systematic review. *Journal of the Academy of Nutrition and Dietetics*, 117 (2): 240–250.

Scott, M., Beck, C. & Rabidou, B., 2011. Complete streets in Delaware: A guide for local governments: www.ipa.udel.edu.

Shafer, L., 2018. The long-lasting benefits of a school garden: Supporting health and wellness, encouraging students to choose nutritious foods. [Online], Available at: https ://www.gse.harvard.edu/news/uk/18/07/let-it-grow, [Accessed 4 January 2020].

Shaftoe, H., 2008. *Convivial Urban Spaces Creating Effective Public Places*. London; Sterling, VA: Earthscan in association with the International Institute for Environment and Development.

Shukla, A. & Navratra, N. D., 2017. Streets as public spaces: A case study of Manek Chowk. *International Journal of Civil Engineering and Technology (IJCIET)*. 8 (5, May): 1367–1376.

Sinn, H., 1986. Vacant land and the role of government intervention. *Regional Science and Urban Economics*, Elsevier, 16 (3): 353–357.

Social Farms & Gardens, 2018. School farms network. [Online], Available at: https:// www.farmgarden.org.uk/resources#filter, [Accessed 4 January 2021].

Somerset, S. M. & Bossard, A., 2009. Variations in prevalence and conduct of school food gardens in tropical and subtropical regions of north-eastern Australia. *Public Health Nutrition*, 12 (9): 1485–1493.

South, E. et al., 2018. Effect of greening vacant land on mental health of community-dwelling adults: A cluster randomized trial. *Public Health*. [online], Available at: https://jamanetwork.com/, [Accessed 1/27/2021].

Sulaiman, N., Zaman, N. H. Q., Hamdani, H. & Abdullah, Y. A., 2016. Rethinking potentials of public space and its management through placemaking in Kuala Lumpur. *MATEC Web of Conferences*, 66, 00056.

Thomaier, S. et al., 2014. Farming in and on urban buildings: Present practice and specific novelties of Zero-Acreage Farming (ZFarming). *Renewable Agriculture and Food Systems*, 30 (1): 43–54.

Thorpe, D., 2017. 10 examples of urban food policies: Feeding the cities, part 2. [Online], Available at: https://www.thefifthestate.com.au/urbanism/environment/ 10-examples-of-urban-food-policies-feeding-the-cities-part-2/, [Accessed 15 October 2020].

Thwaites, K., Porta, S., Romice, O. & Greaves, M., 2007. *Urban Sustainability through Environmental Design*. New York: Routledge.

Trancik, R., 1986. *Finding Lost Space: Theories of Urban Design*. New York: Wiley.

Vallianatos, M., Gottlieb, R. & Haase, M. A., 2004. Farm-to-school: Strategies for urban health, combating sprawl, and establishing a community fod systems approach. *Journal of Planning Education and Research*, 23 (4): 414–423.

Venn, S., 2019. Asking for change-local food and you. [Online], Available at: https://ww w.incredibleedible.org.uk/news/asking-for-change-local-food-and-you/, [Accessed 25 December 2020].

Viljoen, A., Bohn, K. & Howe, J., 2005. More food with less space. In: A. Viljoen, K. Bohn & J. Howe, eds. *Continuous Productive Urban Landscape (CPUL): Essential Infrastructure and Edible Ornament*. Oxford: Architectural Press: 19–29.

Zafarivahid, M. & Shieh, E., 2016. The hierarchy of city spatial organization in terms of establishment of land use factors (Case study: District No. 2 of the Municipality of Hamadan). *Science Arena Publications: Specialty Journal of Architecture and Construction*, 2 (3): 67–77. Available online at www.sciarena.com.

Zaman, N. Q., Samadi, Z. & Azhari, N. F. N., 2012. Opportunity in leftover spaces: Activities under the flyovers of Kuala Lumpur. Egypt. *Procedia Social and Behavioral Sciences*, 68 (19): 451–463.

Zucker, P., 2003. The square in space and time. In: *Time-Saver Standards for Urban Design*. New York: McGraw-Hill Education.

14

INCLUSIVE LEARNING SCHOOL FARM ENVIRONMENT

Alshimaa A. Farag and Iman S. Hamza

Introduction

Inclusion in the learning environment allows all students with different abilities to join a normal, learning, interactive physical environment with a suitable interface between them and their community to develop their diverse abilities and integrate within their society as productive members. The inclusive outdoor learning environment allows for adaptation and integration in the school physical environment to support students with their different disabilities to participate physically, sensorily, and mentally in an inclusive and active learning experience.

One of the significant learning models of using outdoor spaces is the school farm, which is considered one of the vital learning school environments. It allows all students to get hands-on learning opportunities of gardening and knowledge of planting and animal care. It brings them healthy and local food and lets them learn where their food comes from. In addition to learning opportunities, students gain significant aesthetical, environmental, and social benefits by embedding greenery spaces in the school's physical environment. It beautifies the school environment, improves the air quality, and reduces noise levels. It hosts wildlife, reduces stress, provides calm, and promotes socialization between students (Karakoç and Polat, 2019; Farag, Badawi, and Doheim, 2019).

The school farm must be designed with conscious consideration to students with different disabilities, whether physical, mental, or sensory, contributing to creating an efficient and effective physical and learning environment for all students. Allowing students with various disabilities to be active participants in a natural learning environment proves beneficial to their physiological, emotional, and spiritual wellbeing. It enhances students' cognitive level and hands-on experience, stimulates their senses, allows them to be in contact with nature, develops their attitude toward the environment, and improves integration within their

DOI: 10.4324/9781003176558-14

community. In addition to learning opportunities, enabling social interaction between all students in an enjoyable, authentic learning experience allows them to deepen their understanding of their diverse abilities. This can build empathy and respect between all students and contribute to changing possible discriminatory attitudes in the coming generations.

Barriers and challenges face students with disabilities due to the lack of understanding and knowledge of the design and requirements of different spaces to involve them in the learning environment. Many designers and landscape architects still do not know how to design inclusive outdoor spaces that consider all students' abilities and differences (Woolley, 2013). Therefore, this chapter provides a thought-provoking and detailed consideration of guidelines and requirements to design an inclusive learning environment in a school farm, where all students together, regardless of their abilities, could access nature, learn, improve their skills, and participate physically, sensorily, and mentally in an active learning environment.

The chapter aims to identify the design guidelines of an inclusive experience in an outdoor learning environment of the school farm by investigating the available literature review to propose an initial platform of the design guidelines. Then, a survey of 30 experts in the field is used to validate and determine the most effective and significant design guidelines and requirements essential to design the school farm spaces and physical environment to facilitate the accessibility, adaption, and integration for all students within the school farm, regardless of their various abilities and differences.

Inclusive learning school

Inclusive design is the design of a physical environment that enables everyone to participate and engage equally, confidently, and independently in everyday activities and removes any barriers that create an unnecessary effort and causes segregation from the surrounding environment. According to the Inclusive Design Institute (2016), there are three dimensions of inclusive design of the learning school environment:

- Recognize diversity and uniqueness: the inclusive design keeps each student's diversity and uniqueness in mind and recognizes the importance of independence and self-knowledge.
- Inclusive process and tools: the design and the tools should be accessible and usable for all students.
- Broader beneficial impact: inclusive design should prompt a virtuous cycle of inclusion and recognize the interconnectedness of all students and systems.

An inclusive learning school is an education system that includes all students in improving their skills to reach a level of independence, and interact within their community and be sociable. The inclusive learning environment is based on the fact that students with different disabilities do not feel comfortable being treated differently from anyone else, segregated from ordinary education, and deprived of enjoying educational activities with their peers (Hussein, 2012). Therefore, the inclusive design for the learning environment and facilities should consider all students regardless of their different abilities and overcome the stigma attached to being labeled 'disabled' by integrating rather than segregating facilities.

To ensure inclusive learning for all students, UNICEF (2020) demands all parties take essential measures and methods to provide students with disabilities with satisfaction of inclusive learning systems at all levels. UNICEF (2020) determines the required actions, including promoting physical accessibility to the school environment and its facilities. Also, materials and tools need to be made accessible to suit the needs of students with different types of disabilities.

In sum, an inclusive learning school is defined as a school that integrates students with different disabilities with other students in regular schools rather than segregating them into separate schools. Providing inclusive spaces, materials, and tools for all students with different disabilities to join a normal learning environment can result in good interaction between all students with varying learning abilities and develop their leadership and citizenship skills. Everyone is valuable and has the right to learn, access education safely, and interact with others, including all students, regardless of their abilities or disabilities.

School farm: outdoor learning environment

The school farm is a significant and effective learning model of using outdoor spaces in the school as a real-life learning environment (Smeds, Jeronen, and Kurppa, 2015), where students can practice traditional farming activities, explore farm life, and interact with nature. The school farm contains two main sections: the planting section and the livestock section (Iderawumi, 2020):

- In the planting section, students can dig, garden, prepare the soil, grow plants, water plants, and care for plants throughout the growing season. Additionally, they can cook and eat the fresh plants they grow and prepare different types of food.
- In the livestock section, students take care of animals and feed them if the school farm can afford to keep livestock.

In the school farm, the learning process is a structure of comprehensive and contextual learning, personal experiences and emotions, and social interaction between students and their community aiming to teach students to become responsible citizens who can make decisions in their lives and communities. Students can gain a comprehensive learning experience that involves knowledge, activity, emotions, senses, values, and social interaction. They can also learn new things by developing and expanding the existing knowledge in a contextual learning experience (Risku-Norja, Korpela, and Vieraankivi, 2008).

In such an active learning environment, students will acquire personal and emotional experiences and develop their personalities through social integration with their community and interaction with nature. According to Titman (1994), there are four purposes of spaces that students look for in the school farm environment, regardless of their different abilities, to provide them with an effective outdoor learning and physical environment; the researchers presented these four purposes of spaces as shown in Figure 14.1.

- *A space for doing*

The school farm allows students to practice and extend their abilities and skills comprehensively and learn through their own experiences, where they have several opportunities to learn by doing and participating actively with their peers. The school farm is an interesting space where they can play safely, and learn while enjoying planting, watching milking cows, and taking part in pony riding (Mattu, 2016).

- *A space for thinking*

The school farm provides students with a space for thinking, where they practice several farming activities that stimulate them intellectually. In the school farm, they can learn new things about growing plants and taking care of animals, and therefore, they can develop their understanding and strengthen the sensibility by applying what they have learned in practical situations.

- *A space for feeling*

The school farm provides students with an unforgettable emotional experience that provokes their feelings toward their peers and community. They can develop a sense of belonging while cooperating with their peers and being sociable and influential. Taking care of animals can also enrich their cognitive and emotional experience (Risku-Norja, Korpela, and Vieraankivi, 2008).

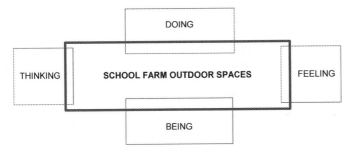

FIGURE 14.1 The four purposes of the school farm outdoor spaces . Source: Researchers.

- *A space for being*

Learning in the school farm allows students to be themselves when they feel free, abled, comfortable, safe, healthy, and involved. In this regard, school farms provide several benefits for students, such as spreading positive energy, reducing stress, and the fresh air affords a state that enables students to concentrate better and enhances cognitive performance (Smeds, Jeronen, and Kurppa, 2015).

All students, regardless of their different abilities, have the right to inclusive spaces and activities within the school farm learning environment. It is crucial to help them have a normal life, enhance their capabilities, improve their skills, and achieve a good education and learning aspects within the different spaces that provide them with all their needs and requirements to be part of their community. Therefore, integrating school farms into school learning facilities would ensure a regular involvement of all students, regardless of their abilities in farming learning activities and continued learning input, enhancing students' cognition, understanding, attitude, and behavior (Lewis, 2013; Bevan, Vitale, and Wengreen, 2012).

Challenges of students' abilities in a learning environment

Students are diverse in their needs due to their different abilities and skills which can classify some of them as 'students with disabilities', and these disabilities affect their way of life, learning, and their needs within any space in the physical environment.

Disability is defined as an umbrella term covering impairments, human activity limitations, and participation boundaries. As impairment is a problem in body function or structure; an activity limitation is a difficulty met by a human in performing a task or action; while a participation boundary is a problem experienced by any person when participating in life situations (WHO, 2011b).

The disability results from several factors that interact with the health condition. The WHO's International Classification of Functioning, Disability and Health (ICF) defines disability as 'a dynamic interaction between health conditions and environmental and personal factors' (WHO, 2001). Disability is, thus, not a health problem as much as it is a complex phenomenon, reflecting the quality of interaction between the persons, activities within their society, and surrounding physical environment.

According to UNICEF (2020), at least 93 million children globally have different types of disabilities that cause them several challenges starting from discrimination within their community to deprivation of the right to education and being part of their community. It is a fact that the physical environment has a significant impact on students' experience and extent of disability as the inaccessible environment leads to exaggerating the status of disability by creating barriers to participation and inclusion. In this regard, the ICF emphasizes the environmental factors to advance the understanding and measurement of disability (WHO, 2011a).

Therefore, the United Nations in the 2030 Agenda for Sustainable Development Goals refers to providing equal access for persons with disabilities to education and outdoor spaces. For example, Goal 4, Quality Education, aims to achieve inclusive and equitable quality education opportunities, ensuring equal access to all teaching and vocational training levels. Goal 11, Sustainable Cities and Communities, calls for providing persons with disabilities with universal access to safe, inclusive, and accessible green and outdoor spaces (United Nations Department of Economic and Social Affairs, 2018).

Kurniawan and Rofiah (2018) stated in their study that the qualified facilities concerning students with disabilities are a factor that affects students' access to the physical environment. Examples of environmental barriers that may hinder students from accessing the learning environment are lack of ramps, insufficient visual or acoustic signaling, and colors that cause an optical illusion.

Accordingly, it is essential to improve the physical learning environment with all facilities, including school farms, to be sensitive to all students regardless of their different abilities and provide them with safe, inclusive, and effective outdoor learning environments (UNICEF, 2017). This means the school environment should be adapted to different types of students to offer the best learning conditions without discrimination (Bessai, 2019), creating a caring, welcoming, safe, and accessible learning environment that responds to each student's needs, including students with different disabilities (Miles et al., 2002).

In this chapter, three different challenging disabilities are considered while designing the school farm as an outdoor learning environment; those disabilities are physical, sensory, and mental disabilities (Universal Design Handbook, 2010). Figure 14.2 is illustrated by the researchers to interpret the relationship between different types of challenging disabilities of students in parallel to the needs and requirements of these students to fulfill their various requirements and needs, so that students with disabilities can participate in their community safely and independently and overcome the limitations caused by their disabilities. This interpretation will be used later to figure out the design guidelines of outdoor spaces in the school farm to achieve an inclusive learning environment.

Several studies demonstrate the effect and influence of involving students with disabilities in outdoor environments on their psychological and physical health and social life. It is noticed that their behavior slightly changes even after a single visit to a farm (Seo, Kaneko, and Kashiwamura, 2013; Kellert, 1997; Marcus and Barnes, 1999).

The school farm has been acknowledged for its therapeutic effects on students with disabilities (Larson, Hancheck, and Vollmar, 1996). For example, it allows a student with a mental disability to discover new things in a joyful learning experience, making them calm, obedient to supervisors, more cheerful, and participative (Akin and Arslan, 2006). In another study focusing on the healing benefits, Karakoç and Polat (2019) suggested that green outdoor spaces can work as a

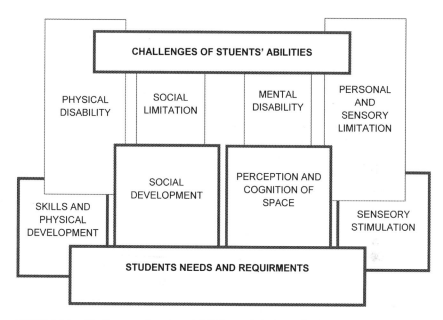

FIGURE 14.2 Challenges of students' abilities and their needs. Source: Researchers.

healing place for children with mental and physical disabilities; it promotes their self-esteem and develops their personality. A case study from Malaysia showed several benefits that students with disabilities would gain by visiting a sensory garden, such as sensory learning experience, physical mobility, and social communication (Hussein, 2012).

A key finding of a similar study is the possibility of farm education to support learners with different learning abilities and preferences. Farm-based education positively impacts students' cognitive skills, enhances the long-term retention of what has been learned and improves understanding, and increases long-term persistence at the learning process level. A study conducted in Finland on Year 5 students assured that an authentic learning environment could deepen the learning capacity of students with different abilities. The study examined the effect of the learning environment on students' performance, as the farm was selected as an authentic learning environment, combined with a classroom to teach 'the route of milk'. The study showed a significant enhancement in learning results even among students with low academic performance and learning difficulties. Students were able to observe, think, walk around, and interact with the environment (Smeds, Jeronen, and Kurppa, 2015).

Likewise, in a study from Oregon, in Wilsonville High School, there is a special farm planned to be used as a learning space for students in a special education program who have physical and mental disabilities. The study results in involving students with disabilities in farm activities which help them build science, math, and problem-solving skills. Besides, it reduces the stress they feel toward education and gives them a sense of satisfaction by working with their hands (Johnson, 2010).

Accordingly, in order to provide students with different disabilities with equal opportunities to safely and independently access the physical environment of the school farm without barriers, all involved parties should increasingly incorporate their efforts and support (United Nations Enable, 2003). And to explore how to innovate or adapt an inclusive school farm to be used easily, efficiently, and equally by all students, designers should understand the nature and causes of disability before embarking on designing a space that aims at improving students' quality of life in general and quality of education in particular (United Nations Department of Economic and Social Affairs, 2018).

Involving all students with different abilities together in an outdoor learning environment in a school farm can provide them with an effective learning experience, especially when the space is adequately designed to fulfill their different needs, requirements, and abilities.

Inclusive experience of students in the school farm

Reviewing the recent relevant literature shows that many features could be used to create outdoor spaces in a learning environment that are inclusive, accessible, and safe for all students with different disabilities. Additionally, the studies focusing on students with disabilities showed that they have different needs and requirements within any space to improve and overcome any barriers and avoid feeling disabled. They need to be provided with having a good perception and cognition and accessibility to any space that encourages sensory development and expansion, and the need to develop their skills and physical development while being socially integrated within their community (Figure 14.2).

An effective, inclusive learning environment experience in a school farm should provide all students, regardless of their abilities, with four sub-experiences, which are spatial experience, sensorial experience, social integration experience, and nature interaction experience, as shown in Figure 14.3. In Figure 14.3, the researchers built a relation between the purpose of the spaces within the school farm (Figure 14.1), students' needs (Figure 14.2), and the quadruple experiences that are suggested according to the relevant literature review. Those experiences are used as a base for the design guidelines of the school farm to achieve an active outdoor experience in an inclusive learning environment for all students regardless of their different disabilities.

Spatial experience

The quality of the spatial experience significantly affects students' perception and feelings toward their school and education (Farag and Badawi, 2019; Tanner, 2009). Therefore, the school farm's design should address the diverse spatial needs of all students regardless of their different abilities so that students can be self-reliant

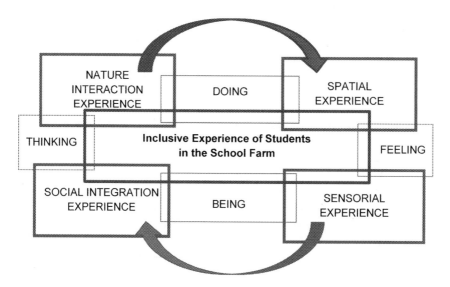

FIGURE 14.3   Inclusive experience of students in the school farm. Source: Researchers.

and effectively participate in a memorable learning spatial experience that increases their interest in education and school farm activities (Harte, 2013). Students with physical disabilities face different challenges to access spaces and need special consideration. For example, some vegetable beds could be raised to enable students in wheelchairs to access and join in without barriers (Johnson, 2010).

To enhance students' spatial experience, it is essential to give each student equal opportunity to access all school farm activities (Rahimi et al., 2018). Easy access to all spaces through simple and continuous pathways without barriers will allow all students to navigate the different spaces, undertake various activities, and use the school farm spaces and tools the way they want to (Hussein, 2012).

The inclusive design principles should be considered to provide all students with a quality of spatial experience in the school farm as follows: 1. Ease of use, 2. Freedom of choice, 3. Independent access to activities, 4. Diversity to meet different needs, 5. Legibility and predictability, 6. Quality of design, and 7. Safety (London Borough of Islington, 2010).

Sensorial experience

Students learn and develop their understanding of their physical environment by using their five senses. Stimulating those senses for learning purposes could foster their understanding of the subject being taught, as well as the place image.

Students with sensory disabilities could experience some limitations in understanding the surrounding environment as their senses are entirely different.

However, students with one impaired sense will try to compensate to some extent by making greater use of another sense. Therefore, providing students with a caring sensory experience in the learning environment will provide students with sensory disabilities with rich opportunities to explore and develop an understanding of the environment through visual, auditory, and tactile stimuli.

In an enjoyable sensory experience, students can have many different kinds of sensory inputs within an inclusive school farm learning environment by providing them with direct contact with animals and plants as well as the landscape elements. All plants, hardscape elements, textures, colors, patterns, scents, and sounds are carefully used to provide a controlled and safe sensory experience (Hussein, 2012). Students can use different senses aligned with their individual learning capacities and preferences while enjoying tasting fruit and vegetables, smelling flowers, touching plants and water, walking around plants and animals, and listening to sounds coming from nature. They can also pet the newborn animals in peace which provides them with a sensory, emotional experience and educates them on taking the responsibility of fragile creatures (Risku-Norja, Korpela, and Vieraankivi, 2008).

The sensory experience can benefit all students in terms of mental development, health improvements, emotional growth, social integration, and increasing students' learning motivation. It can also help calm students, regulate their nervous system, and reduce aggressive behavior, especially in those with mental disabilities (Hussein, 2012). It can also reinforce the learning quality by making each student experience the subject being taught and its interactions on their individual abilities (Smeds, Jeronen, and Kurppa, 2015).

Social integration experience

Social integration experience between students at the school farm can improve their feelings of belonging to their community when their different abilities are recognized by their peers and teachers (Hasugian et al., 2019; Bessai, 2019). The purpose of social integration in the school farm is to extend participation in social relationships with their peers to students with different disabilities and their engagement in the farming activities, which foster a sense of communality and identification with one's social roles (Holt-Lunstad and Uchino, 2015).

In the school farm, all students have an opportunity to improve the social integration with peers. For example, students can share many farming activities, while everyone is assigned to suitable tasks that fit their abilities and differences (Johnson, 2010). And thus, when they all participate to accomplish a hands-on task, this could significantly affect their integration (Smeds, Jeronen, and Kurppa, 2015).

They can also improve social integration with their community. For example, involving students in small farming projects such as herbal packaging, floral arrangements, organic produce, and marketing their products to the community allows further interaction through the available commercial outlets. The social interaction with the surrounding community has benefits to students' social skills and improves their self-esteem (Mostafa, 2014).

Nature interaction experience

Interacting with nature within the school environment has a positive effect on students' emotions, cognition, mental health, learning outcomes, and satisfaction toward the educational institution and learning process (Farag and Badawi, 2019; Larson, Jennings, and Cloutier, 2016; Pfeiffer and Cloutier, 2016; Dutt, 2012; Schäffer and Kistemann, 2012). It enhances friendly, supportive, and helpful attitudes in students, making them less violent and contributes to the feeling of belonging.

There are several opportunities to interact with nature in the school farm through farming activities, including a list of tasks that fit different development levels so that each student can take part in a suitable learning task. There are opportunities to practice cultivating, thinning, weeding, watering, sowing, harvesting plants, and participating in crafting and cooking activities that use farm products. Students can choose to grow fresh fruit, vegetables, and herbs suitable for their cooking lessons (Johnson, 2010). Thus, students can learn and understand the basis of sustainable development and domestic food production (Risku-Norja, Korpela, and Vieraankivi, 2008).

Additionally, interacting with farm animals can help to reduce stress and anxiety and improve social interactions between students (Gee, Griffin, and McCardle, 2017) by learning to take care of the farm animals and feed and pet small animals, which in turn teach students responsibility, and foster their empathy and respect to those who are different from them. Students can also learn about insects that are associated with the cultivation and growth of plants.

The nature interaction experience had a significant impact on students, regardless of their different abilities and behavior and attitude, enhancing their diverse skills and bringing out the good of students, helping them build essential bonds with the surrounding environment (Montgomery, 2013).

Method

The previous discussion revealed the benefits of involving all students with different abilities in an inclusive, active, and outdoor learning environment on their diverse experiences within the school farm and farming activities. Therefore, it is crucial to prepare the dedicated spaces in the school farm to facilitate access and participation of all students regardless of their disabilities (Karakoç and Polat, 2019).

One of the main challenges and barriers of including students with disabilities in outdoor spaces is the lack of information and design guidelines (Woolley, 2013). The researchers reviewed the recent literature that shows no empirical research cited as an evidence base for design guidelines that can be used to generate inclusive school farms as outdoor learning environments designed for all students, including those with disabilities. Therefore, this chapter aims to determine the design guidelines of an inclusive experience in an outdoor learning environment of the school farms that are required to offer equal opportunities for all students regardless of their abilities to safely and easily access and physically, sensorily, and mentally participate in an active learning physical environment. The study focuses on middle and high school level students aged between 11–16 years with different abilities, including those who have physical, sensory, and mental disabilities.

Accordingly, similar studies and relevant reports have been reviewed to investigate design guidelines that consider students' various needs and abilities within similar outdoor areas, including sensory gardens, outdoor play spaces, school grounds, and rehabilitation centers (Hamza, Elgohary, and Dewidar, 2020; Karakoç and Polat, 2019; Hamza and Elgohary, 2019; Hussein, 2012; Ministerial Advisory Committee: Children and Students with Disability, 2020; Johnson, 2010; Mostafa, 2014; Miles et al., 2002; London Borough of Islington, 2010).

The researchers propose a design platform to classify the collected design guidelines. All guidelines are arranged according to the quadruple inclusive experience (Figure 14.3), which are spatial experience, sensorial experience, social integration experience, and nature interaction experience, for easy understanding and implication of the design guidelines.

The guidelines are elucidated in Figure 14.4. Firstly, the spatial experience, which is the main aspect that assists students regardless of their disability to access and navigate within the spaces independently in an easy layout between the different spaces using the access elements, signs, and the hardscapes and farm furniture. The second is the sensorial experience divided into the essential and effective aspects that guide students regardless of their disability within the school farm by using their senses to recognize the space's elements using the color, sound, smell, and texture. Thirdly, the social integration experience is essential to build strong social bonds between students and their peers with their community and the feeling of being accepted and an effective person within social spaces, seating areas, and social integrating spaces within the community. The fourth experience is the nature interaction experience which had a significant effect on students with different disabilities and their attitudes and behavior through integration with nature through planting and caring for animals.

Content validity was established through the opinion of a panel of experts. The researchers used an expert survey method to review and examine the proposed platform and achieve a consensus about the essential design guidelines of the inclusive experience of the outdoor learning environment of school farms. A panel of 30 experts was purposely selected with various types of experience in landscape design (30%), inclusive/special education (30%), school farming (20%), academic research (20%), different cultures, and many years of experience.

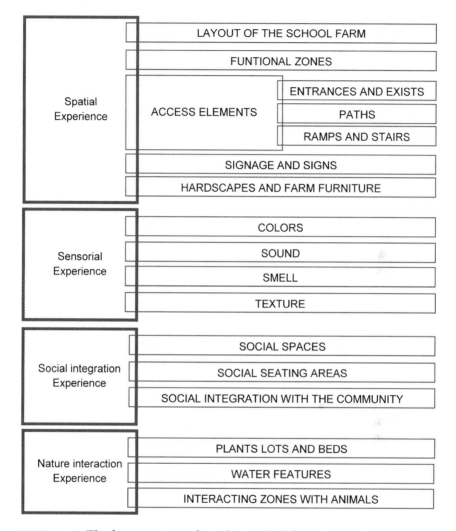

FIGURE 14.4 The four experiences for inclusive school farms. Source: Researchers.

The survey consists of two types of questions: the first type is a Likert scale method including three choices (Essential, Agree, and Disagree) that allows experts to determine the essentiality, preferability, and the unnecessity aspects of each individual design guideline so that the researchers could quantitatively determine the most effective design guidelines and requirements needed to design and adapt the school farm spaces, to facilitate access and practice for all students including those with disabilities (physical, mental, or sensory). The second type is an open-ended question that allows the researchers to benefit from the experts' suggestions and ensure the quality of the proposed guidelines.

Inclusive guidelines of learning school farm environment

The expert survey resulted in consistent consensus about 104 design guidelines for inclusive learning in the school farm environment. According to the quadruple inclusive experience mentioned before (Figure 14.3), they are categorized into four sections, which students need, regardless of their abilities in the school farm, to achieve an effective learning environment and significant experiences. In each section, the design guidelines are listed according to the applicable design elements (Figure 14.4).

Section 1: design guidelines for spatial experience

The spatial experience concerns the quality of spaces that all students can safely and independently access and be involve in all the farming activities within the school farm by implementing the following 47 design guidelines, which are listed in five design elements, divided into the layout of the school farm, functional zones, access elements, signage and signs, and hardscape and farm furniture. All students can potentially access, perceive, and safely use the school farm spaces in an inclusive learning spatial experience, as shown in Table 14.1.

Section 2: design guidelines for a sensorial experience

The sensory experience concerns the quality of spaces to stimulate students in farming activities within the school farm by implementing the following 24 design guidelines, which are listed into four design elements divided into color, sound, smell, and texture. All students can possibly get involved in a rich sensorial experience that meets students' different abilities and needs in an inclusive learning experience, as shown in Table 14.2.

Section 3: design guidelines for social integration experience

Social integration concerns the quality of social engagement of all students within the school farm by.implementing the following 12 design guidelines, which are listed into three design elements, divided into social spaces, social seating areas, and social integration with the community. All students would potentially integrate with their peers and teachers and their surrounding community for an inclusive learning experience, as shown in Table 14.3.

Section 4: design guidelines for nature interaction experience

The nature interaction concerns the quality of the natural environment that involves all students in farming activities within the school farm by implementing

TABLE 14.1 Design guidelines for spatial experience in an inclusive learning school farm environment

LAYOUT OF THE SCHOOL FARM	Simple and legible layout design of the school farm.
	Well-defined and flexible spaces connected to direct access elements and paths.
	School farm layout should be designed so that each space is exposed and visible, without any barriers or blind spots.
	School farm layout should be designed so that a network of unobstructed paths connects directly to all of the school farm's functional zones.
	School farm spaces should be provided with an alarm system to help students in case of an emergency.
FUNCTIONAL ZONES	Clear boundaries separate different zones, spaces, and activities without any visual barriers.
	Each functional zone should be characterized by different landmarks and signs to identify its identity.
	Different colors to differentiate between the zones within the school farm to guide students to navigate easily between them.
	The school farm should be attached to a services zone, including bathrooms and on-spot clinic facilities.
	A closed store within the farm to keep the farm tools, seeds, and organic pest repellents so that students have controlled access to prevent any farm accidents.
ACCESS ELEMENTS — ENTRANCES AND EXITS	Clear entrances and exits with readable information and signs.
	Gates of the school farm should be provided to keep students safe.
	Entrances and exits should be directly linked to the main path network of the school farm.
	Avoid any architectural barriers and obstacles near the entrances and exits.
	Clear emergency exits and legible with clear signs.

(Continued)

TABLE 14.1 (Continued)

PATHS	A clear and continuous network of paths links the different zones and spaces of the school farm.
	Paths should be at least 120–150 cm wide to facilitate access for students with a physical disability.
	Consider a space of 150×150 cm for the maneuvering of wheelchairs.
	Path surfaces should be stable and smooth without any barriers or obstacles.
	Paths should be provided with slip-resistant materials and textures without gaps in joints.
	Use local, sustainable, and durable materials and textures for the path surfaces.
	Paths should not have overgrown or nearby plants that drop berries or seeds.
	Edges of paths should be different colors and textures to be recognized.
	Use tactile guide markers on the path surfaces to help students with visual impairments to navigate easily within the school farm.
	Paths have different colors, textures, or scents to be memorable for all students to guide them within the school farm.
	Provide enough lighting alongside the paths to help all students to access the school farm safely.
RAMPS AND STAIRS	Ramps in the school farm should be added at any changes of level and stairs.
	Ramps should have a maximum slope of 1:12.
	Ramps should be provided with 'non-slip' surfaces.
	Ramps should be provided with handrails at a height of 65–80 cm for safety.
	Clear and attractive signs should be implemented within the school farm at any change of level to assist students with different abilities.
	Use different colors or textures at the beginning and end of the ramps and stairs to be perceived by all students.

SIGNAGE AND SIGNS

Signs should be placed at entrances and exits, junctions, stairs, ramps, and key destinations and facilities.

Signs should be placed in visible and clear points and perpendicular to the paths within the school farm.

Consistent signs and visual pictograms in the school farm guide all students to access any space independently and safely.

Interactive signs should be mounted between 90 and 120 cm above the ground to be reachable for students using wheelchairs.

Signs should provide well-defined and readable information within the school farm.

Use the same terminology and terms to indicate the same spaces within the school farm with appropriate and large contrasting text.

Braille and tactile identification information provided to assist students with visual disabilities.

Provide adequate lighting for signs and avoid any reflection or glaring of the signs' surface.

Signs and labels are provided near the plant lots and beds to provide students with information and details about the types of plants used.

HARDSCAPE AND FARM FURNITURE

Accessibility and usability of hardscape and school furniture are important.

A combination of softscape and hardscape to be adjacent to the paths of the school farm.

The school farm's furniture should be durable, multi-purpose, and should not have sharp or acute edges.

Benches should be designed to allow wheelchair access with incorporated armrests to aid those students with a physical disability to get up.

Enough space on either side of the benches so students in wheelchairs can transfer themselves to the benches.

Access to water at the entrances and exists for students to wash their hands before leaving the farm.

TABLE 14.2 Design guidelines for sensorial experience in inclusive learning school farm environment

COLOR	Use different colors to differentiate between various spaces and activities in the school farm.
	Use basic colors within the school farm that are easy for all students to memorize for a long time.
	Colors must be combined with different shapes and patterns and must not exceed four different colors in the same object.
	Avoid using colors with too much similarity that confuses students with mental disabilities.
	Paths and walls have different colors and guide markers to orient students within the school farm.
	Use different and contrasting color schemes between the school farm's furniture and hardscape.
	Use contrasting colors between the signs, written information, and surroundings.
	Any changes in level and steps should be indicated by a change in colors or texture to alert students.
	Colorful paintings of various farm tools and vegetables should be displayed on the school farm's fences as visual aids.
SOUND	Nature sounds such as bird sounds, wind sounds, plants sounds formed by wind, water sounds, and rain sounds should be considered in the school farm.
	Use equipment that provides different sounds for students with visual disabilities.
	Provide the spaces within the school farm with sound notification systems to guide all students.
	Listening signs provided to guide all students within the school farm.
	Use absorbing sound panels to control sound levels for students with mental disabilities to avoid distracting them.
	High trees surround the school farm area to avoid the surrounding distracting sounds.
SMELL	Scented plants are provided to offer smell stimulation to orient students within the spaces of the school farm.
	A specific smell is used for each space within the school farm to link between memorable smell and space to help students to memorize the spaces.
TEXTURE	Use different textures to differentiate between various spaces and activities for students.
	Use different textures to identify the paths.
	Choose textures that are memorable to assist students to experience the school farm.
	Avoid using reflected or polished surfaces and textures that cause optical illusions and defuse students within the school farm.
	Tapping surfaces are provided when needed for use by students with visual disabilities.
	Any changes in level and steps should be indicated by a change in surface texture.
	Use different textures for equipment and tools to help students with visual and hearing disabilities.

TABLE 14.3 Design guidelines for social integration experience in inclusive learning school farm environment

SOCIAL SPACES	Gathering and social spaces within the school farm for social integration.
	The school farm social spaces should be designed for solo time, one-to-one work, and small and large group work.
	Each social space should be characterized by different landmarks to identify the identity of each space and the social activity done within it.
	Provide suitable spaces for students to gather in a circle around the plant beds so they can interact with each other.
	Graphical media and data exist to guide students with different disabilities to the school farm's social spaces.
SOCIAL SEATING AREAS	Seating areas with special forms should be arranged to encourage inclusive interactions among different students with different needs.
	A double bench is provided for social integration with students within the school farm.
	Shade devices are added, so students will enjoy gathering regardless of the climatic condition.
	Provide a shed to store seeds and materials needed by students within the school farm.
SOCIAL INTEGRATION WITH THE COMMUNITY	Provide secured semi-public spaces to interface between students and the community in controlled gathering events.
	Provide clear access and gathering spaces with extra added services needed to attract people to visit and communicate with students within the school farm.
	Provide particular spaces to serve communal activities for students to interact with the broader community.

the following 21 design guidelines, which are listed into three design elements divided into plant lots and beds, water features, and interacting zones with animals. All students would enjoy learning by interacting with natural elements and caring for animals in the school farm spaces in an inclusive learning experience, as shown in Table 14.4.

Results and discussions

The crucial guidelines to design an inclusive experience in the outdoor learning environment in school farms are presented in ables 14.1, 14.2, 14.3, and 14.4. These guidelines are extracted from the literature review and validated through an expert survey. In addition to these guidelines, the study has raised important issues regarding the effectiveness of the proposed guidelines, as follows.

Local implication of the design guidelines

The resulting 104 design guidelines have achieved consistent consensus among the 30 experts, and thus, they are broadly applicable to learning school farm

TABLE 14.4 Design guidelines for nature interaction experience in inclusive learning school farm environment

PLANT LOTS AND BEDS	Plant lots and beds are provided at different heights, sizes, and shapes in the school farm. Plant beds should be raised at different heights from 60–90 cm to allow students in wheelchairs to access them easily. Plant lots and beds are provided with surrounding space, so students can gather in a circle and have equal interaction with plants. A space at least 90 cm wide is needed between the plant lots and beds to allow free access for all students, especially students in wheelchairs. Consider the position of the plants lots and beds to allow the rotation of the crops. Trees and shrubs should surround the farm space to give a feeling of coming into a protected space. Plants in the school farm should not cause visual barriers for students. Plants should be organized to enable students to enjoy the sun. Plants with various forms, textiles, and striking seasonal colors should be provided in the school farm. No use of growing poisonous and dangerous plants. Reduce and separate plants that attract bees and insects to the school farm. Group plants based on their qualities and types with labels to help students gain information and details about all plants. Small containers, jars, earthen pots, food tins, and any available recyclable containers can be used to grow plants within the school farm.
WATER FEATURES	Provide the school farm with free-standing drinking units and water taps to wash hands and water the plants. The standing drinking unit has a clear knee space under the drinking unit at 74 cm height above the ground, 76 cm wide, and 20 cm deep. The water taps must be from a height of 60–120 cm without any barriers and obstacles. The water taps must be colorful and with contrasting colors to the surroundings. The school farm hoses should be in good order, including nozzles with throttle control. Provide the school farm with a rainwater harvesting system.
INTERACTING ZONES WITH ANIMALs	A separate zone for farm animals is secured by transparent walls or screens at least 120 cm in height. Provide an interaction zone that is well supervised and well-controlled, allowing students to get involved with the farm animals.

environments worldwide. However, those guidelines should be applied with consideration to the local circumstances, as follows:

- The significance of the climatic factor and its impact on the school farm design and students' comfort and safety, especially in harsh climates.
- Use the local environmental materials to set up and furnish the school farm, especially with the financial challenges that could result in difficulties in meeting the design guidelines mentioned in this study.
- Use the local environmental materials could be a sustainable alternative that has a lower impact on the environment.
- Upcycle the wasted resources such as vegetable beds made out of packaging materials and wooden planks; plastic drums can also fulfill the purpose.
- Where adequate land is not available, students can use discarded small containers, jars, earthen pots, and food tins for growing plants.
- Consider local regulations and legislation while implementing the design guidelines.
- Inclusion of the local community and students' voices to determine the optimal design.
- The use of design guidelines may also be affected by the scale of the farm and the school and whether the school farm is designed for a community of the school, campus, neighborhood, district, or city.
- School owners, urban developers, and governments should embolden these guidelines within all the schools to facilitate the integration of all types of students regardless of their different abilities to help them be involved in the education system independently.

Statistical significance of the design elements

The quantitative analysis of the expert survey shows the difference in the statistical significance of the design elements of school farms, as follows:

- Legibility and accessibility of school farm spaces are two crucial principles to design an inclusive outdoor learning environment in school farms. The ability to navigate and access all spaces and activities safely and easily without any barriers is essential for all students.
- The inclusivity-compliant signage is an effective tool to ensure that all students can easily navigate the school farm, feeling respected rather than feeling lost.
- The accessibility and ease of access will let students move freely and abled and can make the school farm a more welcoming environment for active learning.
- A statistical significance for the essentiality of signage and sign elements (70%), following by access elements, including entrances, exits, paths, and ramps (68.5%) as shown in Figure 14.5, followed by the hardscape and farm

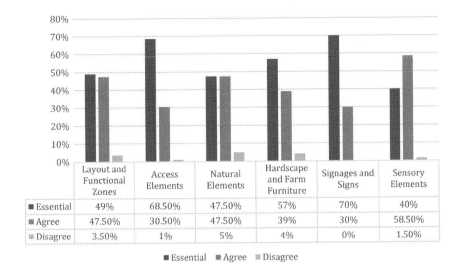

	Layout and Functional Zones	Access Elements	Natural Elements	Hardscape and Farm Furniture	Signages and Signs	Sensory Elements
▩ Essential	49%	68.50%	47.50%	57%	70%	40%
▩ Agree	47.50%	30.50%	47.50%	39%	30%	58.50%
▩ Disagree	3.50%	1%	5%	4%	0%	1.50%

▩ Essential ▩ Agree ▩ Disagree

FIGURE 14.5 The statistical significance of design elements and landscape.

furniture (57%), then the layout and the functional zones (49%), natural elements (47.5%), and finally the sensory elements (40%).

• Despite that the reviewing literature has shown the substantial significance of sensory elements in motivating students with disabilities to learn and clearly recognize the different spaces in the school farm, statistical analysis has not aligned with the literature review. The sensory elements are the last essential design elements, as shown in Figure 14.5; however, they are considered the highly preferable elements (58.5%) rather than essential elements (40%).

Future research potential

This study has opened several directions for future research potential, such as:

• Consider the needs of all students with their different disabilities, including students with a spectrum of neurodiverse disabilities to get them all engaged together in the same space.
• Age and gender, and other demographic factors should be investigated in a further study.
• Consider the visions and views of students with disabilities in the design process.
• Virtual software could be used to examine the design guidelines' applicability by involving students with different abilities and allowing them to participate actively and visualize what the space would potentially be like.
• More investigation is recommended to study the significant impact of the design sensory elements on students with disabilities within an outdoor learning context.

Conclusion

The school farm is a model of an authentic outdoor learning environment, where all students, including students with disabilities, have the opportunity to do, think, feel, and be themselves through the quadruple inclusive experience within a spatial physical environment, using their different senses, through the interaction with nature, in an active social community. These experiences are greatly effective and have a significant impact on students regardless of their abilities, enhancing their behavior and attitudes, improving their skills, teaching them responsibility and leadership skills, and assisting them to navigate between school farm spaces safely and independently. Inclusive guidelines for a learning school farm environment can contribute to involving all students in the farming-based learning experience, maximizing the benefits of the school farm as an educational tool. They could also be developed for cultural, social, environmental, economic, and entertainment purposes. The inclusivity-compliant design of the school farm can have a significant impact on students' attitudes toward their community and the learning process.

References

Akin, Z.Ş.Y. and Arslan, M.T.D., 2006. *Development Gardens for Children* (Doctoral dissertation, Ankara University Graduate School of Natural and Applied Sciences, Department of Landscape Architecture).

Bessai, R., 2019. 'Access to Education for People with Special Needs in Algeria' in *Rethinking Social Action. Core Values in Practice*. Editura Lumen, Asociatia Lumen, pp. 1–12.

Bevan, S., Vitale, T. and Wengreen, H., 2012. 'Farm Field Trips Provide Sensory-based Experiences with Fresh, Local Produce', *Journal of Nutrition Education and Behavior*, 44(3), pp.278–279.

Dutt, I., 2012. 'School Design and Students' Relationships with the Natural World', *Children Youth and Environments*, 22(1), pp.198–226.

Farag, A.A. and Badawi, S., 2019. 'Exploring Students' Cognitive Maps in Different Built Environments of Elementary Schools' *AMPS, Architecture_MPS*, Stevens Institute of Technology. New Jersey/New York, 17-19 June 2019, 17 (1), pp.8–15.

Farag, A.A., Badawi, S.R. and Doheim, R.M., 2019. Assessment of User Happiness in Campus Open Spaces. *The Journal of Public Space*, 4(1), pp.45–64.

Gee, N.R., Griffin, J.A. and McCardle, P., 2017. Human–Animal Interaction Research in School Settings: Current Knowledge and Future Directions. *Aera Open*, 3(3), pp. 1–9.

Hamza, I.S.E.D. and Elgohary, A., 2019. Wayfinders in Barrier Free Environments. *International Journal of Current Research*, 11(6), pp. 4307–4310.

Hamza, I.S.E.D., Elgohary, A. and Dewidar, K., 2020. Mentally Challenged Wayfinders. *Journal of Al-Azhar University Engineering Sector*, 15(54), pp.57–66.

Harte, H.A., 2013. Universal Design and Outdoor Learning. *Dimensions of Early Childhood*, 41(3), pp.18–22.

Hasugian, J.W., Gaurifa, S., Warella, S.B., Kelelufna, J.H. and Waas, J., 2019, March. Education for Children with Special Needs in Indonesia. *Journal of Physics: Conference Series*, 1175(1), p. 012172. IOP Publishing.

Holt-Lunstad, J. and Uchino, B.N., 2015. Social Support and Health. *Health Behavior: Theory, Research and Practice*, pp.183–204.

Hussein, H., 2012. The Influence of Sensory Gardens on the Behaviour of Children with Special Educational Needs. *Procedia-Social and Behavioral Sciences*, 38, pp.343–354.

Iderawumi, A., 2020. Establishment of School Farm and Gardening. In *Introduction to Agricultural Systems: Principles and Practices*. Lanlate, Nigeria: Department of Agricultural Education, The College of Education.

Inclusive Design Institute, 2016. The Inclusive Design Guide. Inclusive Design Research Centre. [online]. Available at: https://guide.inclusivedesign.ca/

Johnson, K.M., 2010. The Use of Horticulture and Gardening as a Special Education Tool at the High School Level. [online]. Available at: https://digitalcommons.calpoly .edu/cgi/viewcontent.cgi?article=1008&context=hcssp.

Karakoç, E. and Polat, A.T., 2019. Design Principles of Healing Gardens for Disabled Children. 6th International Conference on Sustainable Agriculture and Environment, October 3–5, 2019, Konya, Turkey, pp.134–139.

Kellert, S.R., 1997. *The Value of Life: Biological Diversity and Human Society*. Washington, DC: Island Press.

Kurniawan, M.R. and Rofiah, N.H., 2018. Acceptability of Children with Special Needs in the Inclusive Elementary School. *Journal of Education and Learning*, 12(4), pp.589–596.

Larson, J., Hanchek, A. and Vollmar, P., 1996. *Accessible Gardening for Therapeutic Horticulture*. Minneapolis, MN: Minnesota Extension Service, University of Minnesota, College of Agricultural, Food, and Environmental Sciences.

Larson, L.R., Jennings, V. and Cloutier, S.A., 2016. Public Parks and Wellbeing in Urban Areas of the United States. *PLoS One*, 11(4), p.e0153211.

Lewis, L.M., 2013. *Comparative Study of Agricultural Literacy of Urban Vs. Rural Third and Fourth Graders: Before and After an Agricultural Program* (Doctoral dissertation, Oklahoma State University).

London Borough of Islington, 2010. *Inclusive Landscape Design*. Supplementary Planning Document.

Ministerial Advisory Committee: Children and Students with Disability, 2020. Designing Outdoor Learning Spaces. [online]. Available at: https://www.educatio n.sa.gov.au/sites-and-facilities/maintenance-and-design/design-everyone/designing -outdoor-learning-spaces

Marcus, C.C. and Barnes, M. eds., 1999. *Healing Gardens: Therapeutic Benefits and Design Recommendations* (Vol. 4). Hoboken, NJ: Wiley.

Mattu, L.M., 2016. *Farm Visits: Interdisciplinary Outdoor Learning for Primary School Pupils and Scotland's Curriculum for Excellence* (Doctoral dissertation, University of Glasgow).

Miles, S., Miller, S., Lewis, I. and Van der Kroft, M., 2002. *Schools for All: Including Disabled Children in Education*. Save the Children UK. Available at: https://resourcecentre.sa vethechildren.net/library/schools-all-including-disabled-children-education.

Montgomery, C., 2013. *Happy City: Transforming our Lives Through Urban Design*. New York: Macmillan.

Mostafa, M., 2014. Architecture for Autism: Autism ASPECTSS™ in School Design. *International Journal of Architectural Research: ArchNet-IJAR*, 8(1), pp.143–158.

Pfeiffer, D. and Cloutier, S., 2016. Planning for Happy Neighborhoods. *Journal of the American Planning Association*, 82(3), pp.267–279.

Rahimi, F.B., Levy, R.M., Boyd, J.E. and Dadkhahfard, S., 2018. Human Behaviour and Cognition of Spatial Experience: A Model for Enhancing the Quality of Spatial

Experiences in the Built Environment. *International Journal of Industrial Ergonomics*, 68, pp.245–255.

Risku-Norja, H., Korpela, E. and Vieraankivi, M.L., 2008. Farms as Learning Environment: Experiences from School-farm Co-operation. *Suomen Maataloustieteellisen Seuran Tiedote*, (23), pp.1–9.

Schäffer, S.D. and Kistemann, T., 2012. German Forest Kindergartens: Healthy Childcare under the Leafy Canopy. *Children Youth and Environments*, 22(1), pp.270–279.

Seo, T., Kaneko, M. and Kashiwamura, F., 2013. Changes in Intake of Milk and Dairy Products among Elementary Schoolchildren Following Experiential Studies of Dairy Farming. *Animal Science Journal*, 84(2), pp.178–184.

Smeds, P., Jeronen, E. and Kurppa, S., 2015. Farm Education and the Value of Learning in an Authentic Learning Environment. *International Journal of Environmental and Science Education*, 10(3), pp.381–404.

Tanner, C.K., 2009. Effects of School Design on Student Outcomes. *Journal of Educational Administration*, 47(3), pp. 381–399. https://doi.org/10.1108/09578230910955809.

Titman, W., 1994. *Special Places; Special People: The Hidden Curriculum of School Grounds.* Toronto, ON, Canada: WWF UK (World Wide Fund For Nature). M4K 1P1.

UNICEF, 2017. Inclusive Education Including Children with Disabilities in Quality Learning: What Needs to be Done? [online]. Available at: https://www.unicef.org/eca/sites/unicef.org.eca/files/IE_summary_accessible_220917_brief.pdf

UNICEF, 2020. Disabilities. [online]. Available at: https://www.unicef.org/disabilities/

United Nations Department of Economic and Social Affairs, 2018. The United Nations and Disability: 70 Years of the Work Towards a More Inclusive World. [online]. Available at: https://www.un.org/development/desa/disabilities/wp-content/uploads/sites/15/2018/01/History_Disability-in-the-UN_jan23.18-Clean.pdf

United Nations Enable, 2003. The UN and Persons with Disabilities. United Nations, Department of Economic and Social Affairs, Division for Social Policy and Development [online]. Available at: https://www.un.org/esa/socdev/enable/disun.htm.

Universal Design Handbook, 2010. *Building Accessible and Inclusive Environments. Advisory Committee on Accessibility (ACA), Access Design Subcommittee, the City of Calgary.* Available at: https://www.scribd.com/document/46650039/Universal-Design-Handbook.

WHO, 2001. *International Classification of Functioning, Disability and Health (ICF)*, Geneva: World Health Organization.

WHO, 2011a. Understanding Disability in World Report 2011. https://www.who.int/disabilities/world_report/2011/chapter1.pdf?ua=1

WHO, 2011b. World Report on Disability 2011: Technical Appendix A' 295 [online]. Available at: www.unicef.org/ protection/World_report_on_disability_eng.pdf

Woolley, H., 2013. Now Being Social: The Barrier of Designing Outdoor Play Spaces for Disabled Children. *Children & Society*, 27(6), pp.448–458.

15

CONCLUSION

Toward a comprehensive perspective on the role of the school farm

Gurpinder Singh Lalli, Alshimaa A. Farag,and Samaa Badawi

To return to the objectives of this book, four proposed themes (Problem, People, Process, and Place) led to the production of 14 chapters which are closely aligned to issues of hunger, food insecurity, malnutrition, obesity and overweight, healthy community, efficient learning systems, access to learning, and urban sustainability, all in a bid to develop resilience in food systems relating to food in educational spaces. In the opening section of this book, we discussed how school farms consisted of having deep historical roots and how the names changed over time. This was also reflective of the changing nature of the discourses surrounding school farms which are more locally known as school gardens. This international edited collection brings together scholars from Asia, Africa, Europe, and North America. This diversity of perspectives enriches the book with different approaches, emphasizing the significance of the school farms for the students and the broader community. We begin to delve further into each of the four themes, which are introduced as the 4Ps (Problem, People, Process, and Place) in relation to this concept of the school farm.

Problem

The opening chapter of this book introduced food education and food growing in schools. The author highlighted the interdisciplinary importance of research on school farms and illustrates how the power of such spaces is crucial in shaping global citizenship education in terms of sustainable development. Key questions are posed, and a thorough review of the literature supports those questions on how policymakers might think harder about prioritizing food education on the curriculum. In Chapter 2, the author introduced the impact of hunger on children and adolescents based on a study conducted in Nigeria, and the benefits of school farms as a tool for fostering food sustainability and vocational

DOI: 10.4324/9781003176558-15

pedagogical instruments are discussed. The work in this chapter addressed the need for urgency in relation to prioritizing and empowering the school farm system in a bid to empower and save the lives of children and adolescents from hunger. The study identified a number of implications for school-based counselors who were responsible for orientation as well as engaging with training and appropriate counseling approaches. Chapter 3 explored the combined impact of school farming to improve the nutritional status of school children in relation to sustainable development in India, Nepal, and Bhutan. Overall, little data was available for low-income countries of South Asia, and governments should encourage the formation of school farms and private schools in order to provide a better future for young people. The authors explored the impact of school farming on nutritional status during the COVID-19 pandemic and on sustainable development. Overall, findings revealed how school farms in low-income countries could effectively increase children's knowledge, understanding, and preference towards nutrient-rich vegetables alongside shaping understanding of the effect of fresh fruit and vegetables on human nutrition.

People

Chapter 4 presented three specific case studies to highlight current work on school farming across the UK. The recommendations from the chapter highlight the importance of networking and sharing good practices. School farms and gardens are said to provide an important foundation for young people and provide links into the wider agricultural sector and a route to employment related to agriculture and horticulture. With the introduction of technological advancements in school farm activities, the future holds real promise, providing investment takes place. On the whole, in the UK, school farms are identified as a key educational resource as they offer invaluable experiences to future generations. The fifth chapter explored the relationship between land attributes, policy, degradation, agricultural practices, food, and resource access challenges in Bandung, Indonesia. The author argues local communities are best placed and equipped to manage the environments and ecosystems they rely on. In Chapter 6, the author explored the psychological benefits of school farms by providing a case of one successful school farm in the United States. The data presented highlighted the benefits of time spent surrounded by plants, animals, and in nature settings. School farms make sense as a means of giving this same opportunity to students who may not have access to greenspace or gardening at home or elsewhere in their community. However, much work on the psychological benefits of school farms needs to be done as they have not been directly measured. In Chapter 7, the project discussed in the study reveals the significance of informal outdoor education in developing sustainability literacy among campus students. The idea of this study was to spark debate and also model a design for learning activities for sustainable living. Therefore, the 'Harithalayam campus farming mission' project would, in the long term, enable students to develop behavioral changes towards sustainability. The authors argued that while students were able to develop the knowledge and attitudes towards sustainable development, the behavioral change remained low.

Process

A discussion on learning theory was introduced in relation to the cooperation between farms and schools, which relate specifically to Norway and Tanzania. The central argument in Chapter 8 highlighted how learning could lead to permanent behavior change. The authors presented a model for relationship-based experiential learning on farms and identified key points for teachers to consider in the planning phase. These included joint planning and societal relevance. Through the contact to plants, animals, soil, and the people who produce our food, relationship-based experiential learning is not just a model for learning that engages the whole human being, but also a model for learning for sustainable development, empowerment, and self-efficacy that is necessary if we are to find solutions. The research has shown that such learning makes a difference. Students who learn in this way are often inspired to engage actively in issues of sustainability, and are connected, intentionally motivated, and hopefully able to transcend the inadequate practices of our time. The novelty of this work is that learning theories often avoid the question and what motivates students to make a change. In Chapter 9, the authors introduced a case study of outdoor learning in one of the biggest school farms in the UK while trying to critique the contemporary challenge of teenagers' understanding of where food comes from and also in relation to food security and sustainability. The challenges of time management, funding, and the lack of engaging opportunities for teachers were commonplace due to the pressures of the curriculum. The strategies used to develop the curriculum, which involved teacher input, were an important outcome of this study.

Furthermore, the involvement of staff alongside students and the community was pivotal in achieving positive outcomes. Overall, the focus was on promoting the need for fostering a better understanding of the world by encouraging young people to recognize the relationship between outdoor learning and the world through an authentic environment of the school farm. The final chapter in this part presents findings from a case study in the Middle East on the importance of the relationship between healthy minds and healthy bodies. The chapter calls key points into question in relation to the responsibility of parents, the community, and the government. The study calls for a thorough implementation of school farms in schools that do not have the privilege. The chapter highlighted guidelines to minimize the cost of the farm-to-school programs, which are considered to be challenging for those less fortunate schools, and this highlights the complexity in its implementation. Much more investment in terms of resources, time, and money is needed in order to set up a path for long-term benefits, but the author appreciates this comes at a risk to the public purse.

Place

This section of the book introduces key debates on the notion of *place* with an opening chapter on projects of social intervention with a focus on active observation between schools and local institutions in Venice. The study outlines the direct relation between the territory and the school, which can determine the transformative potential of educational reform relating to the landscape. Schools are said to be interwoven into the urban fabric of society, and recognizing territorial influences can support active civic participation in educational reform. Chapter 12 directly returns to the issue of malnutrition as a public health concern and proceeds by reviewing six projects from Vietnam, the United States, England, China, Slovenia, and Canada in relation to the construction of school roof farms and the author identified four pillars of success: people, institutional support, sustainable construction techniques, and precise process. A review of six case studies revealed the realities of the resource involved in order to invest in school roof farms. These projects were said to benefit both the schools and broader community at different levels, so in terms of the environmental level, they are said to reduce heat gain, manage stormwater, and purify the air. While educationally, roof farms provide opportunities for active learning on sustainability and agriculture. Chapter 13 discusses school farms and the impact of neglected urban open spaces (NUOS) with a focus on trying to build community resilience. The chapter highlights the stark realities of urban spaces which are left dead and undeveloped, and it provides further evidence on the financial, economic, planning, and social barriers of school farms. The authors offer a definition of *community resilience*, arguing that the interconnected relationships of social and technical systems can directly impact human society at the community level through engagement with agriculture, and they also highlight the complexity of contemporary cities. The final chapter details a critical discussion on inclusive learning in relation to the school farm environment, arguing that the school farm must be designed with conscious consideration to students with different disabilities, both visible and invisible. The barriers which prevent successful planning and design are identified as a lack of knowledge on the requirements of different spaces within learning environments. More importantly, this chapter reiterates how the school farm is an authentic outdoor learning environment where everyone can get involved regardless of disabilities. The experiences gained empower students and can potentially change behavior and attitudes and help them to navigate as future change-makers and advocates for a more sustainable environment.

Closing thoughts

This book offers comprehensive recommendations to schools, policymakers, and educators around the world for thinking hard about school farms and their transformative potential. This edited collection sheds light on the benefits of establishing a school farm and its significant impact on providing essential food for the community. Clearly, we need a joint-up approach to school farming and to invest in the infrastructure to introduce more of the models through schools across the globe. We need to take account of the contextual differences in the given environment, and for this reason, we need to systematically engage with policy and, through advocacy, raise awareness of the impact on health and hunger. We also need to take account of societal benefits in the long term and need to encourage and convince governments across the globe to avoid adopting short-term approaches in combating a very complex issue such as hunger. We need both short-term and long-term approaches to make a change. The key recommendations from this edited collection and body of important work signal that we as a collective and as a community need to embrace change in a way that will see our future generations prosper, excel, and live healthy lives. We need to consider the school as a microcosm of society and to ensure we pool our resources, time, and energy into educating children and through feeding in societies where food rations are limited. We also need to provide aid and recognize the privileges surrounding those high-income countries based in the global north to support those in the global south. We need to take account of the positive messages in the globalized south and put these to good use in the globalized north; a lesson, which is often neglected and goes ignored. Hunger is experienced in both relative and absolute terms and should be taken more seriously, so the lessons learned during a global pandemic have helped to shine a light on the issue of hunger even more so. The recommendations from this edited collection point to the need for resources, infrastructure, economic stability, and community cohesion; and for us to think about making a greater contribution on a daily basis to the fight against globalization, climate change, and doing so through feeding and educating children and young people.

Future direction

This book has raised many questions and highlighted several concerns that could open new potential for scholars and academics to investigate new solutions for the current challenges. One of the current critical challenges is COVID-19 and its impact on our lives in general and on food sufficiency and education in particular. The advantage of the COVID-19 epidemic is that it has drawn the world's attention to the real challenges that pose threats, so that the world must give them greater priority, such as the food problem. There are many children worldwide, especially in the global south, who depend mainly on the nutritional programs provided by schools for their food. School closures as a result of the pandemic posed a real threat to those children, prompting international organizations to provide more costly alternatives. Schools also have financial burdens on their budgets due to the emergency measures that followed the epidemic. Under such pressure, some schools are unable to provide the necessary food for children, which exposes children to real health and psychological problems, according to this book's chapters. It is important to empower school farm systems to save children's lives. We do not claim the school farm is a decisive solution that can stand alone to provide full food sufficiency for children during the epidemic or afterwards, especially as not all schools have sufficient areas for farming activities. However, the schools can contribute even with limited areas to partially sustain the provision of healthy food for children, in addition to learning opportunities. What distinguishes the school farm is that its role is not limited to providing healthy and fresh food to children, which contributes significantly to their mental, physical, and psychological development, but its role extends beyond that to the idea children and young people can be more influential within their families and the broader community of their neighborhoods and cities. Additionally, the pandemic has challenged educators and revealed the need to rethink the outdoor learning areas of schools and whether these should be engaged deeply in the educational curriculum. More research is needed on the impact of COVID-19 on the sustainability of the food system, community resiliency, and how to remotely educate children on farming skills.

The scope of this book does not include some related topics; therefore, the editors would recommend those topics are investigated further, such as investment in school farms as a local business and small enterprise, growing food on school farms to save energy, reducing transportation, decreasing the heat island effect, eco-friendly and smart strategies, techniques, tools in gardening, harvesting, watering, and monitoring processes, and new planting systems such as hydroponic, aquaponic, and aeroponic.

REVIEWERS

Abdulraheem Iderawumi
Abeer Elshater
Abel Enokela
Adrian Bethune
Ahmed El-kholei
Ahmed Refaat
Catherine Price
Divya Senan
Donna Ashlee
Elaine Swan
Elizabeth Gregory
Fillipo Oncini
Hesham Abusaada
Iman Hamza
Imana Pal
Indjy M. Shawket
Kathryn Terzano
Kelly Rose
Kim McGowan
Linda Jolly
Lobna Abdulaziz
Nurul Rofiah
Rahma Doheim
Samah Elkhateeb
Sarah Dempster
Sarah Mander

DOI: 10.4324/9781003176558-16

INDEX

Note: Page numbers in *italics* indicate figures, **bold** indicate tables and page numbers with "n" indicates the end notes in the text.

Printed in the United States
by Baker & Taylor Publisher Services